C0-AWI-649

THE ANARCHIST PRINCE

PETER KROPOTKIN

Frontispiece

THE
ANARCHIST PRINCE

A BIOGRAPHICAL STUDY OF PETER KROPOTKIN

by

George Woodcock and
Ivan Avakumović

LONDON — NEW YORK

T. V. BOARDMAN & CO. LTD
14 Cockspur Street, London, S.W.1

KRAUS REPRINT CO.
New York
1970

68884

First Printed 1950

TO

MARIE LOUISE BERNERI

a true disciple of Kropotkin,
who died on the 13th April, 1949

LC 51-5772

Reprinted with the permission of the author

KRAUS REPRINT CO.

A U.S. Division of Kraus-Thomson Organization Limited

Printed in U.S.A.

CONTENTS

68884

ILLUSTRATIONS

C0381

CHAPTER I

THE YOUTH

I

THE 'forties of the last century, characterised in Western Europe by change and unrest, were for Russia, in those days always a few steps behind the civilised world, a time of uneasy stability, of waiting for an inevitable storm. In 1842, the year when Peter Alexeivich Kropotkin was born in a mansion of the old aristocratic quarter of Moscow, the military despotism of Nicholas I had hardened into a harsh tyranny that was to continue unbroken until the old Tsar died in disappointment, after the appalling Russian reverses during the Crimean War.

The basic structure of Russian society still maintained the belated feudalism imposed on it by Ivan the Terrible and Peter the Great. It could be divided into three mutually exclusive layers, separated by gulfs of tradition and custom. There were the aristocrats, consisting of the titled nobility—Princes, Counts, and Barons in profusion—and the hereditary noblemen like the fathers of Herzen and Bakunin, who had no titles and supplied the place in Russia of the English country gentlemen. The army, the land, the civil bureaucracy were all vested in the men of this top social layer who, speaking French almost as their native language and influenced by the Prussian methods of organisation favoured by the half-German Nicholas, were as yet, before the impact of Slavophil nationalism during the following decade, hardly conscious of the fact that they were Russian. Their conversation, their interests, their ways of living, their ideas of social efficiency were borrowed from Western Europe, although at times they bore these acquired possessions with all the awkwardness of the *parvenu*, of the

African chieftain parading in the cast-off frock-coat and top-hat of a European traveller. Even their feudal system was alien, for it was a negation of the primitive communal economy of the *mir*, which still existed beside and beneath it, and represented the vital element in the cohesion of rural society.

Next to this motley nobility, many of whose members were merely poor clerks or half-pay officers who earned their livelihood by bribery and by sponging on their more fortunate neighbours, lay a great middle-class stratum of merchants and craftsmen. Free, but deprived of many of the privileges enjoyed by the nobility, these men were as a whole much more consciously Russian. At this period, however, their influence on affairs was slight, and, though they produced some intellectuals and outstanding professional men, they were engaged principally in exploiting the trading possibilities of the industrial and agrarian revolutions that were slowly beginning to reach Russia. Related to and dependent on them was an amorphous class of poorer freemen, artisans, petty traders, porters, still involved in a small-scale industry not yet dominated by the factory system which developed during the next half-century.

At the bottom of the creaking social pyramid moved the mass of the peasants, who represented the majority of the Russian people. Except in a few isolated districts they were serfs, bound to the landowners and saleable like goods and chattels. According to feudal theory they should have been linked inalienably to the land on which they lived; there was an old saying among them that "the peasants belong to the lord, but the land belongs to the peasants". Feudalism in Russia, as elsewhere, had originally implied a reciprocity of obligations. But by the nineteenth century this had almost vanished, and, except for a few enlightened men, the landowners treated the "souls" under their care as movable property, selling them away from the land and sending them into the army at will. Theoretically, there was redress in law for wrongful ill-treatment of serfs, but in fact little real protection existed, and the Russian State, which always favoured the powerful, on the principle that concessions of any kind would merely encourage the poor to be rebellious, usually repulsed any attempt to temper the harshness of the masters. Even after their liberation the peasants generally took it for granted that the bureaucratic machine would always work against them, and those who have read such books on the period as Herzen's *Memoirs* will realise the heart-breaking difficulties facing the isolated men who tried to obtain some genuine improvement of conditions, even on a piecemeal scale. In reality, until the emancipation of 1861, the Russian peasants were usually slaves rather than serfs in the genuine feudal sense of a man tied to his land and bound to render certain services in return for his lord's protection.

Largely illiterate, dominated by a venial and superstitious priesthood, and possessing at best a localised communal consciousness, the Russian peasants as yet represented only a potential force in society—the source of occasional blind insurrections of a savage but inevitable brutality; in no way could they be regarded as an awakened and conscious class. Here the next twenty years were to show some considerable changes.

On this clumsy social edifice, represented at its apex by callous self-interest and at the base by illiterate misery, the despotic Nicholas I, warned by the Decembrist rising of the enlightened nobility in 1825, had sought to impose a rigid and all-pervading military discipline. He regarded the aristocracy as a prætorian class, and every gentleman's son was expected to pass through the military schools and spend at least part of his manhood as an officer, before joining the civil service or retiring to manage his estates. The merchants and other freemen were exempt from military service, but the serfs were forced to supply the common soldiers for an army that was ruled by means of a brutal discipline. Men were chosen by lot from the villages, but disobedient serfs could always be sent straight into the ranks, and this threat acted as a powerful deterrent to individual or mass resistance. The term of twenty-five years' service usually meant that the conscript would never return to his village, and his neighbours would mourn for him when he departed as if he were already a corpse being taken to burial. The life of the common soldier was even harsher than that of the serfs on the land. A rigid Prussian discipline treated the men like automatons, and the "Autocrat of All the Russias" was never so pleased as when he could inspect a regiment of men who behaved like machines. Among the

Russians, with their natural tendency towards indiscipline, this result could only be obtained by the most rigorous brutality, and Kropotkin himself tells in his *Memoirs* that: "Blows from the officers, flogging with birch rods and with sticks, for the slightest fault, were normal affairs. The cruelty that was displayed surpasses all imagination." A common soldier who reached a court martial could expect a really terrible fate, for in most cases:

> "... The sentence was that a thousand men should be placed in two ranks facing each other, every soldier armed with a stick of the thickness of the little finger ... and that the condemned men should be dragged three, four, five, and seven times between these two rows, each soldier administering a blow. Sergeants followed to see that the full force was used. After one or two thousand blows had been given the victim, spitting blood, was taken to the hospital and attended to, in order that the punishment might be finished as soon as he had more or less recovered from the first part of it. If he died under the torture, the execution of the sentence was completed on the corpse."

Yet this blend of Prussian militarism and Oriental barbarism which held together the unformed mass of the Russian peoples under the heartless tyranny of Nicholas failed in its attempt to destroy every spark of rebellion, every expression of independent thought. The last rising, and the first conscious revolutionary movement of nineteenth-century Russia, that of the Decembrists, had occurred in 1825, only seventeen years before, and for many who were young at the time, like Herzen and Ogarev, the executed leaders of this conspiracy attained something of the sanctity of martyrs, while the survivors, exiled in Siberia, represented the living manifestations of a cause that was only submerged, but never died, in the decade after 1825. The Polish insurrections of 1830–1, repressed savagely by the orders of the Tsar, helped to keep alive the spirit of revolt, and very soon the young men of the universities, influenced also by the French revolution of 1830, were again inspired by radical ideas, adopted enthusiastically from the works of French philosophers and early socialist thinkers like Rousseau, Voltaire, Saint-Simon, and Fourier. Discussion circles were formed, and suppressed in 1834 by a scared government, Herzen and his friends being sent to a surprisingly mild administrative exile in the remoter provinces of European Russia.

For a time there was little overt revolutionary or even radical activity. The dissolution of Herzen's circle was followed by a temporary loss among Moscow intellectuals of interest in the French progressive thinkers. German philosophy and romantic fiction and poetry, particularly the writings of the Gothic Terror school, now became the fashion; the young students and littérateurs spent their time discussing the metaphysical tortuosities of Fichte and Hegel, and this tendency was encouraged by the Tsar and his advisers, under the illusion that anything emanating from the Berlin academies must necessarily be favourable to the kind of absolutism they wished to maintain.

But the ferment of intellectual rebellion set going by the Decembrists was by no means dead, and any current of thought from the West was assimilated and transformed in the minds of these restive young men until it served their need to formulate a creed of criticism and resistance. Hegelianism became the fashionable philosophy, and, while some Russians, like Katkov and the Slavophils, eventually followed Hegel's own path to the justification of autocracy, the more energetic spirits, like Bakunin and Belinsky, merely found that it gave an impetus to their iconoclastic urges. Belinsky became the first great Russian critic and, throughout the 1840's until his death in 1848, wrote literary criticism into which he contrived to instil a biting commentary on the existing social structure of his country. Herzen, returning from exile in 1840, once again contributed the matured scepticism of his French philosophy, while this decade also saw the beginning of the great exodus to the West. Bakunin departed to Germany, and only returned home fettered and as a dreaded revolutionary in 1849; Turgenev was for a time his travelling companion and remained under the influence of Western radical thought; Stankevitch, one of the finest characters of this Russian renaissance, died in Italy, having exhausted a great talent in the uncongenial atmosphere of autocratic Moscow.

The tide of thought that was to produce the outstanding outburst of great literature and revolutionary endeavour in nineteenth-century Russia was thus well under way by the

1840's, and the very year of Kropotkin's birth saw two events of great importance in that movement in which he himself was to become so significant a figure.

The first great Russian novel, Gogol's *Dead Souls*, was published in that year, and caused a stir of astonished pleasure at the satirical mockery which it directed against contemporary Russian society. Its reception scared the government and perturbed the rather timid author, who in later years drew back into a virtual support of the existing system. But he had already delivered his blow at the Romanov despotism, and the effect of *Dead Souls* on Russian literature and radical thought could not be negated by his later repentance.

The second significant event of the year took place outside Russia; Michael Bakunin, having come under the radical influence of Arnold Ruge and the young Hegelians in Germany, published his celebrated essay on *The Reaction in Germany*, in which he first put forward his doctrine, later to become influential among the radical groups within Russia, of the necessity for destruction.

> "Let us put our trust", he said, "in the eternal spirit which destroys and annihilates only because it is the unsearchable and eternally creative source of all life. The urge for destruction is also a creative urge."

When, and only when, the destructive urge has done its work, he prophesied in almost religious tones:

> "There will be a qualitative transformation, a new, living, life-giving revelation, a new heaven and a new earth, a new and mighty world in which all our present dissonances will be resolved into a harmonious whole."

It was a gesture of open defiance, the like of which had not been seen among Russians since 1825. It must have filled the Germanophile Nicholas with consternation at the results of his beloved Berlin philosophy, but to some Russians, like Herzen, still confined in the oppressive atmosphere of St Petersburg and Moscow, it came as a grateful and encouraging sign.

It was many years before anybody within Russia could echo in action the spirit of Bakunin's challenge. Not for another quarter of a century, when the reactionary tendencies of

Alexander II had driven the liberals to despair, would come the day of revolutionary action, of the Narodniks going to the people and the Terrorists committing their grim acts of vengeance and propaganda by deed. But the intellectual ferment continued, and was marked during the next few years by two further important works of fiction, Turgenev's *Sportsman's Sketches* (1845) and Dostoevsky's *Poor Folk* (1846), in which the satire contained in *Dead Souls* was reinforced by the revelation that the poor had their feelings and, in the case of Turgenev's book, that serfs were just as human as their masters. The uneasy consciences of the Russian upper classes were a fertile ground in which the twin impulses of literature and radical thought worked strongly, and by the time Kropotkin was born it was already evident that vast social changes were on their way. He came into a society in which the inertia of a century was already beginning to catch the dynamic momentum that carried Western Europe through its age of revolution.

II

Peter Alexeivich Kropotkin was born into the highest rank of the Russian aristocracy. The Kropotkins had been princes of Smolensk, in Western Russia, and the family tradition claimed that once their ancestors had ruled the Principality of Kiev and were descended from the dynasty of Rurik, which had governed Russia before the Romanovs. When Peter Kropotkin became in later years a revolutionary, it was said in jest among his fellow conspirators of the Chaikovsky circle, as we are told by one of its members, "that he had more right to the throne of Russia than the Emperor, Alexander II, who was only a German". Kropotkin himself never set great store by this reputed ancestry, and, though in his *Memoirs* he describes his father showing him the certificate from the Heraldry Department which said that the Kropotkin family descended from a grandson of a certain Prince of Kiev, he adds that his father valued this pedigree "more for its cost than for its historical association", and would remark proudly, "It cost me three hundred roubles to obtain that parchment". The notorious ingenuity of genealogists may well lead us to regard this patent with hesitation, but the Kropotkins were, nevertheless, an ancient family who had played an active part in mediæval Russia, with its loose structure of semi-independent principalities, and had been thrust into the background when the centralising tactics of the Romanov Tsars cut down both the power and the possessions of the old *boyars*.

Perhaps it was a feeling that by right of ancestry they should have held a greater position in modern Russia that had prevented the Kropotkins from playing any distinguished part in Russian public life for many years before Peter's birth. After the brief periods of military service necessary to preserve appearances, they had mostly retired to their country estates, and contented themselves with the life of glorified but not particularly enlightened country gentlemen.

A strain of more adventurous blood entered the family when Peter's grandfather married a Princess Gagarin, who had strong artistic leanings and whose brother had created a scandal by marrying the famous actress Semionova, a serf who insisted on remaining on the stage after her marriage. Whether it must be attributed to the Gagarin influence or to the general intellectual trend of the period, the Kropotkins henceforward showed a marked literary tendency; one of Peter's uncles was a poet and several cousins dabbled in writing of various kinds.

But his father was wholly unaffected by such tastes. He was, Peter tells us, "a typical officer of the time of Nicholas I", enamoured of the mechanical type of military discipline then in fashion. He had, indeed, no record of real combat; during his only campaign, that against the Turks in 1828, his sole adventure was an encounter with pariah dogs when he was riding through a deserted Turkish village with dispatches. He was awarded the Cross of St Anne for gallantry, not because he had done anything himself to deserve it, but because his servant rescued a child from a burning house in the village where the general staff were quartered. A measure of the difference in outlook between two generations of Russians is shown by the fact that, while Alexander Kropotkin himself could see no incongruity in this event, his own children mocked the peculiar code by which the master gained credit for the actions of the man. Yet, in spite of this total lack of real military experience, the Romanov system set such store by a good martinet that he rose eventually to the rank of general.

Alexander Kropotkin has been described as "a coarse and stubborn landowner", and he ruled his twelve hundred serfs in truly despotic manner. For a slight offence he would have a man beaten by the police or sent into the army, and his servants feared him, though in justice it must be said that he was not so bad as many another serf-owner. At the same time, he was often capable of going to great lengths in order to help his own dependants, or even comparative strangers who came to him for assistance; but this can be attributed more to the gratification it gave his sense of self-importance than to any innate kindness of disposition.

His values were those of his master Nicholas, the values of a soldier of that brutal age, and, while there was no trace of real spartanism in his well-fed life among a whole company of servants, he certainly detested anything that seemed intellectual or artistic, was ashamed of the presence of a poet in his family, and hated any kind of liberal thought. He was ignorant and superstitious; once he was deceived by a serf girl who posed as the ghost of his first wife and scared him into setting her free in accordance with a forgotten promise.

Like many stubborn men he was amenable to flattery, and once an influence had been established over him, he could be led easily into almost any course of action. His second wife managed in this way to rule him quite effectively. Towards his children he was harsh and unsympathetic, and his second son, Alexander, probably expressed an often-felt thought when he wrote to Peter in 1860 that their father was "nasty, revengeful, obstinate and mean", and described him as a cheat.

Yet he had at least one virtue, outstanding enough in an age of wholesale corruption, for, as his by no means admiring son tells us, he was "absolutely honest, and, at a time when almost everyone was receiving bribes and making fortunes, had never let himself be bribed". It was a negative merit, but at least it distinguished him from the great mass of Russian officials in his age.

It is clear that neither Peter Kropotkin nor his brother Alexander inherited much from their father. Not only did they belong intellectually to a generation that was a world apart from the ignorant serf-owners whom he represented, but they were wholly different in character, gentle and generous in nature where he was harsh and mean, intellectual and radical in their interests where he was stupid and reactionary.

This difference was undoubtedly due to the influence of their mother. Alexander had met his future wife, Ekaterina Nicholaevna Sulima, when he was serving with the army during the suppression of the Polish rising in 1831. Her father, General Nikolai Semionovich Sulima, was the commander of an army corps, and had taken a prominent part in the war of 1812 against Napoleon, when, at the head of his cavalry regiment, he had "cut his way into an infantry square bristling with bayonets" and had recovered "after having been left for dead on the battle-field". He was a man of rare independence among the high Russian officials of the time, and his lack of venality was shown in the fact that, in spite of a life of service in high military and administrative positions, he was extremely poor and unable to settle any large dowry on his daughter at her marriage. For a while he was governor-general of Western and, later, of Eastern Siberia, and tried to bring some kind of honest dealings into the administration of these provinces, which were then considered "more lucrative than a gold-mine". He failed in this, but himself remained completely unaffected by the prevalent atmosphere.

Sulima's innate independence and integrity, inherited by his daughter and grandchildren, were perhaps due in some measure to the traditions of his own ancestry. For he was a descendant of Ivan Sulima, Hetman of the Zoporozie Cossacks, those independent peasants and freebooters of the Ukraine who in past centuries built their settlements on the banks of the Dnieper and, in these early days, practised a form of society based on primitive communism. Ivan Sulima fought against the Poles for the independence of the Ukraine, and was taken by them to Warsaw, where he was tortured to death. But the Cossacks continued their fight, and succeeded in throwing out the invader. It was only, however, to fall into the hands of the Romanovs; the Sulimas and their kind were too straight-forward to detect what lay behind the blandishments of Catherine the Great and her advisers, so that they allowed the Cossacks to become the servants of the Tsars and, instead of remaining themselves the examples of independence, to act as the destroyers of liberty in others.

With this Cossack blood, Kropotkin mingled in his person the two great branches of the Slav race, the Great Russians and the Ukrainians, and in conversation used often to call himself a Scythian.

Ekaterina Sulima was an attractive and vigorous girl, and it is perhaps not surprising that she melted the heart of Alexander Kropotkin to such an extent that, mean as he was, he accepted her without a substantial marriage settlement. In his *Memoirs*, Peter Kropotkin describes her as "tall, slim, adorned with a mass of dark chestnut hair, with dark brown eyes and a tiny mouth", and this description is confirmed by a portrait which gives, as well, the impression of girlish impulsiveness.

"All who knew her loved her", said her son. Towards the serfs she was always friendly and kind; "the servants worshipped her memory". She was fond of music and painting, and delighted to watch the peasants dancing, and even to join them. Her appreciation of literature was very wide and, many years after her death, Peter discovered in a storeroom of their country house "a mass of papers covered with her firm but pretty handwriting; diaries in which she wrote with delight of the scenery of Germany, and spoke of her sorrows and her thirst for happiness; books which she had filled with Russian verses prohibited by censorship—among them the beautiful historical ballads of Ryleef, the poet whom Nicholas I hanged in 1826; other books containing music, French dramas, verses of Lamartine, and Byron's poems that she had copied; and a great number of water-colour paintings". She seems to have been indeed, as her son claims, "a remarkable woman" for the Russia of her day, inspired by the best in Western romantic culture, and it is not hard to imagine the difficulty and unhappiness of her life with her insensitive husband. But she never allowed such problems to blunt her nature or influence her gentle treatment of those among whom she lived.

She bore four children. Nicholas, the eldest, was born in 1834, and Helen, the only girl, a year later. There followed a lapse of six years, until Alexander was born in 1841, and Peter in the following year. Thus the children were divided by age into two pairs and, while the smaller boys became very intimate and shared all their developing interests, the elder children "kept together, and we knew them very little".

The first fifteen years of Peter's life were spent partly in the large town house in the Old Equerries' Quarter of Moscow, the district favoured by the more old-fashioned aristocracy, and partly on their estate at Nikolskoye, a village in the province of Kaluga, some 160 miles from Moscow. It was a conservative pattern of life, with a regular alternation of urban and rural existence; so attached was Kropotkin's father to familiar environments that, on the two occasions at which the family moved to different Moscow houses during Peter's childhood, they still remained in the same small quarter of the city, within a stone's throw of the church in which the old Prince had himself been baptised.

The life of Russian serf-owners a century ago belongs to an era that was rapidly passing away even in Kropotkin's own childhood, but in his *Memoirs* he has given an imperishably vivid picture of its feudal and semi-barbarian extravagance. His own father, an owner of the "souls" of over a thousand peasants, was a rich man by the standards of the time, and had to entertain accordingly, with the maximum of wasted energy, so that a family of eight was waited on by fifty servants —"four coachmen to attend a dozen horses, three cooks for the masters and two more for the servants, a dozen men to wait upon us at dinner-time (one man, plate in hand, standing behind each person seated at the table), and girls innumerable in the maid-servants' room", as well as a tailor, a piano-tuner, a confectioner, and a band of twelve musicians, all of them serfs who had been expensively trained for their respective positions to the greater glory of their master. Balls, gambling parties, and evening gatherings for tea, to which all the friends of the neighbourhood were freely invited whenever they might be inclined to call, were in the regular routine of town life, and, while the Kropotkins were perhaps not so extravagant as a certain wealthy relative who frittered away a vast fortune on epicurean dainties, they spared no cost in providing entertainments that would bring them credit in the coarse esteem of early nineteenth-century Moscow society. This ostentatious generosity was not considered in the least incompatible with an astonishing stinginess over the daily economy of the house, which involved the servants in continual petty bullying over their alleged mishandling of the master's goods.

Kropotkin has written much on the lives of the Russian magnates of that age, which we must leave the reader to discover for himself in the *Memoirs of a Revolutionist*, but the following passage, describing the country house which provided the other side of his childhood life, is so evocative of the better aspect of that existence as to deserve ample quotation:

"For the quiet life of the landlords of these times Nikolskoye was admirably suited. There was nothing in it of the luxury which is seen in richer estates; but an artistic hand was visible in the planning of the buildings and the gardens, and in the general arrangement of things. Besides the main house, which Father had recently built, there were, round a spacious and well-kept yard, several smaller houses, which gave a greater degree of independence to their inhabitants without destroying the close intercourse of the family life. An immense 'upper garden' was devoted to fruit-trees, and through it the church was reached. The southern slope of the land, which led to the river, was entirely given up to a pleasure garden, where flower-beds were intermingled with alleys of lime-trees, lilacs and acacias. From the balcony of the main house there was a beautiful view of the Siréne, with the ruins of an old earthen fortress where the Russians had offered a stubborn resistance during the Mongol invasion, and farther on, the boundless yellow grain-fields, with copses of woods on the horizon.

". . . The woods; the walks along the river, the climbing over the hills to the old fortress . . . there was no end of new and delightful impressions. Large parties were organised in which all the family took part, sometimes picking mushrooms in the woods, and afterwards having tea in the midst of the forest, where a man a hundred years old lived alone with his little grandson, taking care of the bees. At other times we went to one of my father's villages where a big pond had been dug, in which golden carp were caught by the thousand—part of them being taken for the landlord and the remainder being distributed among all the peasants. My former nurse, Vasilisa, lived in that village. Her family was one of the poorest; besides her husband, she had only a small boy to help her, and a girl, my foster-sister, who became later a preacher and a Virgin in the Nonconformist sect to which they belonged. There was no bound to her joy when I came to see her. Cream, eggs, apples, and honey were all she could offer; but the way in which she offered them, in bright wooden plates, after having covered the table with a fine snow-white linen tablecloth of her own making (with the Russian Nonconformists absolute cleanliness is a matter of religion), and the fond words with which she addressed me, treating me as her own son, left the warmest feelings in my heart."

It was a life that had many idyllic features, and even a certain wealth of colour, but only the completely insensitive could fail to perceive the terrible facts of oppression and misery that underlay it and would precipitate its eventual destruction.

The childhood of the younger Kropotkin boys had from the beginning a certain shiftless independence which probably helped to preserve them from the typical attitude of their class. Their mother died young—from a chill caught while she was dancing, which developed into consumption, and Peter's first memory was of standing at her bedside as she saw her children for the last time, having in her thoughtfulness arranged a little party with the intention of distracting their minds from the sadness of the occasion. Neither he nor his brother understood the significance of this farewell, or of the tears into which their mother burst when she sent them away. A few days later they were moved into a little house in the courtyard of the Moscow mansion, and it was here that they heard of her death.

"The April sun filled the little rooms with its rays, but our German nurse, Madame Burman, and Uliana, our Russian nurse, told us to go to bed. Their faces wet with tears, they were sewing for us black shirts fringed with broad white tassels. We could not sleep: the unknown frightened us, and we listened to their subdued talk. They said something about our mother which we could not understand. We jumped out of our beds, asking, 'Where is Mamma? Where is Mamma?'

"Both of them burst into sobs and began to pat our curly heads, calling us 'poor orphans', until Uliana could hold out no longer, and said, 'Your mother is gone there—to the sky, to the angels.'

"'How to the sky? Why?' our infantile imagination in vain demanded."

After the death of his wife, Alexander Kropotkin devoted himself to outside interests, and his children saw little of him, even at the rare times when he was not engaged on military inspections or other official business that took him away from home. He showed them scanty attention, and during their whole childhood the only toys he gave them were a rifle and a sentry-box, which he hoped would encourage them in soldierly interests! Had it not been for the unremitting devotion of the servants to their mother's memory, these neglected children would indeed have had a bare and unhappy infancy. But they found always "that atmosphere of love which children must have around them", and Madame Burman and the house serfs cared for them and gave them all the little kindnesses their father forgot.

This close and warm contact with the peasants and house serfs, which persisted throughout the childhood of the younger Kropotkin boys, preserved them from the rigid prejudices of their father, and made them receptive to the virtues of those poor Russians with whom they were in daily and intimate relationship. The understanding between them and the domestic serfs became so close that the latter would often risk severe punishment to protect the boys or to do them some personal service that otherwise would have been forbidden. "Few", said Kropotkin in his later days, "know what treasuries of goodness can be found in the hearts of Russian peasants, even after centuries of the most cruel oppression, which might well have embittered them." He had been fortunate enough in his youth to gain access to these generous hearts, and the discovery did much towards making him the passionate defender of the poor and downtrodden he afterwards became.

The years immediately following the death of his mother passed so uneventfully that Kropotkin retained no further outstanding memories until the year 1848, when he was six years old.

This was a year of profound changes in Europe, and even in Russia its effects were not wholly unfelt. It is true that the actual movements of rebellion there were very mild and inconspicuous in character. Nevertheless, it was for participation in activity deemed to be hostile to the rule of Nicholas I that Schedrin, the satirist, was exiled in 1848, and the Petrashevsky circle, with Dostoevsky among its members, was cruelly suppressed in 1849, while a Russian army helped the Hapsburgs to crush the Hungarian insurrection. But outside Russia, Herzen and Bakunin, the future leaders of early Russian resistance, were tempered in the fires and failures of European revolutions, and gained the experience that was to make them so influential in Russian affairs during the next decades. Bakunin, captured after leading the defence of Dresden against the Prussian troops, was immured in solitary confinement in the Peter-and-Paul and Schuesselberg fortresses for six years, becoming a legendary figure among the Russian youth.

Nor was this the only important effect of 1848 on Russian affairs, for, although all the revolutions in Europe of that and the ensuing year were finally defeated, they resulted in some social changes which were not withdrawn after the triumph of the conservative forces. The most important of these was the destruction of serfdom in Germany and Austria, and this change, in its turn, had a deep indirect effect on the social development of Russia, now the only country pretending to European civilisation in which the feudal system continued, and thus gave an important moral support to the liberals in their efforts during the next decade to get rid of this institution. All these factors, the radical propaganda of Herzen, the revolutionary experiences of Bakunin in 1848 and after, and the agitation for the liberation of the serfs, were to have a decisive and direct effect on Kropotkin's later development and his life in manhood. But as yet he was wholly unaware of these portentous events happening around him, for no echo of them seems to have reached the small boys who played that summer of 1848 in the gardens of Nikolskoye. At the time it was another and more personal event that made the year memorable for them.

For in 1848 their father married again. It was a marriage, not of love, nor even of convenience, but of pusillanimity. Alexander Kropotkin, having already married a poor woman for love, was now looking around with rather more circumspection, and "cast his eyes upon a nice-looking young person, this time belonging to a wealthy family . . .". But his plans were frustrated by a sudden visit from the General commanding his army corps, a certain Timofeyev who ruled his men and officers with the terroristic fury beloved of Nicholas. The Prince was abjectly frightened of this formidable man, and immediately agreed to a proposal to marry Elisabeth Koradino, an admiral's daughter even poorer than her predecessor, for, as the old man admitted to his sons in later years, "she had no dowry; only a big trunk filled with ladies' finery, and that Martha, her one serf, dark as a gipsy, sitting upon it".

This stepmother was young and pretty, "but with a rather too sharp southern look". At first she tried to ingratiate herself with the children, playing rather boisterously and crying, "You see what a jolly mamma you will have". The little boys looked at her with suspicion, and answered, "Our mamma has flown away to the sky!"

It was a relationship that started inauspiciously and matured only into estrangement in later years. Elisabeth Kropotkin was a woman of shrewish and vindictive disposition, and many years later Peter was to refer to her as his "cursed stepmother". She began by sweeping away all vestiges of her predecessor's presence, declaring, "Nothing of the Sulimas in my house", and, besides consigning to the lumber-room any object that might hold an association with Ekaterina, she dismissed the kind old German nurse, despite all her pleas to be retained to care for the children she loved, and even went so far as to forbid the boys any contact with their mother's relatives, so that it was many years before they again met their maternal cousins.

Her attitude to Peter and Alexander, and probably also to the elder children, became one of growing hostility, no doubt partly caused by their original aloofness from her, but growing more evident as she felt her own position in the household more secure and gained an ascendancy over her husband. She neglected them greatly, devoting her personal attention almost exclusively to their young half-sister Pauline ; but her attitude was not one of mere indifference, for she seems to have done everything she could to prejudice the Prince against his sons, and particularly against Alexander, towards whom he became extremely antagonistic.

The two boys were taken from their nurses, and put under the charge of French and Russian tutors, both of whom had some influence on their development. The French tutor, Monsieur Poulain, was an old soldier of Napoleon's Grande Armée, who, on being stranded in Russia after the retreat from Moscow, had taken to teaching aristocratic children in order to live. He instructed them in French, history, and geography, by methods which were, by present-day standards, somewhat rough-and-ready.

"M. Poulain had brought with him the grammar of Noel and Chapsal, memorable to more than one generation of Russian boys and girls; a book of French dialogues; a history of the world, in one volume; and a universal geography, also in one volume. We had to commit to memory the grammar, the dialogues, the history and the geography."

Poulain would reinforce this teaching with a liberal use of the cane, until the boys' sister made her most dramatic appearance in their early life by angrily accusing their father of neglect and thus securing a termination of this method of instruction.

Despite his methods, Poulain appears to have succeeded in teaching his subjects quite effectively, and he had the advantage of being a stimulating companion outside the hours of lessons. Much of his conversation seems, indeed, to have been devoted to stories of his campaigns, which fitted in with the general military atmosphere in which the boys were reared, nobody around them ever doubting that they would follow a career in the army. But Poulain was at least something of a liberating influence in that he brought democratic ideas into their thoughts. Although an Orleanist and a great admirer of Napoleon, he nevertheless retained a respect for the ideals of 1789, and seemed to have been considerably shocked by much that he saw in Russia, and particularly by its social stratification, for he told the boys approvingly how some of the French nobility had renounced their titles at the Revolution, and used to relate a story in which Mirabeau, "to show his contempt for aristocratic titles, opened a shop decorated with a signboard which bore the inscription, 'Mirabeau, tailor' ". The tale caught Peter's imagination; he dreamed of following Mirabeau's example, and from the early age of twelve ceased to use the title of Prince.

M. Poulain was dismissed when Peter was ten, after Alexander had left home to join a cadet corps, and a German tutor was engaged. This man only stayed for one winter, but was memorable because he gave his pupil a taste for Schiller's poetry and transmitted to him a certain portion of his own idealism.

The next winter Peter attended classes at a Moscow gymnasium, but after that was left to the care of N. P. Smirnov, the

68884

Russian tutor who had already taught him and Alexander the rudiments of Russian literature and history and also arithmetic.

On his first engagement, Smirnov was one of those students, familiar to readers of nineteenth-century Russian novels, who, being too poor to continue their studies without assistance, devoted part of their time to private teaching. Like many such men he was of considerable intellectual power, and combined liberal ideas with a taste for literature, by which means he was able to wield a very considerable formative influence over his pupil's development.

Literary interests had already been aroused in both Peter and Alexander by an early introduction to the theatre, where they saw Fanny Elssler and the great Russian actors of the day. As they were given few toys and had little companionship of their own age, they had to rely largely on their inventiveness to furnish the means of play, and often, even when very small, would try to reconstruct what they had seen at the theatre, enlivening their performances with representations of hell fire and the wailing of the damned. On the possible effect of these latter performances, Kropotkin remarks:

"I ask myself now whether this extremely concrete representation of hell with a candle and a sheet of paper did not contribute to free us both at an early age from the fear of eternal fire. Our conception of it was too realistic to resist scepticism."

To this early dramatic taste Peter began to add, from the age of eleven, a very active interest in literature, and in this he was much encouraged by Smirnov, whom he would assist to copy out the texts of forbidden works by Gogol and Pushkin. Very soon he became well grounded in this new Russian literature, and gained a certain knowledge of the contemporary writing of Western Europe. He tells us that:

"Pushkin's great poem, *Eugene Onegin*, made but little impression upon me, and I still admire the marvellous simplicity and beauty of his style in that poem more than its contents. But Gogol's works, which I read when I was eleven or twelve, had a powerful effect on my mind, and my first literary essays were in imitation of his humorous manner. An historical novel by Zagoskin, *Young Miloslavsky*, about the times of the great uprising of 1612, Pushkin's *The*

Captain's Daughter, dealing with the Pugachev rising, and Dumas's *Queen Marguerite* awakened in me a lasting interest in history. As to other French novels, I have only begun to read them since Daudet and Zola came to the front. Nekrasov's poetry was my favourite from early years: I knew many of his verses by heart."

As Kropotkin has indicated, his interest in literature did not stop short at reading. Prompted by the active encouragement of Smirnov and by a feeling of emulation for his brother Alexander, who had taken to composing verse, he very soon began to write. In collaboration with Smirnov he produced a Gogolesque *History of a Sixpence*, and later embarked on stories, articles, and even poems, in spite of his early contempt for his brother's efforts in the last direction.

But he was not content to become a mere author, and soon aspired to produce his own journal, anticipating in this the more momentous enterprises of later life.

"In my twelfth year, I began to edit a daily journal. Paper was not to be had at will in our house, and my journal was of Lilliputian size. As the Crimean War had not yet broken out, and the only newspaper which my father used to receive was the *Gazette of the Moscow Police*, I had not a great choice of models. As a result, my own *Gazette* consisted merely of short paragraphs announcing the news of the day: as, 'Went out to the woods. N. P. Smirnov shot two thrushes', and the like.

"This soon ceased to satisfy me, and in 1855 I started a monthly review which contained Alexander's verse, my novelettes, and some sort of 'varieties'. The material existence of this review was fully guaranteed, for it had plenty of subscribers; that is, the editor himself and Smirnov, who regularly paid his subscription of so many sheets of paper, even after he had left our house. In return, I accurately wrote out for my faithful subscriber a second copy."

Peter's review was called *Vremennik* (Chronicle), and was much inspired by the radical review *Sovremennik* (Contemporary) which Chernyshevsky, the author of the famous utopian novel *What is to be Done?*, joined in the late 1850's. The great period of Chernyshevsky's popularity in progressive circles came after he had written his novel in prison during 1863, but already *Sovremennik* was exercising a wide influence comparable to that exerted from outside Russia by Herzen's *Kolokol* (The Bell), and Kropotkin remarked in an unpublished passage of his *Memoirs of a Revolutionist* that it "was read in the guards' regiments scarcely less than in liberal circles".

Kropotkin did all the laborious work of handwriting his review (at least two copies were made, even if these were each passed round among several readers), and he also wrote many of the items which appeared therein. In the introduction to the collection of letters between Kropotkin and his brother Alexander, published in Moscow during 1932, the editor, Kropotkin's disciple N. Lebedev, gives a list of some twenty-five items from Kropotkin's hand which appeared in various issues of the review, and he may well have made other contributions. They include three original poems, as well as translations from Lamartine and other French poets, and a number of tales and stories, entitled, after the fashion of the period, "Infidelity", "Spring Walk", "Tale of an Old Woman", and "It Does Not Happen as We Wish". Also, foreshadowing his interest in social and political questions, there is an article on "Luxury in Paris in the Reign of Louis XIV" (which may well have been aimed obliquely at the St Petersburg of Alexander II), and "A View on the War of 1853–6".

He had many willing assistants; through Smirnov and a medical student, N. M. Pavlov, who also taught him for a while, he obtained collaboration from people in the university, including even (another anticipation of later scientific interests) an unpublished lecture on physical geography by one of the Moscow professors; through Alexander, who was greatly interested in the work, he gained the help of a number of literary aspirants among the corps of cadets to which his brother belonged. This early journalistic venture may have had a very slight influence at its time, but it was typical of the kind of efforts which were being made by the young men and boys of the age, and symptomatic of the rapid awakening taking place at this period among the educated Russian circles of St Petersburg and Moscow.

Vremennik came to an end in August 1857, when Kropotkin left home to begin his preparation for a military career, and here it becomes necessary to glance back over the intervening years to the circumstances which were responsible for this change in the scene of his activities.

III

It began rather unexpectedly. When Peter was eight years old a great feast was held in Moscow to celebrate the silver jubilee of Nicholas I, and the Tsar's visit to that city was marked by a great fancy-dress ball organised by the Muscovite nobility.

"It was agreed that the whole motley crowd of nationalities of which the population of the Russian Empire is composed should be represented at this ball to greet the monarch. Great preparations went on in our house, as well as in all the houses of our neighbourhood. Some sort of remarkable Russian costume was made for our stepmother. Our father, being a military man, had to appear of course in his uniform; but those of our relatives who were not in the military service were as busy with their Russian, Greek, Caucasian and Mongolian costumes as the ladies themselves. When the Moscow nobility gives a ball to the imperial family, it must be something extraordinary."

Peter and his brother were considered too young to attend the ball, but, by an accident, the former actually took quite a prominent part. Madame Nazimov, the wife of a celebrated general and a close friend of Princess Kropotkin, was appearing at the ball as a Persian princess, and intended to be accompanied by her ten-year-old son, dressed "in the costume of a young Persian prince, exceedingly rich, with a belt covered with jewels". But the boy fell ill, and Peter, whom the costume fitted exactly, was taken in his place. At the ball he and the other children were given flags bearing the arms of the Russian provinces, and the little standard-bearers marched to the imperial dais, where they saluted the Emperor and then retired. For some reason, Nicholas noticed Peter and asked to have him on the platform among his suite. Afterwards, to the delight of the Kropotkin family, he ordered that the boy should be inscribed as a candidate for the Corps of Pages, the most select military academy in Russia, which supplied the personal attendants of the imperial family and most of whose pupils found their way eventually into lucrative positions in the court or on the military staff. But he would have to wait several years yet until he reached the suitable age and a vacancy occurred.

His brother Nicholas was already in a corps of cadets at Moscow, and, in the following year, under a special *ukase* of the Emperor, his brother Alexander was ordered to enter a corps at Orel; and only after his father had spent a great deal of money and time in obtaining the favour was it granted that he should be sent to the same corps as Nicholas in Moscow.

The old Prince was very pleased to have his three sons marked for prospective careers as high-ranking officers. But very soon the two younger became less contented with their future; a childish enjoyment of military games began to fade, and, as Kropotkin puts it, "before we were many years older, we simply hated the military career for its absurdity".

It was probably the Crimean War and its manifestly bad effects on the country, obvious even to an intelligent twelve-year-old boy, that started the alteration in Peter's attitude. In his family, while the war had little real effect on Moscow's life, it was naturally a matter for enthusiasm. His sister Helen sang patriotic songs, his female relatives made lint (to be sold to the enemy by corrupt army contractors), his brother Nicholas left the cadet corps before his due time to join the Crimean army, and was never seen again. But it was from his stepmother's sisters, who had been forced to leave their house in Sebastopol, that Peter learned of the physical horrors of war, and he also quickly perceived the sense of tragedy which it caused among his peasant friends.

> "In the country the war caused much gloominess. The lines of recruits followed one another rapidly, and we continually heard the peasant women singing their funeral songs. The Russian people look upon war as a calamity which is sent upon them by Providence, and they accepted this war with a solemnity that contrasted strangely with the levity I saw elsewhere under similar conditions."

Then came the death of Nicholas I, and a wave of mingled fear and hope swept the country. For the landowners it was a moment of apprehension, and Kropotkin perceived a "real terror" among his own relatives, who, like most other landowners, expected a "new uprising of Pugachev". Indeed, very shortly, when the war had ended, there were widespread peasant risings, and Kropotkin tells in the unpublished part of his *Memoirs* of this period that:

"Over the whole of Russia peasant revolts began to attain such proportions that for their 'pacification' not companies nor battalions but entire units with artillery were sent."

Among the intellectuals and liberals, particularly of St Petersburg, the death of the old Tsar was a matter for mutual congratulation, and it was said freely that "the end of the war and the end of the terrible conditions which prevailed under the 'iron despot' were near at hand".

The influence of all these events could not fail to have their effect on Peter Kropotkin; it was greatly reinforced by his literary interests and his reading of those radical Russian authors of the last years of Nicholas I, whose writings, despite the repressive censorship, breathed the free spirit of the rising tide of Russian liberalism. When the time came for Kropotkin to join the Corps of Pages he "already considered it a misfortune" to enter a military school.

Yet, despite all its unpleasant features, Kropotkin's period in the Corps was not without compensations. It is true that the institution had a rigid disciplinary framework of the most tyrannical kind, and that at the time of his entry bullying by the seniors and individually despotic acts by the authorities were common. But a healthier and more independent attitude was growing up among the younger pages, and the helpfulness of some of the teachers (and even of some officers) contributed greatly to Kropotkin's rapid intellectual development.

He himself has devoted a lengthy section of his *Memoirs* to a description of the Corps of Pages; we cannot hope to reproduce in a few paragraphs the spirit of this interesting social document on the Russia of the early days of Alexander II, and shall be content to describe his own development while he was studying there. But for the reader's general guidance it is necessary to say that the Corps was a picked and privileged body of 150 pupils, mostly from the families of St Petersburg courtiers, and "combined the character of a military school endowed with special rights and of a court institution attached to the imperial household". Each year the sixteen highest pupils were chosen as *pages de chambre* and were personally attached to the Emperor and other members of the imperial family. This honour was highly sought, for those who attained it "had every facility for making a brilliant career in the service of the State". Finally, on leaving the Corps after four or five years of study, each candidate had the right to choose a commission in any regiment of the Russian army, guards or line, without regard to the actual number of vacancies.

The Corps was run with all the discipline of a military unit, and, as in the rest of the contemporary Russian army, severe and even savage punishments were often given for offences against the code. But in its educational activity there appeared a completely different spirit. The actual teaching was under the control of the inspector, a colonel of artillery named Winkler, who was an excellent mathematician and a real liberal. Winkler did all he could to encourage the love for study which was awakening among the lower forms, and strove to give them the best instruction available in his day. It was an education that would have been good at any period, and many of the boys developed rapidly under his influence. A number of important university men consented to give classes in their own special subjects. All of them were remarkable teachers, but perhaps the most outstanding was Klassovsky, a great scholar in the classics and in Russian literature, who had on Kropotkin "an immense influence, which only grew with the years". Klassovsky interpreted his province in a broad and liberal way, and not merely gave bare instruction in the subjects he taught, but sought to reveal to his pupils "that generalised conception of the development of the human mind which lies beyond the scope of each of the subjects that are taught separately".

If it had not been for the excellence of his teachers and the reasonable attitude of officers like Winkler, Kropotkin's time at the Corps of Pages would have been unhappy indeed, for from the outset he found himself in a state of rebellion against its absurd authority.

His first reason for discontent came at the beginning when, although he had reached a sufficient standard of general knowledge for the fourth form, he was actually placed in the fifth, because there were already too many pupils for the higher class. Peter was annoyed at this decision, for it meant that his career in a military school, which he did not wish to join in any case, would now be one of five instead of four years.

To the teachers he expressed his objection outspokenly, but this seems only to have made the more liberal members of the educational staff, and particularly Winkler, all the more friendly to him. In the end he did not wholly regret the circumstances that had been the cause of this little rebellion, for being in the lower form and repeating the lessons he had already learnt both gave him a better foundation for extending his studies and allowed more leisure for developing his taste in literature by "reading aloud to a few friends the dramas of Shakespeare or of Ostrovsky".

But, if Kropotkin's relationship with the teaching staff was increasingly cordial, he found himself from the first in enmity towards the disciplinary system, and took an active part in a rebellion of the younger boys against the *pages de chambre* of that time, a generation of bullies and degenerates whose attitude was completely out of harmony with the new spirit of the rest of the school. A suspicion of his rebellious nature earned him the hostility of the Colonel of the Corps, a French martinet named Girardot whom the boys suspected of being a Jesuit and who was much addicted to the court manners of the days of Nicholas I. It was through this man that Kropotkin was for a time kept unjustly in a subordinate position.

Some years after his entry into the school, in the autumn of 1860, Kropotkin took a leading part in a revolt against one of the masters who had made a consistent practice of reporting the students who committed minor offences during his class. When the signal for the preconcerted demonstration had been given, the whole class turned in their seats and beat loudly with their rulers on the desks behind. By this means nobody could be picked out as the ringleader, so Kropotkin, as the head of the form, was put under arrest and confined to the black cell for ten days. He was deprived of books, and "composed (in horrible verses) a poem, in which the deeds of the fourth form were duly glorified". There was, according to Lebedev, some talk of expelling him from the school, and his name was removed from the red board of honour. But, through the intervention of the Director of the Corps, he was eventually allowed to stay.

One of the principal disadvantages of being at the Corps of Pages was the fact that he was separated from his brother

Alexander in Moscow. They had been, as their early tutor Poulain once expressed it, "deux têtes sous un même bonnet", and had shared the thoughts and interests which each developed during boyhood. Yet they were by no means mutually imitative, in spite of the many ideas they had in common. They differed greatly in disposition and mentality, Alexander being of a passive nature and inclined to abstract thought, while Peter, even as a boy, had a far more active and forceful character, and inclined rather to the concrete aspects of science. Their disagreements were reflected in the fact that, while at this time Alexander was turning towards the German philosophy which had been so fashionable in the late 1830's, and was reading Kant and Hegel enthusiastically, Peter could find no sympathetic attraction towards this school of thought, and, like Herzen before him, preferred the rational philosophers of the French Enlightenment, and particularly Voltaire. Their differing attitudes were to result eventually in divergences of political opinion, for in later years Alexander never accepted Peter's advanced views; he was a disciple of Lavrov, and his brother described him as a social democrat.

Nevertheless, during this period of development the two boys found a great bond in their awakening literary and social interests, and Peter's departure for the capital saw the beginning of a long correspondence in which they exchanged their impressions and thoughts. This had not been possible before he left home, since their father read all the letters that entered the house for any member of the family and "he would soon have put an end to any but a commonplace correspondence."

These letters were preserved by Alexander, and transmitted by him to the care of the Russian socialist Lavrov. Kropotkin, at the time of writing his *Memoirs*, seems to have regarded them as lost; but in 1905 they were returned to him by Alexander's widow, and taken by him to Russia in 1917. In 1932 they were published by Nicholas Lebedev, in Moscow.

Though by no means so full of interesting topics and discussions as Kropotkin himself seems to have believed after a lapse of forty years, they do give an insight into the rapid development of his ideas, which was assisted not only by his teachers at the Corps of Pages, but also by Alexander's advice and his occasional presents of books Peter could not afford to buy. In addition, he found much benefit from his access to the library at the house of his sister Helen, who was now married and living in St Petersburg. It was here that, on his Saturday visits, he would sit up long into the night, reading prohibited French books, including the twelve volumes of Voltaire's *Dictionnaire Philosophique*, as well as the writings of the Stoic philosophers of antiquity. These readings reinforced the curiosity regarding nature and its processes which he had already experienced as a young boy wandering through the forests of Kaluga.

Naturally, with such a steady mental development, it was not to be expected that Kropotkin should remain content with the beliefs of his childhood, and he soon began to seek some faith which would suit his rationalist and democratic interests. He visited Roman Catholic and Protestant churches, but the tawdriness of the one and the aridity of the other alike repelled him, and he seems to have moved on to a natural agnosticism, without feeling the same need for a metaphysical substitute for religion which his brother showed in his preoccupation with Kant. At this period Peter attempted to read the German philosopher's *Critique of Pure Reason*, and found it heavy going, mentioning that he had to spend half an hour over two or three pages. Of his own beliefs he tells us that in these years they were influenced by his interest in science, and particularly in astronomy, which he studied intensively during his last year at the Corps.

> "The never-ceasing life of the universe, which I conceived as *life* and evolution, became for me an inexhaustible source of higher poetic thought, and gradually the sense of man's oneness with nature, both animate and inanimate—the poetry of nature—became the philosophy of my life."

This attitude, so reminiscent of Shelley's basic philosophy, was to receive its finest development when, in old age, Kropotkin wrote his monumental last work, *Ethics*.

His reading in these years was very wide, embracing such varied subjects as the natural sciences (mathematics, physics, and astronomy), biology, political economy, and Russian history. He read a great many books on these and other subjects, in Russian, French, and German, and remarks that he "cannot think now without amazement of the number of books, often of a quite special character, which I read, in all branches, but particularly in the domain of history". The evidently incomplete lists in his correspondence give a great range of titles; one letter alone mentions works by Lamartine, Bianchini, the economist A. Blanqui (against whom Proudhon polemicised), Montesquieu, Guizot, Vogt, Buechner, and Marcus Aurelius, as well as several Russian books on history.

It was, indeed, during this period at the Corps of Pages that he gained the basic knowledge on a number of subjects in which he was later to produce works of important scholarship. The enthusiasm of his brother Alexander for Darwinism led him to begin the evolutionary studies which eventually resulted in his own contribution to that field in *Mutual Aid*. His researches into early Russian history in the imperial library not only taught him the rudiments of historical method, but also provided his first contact with the structure of mediæval society and its co-operative institutions—a source of knowledge which again found its place in the pages of later works.

Nor was even the practical military training without its eventual value in developing his mind and his various abilities. In physics he learnt much, and this subject gave him his first introduction to scientific writing; he was entrusted, under the supervision of the lecturer on physics, with the compilation of a new and up-to-date text-book, based on the teacher's lessons, which was printed as a standard work for use in the school. From this it will be seen that Kropotkin must already have possessed an unusual aptitude for grasping the theoretical bases of scientific thought.

He was also much absorbed in mathematics, and at one time even thought of entering an artillery academy in order to continue these studies after leaving the Corps of Pages. However, other influences were eventually to lead him in a very different direction.

In the shaping of his later activities we find important influences in the practical work of the Corps, and particularly the application of scientific theory to concrete practice. Much time was spent on independent surveys and the building of model fortifications, and Kropotkin rightly points to the beneficial nature of such training, if it is used for a constructive purpose. In describing the surveys, he tells us:

"After a few preliminary exercises we were given a reflecting compass and told: 'Go and make a plan of, say, this lake or those roads, or that park, measuring the angles with the compass and the distances with your pace'. . . . For me these surveys were a deep source of enjoyment. That independent work, that isolation under the centuries-old trees, that life of the forest which I could enjoy undisturbed, while there was at the same time the interest in the work—all these left deep traces in my mind; and if I later became an explorer of Siberia and several of my companions became explorers of Central Asia, the ground for it was prepared in these surveys.

"And finally, in the last form, parties of four boys were taken every second day to some villages at a considerable distance from the camp, and there they had to make a detailed survey of several square miles with the aid of the surveyor's table and a telescopic ruler. . . . This life amidst the peasants in the villages had the best effect upon the intellectual and moral development of many boys.

"At the same time, exercises were made in the construction of natural-sized cross-sections of fortifications. . . . We delighted in such work. . . . I mention this to show how children and youths long for real applications of what they learn at school in abstract, and how stupid are the educators who are unable to see what a powerful aid they could find in concrete applications for helping their pupils to grasp the real sense of the things they learn."

Here we can see the origin of the ideas on balanced intellectual and manual work put forward many years later in *Fields, Factories and Workshops*, as part of a plea for the reintegration of rural and urban life.

The influence of these teaching methods was naturally not in itself sufficient to produce the kind of development Kropotkin underwent during his adolescence. Most of the pages became model officers or fine courtiers, and only the few who had already a predisposition towards independence were able to utilise their education for ends certainly not consciously contemplated by the administrators of the school.

Indeed, Kropotkin's life at this time was by no means wholly bound up in the activities of the Corps of Pages, and the most important influences that fostered his development came from outside that institution. As we have seen, he did not abandon his concern for literature, which was indeed enhanced by a growing interest in other arts. For music, in particular, he developed a passion that was to be life-long. Many evenings he would spend at the houses of St Petersburg friends, singing duets, trios and choruses from the Russian and Italian operas, and, in company with other cadets, he became an habitué of the Opera House, which, he tells us, had in those days become a kind of symbolical rallying-place for liberal sentiment, expressed in the stormy applause that greeted the revolutionary recitatives from *William Tell*. "All this", he remarks, "may seem childish; but many higher ideas and pure inspirations were kindled in us by this worship of our favourite artists."

But literature continued to occupy most of Kropotkin's attention, and, although his own personal magazine was at an end, he began to write stories for submission to the various literary reviews of St Petersburg. None of them was ever published, and their manuscripts do not appear to have survived. However, his letters contain certain summaries which allow one to assume that they were rather unoriginally realistic sketches of peasant life as he had already seen it in boyhood. One of the stories, called "The Pupil", was taken from an actual incident which he had been told by one of its principal actors. It concerned a serf girl whom her master took into his house and educated as if she were his own daughter. This displeased his wife, and when he died without freeing the girl, she began to persecute her in every possible way. Finally, when the girl was eighteen, a young nobleman appeared on the scene. The woman wanted him to marry her own daughter, but he fell in love with the serf. When the mistress learned of this, she used her power to marry the girl immediately to a crude and brutal *moujik*.

It was the kind of cruel incident that was happening every day in Russia right up to the end of serfdom, and events of a similar character had taken place even in Kropotkin's own home when he was a boy. The plot might have occurred to any young writer at the time, and its effectiveness would depend wholly on originality of treatment, which we may safely guess was not at this period the writer's strong point.

Rather than on any literary merits it may have possessed or

lacked, this story is interesting as an illustration of the social consciousness that was emerging in the young page. Even in boyhood he had been conscious of the evils of serfdom; this feeling had been enhanced by the influence of Smirnov and of the Russian and French authors he had read, and he could not help realising how, since the end of the Crimean War, emancipation of the serfs had become one of the most urgent questions in Russian public consciousness. The discontent among the peasants themselves, the guilty feelings of the more liberal nobility, and the spirit of radicalism that had been released by the death of Nicholas I, all combined to bring the issue on to the order of the day, and at this time nobody was more conscious of its urgency than the new Tsar, Alexander II, who, as early as 1856, told an assembly of landowners that it would be better for them to initiate the abolition of serfdom from above than to wait for it to happen from below. In 1857 a proclamation of the Governor-General of Lithuania had announced that the Emperor intended to abolish serfdom, and this raised the hopes of the peasants and of all well-disposed people among the upper classes. But Alexander was surrounded by reactionaries, and it was several years yet before the promised liberation became an accomplished fact.

It was in this interim of disappointment and delay that the revolutionary influence of Herzen and his little emigré group made itself felt more openly among the Russian intellectuals and even among sections of the ruling class. Kropotkin encountered Herzen's writings towards the end of 1858, a few months before he wrote "The Pupil". He had a beautiful young cousin of nineteen, belonging to one of the most fashionable families in St Petersburg, who was unfortunate enough to fall in love with one of her other cousins. It was at that time strictly forbidden by the Russian ecclesiastical law for cousins to marry, and the Church authorities refused categorically to grant dispensation in this case. The disappointment turned this gay and fashionable young girl into a rebel, and it was she who introduced Peter to Herzen's first magazine, *The Polar Star*. Neither of them was at that time, or for some years to come, connected in any way with the radical circles of the period, but the ideas then put forward by men like Herzen and Chernyshevsky made their insidious way into almost every family and every college room in Russia, and it was no accident that brought Kropotkin for the first time into contact with the works of the remarkable man whose role as the most distinguished Russian exile he was in later years to assume. It was, indeed, not very long before he heard discussion of Herzen's emancipationist arguments even among the officers who frequented the house of his cousin, Dmitri Kropotkin, who could in no way be regarded as a revolutionary and who, as governer of Kharkov, was later to be assassinated by members of *Narodnaya Volya* for allowing ill-treatment of political prisoners in the gaols of the city.

Herzen's writings had an immediate and profound influence on Kropotkin's trend of thought. "The beauty of the style of Herzen . . . the breadth of his ideas, and his love of Russia took possession of me, and I used to read and re-read those pages, even more full of heart than of brain." He also tells us that, "with a feeling akin to worship I used to look on the medallion which was printed on the paper cover of *The Polar Star*, and which represented the noble heads of the five 'Decembrists' whom Nicholas I had hanged after the rebellion of 14th December, 1825. . . ."

The progressive conceptions which he had been forming vaguely under the influence of Western ideas rapidly crystallised; and it is ironical that at this time of development, towards the end of 1859, his brother Alexander, still on the transcendental summits of German metaphysics, should have written to him "your mind is frightfully clumsy and frightfully sluggish". In fact, the brothers were now beginning to draw apart in ideas and interests, although there was never any personal conflict between them or any lessening of the affectionate loyalty they maintained towards each other. Peter was emerging from his brother's influence; other trends of thought were working in his mind, and his action became more independent. Henceforward he did more things on his own initiative, and rapidly showed himself a more determined rebel than Alexander.

Under the impulse given by his reading of Herzen, he took to journalism again. This time his work was inevitably coloured by his developed ideas, and at the end of 1859 or the beginning of 1860 he prepared a handwritten radical paper.

"At that age, what could I be but a constitutionalist?—and my paper advocated the necessity of a constitution for Russia. I wrote about the foolish expenses at the Court, and the sums of money which were spent at Nice to keep quite a squadron of the navy in attendance on the dowager Empress, who died in 1860; I mentioned the misdeeds of the functionaries which I continually heard spoken of, and I urged the necessity of constitutional rule."

Three copies of the paper were handwritten, and slipped into the desks of pages who were likely to be sympathetic. Two replied by leaving, in a hiding place indicated by the editor, notes expressing their sympathy but advising caution. Kropotkin prepared a second number, and then his two sympathisers came to him and suggested that, instead of putting them all in danger by continuing with the journal, they should form a circle, in the traditional manner of the early Russian radicals; this they did, reading the same books and discussing questions of social urgency. It is significant that this activity is not mentioned, even obliquely, in Kropotkin's letters to his brother, who was becoming steadily more of a metaphysician, studying Feuerbach and disclaiming, in 1861, any further interest in the natural sciences.

Kropotkin did not give up his literary activities, and at the end of 1861 his first printed article appeared. As we might expect, it was on a social subject. Early in the year, Chernyshevsky's magazine, *Sovremennik*, had published an exposition by Shelgunov of Engels's *The Position of the Working Class in England*. Just as Bakunin had been impressed on his first introduction to the work of Marx, so Kropotkin, later to become an equally devoted anti-Marxist, was impressed by his first introduction to the work of Marx's principal collaborator. Shelgunov's article interested him greatly, and he immediately wrote a review of it which was published in *Knizhni Vestnik* on the 31st December, 1861.

IV

On the 5th March (old style), 1861, the long-awaited emancipation of the serfs was at last decreed. The announcement was received in St Petersburg with delight, and the students of the Corps of Pages were united in their approval. Before the day was over peasant delegations began to appear in the capital, bearing thanks to the Tsar, who was applauded by the people as he rode through the streets, while mingled crowds stood cheering outside the Palace. At the opera a great demonstration took place, and the sounds of the orchestra playing "God Save the Tsar" were completely drowned by the rejoicings of the audience.

It seemed as though a new age had dawned in Russia, and at first nobody, even among the peasants, quite realised how far the oppressive redemption clauses would impose an even heavier economic weight on the landworkers, and make them, where they did not remain subservient to their old masters, the financial prey to a new generation of usurers and land-grabbers, which arose with extraordinary rapidity during the 1860's.

Kropotkin naturally heard the news with great satisfaction, and spoke, both in letters at the time and also years later in his *Memoirs*, of the enthusiasm with which the decree was received, even among the exclusive young aristocrats of the military schools and the officers of the élite regiments, whom he saw cheering the Tsar at the end of a military parade. He described the patience with which the peasants waited for their own freedom, and the dignity with which they bore themselves. On the morning when the manifesto was read at early mass in the Isaac Cathedral in St Petersburg, one of the pages was present, and told Kropotkin that, "when I came out of the church, two peasants, who stood in the gateway, said to me in such a droll way, 'Well, sir, all gone?'" As Kropotkin remarked, "Years of expectation were in that gesture of sending away the master".

Many educated men immediately rallied to do what was in their power to help the peasants use their liberation to full advantage. The most urgent need was for education, since the great majority of the people were illiterate; a movement arose very rapidly for the foundation of Sunday schools at which town and rural workers were taught the rudiments of letters. Thousand of officers, students, and even pages offered their services freely for this work, and the workers flocked to the new schools, eager for the most elementary education. Kropotkin, with a few comrades from the Corps, was among the enthusiastic body of teachers, and he tells us that "such excellent methods were worked out that (Russian having a phonetic spelling) we succeeded in teaching the peasants to read in nine or ten lessons". The mass of peasant illiteracy might, in his opinion, have been ended in a very few years, if only this band of disinterested volunteers had been left without interference from the authorities, who were ever fearful that any kind of movement towards the people might result in subversive activity.

In the months that followed the publication of the emancipation decree, he saw the peaceful but completely independent restraint with which the peasants behaved, although the new law, with its complications, gave them by no means all they felt was justly due to them. Describing visits to his father's estates, he remarks that:

> "I was at Nikolskoye in August 1861, and again in the summer of 1862, and I was struck with the quiet, intelligent way in which the peasants had accepted the new conditions. They knew perfectly well how difficult it would be to pay the redemption tax for the land, which was in reality an indemnity to the nobles in lieu of the obligations of serfdom. But they so much valued the abolition of their personal enslavement that they accepted the ruinous charges —not without murmuring, but as a hard necessity—the moment that personal freedom was obtained. . . .
>
> "When I saw our Nikolskoye peasants, fifteen months after the liberation, I could not but admire them. Their inborn good nature and softness remained with them, but all traces of servility had disappeared. They talked to their masters as equals talk to equals, as if they never had stood in different relations. Besides, such men came out from among them as could make a stand for their rights."

Kropotkin's own father, despite his autocratic character, accepted the change with a fairly even temper, and the family as a whole seem to have maintained good relations with the former serfs. All their house servants departed, to take up employment elsewhere or to follow their trades in the towns, for, although in some ways their new life might be less secure, they were too glad of their freedom to remain in a condition that reminded them in any way of their past slavery. Yet there was no ill-feeling, and the old serf orchestra of Prince Kropotkin, now working as a professional band in the provincial capital of Kaluga, remained on a friendly footing with him.

In fact, the old Prince, like a number of the more astute landowners, did not lose very much from the emancipation. His son tells us that, from fields which were rented by the village *mir* on his Tambov estate, he obtained a rent twice the value of the return he had gained from cultivating them with serf labour. And in one way and another he, and later his widow, managed to grab back so much land from the peasants that, while these unfortunate people had their personal freedom, they were actually economically worse off than before the emancipation. Because of the alienation of meadow land, families who formerly had six or seven horses were reduced to three, and fewer animals meant less manure for cultivation. Moreover, while the peasants were hungry for land to work, and ruined by the redemption charges and a heavy taxation, arable land taken by the Princess under the Law of Minimum ("that diabolical clause inserted by the serf-owners when they were allowed to revise the emancipation law") was allowed to become an uncultivated wilderness covered with thistles.

Kropotkin was one of the tiny minority of Russian noblemen who were ashamed and angry at the chicanery with which the peasants were defrauded of their moral rights after the liberation. He and his brother Alexander, who had been friendly with the peasants since boyhood, were both profoundly shocked by this pretence, which freed the peasants from the landowners only to enslave them to moneylenders, and it was certainly Peter's disappointment with the fiasco of the reform movement, of which the emancipation represented the chief plank, that drove him at last to a more extreme social attitude.

Nevertheless, the end of serfdom meant a real advance in the social evolution of Russia. Feudalism in its more extreme form was ended for ever. Within the limits of the Tsarist passport system men were free to travel where they wished, and could take up what employment they might find. The result was an immense increase in the industrial population, while the middle class, made rich by speculation in land and railways, by usury among the peasants, and by the spread of factory work due to the extra labour of many freed serfs, took a much higher place in Russian society, and began to challenge the authority of the court and the aristocracy. Bowing to necessity, Alexander II had granted the liberation; perhaps a premonition that in doing this he sealed the doom of his own dynasty was at least partly responsible for the reaction into which his reign soon declined.

A fairly close personal contact with this enigmatic figure in Russian history was one of the most important factors in Kropotkin's life at the Corps of Pages, and in some ways the most educative, since it robbed him for good of a number of illusions he might otherwise have retained for a much longer period. His scholastic powers, which had brought him to the head of his form in each successive year, eventually made him the leading boy of the school, and he was accordingly appointed sergeant of the Corps. This caused certain misgivings among some of the officers, who had no high opinion of his capabilities in drill and other more esoteric branches of the military art, and who may also have gained an inkling of the radical lines along which his mind was already beginning to develop.They declared that with Kropotkin in this post there would be no discipline in the Corps. But the custom was that the first boy of the highest form should be the sergeant, and there was no reasonable excuse on which a departure could be made from this rule. So Kropotkin found himself, not very willingly, in this envied post.

The sergeant enjoyed certain privileges. He was treated as an officer, and relieved of the routine duties of internal administration, which were conducted by his fellows of the upper form, while for study he had a separate room. The dignity of the office irked Kropotkin, but he was quick to put his relationship with his friends on a "new comrade-like footing".

But the principal attribute of the office, which made it so much desired in the Corps, was that its holder also acted as the Emperor's personal *page de chambre*: this was regarded as a fine stepping-stone to further distinction, and Kropotkin's family were delighted at this additional opportunity conferred on one of their members.

As for Kropotkin himself, he was at first impressed by the glamour of court life, in spite of his liberal ideas and the fact that he himself, even while in the Corps of Pages, had resolutely refused to use his own title of Prince, earning in this way the evident displeasure of many of his superiors. He remarks that:

"Court life has undoubtedly much that is picturesque about it. With its elegant refinement of manners—superficial though it may be—its strict etiquette, and its brilliant surroundings, it is certainly meant to be impressive. . . . To be an actor in the court ceremonies, in attendance upon the chief personages, offered something more than the mere interest of curiosity for a boy of my age. Besides, I then looked upon Alexander II as a sort of hero; a man who attached no importance to the court ceremonies, but who, at this period of his reign, began his working day at six in the morning, and was engaged in a hard struggle with a powerful reactionary party in order to carry through a series of reforms in which the abolition of serfdom was only the first step."

However, there was nothing like a period of direct experience of court life and of close contact with the Tsar himself to take from a youth of Kropotkin's earnest character any illusions on either of these points. The profligacy of the court offended his naturally puritanical mind, while at the levées, in which he took a fairly conspicuous part, he was disgusted by the competition among so-called responsible men to obtain the favour of a glance or a word from the Emperor that might mean an advancement of their careers. Moreover, proximity to Alexander enabled him to see how far policy was dictated by the whim of that highly neurotic individual, while the latter's attitude towards the peasants who approached him with petitions led Kropotkin to realise that, fundamentally, the Emperor's interest in emancipation had been motivated rather by policy and fear than by any essential humanity of outlook.

He was further repelled by the events of the latter end of 1861, which spoke too clearly of the continuance of naked tyranny to be passed over lightly by a young man of sensitive conscience. In October the students of St Petersburg, Moscow, and Kazan, discontented by the reactionary way in which the universities were treated, held demonstrations to express their annoyance. These were suppressed with the greatest severity, and in a letter to his brother on the 4th October Kropotkin described the police patrols which were brought into the streets to deal with the students, and said that it was only the opposition of the Tsar's brother, the Grand Duke Constantine, which prevented the use of the army. The university of St Petersburg was closed for a time, but many professors supported the students and opened courses in the Town Hall. These were likewise suppressed, and many of the best teachers resigned in protest. At the same time a general attack on any kind of independent education was instituted, and the Sunday schools for teaching the peasants, in which Kropotkin took part, were closed down because the authorities thought that the mere reduction of illiteracy might lead to subversive activities. Kropotkin at the time expressed his utmost disgust with these proceedings, and the last paragraph of the letter in which he described them to his brother contained only the three words: "Meanness—abomination—nastiness!"

At the same time, the brutality of the regime was once again manifested openly in the ruthless cruelty with which the army, and particularly the Cossacks, were ordered to suppress the patriotic demonstrations which took place in Poland, and also the few risings among those peasants who had already begun to realise how they had been defrauded by the redemption. In Warsaw the demonstrators were attacked with whips, hundreds of them were arrested, Roman Catholic churches were attacked by the soldiers and, finally, patriots were shot down in the streets. All this prepared the way for the terrible Polish rising of 1863, which might have been prevented had Alexander been really sincere and consistent in his avowed policy of reform and conciliation. As for the peasants, many of them were killed by the brutal punishment of flogging through the ranks. With such events happening around him in Russia, negating all the line of progress which seemed to have been indicated by the emancipation decree, it was little wonder that Kropotkin's devotion should soon have begun to wear thin.

At the beginning his admiration for Alexander II as the "Liberator" was so great that, he tells us, he would willingly have given his own life to save the Tsar's had any attempt been made on him. But these illusions faded rapidly, and by the end of the year Kropotkin had ceased to regard Alexander as a hero, or as anything more than a man swayed by terrible fears and inner conflicts. He realised that there was, in the circumstances then obtaining, little chance of doing any "useful activity in the spheres nearest the palace".

Undoubtedly, this revealing year at the court did much to complete that preliminary education in life which Kropotkin received at the Corps of Pages. It was his first lesson in the uselessness of expecting anything from the hands of those in power; and by showing him the utter venality of courtly administration and the more than ordinarily human weakness of Alexander, it not only laid the foundations of his distrust of government and authority in general, but also formed the pattern in which the next period of his career was moulded. For, had it not been for this year of close contact with the Tsar, he might well have hoped to promote liberal aims by work at the centre of affairs, instead of, as he did, carrying them to the extreme periphery of the Russian empire, to the distant confines of Siberia.

Yet, though this experience gave him a full knowledge of the Tsar's weakness as ruler and person, it also gave a human contact with that unhappy man, and prevented him from feeling in later years the completely blind hatred which so many of the Russian revolutionaries held towards Alexander. However he may have condemned the later tyrannies of the reign, Kropotkin could never completely forget the anxious neurotic whom he had followed through the corridors of the Winter Palace; in after years, as Annie Besant and others have recorded, he would often say that the blame for the terrible reaction that followed 1863 lay not so much with Alexander as with the evil advisers who surrounded him.

It is perhaps because he, almost more than any other of the Russian revolutionaries, realised fully the dual character of Alexander that he was able to set his faults in a true perspective, and few better estimates of that ruler have been given than the following paragraph, which might be regarded as an epigraph on the period of Kropotkin's life when he, like so many others, still hoped that from above would come a real liberation of the suffering Russian people.

"It has often been said that Alexander II committed a great fault, and brought about his own ruin, by raising so many hopes which later he did not satisfy. . . . It was not merely that he raised hopes. Yielding for a moment to the current of public opinion around him, he induced men all over Russia to set to work, to issue from the domain of mere hopes and dreams, and to touch with the finger the reforms that were required. He made them realise what could be done immediately, and how easy it was to do it; he induced them to sacrifice whatever of their ideals could not be immediately realised, and to demand only what was practically possible at the time. And when they had framed their ideas, and had shaped them into laws which merely required his signature to become realities, then he refused that signature. No reactionist could raise, or even has raised, his voice to assert that what was left—the unreformed tribunals, the absence of municipal government, or the system of exile—was good and was worth maintaining: no one has dared to say that. And yet, owing to the fear of doing, all was left as it was. . . ."

It was small wonder that in a very few years the active youth of Russia were to turn against Alexander, to make his fears into reality, and hunt him to that violent death for which only his own actions can be held to blame.

CHAPTER II

THE EXPLORER

I

KROPOTKIN'S course at the Corps of Pages was due to end in the middle of 1862. He had entered the Corps with no illusions regarding a military career, and his experiences had in no way increased his leaning towards such a vocation. In March 1860, in the middle of his course, he was writing to his brother that "military science does not interest me. . . . I will busy myself with it out of sheer necessity." And his ideas underwent no fundamental change.

But there seemed no alternative to becoming an officer. Neither he nor his brother had any means of subsistence but what their father provided, and the old Prince was wholly determined that all his sons should pursue distinguished military careers. Rebellion against this future would have meant the immediate end of financial support, which was in any case so meagre that Alexander, whom his father disliked, was usually penniless and often in debt.

What Peter really wanted was to remove himself entirely from military life and continue his scientific studies at the university. But this presented difficulties which seemed almost insuperable. It would have meant following the example of many thousands of Russian students and maintaining himself by private teaching while he pursued his own work. Kropotkin, who had no sense of pride in such matters, would not have found this difficult, but he was in an even worse position than the average poor student, since despite all his family's wealth he had neither a civilian suit of his own nor the money to buy one or take lodgings or buy the few small items, such as books and paper, which were necessary to make a start. Klassovsky, his professor of Russian literature, begged him to go to the university, saying: "Believe me, you will be the pride of Russia." But Kropotkin had reluctantly to reject, for the time being at least, the advice of his respected teacher, and he did not even dare to explain his true position, since he knew that Klassovsky would have contributed from his own means to assist him. All that remained, then, was to find the most congenial position in the army, where, if possible, he might find the means to satisfy his twin passions for scientific study and social reform, and also his youthful love of adventure.

He had first thought of entering the Artillery Academy, which would have meant two years of extended study in mathematics and physics and a postponement of the irksome duties of military service. But his experience of court life and the reactionary happenings of recent months had left him with no desire to stay at the centres of the Russian autocracy, besides which life in the military academies had become as frustrating as anywhere else in the metropolitan areas: "The officers of the academies had been treated during the previous winter as if they were schoolboys; in two academies they had revolted, and in one of them they had left in a body."

There was one region in which it seemed possible both to escape from the constricting prison of metropolitan Russia and to do work which would indulge his real interests.

> "My thoughts turned more and more towards Siberia. The Amur region had recently been annexed by Russia; I had read all about that Mississippi of the East, the mountains it pierces, the sub-tropical vegetation of its tributary, the Usuri, and my thoughts went further—to the tropical regions which Humboldt had described, and to the great generalisations of Ritter, which I delighted to read. Besides, I reasoned, there is in Siberia an immense field for the application of the great reforms which have been made or are coming; the workers must be few there, and I shall find a field of action to my tastes."

For these reasons Kropotkin finally decided to apply for a commission in a Siberian regiment, and selected the Mounted Cossacks of the Amur. But he was not to have his way without difficulty. The regiment had little prestige—it was the youngest in the Russian army—and that the head boy of the school, who had passed out highest and for a year had been the personal page of the Emperor, should elect to join this almost disreputable unit was a subject of consternation both to his fellow pages and to the authorities of the school. The director at first regarded it as a jest in bad taste. Kropotkin's father was even more indignant to see all the fine opportunities provided by a life at the court thrown away in this manner; he immediately sent an explosive telegram to the Grand Duke Michael, then commander of the military schools, saying, "I forbid my son to go to the Amur".

Russian absolutism automatically upheld parental authority against the rebellion of the young, and it is very likely that Kropotkin would not have been able to make the journey to Siberia, which was such a turning-point in his life, had it not been for the opportune outbreak of an historic fire in the Apraxin Dvor on the 26th May which threatened the Corps of Pages, as well as some of the ministries and other official buildings.

The origin of this mysterious fire has never been traced; it was certainly the work of incendiaries, and the reactionaries were quick to accuse the liberals. However, at this time there was little reason for the opposition to use such extreme tactics, and there is a great deal of evidence to support the view, held by Kropotkin and many others, that the fire was actually the work of counter-revolutionary groups, ancestors of the Black Hundreds, who sought to frighten the Tsar out of any further liberal measures in the line of the emancipation of the serfs. However that may be, the actual result of the fire was certainly to deepen the reactionary tendencies of the administration, and to heighten the impetus of that retrogression towards naked despotism which had already become evident at the end of the preceding year.

The conflagration, starting in a comparatively small way, was fed by inflammable materials of all kinds—second-hand rubbish, oils, etc., with which the wooden booths and warehouses of the area were filled, and it rapidly assumed very dangerous proportions. The authorities displayed their usual incompetence; few fire engines were available, and these were used at the wrong places, while water supplies were miserably inadequate. It was, Kropotkin says, the common people, working without pause to move inflammable goods, who prevented it from spreading with disastrous rapidity. Despite these spontaneous efforts, the flames reached the archives of the Ministry of the Interior, and began to affect the timber-yards in the vicinity. The Corps of Pages itself was threatened, and it seemed likely that from thence the fire, if unchecked, would sweep to the National Library and up the Nevsky Prospect. Already the window frames of the Corps buildings were beginning to smoulder. It was eventually only through the initiative of the pages themselves, and particularly of Kropotkin, that the inertia of the authorities was overcome and adequate means were brought to prevent the fire from spreading farther.

Next morning the Grand Duke Michael arrived to inspect the damage at the Corps, and Kropotkin, in accordance with routine, attended his rounds. The Grand Duke showed an interest in Kropotkin's plans, asked his reasons for wishing to visit the Amur, and, on hearing that he had no relatives or friends in Siberia, remarked: "But how are you going, then? They may send you to a lonely Cossack village. What will you be doing there? I had better write about you to the Governor-General, to recommend you."

This offer was sufficient to remove the parental objections, and on the 13th of June Kropotkin was duly appointed an officer in the regiment of his choice. On the same day he took part in a final parade, riding on horseback at the head of the battalion and leading the military evolutions before the Tsar. At the end of the parade an incident occurred which strengthened his desire to escape from the capital, with its atmosphere of steadily increasing oppression.

Alexander II called out, "The promoted officers to me!", and, when they had gathered round him, began to speak, still sitting upon his horse.

"He began in a quiet tone. 'I congratulate you: you are officers.' He spoke about military duty and loyalty as they are usually spoken of on such occasions. 'But if any one of you,' he went on, 'but if any one of you—which God preserve you from—should under any circumstances prove disloyal to the Tsar, the throne, and the fatherland—take heed of what I say—he will be treated with all the se-ve-ri-ty of the laws, without the slightest com-mi-se-ra-tion!'

"His voice failed; his face was peevish, full of that expression of blind rage, which I saw in my childhood on the faces of landlords when they threatened their serfs 'to skin them under the rods'. He violently spurred his horse, and rode out of our circle.

" 'Reaction, full speed backwards', I said to myself as we made our way back to the Corps."

A few days later, Kropotkin saw the Emperor for the last time at a Palace levée for the newly appointed officers, and he gives his impressions of this final meeting with the man against whom he was in later years to become an uncompromising but almost regretful rebel.

"Alexander II found me and asked, 'So you go to Siberia? Did your father consent to it, after all?' I answered in the affirmative. 'Are you not afraid to go so far?' I warmly replied: 'No, I want to work. There must be so much to do in Siberia to apply the great reforms which are going to be made.' He looked straight at me; he became pensive; at last he said, 'Well, go; one can be useful everywhere', and his face took on such a character of complete surrender that I thought at once, 'He is a used-up man; he is going to give it all up'."

This interview marked the end of Kropotkin's life as a courtier, and he was impatient to get away from close contact with tendencies that betrayed all the hopes raised by the emancipation, and all the promises of reforms which the liberals had been expecting for the past few years. The St Petersburg fire had been used as an excuse for widespread repression; the city had been placed under martial law, wholesale arrests of suspected radicals had taken place, Chernyshevsky's *Sovremennik*, the one progressive magazine in Russia, had been suppressed, and, on the 14th of June, three disaffected officers were shot in Poland. "St Petersburg had assumed a gloomy aspect. Soldiers marched in the streets. Cossack patrols rode round the palace, the fortress was filled with prisoners. Whereever I went I saw the same thing—the triumph of the reaction." Kropotkin hastened to escape from this sombre atmosphere, and "left St Petersburg without regret" on the 24th June, 1862, travelling via Moscow, where he stopped to see his brother Alexander before proceeding to Siberia.

He went first to Irkutsk and there found himself in more congenial surroundings which were not yet overshadowed by the mounting reaction he had left in St Petersburg. " 'Reforms' were on all lips", and among those most often mentioned was a thorough reorganisation of the system of exile.

The celebrated Nicholas Muraviev, who had added the territories of the Amur to the Russian empire, had just returned from Siberia to Moscow, and his place was taken by a young general, Korsakov, but the spirit of the administration was not changed, and the Governor-General welcomed Kropotkin personally and with great friendliness, remarking that he was very glad to have around him men of liberal opinions. Kropotkin's first appointment was that of *aide-de-camp* to General Kukel, the head of the General Staff, a brilliant young Lithuanian of thirty-five who was already well known for his radical opinions. Kropotkin, although only a junior officer, was treated immediately with great warmth by this remarkable man, and they soon became intimate friends. Kukel, says Kropotkin, "at once took me to a room in his house, where I found, together with the best Russian reviews, complete collections of the London revolutionary editions of Herzen".

Kukel had been friendly with Bakunin during his exile, and through him Kropotkin learnt a great deal about that famous revolutionary, who had recently escaped from Siberia, down the Amur and across to Japan and the United States. He also met Bakunin's Polish wife, Antonia, who had stayed on in Irkutsk after her husband's escape, and who experienced great difficulty in leaving Siberia for Western Europe to rejoin Bakunin. But at this time Kropotkin learnt little of Bakunin's anarchist views, which the latter did not, indeed, develop fully until his return to Western Europe and his great struggle with Marx within the International Workingmen's Association.

Kukel was appointed temporary governor of the distant province of Transbaikalia, and, a few weeks after reaching Irkutsk, Kropotkin accompanied him across Lake Baikal to the tiny wooden town of Chita, which was the capital of the vast territory.

II

Much work lay before them, for all the officials then in Chita took very seriously the reforms which they expected to achieve under the Tsar's avowed policy, and by which they saw Siberia becoming an example for the rest of the empire. In Russia of that period it must have been difficult to find a more industrious and disinterested set of officials; Kukel would say to Kropotkin, "It is a great epoch we live in; work, my dear friend", and he followed his own advice to the letter, for he was active all day long and often worked far into the night.

Kropotkin soon found himself involved in responsible work rarely entrusted to a youth of twenty. One day Kukel said: "Here is a circular from the Ministry. They ask us to collect all possible information about the state of prisons, and to express our opinions as to the reforms to be made. There is no one here to undertake the work; you know how fully we are all occupied. We have asked for information in the usual way, but receive nothing in reply. Will you take up the work?"

Kropotkin objected that he was too inexperienced, but Kukel would hear nothing of this and, wisely trusting to the young man's initiative, told him: "Study! In the *Journal of the Ministry of Justice* you will find, to guide you, elaborate reports on all possible systems of prisons. As to the practical side of the work, let us gather, first, reliable information as to where we stand. Then we all—Colonel Pedashenko, Mr A. and Y., and the mining authorities also—will help you. We will discuss everything in detail with people having practical knowledge of the matter; but gather, first, the data—prepare material for discussion."

For several months Kropotkin worked at his investigations. He encountered far more difficulties than he had anticipated, for the mining authorities, who controlled a great deal of the convict labour, were responsible directly to St Petersburg, and by no means anxious to cooperate in reforms which would complicate their own work and perhaps deprive them of the opportunities for corruption which characterised their part of the Siberian administration. They delayed submitting the information for which they were asked, and then, when they could decently procrastinate no longer, sent reports so obscure as to be almost useless.

However, Kropotkin and the small committee of "well-intentioned men" with whom he worked made great efforts to collect the necessary information. He himself travelled tirelessly in search of first-hand impressions and facts. He visited a number of prisons and found that, with their unbelievable filth, overcrowding, inadequate food, unhealthy buildings, tyrannical officers, and the excessive work which convicts were forced to perform, they "all answered literally to the well-known description of Dostoevsky in his *Buried Alive* ".

He visited the *etapes*, or lockups, on the route from Russia to Siberia, where the prisoners stopped for the night during their terrible march of thousands of miles from the Urals to the prison camps, and found the buildings both rotten in structure and completely inadequate in size for the large numbers of prisoners, who were often accompanied, according to the Russian custom of that period, by their wives and children.

He watched the "Trains", or processions of convicts, loaded with chains and guarded by soldiers, crossing the frozen steppes on foot, beheld the sufferings of these unfortunate men and their still more miserable companions from cold, hunger, and the sheer brutality of their guards, and heard the pitiful *miloserdnaya*, the traditional song for charity which the prisoners raised as they passed through the villages. And he was lastingly impressed by the impulsive and unvarying generosity with which the poor answered the call of these unfortunates.

> "The peasants of the villages on the Siberian highway understand these tones; they know their true meaning from their own experience, and the appeal of the *nestchastnyie*—of the 'sufferers', as our people call all prisoners—is answered by the poor; the most destitute widow, signing herself with the cross, brings her coppers, or her piece of bread, and deeply bows before the chained 'sufferer', grateful to him for not disdaining her small offering."

He visited the gold mines and saw the convicts working in frozen and icy water "that covers their feet to the knees, and sometimes to the stomach", and returning to the prison to sleep in their drenched clothes. Worst of all, he saw the terrible conditions of the salt mines, where the Polish exiles were employed, and in which all but a few inevitably died in a short time from either consumption or scurvy.

All these experiences had a profound effect in increasing Kropotkin's horror at the system of government then in power, but, like many another Russian liberal at that time, he still hoped that something would come of his efforts, and felt that it was possible to deal with the evils of prison life by reform. Kukel and the committee shared his ideas, and prepared a report making drastic recommendations for improvement. They condemned the exile system wholeheartedly, both on humanitarian grounds and because it inflicted a heavy burden on Siberia. This recommendation would in itself have involved a complete change in the Russian judicial procedure and penal organisation, but the committee, under the enthusiastic guidance of Kropotkin, went farther still. It condemned cellular confinement, advocated the classification of prisoners, recommended the provision of productive and paid work in common, and in general laid down a plan for the transformation of prisons into reformatories.

The final submission of the document was, however, delayed by an event which showed that the reaction of St Petersburg was already, in 1863, beginning to penetrate into the more remote regions. Kukel, having been denounced, was ordered to return to Irkutsk, where he was kept waiting until further orders, without being allowed to resume his position on the general staff. The intention was to imprison him in the Peter-and-Paul fortress as a dangerous radical, and it was only the intervention of Nicholas Muraviev, still one of the most influential men in Russia, that persuaded the Tsar to abandon this plan.

The principal reason for this dismissal was Kukel's sympathy for the political exiles in general and particularly for the celebrated Russian poet, M. L. Mikhailov, who had been condemned to hard labour in 1861 for issuing a revolutionary proclamation. Mikhailov's case aroused so much sympathy that the Governor of Tobolsk gave a dinner in his honour when he arrived in Western Siberia, at which all the local officials paid tribute to the exile. Mikhailov, who was suffering from consumption, of which he was to die in 1865, was relieved from hard labour, and officially allowed to stay in the prison hospital of Narchinsk. But Kukel let him live in the house of his brother, who was a mining engineer, and here he was visited by Kropotkin, on whom he had some influence. It was Mikhailov who first introduced him to anarchist ideas, in the shape of Proudhon's *Système des Contradictions Economiques*, which he recommended him to read. After Mikhailov's death Kropotkin bought his copy of this book, which the poet had annotated. He also read

N. Sokolov's comments on Proudhon; it was the introduction to this thinker's ideas that made the young officer first regard himself as a socialist.

Like all the liberals in Siberia, Kropotkin was deeply affected by his parting with Kukel. "I not only lost in him a dear friend, but I felt also that this parting was the burial of a whole epoch, full of long-cherished hopes—'full of illusions', as it became the fashion to say."

Meanwhile, the Polish insurrection made the reform of the prisons all the more urgent, since to Transbaikalia alone some 11,000 new exiles were sent. But the insurrection, which in Russia established the final ascendancy of the party of reaction, including such terrible figures as Michael Muraviev (called 'the Butcher' because of his hanging progress through Poland), and Generals Shuvalov and Trepov, the police chiefs who scared Alexander into conniving at their corrupt administration, meant the end of the schemes of reform which it was intended should follow the emancipation. The proposals of Kropotkin's committee, after being subjected to a few formal objections from the new governor, an amiable but ineffective man, were sent to St Petersburg, where they were quietly shelved. Except for one or two show-prisons of European Russia, the penal system remained unchanged, and the recommendations on which Kropotkin had worked so hard were forgotten.

A similar fate befell his other efforts at reform. Kukel had appointed him secretary of a second committee, this time to prepare a scheme of municipal self-goverment. The committee was "composed of citizens of Chita, elected by all the population, as freely as they might have been elected in the United States", and its members showed intelligence and enthusiasm. Seeing the oncoming reaction, Kropotkin hastened to complete this report, and very quickly a comprehensive scheme for municipal reform was sent forward. Like that on the prisons, it was never heard of again.

Even more frustrating were the occasions when his efforts actually appeared to bear fruit, to be withered by corruption, inefficiency, or mere indifference. An example of the influence of corruption was shown in the case of a police chief whom, after a great deal of effort, Kropotkin and Kukel managed to expel from Transbaikalia for flagrant maladministration—only to learn a few months later that the same man had, through influence at St Petersburg, been appointed to an even higher position in Kamchatka, from which he retired very shortly as a rich man. An instance of monstrous inefficiency took place during the later period of Kropotkin's stay in Siberia, when he was attaché for Cossack Affairs to the Governor-General in Irkutsk. In this capacity he made an intensive investigation of the recent famines on the Usuri. He prepared an elaborate report, and received official congratulations, being promoted to the rank of captain and given special rewards. But his efforts proved useless, as he tells us:

"All the measures I recommended were accepted, and special grants of money were given for aiding the emigration of some and for supplying cattle to others, as I had suggested. But the practical realisation of the measures went into the hands of some old drunkard who would squander the money and pitilessly flog the unfortunate Cossacks for the purpose of converting them into good agriculturists."

It was small wonder that Kropotkin began to despair of achieving anything when he saw such a vast combination of reaction in St Petersburg, corruption in the provinces, and gross inefficiency in both. But there were few experiences in his career which he did not turn to some use, and it was through such lessons in Siberia that he gained the mental outlook which later made him such a steadfast opponent of governmental interference and such a warm advocate of voluntary initiative. Time and again in these years he saw his reliance on the State to carry out reforms frustrated by some vested interest, or found that schemes which seemed well started vanish in the wastes of bureaucratic inefficiency, like rivers disappearing in the sand. But he also found that direct co-operation with individual peasants or hunters was almost always fruitful. From the ending of his illusion that the administrative machine of the State could ever serve the interests of the people as a whole, he dates his first glimmerings of understanding of the natural working of human society. But, to balance this negative lesson, he tells us that:

"The constructive work of the unknown masses, which so seldom finds any mention in books, and the importance of that constructive work in the growth of forms of society, appeared before my eyes in a clear light. To witness, for instance, the ways in which the communities of Dukhobortsy . . . migrated to the Amur region; to see the immense advantages which they got from their semi-communistic brotherly organisation; and to realise what a success the colonisation was, amidst all the failures of State colonisation, was learning something which cannot be learned from books. Again, to live with natives, to see at work the complex forms of social organisation which they have elaborated far away from the influence of any civilisation, was, as it were, to store up floods of light which illuminated my subsequent reading. The part which the unknown masses play in the accomplishment of all important historical events, and even in war, became evident to me from direct observation, and I came to hold ideas similar to those which Tolstoy expressed concerning the leaders and the masses in his monumental work, *War and Peace*.

"Having been brought up in a serf-owner's family, I entered active life, like all young men of my time, with a great deal of confidence in the necessity of commanding, ordering, scolding, punishing, and the like. But when, at an early stage, I had to manage serious enterprises and to deal with men, and when each mistake would lead at once to heavy consequences, I began to appreciate the difference between acting on the principle of command and discipline and acting on the principle of common understanding. The former works admirably in a military parade, but it is worth nothing where real life is concerned and the aim can be achieved only through the severe effort of many converging wills. Although I did not then formulate my observations in terms from party struggles, I may say now that I lost in Siberia whatever faith in State discipline I had cherished before. I was prepared to become an anarchist."

But it was a matter of some years before these realisations were to bear fruit in open rebellion against the system. In the meantime a series of opportunities to follow his scientific inclinations by exploring the little-known parts of Eastern Siberia occurred, and he was not slow to seize the chance of work likely to be more productive and personally satisfying than his attempts at reform, and to enable him to act on his own responsibility in situations distant from the influences which were growing steadily more distasteful to him.

Besides, with Kukel's departure and the steady permeation of St Petersburg reaction into the remoter parts of the empire, the atmosphere of the towns, Irkutsk and Chita, had become steadily less congenial. At best the social life of these little Russian communities was restricted to official circles. Now, since radical ideas and discussion of the serious problems which faced Russia and Siberia alike had become less popular, their communal life appeared more frivolous and pointless than ever; gambling, spiritualism, idle gossip, and philandering held the day, and disgusted all men of serious thought. Kropotkin was by no means a killjoy; he would dance with the young people until the small hours, and he enjoyed taking part in the amateur theatricals in Irkutsk. But the prevalent atmosphere of unthinking folly as a mask for deepening reaction led him to dislike these centres of administration, and to grasp eagerly at any chance that might be offered to go into the remote and little-known parts of the Far Eastern provinces. Indeed, the only thing that reconciled him to continued life in Siberia, besides the joy of creative geographical work, was the arrival of his brother Alexander, who commanded a squadron of Cossacks in Irkutsk. They eagerly discussed once again "all the philosophical, social, and sociological questions of the day", and, though their ideas had grown somewhat apart in the intervening years, were very happy to be together once more and to resume their old companionship.

III

Kropotkin's travels in the Far East were extensive, and not without risk and excitement. He made five major journeys, as well as a number of smaller expeditions, and estimated that he travelled, in all, "over fifty thousand miles in carts, on board steamers, in boats, but chiefly on horseback". His journeys often involved him in dangerous situations, but were always undertaken with the maximum simplicity, and completely without the elaborate equipment which is so often associated with explorers. This was partly due to lack of resources, for the St Petersburg government, extravagant in so many things, was always parsimonious in its expenditure on scientific expeditions, except in the direction of Afghanistan and Persia, where they had some strategic significance in connection with the Russian imperialist designs on the Near

East and India. The Russian drive in the Far East, which had such disastrous results in the Russo-Japanese war, had not yet excited ambition in the capital. The territories of the Amur had been gained, almost against the will of the Tsar's advisers, by the initiative of Nicholas Muraviev, Governor-General of Eastern Siberia before Kropotkin's arrival, and nobody in St Petersburg was anxious to devote any cash to expeditions which might well lead to clashes with the neighbouring Chinese empire, jealously suspicious, since Muraviev's infringements, of activities on its Manchurian frontiers.

However, Kropotkin himself seems to have preferred the greatest simplicity in his expeditions. Always he was ready to take the means which lay at hand and to travel as lightly as possible. When he had control he went without any armed escort and did not carry weapons, since he considered that the local inhabitants were always irritated by the presence of an armed stranger, and that friendliness was a much better protection. Certainly his own experience supported his theories in this respect. As for elaborate equipment, he soon learnt "how little man really needs as soon as he comes out of the enchanted circle of conventional civilisation", and realised that, "with a few pounds of bread and a few ounces of tea in a leather bag, a kettle and a hatchet hanging at the side of the saddle, and under the saddle a blanket, to be spread at the camp fire upon a bed of freshly cut spruce twigs, a man feels wonderfully independent, even amidst unknown mountains thickly covered with woods or capped with snow".

The first expedition, although of little geographical consequence since the ground it covered had already been surveyed, militarily occupied and partly settled by Europeans, was nevertheless of great value as a training in initiative and individual responsibility.

In order to make his occupation of the Lower Amur and the Usuri more than merely nominal, Muraviev had sent there some thousands of ex-convicts, who accepted their freedom on the condition of settling this wild land, which consisted largely of virgin forest. Although most of the men were of peasant extraction, the years of prison and army life had demoralised them to such an extent that they were unable to make their way against the circumstances which, in these regions of luxuriant and even sub-tropical flora, with abnormally heavy rainfalls, would have been hard to overcome quickly with even the best resources. The difficulty of clearing the forests and the steady destruction of crops by various natural agencies resulted in famine conditions, and large quantities of food had to be sent periodically to provide for the needs of soldiers and settlers.

Each year a small fleet of a hundred and fifty barges was built at Chita, loaded with stores and taken down the rivers on the early spring floods. The flotilla was divided into groups of twenty or more barges, and these were put under the charge of those officers who seemed reasonably honest. Hardly any of them were conversant with navigation, but at least "they could be trusted . . . not to steal the provisions and then report them as lost".

Kropotkin was appointed assistant to the major in charge, and his first assignment was to take a small batch of vessels quickly down to a certain point on the Amur. He had no experience in sailing on a large and swiftly flowing river with dangerous rocky banks, and the only crews he could find were the equally inexperienced and notoriously lazy ex-soldiers of the Amur settlements. On the morning of departure the men were collected from the taverns of Chita; most of them were so drunk that they had to be ducked in the river to bring them to their senses. However, Kropotkin's flair for practical work soon taught him all that was necessary, and he managed to instruct his "sons" to such effect that only one barge was sunk. It was his first introduction to the Lower Amur, and he was deeply impressed by the "most beautiful, wide, and swift river flowing amidst mountains rising in steep wooded cliffs a couple of thousand feet above the water".

Having delivered his barges in safety, he had to proceed down the river for another thousand miles in a swift post boat. It was a primitive craft, with "a light shed in its back end, and . . . on its stem a box filled with earth upon which a fire is kept to cook the food". As crew he had "three tramps who had the reputation of being incorrigible thieves and robbers". But, although he carried a heavy sack of banknotes and silver, Kropotkin followed his usual practice of not bearing arms, and found his men excellent company. They rowed hard all day, while at night Kropotkin kept watch and steered the drifting boat down river through a landscape which, with "the full moon shining above, and the dark hills reflected in the river", seemed to him "beautiful beyond description". The journey was accomplished rapidly and without incident, the rowers carrying out their task in the most exemplary manner until they reached the destination of Blagoveshchensk, where they got into trouble from drinking too much Chinese brandy and one of them was eventually locked up, to be extricated from prison and sent home by one of Kropotkin's friends.

At Blagoveschensk Kropotkin joined the commander of the flotilla, and, on a large decked boat, they proceeded down the swollen river, which in places extended to a width of five miles with the monsoon floods, disturbed by tremendous waves whenever an easterly wind blew against the current. Running into a typhoon, they managed to sail the boat into a sheltered tributary, where they were held up for two days while the storm raged so fiercely that when Kropotkin ventured into the forest he had to retreat "on account of the number of immense trees which the wind was blowing down".

As a result of this storm more than forty barges, containing two thousand tons of food, were lost, and a famine threatened the Lower Amur settlements unless additional supplies could be brought down before the upper reaches of the river froze.

They were two thousand miles away from Chita, with no telegraph and no means of carrying the news more quickly than by messenger. So it was decided that, while the major went down river to try and buy grain in Japan, Kropotkin should travel back to Chita by the swiftest means he could find.

He proceeded at first by boat, changing his rowers at the villages, roughly twenty miles apart. This type of travelling involved considerable risk, since the weather was still extremely stormy and the village boats very flimsy. Often the danger became really acute, particularly when they had to cross the mouths of tributaries or branches of the river, in which the waves rode very high.

"One day we had to cross a branch of the Amur nearly half a mile wide. Chopped waves rose like mountains as they rolled up that branch. My rowers, two peasants, were seized with terror; their faces were white as paper, their blue lips trembled, they murmured prayers. Only a boy of fifteen, who held the rudder, calmly kept a watchful eye on the waves. He glided between them as they seemed to sink around us for a moment; but when he saw them rising to a menacing height in front of us he gave a slight turn to the boat and steadied it across the waves. The boat shipped water from each wave, and I threw it out with an old ladle, noting at times that it accumulated more rapidly than I could get rid of it. There was a moment when the boat shipped two such great waves that, on a sign given to me by one of the trembling rowers, I unfastened the heavy sack full of copper and silver that I carried across my shoulder. . . . For several days in succession we had such crossings. I never forced the men to cross, but they themselves, knowing why I had to hurry, would decide at a given moment that an attempt must be made. 'There are not seven deaths in one's life, and one cannot be avoided', they would say, and, signing themselves with the cross, would seize the oars and pull over."

The almost nightmare quality of this journey was enhanced when Kropotkin and his rowers were overtaken by a small steamer proceeding up the Shilka, a major branch of the Amur, in the direction of Chita. The captain had jumped overboard in a fit of *delirium tremens*. He had been rescued, and now lay incapable in his bunk. The crew asked Kropotkin to take charge of the steamer, and, somewhat unwillingly in view of his inexperience, he accepted. But he soon found that the crew knew their work so well that they were able to carry on with almost no need for him to interfere.

But he was perpetually obsessed by the urgency of his mission, and the slowness with which the steamer made its way against the swift current of the Shilka did not satisfy him. In order to gain twenty hours which might make all the difference in getting supplies away before navigation ended, he took to horseback, riding with a Cossack two hundred miles up the Argun, "along one of the wildest mountain tracks in Siberia, stopping to light our camp fire only after midnight had overtaken us in the woods". Already ice was forming on the river at night, and his anxiety was becoming desperate when he encountered the Governor and his old friend Pedashenko at Kara on the Shilka, and the latter immediately put in hand the sending of the necessary supplies.

Meanwhile, Kropotkin was sent on to Irkutsk, to report to the Governor-General. At the end of this journey, during which he had taken little rest, he felt completely worn out. But he had hardly been in Irkutsk a week before the Governor-General called on him to go to St Petersburg, more than four thousand miles away, to report personally the loss of the barges. This journey as well had to be completed at breakneck speed, which meant that the 3,200 miles from Irkutsk to the railway at Nijni-Novgorod, over freezing Siberian roads, must be done by fast post-carts within twenty days.

It was difficult weather for travelling, since sleighs could not yet be used, while the frozen ruts over which the post-carts had to travel at full speed made riding uncomfortable and even dangerous, the wheels of the carts often being broken by the rough usage. Moreover, the half-frozen state of the rivers presented difficulties and dangers. One, the Ob, Kropotkin had to cross in a boat among great cakes of floating ice which threatened to crush the tiny boat. On the next river, the Tom, the ice had frozen only the preceding night, and the peasants refused to take him over unless he gave them a "receipt" saying, "I, the undersigned, hereby testify that I was drowned by the will of God, and by no fault of the peasants".

At last he reached Moscow, where his brother joined him for the journey to St Petersburg. There he found the government officials at first incredulous of his story of the disaster; corruption had eaten so far into the Tsarist administration that the first reaction on receiving such a report was to imagine that some local official had stolen the goods and pocketed the money. But Kropotkin was well known at court, where there was a high opinion of his integrity, and the Count Ignatiev revealed in a chance remark that this was obviously why the Governor-General had chosen to send him. " . . . People say that you were well known as a page, and you have only been a few months in Siberia; so you would not shelter the people there if it were swindling. They trust in you." Dmitri Miliutin, the Minister of War, listened to him with attention, and asked him to submit a report giving his recommendations as to how the repetition of such occurrences might be avoided.

Undoubtedly Kropotkin was receiving flattering notice for a young official of twenty-one, and such incidents might have been used by a more scheming mind to build a distinguished and profitable career in the service of the Tsar. But his ambitions already lay in other directions, and the attentions of statesmen were less important to him than the disquieting news that the great socialist writer, Chernyshevsky, had just been taken away to prison because the administration were jealous of his influence over the Russian youth.

He was not anxious to stay in the capital, and, as soon as the winter had set in, travelled back by sleigh, completing the whole journey to Irkutsk in nineteen days. Lying full-length and well wrapped in furs, he found the travelling on the smooth snow roads more comfortable than at any other season, even the forty or sixty degrees of frost being quite bearable.

After these feats of endurance, in which he had travelled more than ten thousand miles in a few weeks by the most arduous forms of transport, Kropotkin was given the post of attaché for Cossack Affairs. But, as we have already seen, he found this work, in which the inadequacy of the system allowed him to do only a fraction of what he desired to improve the lives of the settlers, extremely frustrating and when, in 1864, it was proposed that he should make a geographical expedition into Manchuria, he accepted without hesitation. This journey would involve the first observation of a considerable portion of territory unknown to Europeans, and Kropotkin was sensible of the great opportunity it gave him as a young and self-taught geographer.

The object of the expedition was to find a direct way across the triangular enclave of Chinese-Manchurian territory which projected into the Russian lands—owing to the frontier departing, in a diversion nearly three hundred miles deep, down the Argun and Amur rivers, from the line of the 50th parallel. The direct distance between the Russian posts of Tsurukhaitu in Transbaikalia and Blagoveschensk on the Amur was only five hundred miles, but by the river tracks it was twice as far, besides which the Argun was not navigable, so that travelling down its course had to be done by difficult paths along the precipitous banks.

The ostensible reason for Kropotkin's expedition was to find a track which, according to the Mongols, went over the Great Khingan range and passed via the Chinese town of Merghen, and which might enable the Cossack drovers to take their cattle more quickly from Transbaikalia into the Amur province.

There may well have been in the minds of the officials some ulterior strategic aim, but, if this existed, Kropotkin does not seem to have been conscious of it.

His journey presented considerable difficulties. Only two Europeans, Jesuit missionaries, had penetrated, many years ago, as far as Merghen, and the great area, as large as England, which lay between that city and the angle of the Russian frontier was completely unknown. Kropotkin could discover no information concerning it; even the Chinese geographers yielded him nothing of practical value. An added difficulty arose owing to the fact that the area he must cross was Manchurian territory, part of the Chinese empire, and, according to the Chinese frontier authorities, was not covered by the treaty allowing free trade between Siberia, Mongolia and China. Moreover, even if a Russian trader were allowed to enter the country, a Russian officer certainly would not be admitted. It was therefore necessary to practise deception, and Kropotkin decided to take the risk of travelling disguised as "the Irkutsk second guild merchant, Peter Alexeiev". He adopted the dress and aped the manners of the nineteenth-century Russian merchants and, largely owing to his having often played such parts in amateur performances of Ostrovsky, found that his imitation was successful enough to convince even the inquisitive Cossack peasants he encountered in the frontier areas. On leaving Irkutsk he was warned by the Governor-General not to reveal his identity if taken prisoner by the Chinese authorities, but he did not allow the latter possibility to deter him from such an opportunity of original exploration.

He went to the frontier, already in disguise, and there formed a caravan of eleven Cossack traders and one Tungus hunter. They took a convoy of forty horses for sale, and two carts, in one of which Kropotkin carried the velveteen, gold braid, and cloth he intended to use for trading. As the purpose of the expedition was to be closely hidden, it was impossible to take any conspicuous scientific equipment, and at times, when Chinese soldiers were about, Kropotkin even had to go to the extent of glancing furtively at his compass and writing the bearings and distances in his pocket, without showing the paper concealed there.

The party crossed the frontier without interference, except

from the Chinese soldiers who tried to beg spirits. Then they proceeded for four or five days straight across an undulating plateau about a hundred and thirty miles wide, until they reached an old Chinese road which led into the Great Khingan. They found the crossing of the ridge, which from a distance had seemed so very "black and terrible", relatively easy, as they travelled in the company of an old Chinese functionary whom they had overtaken on the road.

"Mountains devoid of forest rose right and left, and we thought already of the difficulties we should experience in crossing the ridge, when we saw the old Chinese functionary alighting from his cart before an *obo*—that is, before a heap made of stones and branches of trees to which bundles of horse-hair and small rags had been attached. He drew several hairs out of the mane of his horse and attached them to the branches.

" 'What is that?' we asked.

" 'The *obo*—the waters before us flow now to the Amur.'

" 'Is that all of the Khingan?'

" 'Yes! No mountains more to cross as far as the Amur: only hills!' "

They descended a steep zigzag road to the river Gan, and thence, for some seventy miles, crossed "a chopped sea of mountains". The vegetation was more temperate than that of Siberia, the trees of strange species, the grass luxuriant. And their journey was attended by only one real difficulty—a somewhat amusing one—when, after they had crossed the Great Khingan, the old Chinese official assumed his glass-buttoned hat of office and forbade them to go farther. A long altercation followed, in which a copy of the *Moscow Gazette* was made to serve as a passport sufficiently verbose to impress the Chinese. When he continued in his obstruction the party went on its way, having promised to report that he had done everything he could to stop them—a typical example of Chinese face-saving.

Out of the mountain region they entered the high plains of Merghen, and completed their trading business in the city of that name. The horses were sold there at such profit that, in the end, the expedition cost a little over two pounds. It was in this cheap but efficient way that practically all the great Russian travellers of this period worked, making their journeys more like nomads than ordinary explorers because they could not obtain sufficient grants from the government.

After leaving Merghen they passed over the low hills of the Ilkhuri-Alin, explored the remarkable tertiary volcanoes of the Uyian Kholdontsi, and eventually reached the Chinese town of Aigun, on the right bank of the Amur, whence they crossed to Blagoveschensk.

It was an important journey, not only for the new ground it recorded, but also because it revealed some unexpected facts about the watershed of the Siberian rivers, which could not lie on the comparatively low Khingan ridge, and set Kropotkin thinking on unorthodox but fruitful lines about the structure of the Asiatic continent, as we shall see later.

The rest of that summer Kropotkin spent travelling up and down the Amur, going as far as Nikolaevsk on its estuary, and returning thence by steamer up the Usuri. Then, in the autumn, followed another exploratory expedition into Manchuria, this time up the Sungari from its junction with the Amur to the Chinese town of Kirin in the heart of Manchuria. Again, it was a region which, except for pioneering Jesuits, no European had ever investigated.

The expedition was of a somewhat different character from that carried out by Kropotkin's peaceful group of traders. Ostensibly it was to be a mission of friendship, during which a message of goodwill would be delivered to the Chinese Governor-General. A staff colonel was in charge, and, besides Kropotkin, there were an astronomer, a doctor, and two topographers. But the friendly appearance of the party was belied by the fact that the little steamer in which the expedition sailed towed a barge containing twenty-five soldiers, whose rifles had been hidden carefully under the coal.

There were many difficulties. Firstly, the accommodation in the steamer was too slight for the personnel, and supplies had been prepared so inefficiently that there were not even enough knives and spoons. Then the lower part of the Sungari, although wide, was in parts so silted that the small craft, with a draught of only three feet, could not always find a sufficiently deep channel. However, as they advanced up the river and it grew narrower, navigation became more easy, and in a few weeks they reached Kirin, having made the first map of the river.

In the end, any hope of establishing friendly relations with the Manchurian authorities was frustrated. Not unnaturally, after Muraviev's exploits a few years before, the Chinese regarded such an expedition with great mistrust, particularly as, with the rapidity usual in semi-civilised countries, news of the twenty-five rifles hidden so carefully had preceded the Russians. Consequently, the mission arrived at Kirin to find the merchants armed to the teeth, and its members were sent to Coventry in the native style when they walked through the city or attempted to trade. But in the Chinese villages down the river, peopled with political exiles, the travellers were received with great friendliness. It was Kropotkin's first contact with foreign peoples on their own soil, and he was impressed by the natural fellowship which exists among men of different races as soon as the interests of national states are forgotten.

Politically this expedition was useless, but its geographical findings were important. They were reported by Kropotkin in an article in the *Memoirs of the Siberian Geographical Society*, his first published essay in geography, unearthed thirty years later and utilised by the planners of the Trans-Manchurian railway.

A fourth journey, in 1865, took Kropotkin to the Tunkinsk valley and the Sayans, a range of highlands reaching down to the Chinese frontier, in which he surveyed the area and gained further information on the structure of the Siberian mountains.

But his most important expedition, and the most fruitful in providing material for his geographical and biological theories, was that in which he explored the vast and deserted mountain region between the Lena in northern Siberia and the higher reaches of the Amur near Chita. The object was to discover a direct means of communication between the Lena gold mines and Transbaikalia. For four years the Siberian expedition of 1860–4 had tried to find such a passage, but had always been baffled by the complicated and trackless mass of wild ridges which they had approached from the south. Kropotkin, having considered all the difficulties the previous explorers had encountered, decided that the problem might be solved by reversing the process, by finding a way from north to south, "from the dreary unknown wilderness to the warmer and populated regions".

While preparing this expedition he saw by chance a map drawn by a Tungus hunter with the point of his knife on a piece of bark. Kropotkin had never any of that intellectual snobbery which despises the abilities of primitive people; on the contrary, he always esteemed their judgment on matters where they had direct knowledge. "This little map", he says, "so struck me by its seeming truth to nature that I fully trusted to it." His confidence was wholly justified.

He left Irkutsk in the company of his close friend, the young zoologist Poliakov, and a topographer, Maskinski. They travelled first by boat down the Lena, northwards in the direction of the Olekma gold-mining area, passing through sandstone gorges and wide limestone valleys, with very wild and at times beautiful scenery, until they came to the mouth of the Vitim, a tributary of the Lena, where they landed, and rode on horseback for nearly two hundred miles to the Tikono-Zadonsk gold mine. This was the last post of civilisation before entering the wilderness, and here they organised and equipped the expedition. A second piece of good fortune brought them into contact with an old Yakut hunter who, twenty years before, had actually crossed the mountains by the passage indicated on the Tungus map. He consented to act as a guide, and with ten Cossacks and a caravan of fifty horses, carrying food for three months, they started southward into a wild region never before crossed in its entirety by any European, and in which a Russian explorer had been killed by the natives less than five years before.

They crossed in all more than eight hundred miles of uncharted mountains, and it was only the extraordinary memory and sense of direction exhibited by their native guide that enabled them to complete their journey so successfully, for "there was no track of any sort to follow, and all the valleys that one saw from the top of a mountain pass, all equally covered with wood, seemed to be absolutely alike". They went southward in an almost straight line. The first part of the journey led them across an Alpine region of great wildness, in which Kropotkin was able to distinguish no less than four great parallel mountain ranges, each, to his surprise, running from south-west to north-east. This region was nearly four hundred miles across, and led them eventually to the deep valley of the

Muya. After descending they climbed once again to the top of a lofty granite ridge over 5,000 feet high, and thence descended to a plateau, whose marshy surface, broken by low ridges, they traversed for another 350 miles, still with no tracks to follow, until, on crossing the last low ridge of the Yablonovoi, they came down by a very steep slope into Chita.

This journey was important for a number of reasons. Firstly, taken in conjunction with Kropotkin's earlier journeys, it gave him a complete cross-section of North Eastern Asia which, as we shall see, was invaluable as a basis for his theories on the structure of this region and of Eurasia in general. Secondly, Poliakov's discoveries of palæolithic remains in the dried beds of shrunken lakes, and other similar observations gave evidence on the desiccation of Asia, which Kropotkin was later to use in connection with his glacial theories. Thirdly, their observations of animal life raised considerable doubts in the minds of both Kropotkin and Poliakov as to the emphasis placed by Darwin on the struggle for existence as a factor in evolution, and thus provided the first facts on which Kropotkin was later to build his own evolutionary theory of mutual aid. Indeed, in the book which bears that title, he actually refers to this expedition in the following terms:

> "I recollect myself the impressions produced upon me by the animal world of Siberia when I explored the Vitim regions in the company of so accomplished a zoologist as my friend Poliakov. We were both under the fresh impression of the *Origin of Species*, but we looked vainly for the keen competition between animals of the same species which the reading of Darwin's work had prepared us to expect. . . . We saw plenty of adaptations for struggling, very often in common, against the adverse circumstances of climate, or against various enemies, and Poliakov wrote many a good page upon the mutual dependency of carnivores, ruminants, and rodents in their geographical distribution; we witnessed numbers of facts of mutual support, especially during the migration of birds and ruminants; but even in the Amur and Usuri regions, where animal life swarms in abundance, facts of real competition and struggle between higher animals of the same species came very seldom under my notice, though I eagerly searched for them."

The fourth result of the expedition was a practical one; it opened a path by which cattle could be taken during the summer from the pastures of Transbaikalia to the barren tundras of the north.

These were the major expeditions which Kropotkin made in Siberia, though he undertook a number of less spectacular journeys, travelling by boat on the rivers, crossing on horseback the prairies of the Amur, where "man and horse are really concealed by the grasses of gigantic size", and the monsoon areas of the Usuri, where temperate and sub-tropical vegetation mingle and "a rich underwood of lianas, ivies, wild vines, roses, and so on, renders the forests quite impassable". It was on one of these minor journeys that he perceived a phenomenal migration of deer from the Manchurian highlands into the prairies.

> "I found the Cossacks", he says, ". . . in the greatest excitement, because thousands and thousands of fallow deer were crossing the Amur where it is narrowest, in order to reach the lowlands. For several days in succession, upon a length of some forty miles up the river, the Cossacks were butchering the deer as they crossed the Amur, in which already floated a good deal of ice. Thousands were killed every day, and the exodus nevertheless continued. Like migrations were never seen either before or since, and this one must have been called for by an early and heavy snowfall in the Great Khingan, which compelled the deer to make a desperate attempt at reaching the lowlands."

The incident impressed Kropotkin deeply as an illustration of the sociability displayed by these animals, and was one of the many observations from personal experience which his travels enabled him to use later in the elaboration of his biological theories.

IV

At the end of 1866 there occurred an incident which caused an abrupt yet not wholly undesired end to Kropotkin's sojourn in Siberia.

The Polish insurrection of 1863 had brought, as we have seen, a large number of Polish exiles to Eastern Siberia, and, on the whole, these men were treated with exceptional harshness. Many of them were sent to the living death of the salt mines; others were set to work building a road along the shores of Lake Baikal which would make a direct communication between

Irkutsk and Chita during the seasons when navigation on the lake was impossible. In the winter of 1866 the Poles employed on part of this road decided on an insurrection, an idea then unheard-of among the political exiles of Siberia, who had previously confined their efforts at liberation to individual escapes. The plan elaborated by the Poles was to make their way across the mountains into Mongolia and thence to China, where they hoped to board an English ship that would transport them to Western Europe. They succeeded in disarming their guards, but were intercepted by a contingent of Cossacks sent across the lake from Irkutsk. A skirmish took place in which a Russian officer was killed; then the Poles surrendered and their insurrection was at an end.

Peter Kropotkin was away on the Vitim plateau at the time, and the Governor-General tactfully passed over Alexander in selecting the officers for the expedition against the Poles. Otherwise they would both have refused to march, and, as it was, the affair "opened our eyes to the false position we both occupied as officers", and made them realise very emphatically "what it meant to belong in any way to the army".

There was little they could do to help the Poles, fifty of whom were tried by court martial. Peter attended the public trial and took extensive notes of the proceedings, which he sent to one of the St Petersburg newspapers for which he had been writing on Siberian affairs since 1862. Much to the annoyance of the Siberian authorities, his account was published in full, and in this way the brutalities which had been practised on the exiled Poles became known, not only to all educated people in Russia but also to the world outside, where the news caused a considerable sensation and stirred many people, including Herbert Spencer, to protest. Five of the Poles were sentenced to death. The Governor-General telegraphed for permission to reprieve them, and in the meantime promised the Kropotkins not to carry out the execution. But no reply coming within five days, he had them shot secretly early in the morning. A month later a letter arrived from St Petersburg telling him to act as he thought fit.

The wanton brutality of the whole incident shocked and disgusted the two brothers, and they decided to leave the military service as quickly as possible and return to Russia. It was, in fact, the incident necessary to precipitate a decision towards which they had been tending for a long time. Siberian society and its administration were now just as reactionary as those of the great Russian cities, without any cultural compensations. In Siberia there was a dearth of scientific equipment, of books, of foreign magazines, while, although a few amateurs were to be found, only two scientists of real standing, Pumpelly and Bastian, had made brief visits during the past five years. Peter, in particular, felt it necessary to acquire the theoretical background against which to work out the implications of his practical field work. Besides, he was already experiencing that yearning towards Western Europe which sooner or later seized almost every Russian intellectual of consequence during the nineteenth century, including even nationalists like Dostoevsky.

It took some time to arrange the departure, which was complicated by the fact that Alexander had married in Siberia, but at last, in 1867, it was all arranged, and by the autumn of that year they were settled in St Petersburg again. Alexander did not definitely leave the army, but compromised by entering the Military School of Jurisprudence. Peter decided to resign completely from the military service, and this was achieved by the polite fiction of transferring him to the ranks of the civilian service. In January 1868 he nominally entered the Ministry of the Interior as a Titular Councillor, and in November was transferred to the Central Statistical Committee. He was not to end his tenuous connection with the civil service until 1872; in May of that year he resigned from the Ministry of the Interior, and in August received the honorary title of Collegiate Assessor.

It all meant little except that, in the fantastic bureaucratic state of the Romanovs, everybody had to have some official title to fit him into the pattern, even if it corresponded to no actual duties. Kropotkin did nothing in his civil-service career, and received no benefit, except that it allowed him to follow his own inclinations, and to realise his own hopes of five years before and follow Klassovsky's advice by entering the university.

In some ways he found St Petersburg more depressing than he had anticipated. Friends who had been outspoken radicals when he left were now frightened to admit their views, and lived in an atmosphere of cautious withdrawal, while he had not yet made contact with the active spirits of the younger generation. Culturally there had been a great debasement; Offenbach was all the rage, while the Italian and Russian operas were neglected. But he soon became oblivious to this when, among men several years younger than himself, he sat and studied mathematics, a complete understanding of which he regarded as essential for a scientific career. His activities were by no means confined to the university, for he continued vigorously the geographical studies he had commenced as an untrained field worker in Siberia.

He was given a cordial welcome by the geographers of the capital. To the Russian Geographical Society he presented a report of his Vitim expedition, which was subsequently published, and for this he was awarded one of the Society's gold medals, and offered the secretaryship of the Physical Geography section, a part-time position which he accepted gladly. As he received no money from his father and probably ceased to gain any payment from the government, the little money he needed to continue his lessons came from this source and from his translations of Herbert Spencer. He certainly lived very simply, for Nicholas Chaikovsky, who met him for the first time at this period, describes him as inhabiting "one room with a bare ottoman that plainly served our host as bed also. There were books upon the shelves, the table and even the chairs, and on a large work table was a pile of geographical charts." Catherine Breshkovskaya gives a very similar account of "a simple worker's lodging, a room where four people could hardly find space . . . furnished with a table of white wood, a wicker armchair and a great drawing bench on which he executed the charts of the rivers and mountains of our Siberian steppes". No doubt it was partly necessity that made Kropotkin live in this way, but there was also a natural frugality in his character that enabled him easily to do without the kind of crude luxury with which he had been surrounded in youth. He was a worker by nature and the facilities, no matter how simple, for carrying out the job in hand were always much more important to him than any physical abundance. His feeling of lack, when it arose, was in a completely different direction.

In Russia, as elsewhere, it was a period of intense geographical activity, when explorers were pushing out from every frontier into the little-known peripheral regions. Kropotkin, in his secretarial capacity, was able to meet and converse with many of the more important geographers, and in his *Memoirs* he mentions with particular appreciation the names of Syevertov, the explorer of Turkestan and the Pamirs, Miklukho Maklay, who lived for years among the cannibals of New Guinea and was one of the first anthropologists to make an intensive study of these people, Fedchenko, famous as a mountaineer in Turkestan, and Przemalsky, a noted big-game hunter who pushed his expeditions to the frontiers of Tibet. Indeed, he tells us that at this period the Geographical Society was "besieged" with proposals for expeditions in all directions, which it had to consider and sponsor with the hope of gaining that government support without which it was difficult to finance explorations. The government policy varied according to its political interests; while expeditions to north or east were neglected, those to the south were lavishly supported.

But at the time Kropotkin did not realise the way in which the Russian geographers were being deliberately exploited in order to further the expansionist policy of the Tsarist government, and he entered with great enthusiasm into this wave of exploratory activity which was pushing forward rapidly the area of geographical knowledge. Besides, it all helped his own geographical education; not only did he meet daily men who had seen at first hand the geographical and zoological conditions of every corner of Eurasia and beyond, but also, in his secretarial capacity, he had access to all the varied reports which passed through the hands of the society. In this way he was made familiar with many facts and ideas which he later found extremely useful in elaborating his own geological and biological theories, while the studies of physics and mathematics at the university gave a breadth to his scientific education, which accounts in great part for the remarkable versatility of his interests in later years.

But his most important work at this time was his study of the orographical structure of Asia, in which he made a contribution to science whose value is now recognised unanimously among geographers.

Up to the 1870's the maps of Eastern Asia had been drawn

up by European cartographers from incomplete information, due partly to the lack of full exploration, but mostly to the fact that Western geographers had assumed that the mountains of Asia were of an Alpine pattern, with "the highest mountain ridges running along the chief water partings". In consequence, as Kropotkin discovered in his personal observations, these maps were "mostly fantastic", neglecting the true plateau formation of the country, in which the rivers rise from marshes and not from mountain glaciers, and showing a number of great ridges, "black worms" on the maps, having "no existence in nature".

He therefore set himself to discover "the true leading principles of the mountains of Asia—the harmony of mountain formation", and was encouraged in this not only by his Russian colleagues but also by Petermann, the celebrated German topographer, who saw immediately the relevance of his objections to the existing system.

It was a formidable task, for the only reliable information available was a vast mass of unarranged travellers' observations. In an address to the Royal Geographical Society of London in 1903, Kropotkin told in some detail how he set to work:

> "Schwartz gave me all the original meteorological diaries of the members of the Siberian expedition, as well as his own, very precious, full diary of the Akhte Expedition (1851). Utilising, in addition to these, all published barometric observations, and those which I had made myself during my journeys, I calculated a catalogue of about 800 altitudes. . . . With the aid of these altitudes I prepared a number of cross-sections of Siberia. Then taking all the original journeys I traced on the large map of Schwartz all orographic and geological remarks which these records contained; and when I saw that a traveller had crossed a range of mountains which had such and such an orographical and geological structure, I endeavoured to discover which of the ranges crossed by other travellers a hundred miles farther east or west would best answer to the same structure and character. I proceeded, in short, in a strongly inductive way."

But, as Kropotkin remarks, "each inductive research is also guided by some deductive hypotheses", and, while already recognising the wrongness of the current ideas expressed by topographers in their maps covered with high ridges between each pair of rivers, he still worked for long on another inexact hypothesis. The great Alexander Humboldt, whose books had inspired Kropotkin in youth with a passion for travel, had worked out a representation of the mountains of Asia in the form of a network of ranges, some running due north and south and others along the east to west parallels. No doubt it was natural that Kropotkin should at first rely on the work of so revered a master, and endeavour "for a long time to make the plateaux and mountain ranges of Northern Asia fall in accordance with the system of Humboldt", particularly as the earlier geographer had based his ideas on a close study of ancient and modern Chinese maps. However, after two years of hard and bewildering work, he found that the information he had gathered so laboriously completely failed to fit into any scheme based on Humboldt's system. This hypothesis having been proved invalid, he was left once again with his "bewildering chaos of scattered observations".

For months he worked and thought on these facts, until one day he experienced an intuitional realisation which enabled him to see the whole solution as clearly "as if it were illumined with a flash of light". He perceived that:

"The main structural lines of Asia are *not* north and south, or west and east; they are from the south-west to the north-east—just as in the Rocky Mountains and the plateaux of America the lines are north-west to south-east; only secondary ridges shoot out north-west. Moreover, the mountains of Asia are not bundles of independent ridges, like the Alps, but are subordinated to an immense plateau —an old continent which once pointed towards Behring Strait. High border ridges have towered up along its fringes, and in the course of ages terraces, formed by later sediments, have emerged from the sea, thus adding on both sides to the width of that primitive backbone of Asia."

The result of this generalisation was the conception of Asia having been built up round an ancient primary massif, itself the remnant of a still older circumpolar continent. Far from being, as many people generally suppose, a vast plain stretching from the Urals to the Pacific, Siberia was in fact a series of plateaux, built up in steps; the inner and higher series, representing the ancient massif and rising in places to ten or twelve thousand feet, stretching from Tibet up to Siberia and including the Central Asian tablelands, and the lower series, the east, representing the rest of Eastern Siberia, Manchuria, and a great deal of the Chinese highlands. These plateaux were edged by ancient mountain ranges, of the pre-Silurian, Silurian, and Devonian eras, and running in the same north-easterly direction, while at right angles to them ran a later series of upheavals, moving north-westerly and dating from Mesozoic times. As a result of this new presentation of the map of Asia some mountain ranges, like the Great Stanovoi, which had stirred the inventive talents of cartographers, were reduced to minor ridges, and others, like the Great Khingan, were shown to follow a quite different direction from that originally assumed. Indeed, taken as a whole, Kropotkin's conception was a revolutionary advance in geographical ideas, and eventually affected the ideas of geographers relating to the whole world structure.

Since Kropotkin's day there have been alterations in detail to the map of Asia which he drew up. The actual structure of the continent has been shown to be more complicated than he at first imagined, but his general lines remain undisputed and have been confirmed by later explorers of the mountain ranges of Central and East Asia; so that a leading authority like Professor Dudley Stamp speaks for modern geographical opinion when, in his own work on the geography of Asia, he acknowledges our indebtedness to Kropotkin for bringing forward a new and truer view of Asiatic structure, and refers in appreciative terms to his "excellent summary" of these views in his classic address to the London Geographical Society. Kropotkin himself considered this his "chief contribution to science"; it is certainly the achievement on whose value and originality the scientific world is most fully unanimous.

To have made and perfected such a theory was a notable achievement for a young man of less than thirty, and Kropotkin tells of the elation and almost æsthetic pleasure which he experienced on conceiving it.

"There are not many joys in human life equal to the joy of the sudden birth of a generalisation, illuminating the mind after a long period of patient research. What has seemed for years so chaotic, so contradictory, and so problematic takes at once its proper position within an harmonious whole. Out of the wild confusion of facts and from behind the fog of guesses—contradicted almost as soon as they are born—a stately picture makes its appearance, like an Alpine chain suddenly emerging in all its grandeur from the mists which concealed it the moment before, glittering under the rays of the sun in all its simplicity and variety, in all its mightiness and beauty. . . .

"He who has once in his life experienced this joy of scientific creation will never forget it; he will be longing to renew it; and he cannot but feel with pain that this sort of happiness is the lot of so few of us, while so many could also live through it—on a small or on a grand scale—if scientific methods and leisure were not limited to a handful of men."

Kropotkin was never to have the time or peace to write the "bulky volume" he had intended, "in which the new ideas about the mountains and plateaux of Northern Asia should be supported by a detailed examination of each separate region". By the time he had finally reached his conclusions and marshalled his facts to illustrate them the tide of events, which we shall describe more fully in the next chapter, was pressing heavily against him, and he had only the time to prepare, in 1873, a map embodying his views and an explanatory paper, which was published by the Russian Geographical Society after he had been imprisoned by the secret police; its value was immediately recognised by Petermann, who adopted it as the basis for his own map of Asia in Stieler's Atlas, and in this way it became adopted by subsequent cartographers, many of whom did not have the remotest idea of the origin of this conception of Asia until Kropotkin restated his theory in London in 1903.

But while he was elaborating these ideas, other important geographical work shared Kropotkin's attention. He became extremely interested in the revival of Arctic exploration which took place round about 1870. At this period the Norwegian seal hunters had astonished Russian geographers by navigating their ships through what had once been regarded as the more or less permanently frozen sea between Novaya Zemlya and the Siberian coast. The Russian Geographical Society, largely on Kropotkin's insistence, proposed that an Arctic expedition should be equipped and sent out, and a committee was nominated to investigate the work to be done. Kropotkin was the most active member of this committee, and, as several of the experts had not submitted their reports in time, he had to investigate the facts on a number of subjects and write the appropriate sections himself. He tells us, with a pardonable touch of self-complacency, "Several subjects, such as marine zoology, the tides, pedulum observations, and terrestrial magnetism, were quite new to me; but the amount of work which a healthy man can accomplish in a short time, if he strains all his forces and goes straight to the root of the subject, no one could suppose beforehand—and so my report was ready".

At the end of this report Kropotkin set forth an important theory on Arctic geography. He suggested that one of the objects of the expedition must be to try and reach an unknown land which seemed to lie near to Novaya Zemlya. He had come to this conclusion from studying the currents of the Arctic ocean, and the disposition of ice on the coast of Novaya Zemlya. The account won great approval with the Geographical Society, and it was decided to precede the main enterprise by sending out a smaller reconnoitring expedition, to push north or north-east of Novaya Zemlya. A Norwegian schooner was chartered for this purpose, and, to his surprise, Kropotkin was offered the leadership. He protested that he had never been to sea, but the committee replied that, by combining the experience of a Norwegian sailor with the initiative of a scientist, "something valuable could be done". He then decided to accept the assignment, but the expedition never sailed, for the Ministry of Finance abruptly declared that it was unable to grant the relatively small sum of three or four thousand pounds needed to meet the costs.

Kropotkin's report was, however, published, and his contentions were vindicated two years later when an Austrian polar expedition, headed by Payer and Weyprecht, advanced along the route he had indicated and discovered an archipelago, which they named Franz Joseph Land. The modern Russian commentator on Kropotkin's geographical writings, Anisimov, follows the current trend of Soviet patriotism by claiming that this polar country "should in all fairness be called Kropotkin land, since it was he who had discovered it theoretically in 1870". But on this subject it is necessary to bear in mind Kropotkin's own contention, put forward more than once in his later books, that inventions and discoveries are often due more to the prevalent intellectual atmosphere of the age than to any particular achievement on the part of individuals; a contention which is borne out by the frequency with which the same line of research is followed at the same time by quite independent scientists, resulting often in the more or less simultaneous announcement of the same discovery from completely different quarters. While it is true that the Austrians may have been guided by Kropotkin's published report on the possibilities of investigation in the Arctic seas, it is equally likely that they proceeded on their own deductions from facts which were, after all, available to the entire geographical world at the time. This admission does not in any way reduce the credit due to Kropotkin. It is more probable that his ideas on the sea route along the northern shores of Eurasia had some influence on the explorer Nordenskjold, with whom he spent "many happy hours" in Sweden in 1871, and who, in 1878–80, circumnavigated the double continent for the first time.

The scheme for the Polar expedition having been abandoned, Kropotkin was sent by the Russian Geographical Society on a journey to examine the ridges of glacial drift which are so abundant in the Baltic regions. He went into Sweden, as far as Upsala, but most of his time was spent in Finland, examining the many *eskers* which are to be found in that country. It was a task which gave him much enjoyment, for he found Finland an enchanting place. In a much later article in *The Nineteenth Century* (1885), he describes it with an appreciation that leaves no doubt as to the deep impression its natural grandeur made upon him. He tells us that:

"Finland is a poor country, but it is a fine country, and has a stamp of originality. Its like may be sought for in vain even in the lake district of England or among the inland seas of Canada. Where else, indeed, can the Finns find this network of land and water, this tangled skein of lake, and sea, and shore, so full of contrasts, and yet forming an inseparable and enchanting whole? Where find these millions of islands—of lonely rocks giving footing to a few pines and birches which seem to grow from beneath the water; these thousands and thousands of ever-varying tints spreading over the lakes as the sun slowly moves almost on the horizon, unwilling to go down, or leaving behind it the shining twilight which meets in the north with the aurora of the morning? Nowhere else will the Finn find a country which breathes the same mild and sweet harmony, grave and melancholy, which matches so well with the dreamy pensiveness of his character."

To this æsthetic appreciation of the landscape he added an admiration for the people, whom he found, despite the traditions of their "slowness of thought and indifference", to be intelligent, independent, and honest to a far greater degree than their Russian fellows. The fact that feudalism had never been extended to Finland prevented them from becoming servile, and, in spite of the great poverty which existed among the lower classes, he found that they had an habitual cleanliness "not devoid of an æsthetic tint"; simplicity of life and an absence of unhealthy habits of luxury were universal in all ranks of society, while the official corruption of Moscow and St Petersburg was unknown in Helsingfors and the smaller Finnish towns.

But the principal pleasure of this journey lay in his scientific work, which was very productive. He found that, while the outer mantles of the *eskers* consisted of gravel or sand deposited by the action of running water, the great cores upon which they were built were invariably made up of unwashed and unstratified fragments of stone, and were clearly of morainic origin, having been deposited by the action of moving ice.

Kropotkin was not content merely to record isolated observations. His powerful intuition sought the generalised meaning behind these phenomena, and he tells us in his *Memoirs* that:

"Even now, as I was looking on the lakes and hillocks of Finland, new and beautiful generalisations arose before my eyes. I saw in a remote past, at the very dawn of mankind, the ice accumulating from year to year in the northern archipelagos, over Scandinavia and Finland. An immense growth of ice invaded the north of Europe and slowly spread as far as the middle portions. Life dwindled in that part of the Northern Hemisphere, and, wretchedly poor, uncertain, it fled farther and farther south before the icy breath which came from that immense frozen mass. Man—miserable, weak, ignorant—had every difficulty in maintaining a precarious existence. Ages passed away, till the melting of the ice began, and with it came the lake period, when countless lakes were formed in the cavities, and a wretched sub-polar vegetation began timidly to invade the unfathomable marshes with which every lake was surrounded. Another series of ages passed before an extremely slow process of drying up set in, and vegetation began its slow invasion from the south. And now we are fully in the period of a rapid desiccation, accompanied by the formation of dry prairies and steppes, and man has to find out the means to put a check to that desiccation to which Central Asia has fallen, and which menaces South-Eastern Europe."

On returning in September from Finland where he had spent three months, he prepared a report on the results of his expedition, in which he put forward his theory of the ice-cap reaching Middle Europe, which, he says, "was at that time rank heresy". At a meeting of the Geographical Society in 1874, just before his arrest by the Third Section, he gave an address in which he outlined this theory; it aroused much controversy, and led to a general recognition of the fact that previous ideas of ice action needed substantial revision, while a growing number of geologists were convinced of the justice of Kropotkin's ideas, and in a few years they became the accepted basis for further investigations into glaciation in the Northern Hemisphere. Swedish geographers were particularly interested, one of them, Torrel, delivering in 1875 before the German Geographical Society a lecture in which he applied Kropotkin's thesis to evidence gathered in North Germany. The Russian scientific world was also so far impressed that Kropotkin, on presenting his original paper, was nominated for the presidency of the Physical Geography section of the Russian Geographical Society, while during his imprisonment the Russian Academy of Sciences even persuaded the Tsar to allow him the facilities for writing in prison the fuller report he had contemplated. The complete work on his glacial theories ran into two volumes; the first was published by the Geographical Society in 1876, while he was still in prison; the second was seized by the Third Section on his escape, and did not see the light of day until 1895, when the police handed it over to the Russian Geographical Society, who sent it to Kropotkin in England. By this time, however, his ideas had become common currency among scientists, others had completed the investigations necessary to fill in the details of the picture, and the time for publication had passed.

His original contention was that an ice coat, sometimes as much as a thousand metres thick, stretched in an uninterrupted flow from Scandinavia across European Russia as far south as the Voronezh and Kiev provinces. His travels in Siberia had also led him to suppose that in that area, "All regions now over 3,000 feet of altitude have been covered either with ice caps on the plateaux or with large glaciers in the Alpine tracts, the glaciers in the valleys reaching to levels of about 1,000 feet above the sea". The lower-lying regions of this area were probably not glaciated, since it is unlikely that at this time they had yet risen above the sea. A later investigation by independent scientists of the glaciers of Greenland, Switzerland, Germany, England, and Scandinavia brought confirmation of Kropotkin's theory, so that in 1904 he was able, in an address to the Royal Geographical Society in London, to summarise without any dissenting voice the results of these investigations in the terms of his own theory.

"It has been established by the researches of the last fifty years that considerable portions of Eurasia were covered during the Ice Age with a mighty ice-sheet. Its southern limits in Central Europe and European Russia are now traced by geologists approximately along the 50th degree of latitude, with 'tongues' of ice which were protruding in Russia along the main valleys (Dnieper, Don) in a south-eastern direction so as to reach the 47th or the 48th degree of latitude. In France, it has lately been proved that the whole of the Central Plateau and the Vosges were also covered with a thick ice-sheet. The glaciation of the northern section of the Urals is no more doubted upon, and it is only the glaciation of the middle portion of these mountains which still remains a point of contest. As to the great West Siberian depression, it is now certain that during the Great Ice Age most of it was under the Arctic Ocean, which reached, in Western Siberia, roughly speaking, the 52nd degree of latitude, while in Eastern Siberia, which is covered with high plains, this same latitude was reached by narrow gulfs of the Arctic Ocean now occupied by the valleys of the main rivers."

From this conception of the Ice Age it was a natural transition to Kropotkin's theory of the desiccation of Eurasia. In his travels in Siberia he had been impressed by the evidence that not only had the existing lakes been at one time—and even within recent centuries—of considerably greater extent, but also that much wider areas, now dried into steppes and deserts, bore evidence of having once formed part of lake beds and marshes.

Linking this fact with his observations of glacial deposits, he realised that, as the ice cap began to thaw and recede, the water must have collected either in lakes formed by depressions or else in swamps where the ground was more level, and he applied to this period, when the land masses of the Northern Hemisphere were covered by innumerable sheets of water, the name of *The Lake Age*. In that period, he showed, the Baltic Sea covered large portions of Sweden and the lake area of Finland, while the Caspian was united with the Sea of Aral and projected, in the form of an inlet along the course of the Volga, as far as Kazan. Similarly, other great water masses existed which have since entirely disappeared.

As the rivers washed out permanent channels and their flow became steadily more full, the lakes began to diminish, large areas of them turned into marshes, and these in turn dried out and became moors or forests. But the process of desiccation did not cease, and there is evidence all over Eurasia of once fertile lands which have now become desert, so that even in historical times lands that were the homes of flourishing cultures have been abandoned before the steady advance of drought.

This desiccation, Kropotkin indicated, is still going on, and must be expected to continue for some considerable period. He remarked in 1904:

"It is not with a temporary fact that we have to deal. It is a geological epoch of desiccation that we are living in—an epoch as characterised by desiccation as the glacial period was characterised by the accumulation from year to year of unevaporated and frozen precipitation. More than that, this epoch of desiccation is a necessary outcome of the preceding epoch of glaciation.

"Nor is the phenomenon of desiccation limited to a small portion of the continent. It embraces the whole of the region that has once been glaciated. It is not only Central Asia that is desiccating; the same future is in store now for the Caspian steppes of the lower Volga and for South-Western Russia altogether. Desiccation in these regions becomes more and more apparent. But it cannot be attributed, as is often done, to the destruction of the forests in Northern Russia. We must see in it a geological fact, independent of the will of man; and while indicating this fact to men of science as an important line of future research, it would be worth while, at the same time, to think of the measures which should be taken for combating —at least within the limits of what is possible—the coming drought. Such measures, I mean, as tree planting on a large scale in the menaced regions, with the aid of artesian wells, which seems to have given good results in North Africa, or any other measures which the knowledge of the danger and further research may suggest."

As will be seen from the last sentence, Kropotkin was never the "pure" scientist who worked in a social vacuum. He contemplated the value to humanity of his investigations, and was always deeply concerned at the possible effects on human fortunes of the desiccation which is transforming the character of large parts of Russian soil at a comparatively rapid pace, and which has undoubtedly been largely responsible for the terrible series of droughts and famines that have struck Southern Russia during the past century.

These three theories, of glaciation, of desiccation, and of the orography of Asia, represent Kropotkin's main contributions to the science of geography. He himself would have been the last to claim undue credit for theories which were the result of a mass of investigations proceeding at the same time in these directions. Nevertheless, the fact remains that his intuitive power made him the first to put these ideas before the world, and while it may perhaps be contended that other men were working in parallel lines on the question of glaciation and desiccation, and might soon have reached the conclusions which Kropotkin published first, his theory of the structure of Asia was a completely original generalisation which revolutionised geographical ideas on the nature of the world's largest land mass.

These theories were already conceived in the essential forms when Kropotkin was still a young man of less than thirty, and his significant explorations had been completed some time before. It is hard to imagine what such an active scientific talent might have produced, had Kropotkin continued longer to devote his energies exclusively to practical and theoretical geography. Even in 1871 he had great schemes of future work in this direction, and he considered writing "an exhaustive physical geography" of Russia which would not merely give a description of the country's structure but would also recommend measures to utilise the various economic regions to their best advantage.

> "Take, for instance, the wide prairies of Southern Russia, so often visited by droughts and failures of crops. These droughts and failures must not be treated as accidental calamities: they are as much a natural feature of that region as its position on a southern slope, its fertility and the rest; and the whole of the economic life of the southern prairies ought to be organised in prevision of the unavoidable recurrence of periodical droughts."

Kropotkin proposed this work to the Geographical Society, and hoped that one day he might be appointed secretary to the society, a position which would give him the income and leisure necessary to undertake such a task. But, ironically enough, when the opportunity did arise for him to receive this appointment, he had reached a stage in his development when it was impossible to accept it.

It was while he was away on his investigation of the glacial deposits in Finland that a telegram reached him from St Petersburg saying, "The Council begs you to accept the position of secretary to the society". It was a chance which six months before he would have grasped eagerly. But during the recent months of solitude he had been thinking over his position and had decided that, for the present at least, his duty lay elsewhere than in scientific research. The full discussion of this change of attitude belongs to the next chapter, and here let it suffice to say that, as a result, Kropotkin refused the offer.

It was the virtual end of his career as an original geographer. Henceforward he would undertake no journeys of exploration, and his geographical work would consist principally of elaborating the theories he had already put forward in his twenties and of discussing and expounding the knowledge acquired and presented by others. Later, in Western Europe, he wrote geographical contributions to Elisée Reclus's *Géographie Universelle*, the *Encyclopædia Britannica*, and *Chambers's Encyclopædia*, as well as many articles in English and foreign scientific magazines, and delivered lectures to learned societies in Britain, Canada, and the United States. But he never expanded his knowledge in any original way, or used it for the production of further geographical theories. His time and energy were to be taken up with other activities, nor was he ever again presented with the fine opportunities for the original exploration which he had enjoyed as a young man.

But although geographical studies did not resume first place in his activities, the experience they had given him had a deep influence on his later years. His expeditions had developed in him resourcefulness, independence, and the understanding of men in widely differing communities and circumstances, while the theoretical problems he encountered had matured his powers of thought and given him a feeling for scientific method which was to characterise his subsequent thinking, whether revolutionary or biological, sociological or ethical. Moreover, it is difficult to imagine a science better fitted than geography to lay the foundations of his very wide understanding of the sciences; if he later made significant contributions to our biological, sociological, and anthropological ideas, the ground work for these developments had been done in his early career as a practical explorer and a geographical thinker.

CHAPTER III

THE CONVERT

I

In 1871, as we have seen, Peter Kropotkin took the decision which changed the course of his life, and from this time he entered fully into that stream of rebellion which swept in its course the Russian youth of the second half of the nineteenth century.

To describe this as a sudden or in any way unpredictable conversion would be inaccurate. Kropotkin's development followed a steady progress from boyhood, at times expanding quickly as he reached new aspects of thought and realisation, but at no period showing that completely unexpected "overnight change of heart" by which so many converts have suddenly manifested a development long maturing on the subconscious levels of their personalities. Kropotkin's growth is easy to trace, and perhaps the best answer to those who seek the exact point at which he set out upon his path of rebellion can be found in his own reply to the Grand Duke Nicholas, brother of the Tsar, who paid him a visit three years later when he was imprisoned in the Peter-and-Paul fortress.

The Grand Duke Nicholas, filled with curiosity as to how a former personal attendant of the Emperor and ornament of the Corps of Pages could have become involved in revolutionary activity, remarked to Kropotkin:

> "Was it in Siberia, with the Decembrists, that you began to entertain such ideas?"
>
> "No. I knew only one Decembrist, and with him I had no conversation worth speaking of."
>
> "Was it then in St Petersburg that you got them?"
>
> "I was always the same."

This answer really scared the Grand Duke, who then asked anxiously, "Why! Were you such in the Corps of Pages?"

Kropotkin replied: "In the Corps I was a boy, and what is indefinite in boyhood grows definite in manhood."

When we look back briefly over Kropotkin's youth, we can see the literal exactitude of this answer. The circumstances of childhood—his mother's gentle intelligence, his father's harsh neglect, his own close personal contact with the tyrannised serfs, the fostering influence of Smirnov and the books he read in this early period—all contributed to a character predisposed towards independence of thought and compassion for the unfortunate, and therefore towards rebellion against authority.

The experiences of later years all gave added direction and decision to Kropotkin's divergence from the political and social orthodoxies of his time. His discovery of Herzen, Chernyshevsky, and Proudhon, his enthusiasm for the emancipation of the serfs and the contrasting bitterness he felt at the reaction which followed it, his year of close and revealing contact with the Emperor, his acquaintanceship with Kukel and Mikhailov and the very varied experiences of Siberia, were all merely stations on a journey whose destination had already been decided from an early age. By the end of his twenty-first year Kropotkin was certainly convinced by experience of the harmfulness of autocratic administration and no longer expected anything from governmental reforms. We can gather this not only from his own accounts but also from the independent evidence of Catherine Breshkovskaya, better known as the "grandmother of the Russian Revolution". During 1863 she chanced to travel in the same railway carriage as Kropotkin, who was then returning from Siberia on his special mission to report the loss of the barges on the Amur. She conversed with the "handsome young prince", and tells us that: "For hours he discussed with me the problems that were rushing upon us. His words thrilled me like fire. Our excited voices rose steadily higher, until my mother begged me, as my nurse had done before, to speak low."

Yet though Kropotkin's action in 1871 need not have been unexpected to anyone who had observed his development carefully, it represented a more radical decision than any he had taken before, and this was largely because the environment where he was then placed enabled him to consider in perspective the whole series of events in which he had been involved during the last few years. He tells us how, in Finland, he enjoyed a mental leisure such as he had not experienced during all the active years since he left the Corps of Pages, and that in this situation he was able to give more complete consideration to those thoughts that had existed for years on the edge of his consciousness.

"... One idea, which appealed far more strongly to my inner self than geology, persistently worked in my mind.

"I saw what an immense amount of labour the Finnish peasant spends in clearing the land ... and I said to myself, 'I will write, let me say, the physical geography of this part of Russia, and tell the peasant the best means of cultivating his soil. ... But what is the use of talking to this peasant about American machines, when he had barely enough bread to live upon from one crop to the next; when the rent which he has to pay for that boulder clay grows heavier and heavier in proportion to his success in improving the soil? ... He needs me to live with him, to help him to become the owner or the free occupier of that land. Then he will read books with profit, but not now.' "

Kropotkin was beginning to realise that however important his scientific work might appear, there was another task which to him was more urgent, and which made the indulgence of his scholastic leanings seem an unjustifiable luxury, particularly as the common people were denied the very facilities to attain this scientific learning.

"... What right had I to these higher joys when all round me was nothing but misery and struggle for a mouldy bit of bread; when whatsoever I should spend to enable me to live in that world of higher emotions must needs be taken from the very mouths of those who grew the wheat and had not bread enough for their children? ...

"The masses want to know: ... they are ready to widen their knowledge; only give it to them; only give them the means of getting leisure. This is the direction in which, and these are the kind of people for whom, I must work."

The young scientist was feeling, as he has expressed in these sentences, that urge "to the people", that desire to expiate a sense of social guilt by devoting himself to the most downtrodden members of society, which was such a distinctive feature of the *narodnik* intelligentsia in his age. He made the decision of self-abnegation, cast aside the ambitions that seemed most precious to him, and rejected the offer from the Geographical Society which would have assured his future in his own branch of science. By doing this he laid the foundations of a wider fame than he was ever likely to achieve in his specialised field of knowledge, but he clearly did not anticipate this at the time. The path of the *narodnik*, of a man who seeks out the people, was in the Russia of those days a hard and thankless one, and there is no reason to believe that anything but the most sincere desire to serve humanity motivated Kropotkin's decision. It may be admitted that he probably gained some sense of self-fulfilment in having performed his sacrifice; such a satisfaction is inevitable in any act that is done with the full force of personal conviction—it is the tribute to the ego which is exacted from the highest altruism.

This decision represented a break more definite than any before in Kropotkin's life. Previously he was certainly motivated in part by a desire to repudiate the reaction he saw around him, but such acts as his joining a Siberian regiment and leaving the army were only negative in their protest. They did not lead him to take up active work for the cause that was gradually assuming importance in his mind; instead, they were means by which he took the freedom to pursue those scientific occupations from which he gained greatest personal satisfaction. The decision he reached in Finland was, on the contrary, a positive one. This time he was renouncing, not a condition that was irksome like army life, but a pursuit from which he gained great joy, and he did it with the intention of following a course of definite action in order to implement his social beliefs in concrete action.

He decided to devote himself to the oppressed peoples of Russia. But he was not yet a revolutionary if by that term we mean one who aims, whether by violence or otherwise, to procure a fundamental change in the structure of a given society. For the present he seems to have been impelled by no clear ideas beyond those of freeing the peasants from the immediate burden of taxation and landlordism which weighed most heavily upon them. He had not yet come to the conclusion that these burdens could be removed, not by gradual reforms, but only by an overthrow of the order of which they formed an essential part.

He went back to Russia and hurried to Moscow, where his father was dying. He had last seen the old Prince on the eve of the Finnish expedition, when he and Alexander had visited the sick man, who was half enraged and half admiring at their completely independent attitude. "He looked for a scene in the old style—his sons begging pardon, and money—perhaps he even regretted for a moment that this did not happen, but he regarded us with greater esteem."

When Peter reached Moscow it was only in time to follow his father's funeral through the old patrician streets. The last tie with his former life was broken, and he found himself not only free but also wealthy, the owner of an estate in Tambov. But it never so much as entered his head to be content with gaining from his land the income of an idle nobleman, as many of his contemporaries continued to do. On the contrary, he set out to find some part to play in the wave of revolutionary activity which was breaking over Russia during the 1870's.

And here it is necessary to turn aside for a brief consideration of the Russian movements of rebellion during the past decade, and to show how, while Kropotkin had been personally isolated from these developments, he had moved forward mentally along almost parallel lines.

He appears to have been in actual contact with none of the radical circle before his departure to Siberia. His life at the Corps of Pages and in the court tended to isolate him from the *ragno-chintsi*, the *declassé* elements among the students who then formed the main body of Russian progressive movements. While reading with enthusiasm the works of Chernyshevsky and Herzen he had not encountered, until he met Mikhailov in Siberia, any of the leading figures in the circles of the early 1860's, and his position had been superficially similar to that of the many young noblemen who were attracted by liberal ideas while they seemed to be approved by the Autocrat of All the Russias. There was, however, this important difference, that while the others were mostly fair-weather progressives, ready to veer when a return to conservatism was decreed, Kropotkin was fully convinced and retained his opinions in face of the mounting reaction.

PETER KROPOTKIN IN 1861 IN PAGE'S UNIFORM

The emancipation of the serfs was followed by a steady attack on the dissident groups, growing in intensity after the St Petersburg fires of 1863. Mikhailov and Chernyshevsky were by no means the only victims of this reaction; a confidential *Chronique du Mouvemente Socialiste en Russie,* of which only a hundred copies were printed by the Russian Ministry of the Interior in 1890, admitted that at the period:

"The underground movement was clearly beginning to take on solidity; the political trials followed each other without interruption; there were two in the year 1861, eight in 1862, six in 1863, four in 1864. It was clear that there existed a certain force, if not organised, at least very widespread, which had invaded a section of society, particularly the young. . . ."

The groups involved in this movement were of varied types; some merely called for democratic reforms, others went through gradations of revolutionary intensity, to that extreme and no doubt ephemeral circle which in 1862 issued a call for "an immediate revolution, a bloody and implacable revolution which is bound to change fundamentally the whole basis of existing society and to crush the adherents of the present system". All these fragmentary bodies were vague in aims and methods; no clear programme, no defined movement had yet arisen, and perhaps their most important practical activities were the experiments in co-operative lodgings and workshops which they attempted under the influence of the Fourierist "phalansterism" that had survived from the Petrashevtsi.

Under the pressure of renewed persecution these scattered tendencies began to take shape in two different directions, firstly towards drastic action against the autocracy, and secondly, towards an attack upon established forms of behaviour and thought, an attack more elusive but no less insidious in its effect because it seemed at first to have no direct political aim.

The tendency towards direct action during the 1860's reached its climax in 1866, when a young aristocrat, Karakazov, and a number of his associates, including Cherkesov, a Georgian prince, who later became a well-known anarchist and the close friend of Kropotkin, planned an attempt on the life of the Tsar. It was a typical conspiratorial group, closely knit and with no evident affiliations to the wider progressive movements. The men involved, although for the most part wealthy aristocrats, lived in the utmost simplicity, dwelling, according to Kropotkin, "three or four in the same room, never spending more than ten roubles (one pound) apiece a month for all their needs, and giving at the same time their fortunes for co-operative associations, co-operative workshops (where they themselves worked), and the like." Karakazov fired at Alexander II as he was leaving the Summer Garden; the shot missed, and the would-be assassin was immediately arrested. Later he was hanged, and it was universally believed in St Petersburg that he had been tortured beforehand, but had refused to divulge any information.

The attempt was the signal for a great intensification of repressive activity. Shuvalov, one of the most sinister statesmen of this period, was appointed to control both the gendarmerie and the Third Section, the notorious secret bureau for the investigation of political dissension. Michael Muraviev, the "butcher" of Poland, was charged to investigate the Karakazov plot, and took the opportunity to carry out hundreds of arrests and searches among people suspected of the mildest progressive sentiments, and to institute a terror which destroyed any open manifestation of radical feeling among those who had been eloquent followers of Herzen and Chernyshevsky. This campaign was so effective that the police were able to boast, "In the year 1867 there was only a single political trial, with no aftermath; in the years 1868, 1869, and 1870, not a single trial". But it must be borne in mind that there was also a considerable increase of administrative exile, without trial, by the largely autonomous Third Section, a practice encouraged by the fact that Karakazov's trial, with its revelations of the high ideals of the defendants, had created wide sympathy for the revolutionaries. Ten years later, in fact, Karakazov's methods were to be resumed on a much greater scale when the *Narodnaya Volya** began its widespread campaign of terrorism, culminating in the killing of Alexander II. Kropotkin was in Siberia at the time of the Karakazov affair, and followed it with great interest.

The other important movement of the 1860's was that of nihilism. The word "nihilism" has often been used in a mis-

* The People's Will.

leading way to include the terrorists of the late 1870's, the anarchists, and even such complex writers as Dostoevsky and, farther afield, Nietzsche. In fact, while nihilism had some similarities with Bakunin's fundamental teachings and certainly influenced the ideas of the terrorists, it was a distinct movement, and its role was philosophical and ethical rather than political in the direct sense. The nihilist was not primarily concerned with changing the form of society; his first preoccupation was with social behaviour and ways of thought.

Chernyshevsky and his disciple Dobrolubov both made their contributions to nihilist ideas, but the characteristic philosopher of the movement was Pisarev, a brilliant young nobleman who died in 1868. From 1862 until his death Pisarev's ideas were extremely influential among the younger intelligentsia, and they coloured the outlook of many Russian revolutionaries in subsequent decades.

Pisarev's fundamental doctrine was not widely different from that underlying Bakunin's famous call for destruction. In fact, in 1861 Pisarev made a similar declaration when he said: "What can be smashed must be smashed; whatever withstands the blow is fit to survive; what flies into pieces is rubbish; in any case, hit right and left; from that no harm can or will come."

But as has been indicated, Pisarev and his followers carried out their destruction in the realms of philosophy and ethics. Idealist philosophy, metaphysics, and religion were thrown aside, and science, the rule of reason, elevated in their place. Pisarev then attacked the "moral despotism" of the family and the subjection of women, rejected current educational ideas in the name of the rights of children, exposed the insincerity of conventional social customs, and made a violent denial of æsthetic standards, reducing literature to a merely utilitarian function and discarding music, painting, and sculpture as wholly useless.

It will be seen that, even if Pisarev did, like Belinsky, avoid directly political issues, there was enough intellectual dynamite in all this body of philosophical and moral iconoclasm to scare the custodians of autocracy; and when he stepped into the field of social criticism with his pamphlet defending Herzen against the Tsarist writer, Baron Fircks, the logical revolutionary conclusion of nihilism became evident. It is difficult to obtain the text of this document, which was suppressed on publication, but the following extracts, reproduced in an article by F. C. Barghorn (*Review of Politics*, April 1948), give some idea of its forthrightness, which earned its author imprisonment in the Peter-and-Paul fortress.

Pisarev says that the autocracy "fights with two weapons, printed propaganda and brute force, while the public . . . is left with the choice of either playing liberal with the censor or of following the path of secret propaganda . . . ". After defending the Decembrists and Bakunin, and attacking the pretensions and impositions of unlimited monarchy, he continues:

". . . May there fall in the name of reason decrepit despotism, decrepit religion, and the decayed timbers of contemporary official morality . . . the dynasty of the Romanovs and the St Petersburg bureaucracy must perish. . . . That which is decaying and dying must by itself fall into the grave. We have only to give them the last push and throw dirt on their stinking corpses."

It must not be thought that nihilism was a creed of libertinism or of negative free thought. On the contrary, it had a strict and puritanical morality and was as much a religion as, say, the more austere types of Buddhism. A revealing analysis, recognising these factors, has been made by Nicholas Berdyaev in *The Origins of Russian Communism.* He tells us that:

"Russian nihilism denied God, the soul, the spirit, ideas, standards and the highest values. And none the less, nihilism must be recognised as a religious phenomenon. . . . At the base of Russian nihilism, when grasped in its purity and depth, lies the Orthodox rejection of the world, its sense of the truth that 'the whole world lieth in wickedness', the acknowledgment of the sinfulness of all riches and luxury, of all creative profusion of art and thought. Like Orthodox asceticism, nihilism was an individualist movement, but it was also directed against the fullness and richness of life. Nihilism considers as sinful luxury not only art, metaphysics, and spiritual values, but religion also. . . .

". . . Nihilism is a demand for nakedness, for the stripping from oneself of all the trappings of culture, for the annihilation of all historical traditions, for the setting free of the natural man, upon whom there will no longer be fetters of any sort. The intellectual asceticism of nihilism found expression in materialism; any more subtle philosophy was proclaimed a sin. . . . The attitude of the Russian nihilists to science was idolatrous. . . . There was nothing sceptical in Russian nihilism, it was a faith. . . ."

Tempered by this godless faith, the Russian intelligentsia of a whole generation went to the gallows or the penal fortresses with the courage of martyrs. They lived their daily lives with the asceticism of mystics, and gave up wealth and comfort in order to preach their gospel with the eagerness of apostles. Demanding complete freedom, they nevertheless were puritanical in their attitude to life, and had often, in their contempt for polite forms, much of the crudeness of personal intercourse which accompanies such an ascetic attitude.

Kropotkin had encountered nihilists in Siberia, and was impressed by their sincerity and the fearlessness with which they expressed their blunt opinions and trod down fashionable conventions. And like most of his contemporaries, he was influenced by them. There is a certain similarity of outlook between the anarchism to which he later adhered and the doctrines of the nihilists, in so far as these touched on social matters, with the important difference that anarchism, following Bakunin's lead, has never put its faith wholly in reason but has always, tacitly at least, given a place to instinct and intuition as qualities essential for the full life.

Personally, Kropotkin shared many nihilist characteristics. He too was intensely concerned with social ethics and sought to find them in natural and candid behaviour; he too complemented his belief in freedom with an essential puritanism—a quality to be found often among libertarian apostles—including Godwin, Proudhon, and Bakunin. He too had an almost religious veneration for science, and was ready to live hardly and to risk imprisonment or death in a cause wherein he believed.

Nevertheless, he contrived to avoid many of the more dangerous pitfalls of the nihilist path. For while nihilism had initially an enormous liberating influence on the minds of Russian youth, it was rather like the geological process described by Kropotkin in that it superseded the glaciation of the mind by its desiccation, for, as Berdyaev has justly remarked of its exponents, "on behalf of the liberation of personality, they emptied it of its qualitative content, devastated its inner life, and denied it its right to creativeness and spiritual enrichment . . .".

Kropotkin, unlike the nihilists, saw the value of cultural and creative work in developing the personality, and art in various forms was always a necessity for him. Moreover, there was a pantheistic emotion in his love for nature which was removed from the strict nihilist contempt for such feelings. He perceived that life must have other satisfactions than the merely utilitarian. Besides, his essential optimism differed widely from the pessimism with which the real nihilist regarded life around him. And, finally, while he had all the sincerity that could be desired, he never affected the crudeness of manners favoured by so many nihilists, and always behaved, particularly towards women, with a politeness that bordered on chivalry.

The nihilist movement undoubtedly played a great part in shaping Kropotkin's critical attitude towards Russian social institutions. But the next phase of Russian radical activity did not influence him in any way, except to provoke his aversion. In 1869 there was much discontent among the students of both Moscow and St Petersburg, because the authorities were reluctant to allow them the kind of fraternities which are customary in Western countries. This dissatisfaction eventually produced a number of political circles which played a considerable role in the next few years. Among the students at St Petersburg was a certain Serghei Nechaev, a serf's son who had come in contact with a group of intellectuals which included Cherkesov, a survivor of the Karakazov circle, and Peter Tkachev, a young man who kept apart from the populist stream of the period and later expounded a doctrine of seizure of power by a revolutionary minority—a kind of Blanquism which became the remote ancestor of Bolshevism.

Nechaev, an embittered young fanatic, was much influenced by Tkachev, whose philosophy he united to a Jesuitism of his own invention. Unlimited amoralism was the basis of his creed—he regarded the revolutionary as justified in using literally *any* means to attain his end. He has been immortalised by Dostoevsky as Verchovensky in *The Possessed*; this portrait has enough of pettiness to be unjust (for Nechaev had his own nobility when he refused to be broken down by the decade of rigorous imprisonment which ended his life), yet there was some justice in Dostoevsky's recognition of the essential evil in his gospel.

Nechaev succeeded in forming a small group in St Petersburg during 1869, but on the police becoming active against the student movement, he came to Western Europe, where by a series of audacious bluffs he managed to ingratiate himself with Bakunin and for a while to dazzle the veteran revolutionary by his dynamic character. It was during this period that they composed the celebrated Revolutionary Catechism which provided a theoretical background to Nechaev's subsequent activities and a justification of everything in order to attain the desired end. The young Russian revolutionary did not realise that such a doctrine meant in itself a restoration of "the Hobbesian war of each against all", and that its entire rejection of moral values removed any basis on which a just society could arise. His own practical development of this programme involved the use of fraud, not against the autocrats but against his fellow revolutionaries, while he deliberately sent dangerous letters and literature to acquaintances in Russia in order to compromise them with the police and thus involve them willy-nilly in his plans. The culminating point of his effort was the murder, in Moscow, of a student who had dared to oppose his will. Although he himself succeeded in escaping to Western Europe with the aid of Cherkesov, his companions in murder and some three hundred other men and women who had been in some way connected with him were arrested. In July 1871, eighty-four were brought to trial, and, with a few exceptions, sentenced to imprisonment. It was the end of Nechaevism for the time being in the Russian revolutionary movement; the *narodniks* recoiled from his cynical amoralism and were too libertarian to accept the dictatorial party organisation which he demanded, in such words as these, reported by a witness at the trial of his associates:

> "This is not the time to work out theories; you talked enough in 1862 without doing anything; times have changed. It is your business now not to talk but to do, and to do as you are told by men who are more competent than you are in this matter; your duty is to obey and not to argue."

Nechaev's doctrine was eclipsed rather than destroyed; in the party organisation and tactical outlook of the Bolsheviks he took his due place in the corruption of the Russian revolutionary movement.

At no time did Nechaev's personal influence extend over more than a minority of Russian radicals. Kropotkin never had direct contact with him, but his honourable and gentle character could not fail to be repelled by such extirpation of ethical considerations, and he remarked that "a morally developed individuality must be the foundation of every organisation, whatever political character it may take afterwards and whatever programme of action it may adopt in the course of future events".

The disappearance of Nechaevism left a clear field for the development of the *narodnik* movement in all its varied forms, and it was with this tendency that Kropotkin entered the ranks of Russian revolutionaries. The basic idea of the *narodniks* was fundamentally opposed to that of such tacticians as Tkachev and Nechaev, for while the latter believed in the seizure of power by a trained minority, the former advocated going "to the people" from whom, they contended, every revolution must gain its strength. More even than that, there was implicit in the doctrines of the *narodniks* a deep reverence for the people, and a feeling that among the uncultured masses was an innate wisdom which the intelligentsia lacked. This love for the people led to an approval of the primitive communal economy of the Russian peasant, based on the *mir*, and, thence the *narodniks* were impelled to advocate the voluntary association of producers. The populism which was the essential mark of the *narodnik* brings into the ambit of the movement a wide variety of groups from the anarchists to the terrorists, and of thinkers from Bakunin to Lavrov, with even Dostoevsky and some Slavophils approaching on the right.

Kropotkin, with the love and understanding of common people which had been nurtured in his childhood and brought to maturity in Siberia, had already, on his own account, reached conclusions which made him accept eagerly the *narodnik* philosophy. With his extreme sensitiveness to currents of thought, he adopted the populist attitude even before his introduction to any circle of active propagandists, and came quite independently to his decision to devote his life to the poor.

There remained the question of how he would put his decision into practice. He had no friends whom he knew to be active in *narodnik* circles. Most men of his own generation had been frightened away by earlier persecutions from the expression of radical views, and were even less inclined to put such views into action. When in the literary circles of the capital Kropotkin attempted to bring forward progressive arguments, he usually found himself rebuffed by an abrupt turning of the conversation towards food or the latest French opera, or, if he talked privately, his friends would remark, rather in the tone of Stepan Trofimovitch in *The Possessed*, "We have done something in our life: ask no more from us".

On the other hand, he seems to have been completely isolated until 1872 from the contemporary ferment among the young intelligentsia. This was due partly to his immersion in scientific activities, but also to his greater age, which marked him off from the rest of the students. "At the university I had no friends, properly speaking; I was older than most of my companions, and among young people a difference of a few years is always an obstacle to complete comradeship."

The number of radically active students was small in proportion to the total number, and these few Kropotkin failed to meet until later. It was in the movement for the emancipation and education of women, with which his sister-in-law was closely connected, that he first saw the new spirit of the young.

> "Every evening the young wife of my brother, on her return from the women's pedagogical courses which she followed, had something new to tell us about the animation that prevailed there. Schemes were laid for opening a medical academy and universities for women; debates upon schools or upon different methods of education were organised in connection with the course, and hundreds of women took a passionate interest in these questions, discussing them over and over again in private. . . . A vigorous, exuberant life reigned in those feminine centres, in striking contrast to what I met elsewhere."

Kropotkin's first thoughts turned towards rural administration. One of the abortive reforms which followed the emancipation of the serfs had been the foundation of *Zemstvos*, a Russian equivalent of county councils. At first it was intended that these bodies should have considerable powers of initiative, but very soon all autonomy was taken away, and they became little more than local tax-collecting agencies. At the time, however, Kropotkin still thought something might be done through these channels, and considered settling on his Tambov estate and trying to help the peasants of the area, from some of whom he had received a request for advice; with typical *narodnik* spirit he says: "I should have been content with anything I could do, no matter how small it might be, if only it would help to raise the intellectual level and the well-being of the peasants."

But there seemed little real scope for his good intentions. The foundation of "a school, an experimental farm, a co-operative enterprise" would have been impossible; all such efforts were regarded by the authorities as manifestations of dangerous tendencies. And Kropotkin's peasant friends were agreed that little would come of efforts to gain the rectification of individual injustices. He recounts that, a few days after this disappointing decision:

> "An old grey-haired priest, a man who was held in great esteem in our neighbourhood, came to me . . . with two influential dissenting leaders, and said: 'Talk with these two men. If you can manage it, go with them, Bible in hand, and preach to the peasants. . . . Well, you know what to preach. . . . No police in the world will find you, if they conceal you. . . . There's nothing to be done besides; that's what I, an old man, advise you'."

The idea of going as a Christian, even to preach resistance to the State, was repugnant to Kropotkin's rationalist opinions, and he refused the suggestion, frankly telling his reasons. "But", as he was to admit later when the *narodniks* were all going into the country like the early Christian preachers, "the old man was right."

Seeing that he could do nothing immediately among the peasants, Kropotkin decided to pay a long-planned visit to Western Europe. In his attitude he was already more of a Westerner than most of his contemporaries. Such movements as nihilism and populism were characteristically Russian phenomena, and most of the intellectual proletariat of classless students were as closely bound to Russia as the Slavophils. When they went abroad it was to gain knowledge they could apply at home, and the degree of their absorption in Russian affairs can be seen in the fact that when forced into exile few of them became, like Kropotkin, active in an international sphere; instead, they remained permanent Russian emigrés, waiting always for the day of return.

Kropotkin had been brought up in that more cosmopolitan background of the Russian aristocracy which also produced Herzen and Turgenev, and his tendency to think internationally was increased by his intellectual pursuits; a good scientist cannot be parochial. Interest in the intellectual life of Western Europe could not fail to make him realise the comparative freedom of literary and political expression existing there; it also revealed, even through the guarded reports in Russian newspapers, the social ferment that was covering the lands west of the Russian frontier with a network of new and vigorous revolutionary movements. Already in Siberia he had been stirred by news of the International Workingmen's Association, and in 1871 the Paris Commune, with its dramatic defence by the workers and the terrible massacres that signalised its defeat, had fired his imagination, particularly as the conservative press, seeking a scapegoat, had given the International an undeserved prominence in the events in France.

Up to this time Kropotkin had been too busy and also too poor to undertake another journey, but his abandonment of scientific work and his recent acquisition of ample means had removed these obstacles, and he felt nothing would be a better preparation for his career in the popular cause than a first-hand knowledge of the movements among the working classes of Western Europe. Accordingly, he decided to spend a short period in Switzerland. There were two principal reasons for his choice of this country.

Firstly, it was at that time the centre of the most active sections of the International, since within its boundaries were concentrated not only the Swiss Internationalists, but also a great number of French refugees from the Commune, most of the Russians who concerned themselves with activity on an international scale, and a shifting contingent of Italian revolutionaries, periodically augmented after the failure of one or other of the small insurrections which then formed a regular feature of Italian political life.

And secondly, Switzerland, whose doors were still open to the foreigner, was the Mecca of Russians who came to Western Europe seeking the learning they could not gain at home. Bakunin spent the last years of his life there, Herzen actually became a Swiss citizen, and to Zurich university came a whole exodus of Russian students thirsting for knowledge, and particularly women who were anxious for higher education and who found the Swiss professors willing to teach them. In 1872, according to one of the leaders of the People's Will, Vera Figner, there were about three hundred students of Slav origin (including Serbs and Poles, as well as Russians) in Zurich alone.

The representative of the secret police, whose *Chronique du Mouvement Socialiste* we have already quoted, laments the fact that:

> "Since the year 1860, republican Switzerland began to become gradually the meeting place of a mass of exiles, of anarchists and Russian revolutionaries, among others a quantity of young women, who from the beginning of the Socialist movement came forward to bring serious agreement and devoted activity to the cause of the anarchists. A stay in a country which had for long served as the meeting place for the adepts of the most advanced political principles was found to be both convenient and agreeable; it was there that the plots began to be hatched, it was from there that the emissaries went out; Switzerland, and principally Geneva and Zurich, became a focus of propaganda far from the reach of the Russian government."

There was some falsehood in this picture, since the writer was trying the old device of representing unrest in one's own country as due, not to any faults of the regime at home, but to influences from outside. In fact, although emigrés like Bakunin and Lavrov undoubtedly had a great *ideological* influence on the movement in Russia, the part played by the emigration in directing the actual activities of circles at home was relatively slight. The realities of the situation would have made it ridiculous for men in Zurich to concoct plots to be carried out in St Petersburg, and both the organisation of the circles and the shaping of their activity was left to young people within Russia who had often no direct connection with the exiles and sometimes only a vague idea of their teachings. Furthermore, of those who went to Zurich, by no means all were actually involved in conspiratorial activities; there were many who went merely to gain a better education than Russia could offer. Yet there was perhaps more in the policeman's lament than at first seems evident, for he rightly regarded any form of liberal education as a threat to autocracy; no student who had lived in Switzerland was likely to return with any great enthusiasm for Romanov Russia.

II

Kropotkin started from St Petersburg early in February 1872, and at first intended to stay away only four weeks. However, he found so much to interest him abroad that he did not return for three months. He travelled via Wirballen and Berlin, and as it was his first journey into Western Europe he was impressed, "even more intensely" than he had anticipated, by the contrast between the two parts of the continent. Passing through the thinly populated northern provinces of Russia, he had "the feeling of crossing a desert", for the forests were slight, and it was only rarely that he saw "a small, miserably poor village, buried in snow, or an impracticable, muddy, narrow and winding village road". From this it was an abrupt change to the landscape of Prussia "with its clean-looking villages and farms, its gardens and its paved roads", and he found "even dull Berlin . . . animated after our Russian towns". He went across Germany, enjoying the warm climate after the thick snow he had left at St Petersburg, reached the Rhine, and thence came to Switzerland, "bathed in the rays of a bright sun, with its small, clean hotels, where breakfast was served out of doors in view of the snow-clad mountains".

In Zurich he was immediately among friends. His brother's sister-in-law, Madame Sophie Nicholaevna Lavrov, was studying there; she lived with another Russian, Nadeshda Smezkaya, a wealthy woman who later financed some of the insurrectionary efforts of the Italian anarchists and who was already a disciple of Bakunin.

Kropotkin took "a tiny clean room in the Oberstrasse, commanding from a window a view of the lake, with the mountains beyond it, where the Swiss fought for their independence, and the spires of the old town—that scene of so many religious struggles". This street, which lies close to the Polytechnic, had become a favourite haunt of Russians and he found himself in a familiar atmosphere, for the students had transplanted from St Petersburg and Moscow not only their language but also their ascetic way of life.

"Tea and bread, some milk, and a thin slice of meat cooked over a spirit lamp, amidst animated discussions about the latest news of the socialistic world or the last book read, that was their regular fare. Those who had more money than was needed for such a mode of living gave it for 'the common cause'—the library, the Russian review which was going to be published, the support of the Swiss labour papers. As to their dress, the most parsimonious economy reigned in that direction."

Kropotkin himself was no less dominated by this urge and he wasted no time in the idle occupations of the tourist. He had come with a burning desire to learn of the work that was being done by the International, and he was determined to lose no time in increasing his knowledge.

He was assisted by his sister-in-law, who had already entered fully into the life of the emigré circles, and introduced him to other Russians connected with the International—in particular to Michael Sazhin, known more widely as Armand Ross, who was then one of Bakunin's close disciples.

The advice of these friends was to read, and Kropotkin took to his room armfuls of books, pamphlets, and newspapers which his sister-in-law gave him. It was a period of great activity in the young socialist movement, when many small groups in all countries of Western Europe were busy producing ephemeral newspapers and pamphlets, usually sketchy in argument, but alive with the conviction of a new faith. By reading these publications, by paying attention not only to the theories but also to the activities of the working men connected with these groups, Kropotkin was impressed with "the depth and the moral force of the movement", and he tells us that:

"The more I read the more I saw that there was before me a new world, unknown to me, and totally unknown to the learned makers of sociological theories—a world that I could know only by living in the Workingmen's Association and by meeting the workers in their everyday life. I decided, accordingly, to spend a couple of months in such a life."

His new friends encouraged him in his idea, and he went on to Geneva, which was at that time one of the centres of the international socialist movement.

In Geneva Kropotkin first became fully aware of the great division of opinion that existed at this time within the ranks of the movement, and which a few months later was to cause an irreconcilable cleavage in its forces. The conflict crystallised around the leading figures of the organisation, Karl Marx and Michael Bakunin. The two men were as different in character as in ideas. Marx, the bitter, dictatorial scholar, with a great power of social analysis that had been submerged in a messianic conception of history; Bakunin, the hero of insurrections and prisons, the generous and able orator, extravagant in his enthusiasm, too impatient to be a systematic thinker, but possessed of a political clairvoyance that enabled him to see with remarkable accuracy the defects of his opponents and their teachings. But it was much more than a struggle of personalities; it was also a clash of two wholly different conceptions of social organisation, two mutually alien philosophies of life. Marx believed in State socialism, based on authority; he looked to a dictatorship of the proletariat; he advocated the socialists taking over the machinery of the State, and his dream of its eventual "withering away" was vague and distant, a mere concession to the libertarian tradition of socialism in the nineteenth century. From his conception stemmed the theories of the various Continental social-democratic movements, and, after a certain inoculation of Blanquism and Nechaevism, the authoritarian socialism of the Bolsheviks. Bakunin, on the other hand, believed in the abolition of the State and its replacement by a federal society based on free communes and associations of producers. He elevated the principle of voluntary co-operation in place of authority, and he rejected political activity in favour of direct economic action. From his conception originated anarchism, syndicalism, and indirectly the various populist doctrines of the Russian revolutionaries in the subsequent decades.

The story of the struggle between Marx and Bakunin does

not belong to this book, although the differences between the two separate movements which emerged, and between the conceptions of authoritarian and libertarian socialism will necessarily play a prominent part in the subsequent narrative. Here let it suffice to remark that, although history has given Marx a greater number of worshippers in the world today and has provided at least lip service to his aims in "the socialist sixth of the world", it has also brought adequate proof of Bakunin's arguments. For Bakunin indicated with prophetic insight the exact manner in which the acceptance of the principle of State authority would turn Marxian socialism into a political tyranny and deprive the workers of the very liberty and economic security they had hoped to gain. Nearly eighty years ago (in 1873), he said:

"That minority [the rulers], the Marxists say, will consist of workers. Yes, perhaps of *former* workers. And these, as soon as they become rulers or representatives of the people, will cease to be workers, and will begin to look down upon the entire world of manual workers from the heights of the State. They will no longer represent the people, but themselves and their own pretensions to rule the people. Whoever has any doubts about that does not know human nature. But these selected men will be ardently convinced, and at the same time learned, socialists. The term 'scientific socialism', which continually occurs in the works of Lassalle and of the Marxists, proves that the alleged People's State will be nothing else but the quite despotic rule over the popular masses by a new and not very numerous aristocracy of real or spurious savants. The mass is uneducated, which means that it will be completely free from the worries of government; that it will be included in the ruled herd. . . .

"They [the Marxists] will concentrate the reins of government in a strong hand, because the ignorant people are in need of quite a firm guardianship. They will establish a single State Bank that will concentrate in its hands all commercial-industrial, agricultural and even scientific production; and the mass of the people will be divided into two armies, the industrial and the agricultural, which will be under the direct command of government engineers who will constitute a new privileged class."

Intuitively, Bakunin and his followers realised the whole tendency of development which was to lead Marxism to the

ALEXANDER KROPOTKIN

communist State and the Kremlin dictatorship of bureaucrats and managers.

In 1872, however, when Kropotkin reached Switzerland, these words had not been written, and the split in the International was not complete. But the division already existed; the Internationalists of Spain, Italy, and Belgium, as well as part of the French movement, stood on the libertarian side. The Germans were behind Marx. The English trade unionists were in the centre, but distrusted Marx's authoritarian attitude and therefore tended to act in conjunction with the Bakuninists. In Switzerland, which presented a cross-section of the movement as a whole, forces were almost equally divided. In Geneva, although there was a libertarian grouping led by Zhukovsky, Elisée Reclus, the celebrated French geographer, and Lefrançais, a veteran of the Commune, the main strength of the movement was in the hands of the Marxists, led by Utin, a Russian of dubious sincerity, who later made his peace with the Tsar, returned to Russia, amassed a fortune as an army contractor in the Russo-Turkish war of 1877, and who has been described by the well-known Marxist historian, Franz Mehring, as a "master of intrigue", whose successes were "exclusively in the field of tittle-tattle".

But among the watchmakers of the Jura, semi-independent craftsmen who resented any system that smelt of dictation, there was a very strong libertarian movement led by a number of Bakunin's close disciples and intimate personal friends. Nevertheless, the bitterness of later years had not yet entered fully into the struggle. The rank and file of the two sections were still on fairly cordial terms, and when Kropotkin left Zurich his Bakuninist friends do not seem in any way to have prejudiced him, for it was to the Marxist section in Geneva that he first went.

This movement carried on its activity in the Masonic *Temple Unique*. There Kropotkin was welcomed by Utin, whom he generously describes as "a bright, clever and active man", and also by "a most sympathetic Russian lady, who was known far and wide amongst the workers as Madame Olga". These were the first representatives of that Russian Marxism which did not bear fruit for another decade, when the former anarchist, George Plekhanov, formed the first Marxist group and later succeeded in founding a Russian social democratic party, from which eventually sprang the Bolsheviks and the Mensheviks.

Utin and his friends were anxious to make a good impression on a promising recruit, and they willingly gave Kropotkin all the facilities he asked, introducing him to the more active workmen and inviting him to meetings of various committees. He attended conscientiously but does not seem to have found such routines wholly to his taste, and confesses that he preferred personal contact with the working men. His habitual ease of contact with common people quickly won him their confidence. "Taking a glass of sour wine at one of the tables in the hall, I used to sit there every evening amid the workers, and soon became friendly with several of them . . . I could thus follow the movement from the inside, and know the workers' view of it."

He found among these simple men an inspiring combination of devotion and confidence. They were all passionately interested in the International, placed their trust in its promises of a better future, and hoped that very soon would come a social revolution that would "totally change the economic conditions". Kropotkin found them lacking in direct hatred; "no one desired class war", but they all felt that if the rulers persisted in obstinately resisting change, some form of struggle, even a violent one, would have to be entered upon, "provided it would bring with it well-being and liberty to the masses".

Such an attitude naturally found a response in Kropotkin's optimistic temperament. And his *narodnik* love of the people was solidified into a positive admiration of the workers, caused by the impressive self-sacrifice shown by these simple men at this period of enthusiasm.

"One must have lived among the workers at that time to realise the effect which the sudden growth of the Association had upon their minds—the trust they put in it, the love with which they spoke of it, the sacrifices they made for it. Every day, week after week and year after year, thousands of workers gave their time and their coppers, taken from their very food, in order to support the life of each group, to secure the appearance of the papers, to defray the expenses of the congresses, to support the comrades who had suffered for the Association. . . . The mean, the trivial disappeared to leave room for the grand, the elevating emotions."

It is easy to understand how intoxicating all this must have been to a Russian radical. For the peasants in whom the *narodniks* placed their trust still slumbered; far from being roused by the disinterested efforts of the upper- and middle-class missionaries who gave up all comfort to travel and preach among the poor, the peasants regarded them as interfering strangers and sometimes even handed them over to the police. But here were conscious workers, striving actively for their own liberation, and Kropotkin was deeply moved by this vindication of his populist faith.

He absorbed the new ideas that were presented to him, and fell steadily under the influence of the simple revolutionary creed he encountered. His conscience was more than ever stirred by a need to act not merely for, but also with the poor. It was in this state of enthusiasm that he reached the point at which we can justly regard him as a revolutionary, dedicated to the achievement of social justice by means of a complete revolution in social relations, attained by peaceful or forceful means.

"I found this devotion a standing reproach. . . . More and more I began to feel that I was bound to cast in my lot with them. Stepniak says, in his *Career of a Nihilist*, that every revolutionist has had a moment in his life when some circumstance, maybe unimportant in itself, has brought him to pronounce his oath of giving himself to the cause of the revolution. I knew that moment; I lived through it after one of the meetings at the Temple Unique, when I felt more acutely than ever before how cowardly are the educated men who refuse to put their education, their knowledge, their energy at the service of those who are so much in need of that education and that energy."

From this time onwards he was committed to the idea of reconstructing society so that inequality and servitude would be ended by the abolition of property and of the political domination of man by man. It only remained now for him to decide the *kind* of activity which would best bring about this revolutionary change. And it was here that he encountered tendencies among the Genevan Marxists which aroused his disquiet.

While he was in that city the International received a strange recruit, the Genevan lawyer Ambery. This man had long been seeking a career in Swiss politics, and, having been defeated at a previous election where he failed to gain the radical vote, now hoped to reach the same end with the support of the socialistic workers. Kropotkin was shocked by his statement that he had waited until a satisfactory conclusion of his business affairs before joining the International, and only slightly less disturbed by the opportunistic attitude of many Marxists who recognised that Ambery was a careerist but complacently remarked, "We accept their services for the present, but when the revolution comes our first move will be to throw all of them overboard". However, the political game is not so simple, and soon it became apparent to Kropotkin that, far from Ambery serving the International, he was using it for his own ends.

Very shortly after the advent of this politician, a large public meeting was called by Utin. Its object was to deny the statement by the *Journal de Genève* that the building workers connected with the International Workingmen's Association intended to strike for better pay. Hundreds of workers packed the hall, and Utin tried to rush them into passing a resolution protesting against the "calumnious" suggestion that a strike was intended, ending his speech by saying, "If you agree with it, citizens, I will send it at once to the Press". Kropotkin was puzzled by this stir about a matter which seemed to him quite inoffensive. "Why should this statement be described as a calumny? Is it, then, a crime to strike?" he thought to himself. And his perturbation was increased when the representatives of the building trades stood up one after the other to protest that "the wages had lately been so low that they could hardly live upon them; that with the opening of the spring there was plenty of work in view, of which they intended to take advantage to increase their wages; and that if an increase were refused they intended to begin a general strike."

Kropotkin was furious at Utin's duplicity, and next day reproached him, saying: "As a leader, you were bound to know that a strike had really been spoken of." Utin admitted his motives, telling Kropotkin that a strike at this moment would have spoilt Ambery's chances of election, and that the cantonal committee of the International had therefore promised to do their best to prevent it. Kropotkin, who up to then "did not suspect the real motives of the leaders", was disheartened by this revelation of political manœuvring among men who made such "burning speeches" from the platform and practised such cowardly tactics in their daily activities.

Accordingly, after five weeks with the Marxists, he felt it was time to make himself acquainted with the rival trend in the International, and told Utin of his intention to investigate the work of the Bakuninists. Utin, who seems to have behaved in a friendly way towards Kropotkin throughout their brief relationship, gave him a letter of introduction to the libertarian, Zhukovsky. He remarked, with exact foresight, "Well, you won't return to us; you will remain with them".

Zhukovsky was a member of the earlier generation of Westernising Russian noblemen; he had come under Bakunin's influence at an early date. On the triumph of the Marxists he was expelled from the Geneva section, and became the centre of a small group of Bakuninists, mainly exiles from Paris. He remained an anarchist all his life, but adopted a theoretical purism which led him to perpetual and often barren criticism of all his friends and comrades.

At this first meeting Zhukovsky advised Kropotkin, since there was little activity in the libertarian group of Geneva, to go to the Jura, where the movement had its strongest nuclei. The Jura federation was the centre of revolt against the Marxist-controlled General Council of the International. Its members preserved a close personal loyalty towards Bakunin—not the loyalty of followers for a revered chief, Kropotkin says, so much as that of equals for "a personal friend of whom every one spoke with love, in a spirit of comradeship". One other man had played a greater part than Bakunin in inspiring the libertarian movement of the Jura. This was James Guillaume, a former school teacher who, having lost his employment for his opinions, was now working as the manager of a small printing works in Neuchâtel.

Here Kropotkin sought him. Guillaume, who found it difficult to earn his living and carry on propaganda at the same time, seems to have been curt with his visitor. When Kropotkin arrived, early in April, he was bringing out the first number of a local literary paper, *Lectures Populaires*, by means of which he hoped to establish his printing office and so assure a friendly press on which the *Bulletin of the Jura Federation* could always be printed; that afternoon, the first issues of this magazine had come off the press, and "in addition to his usual duties of proof-reader and co-editor, he had to write on the wrappers a thousand addresses of persons to whom the first three numbers would be sent, and to fasten the wrappers himself".

Kropotkin offered help, on condition that Guillaume gave the time saved to telling about the Jura federation.

"We understood each other. Guillaume warmly shook my hand, and that was the beginning of our friendship. We spent all the afternoon in the office, he writing the addresses, I fastening the wrappers, and a French Communard, who was a compositor, chatting with us all the while as he rapidly composed a novel, intermingling his conversation with the sentences which he had to put in the type and which he read aloud. . . .

"It was late in the evening that Guillaume took off his working blouse and we went out for a friendly chat for a couple of hours, when he had to resume his work as editor of the *Bulletin of the Jura Federation.*"

From Guillaume he learnt the main outline of the activities and ideas of the Jura federation, while from the compositor, Bastelica, and from Benoit Malon, another leading Communard who worked as a basket-maker in Neuchâtel, he heard the inner history of the Paris Commune, its heroism and its errors; he was particularly impressed by the high moral integrity of these defeated revolutionaries, exemplified in "that absence of hatred, that confidence in the final triumph of their ideas, that calm though sad gaze of their eyes directed towards the future, that readiness to forget the nightmare of the past which struck me in Malon".

In a day or two he went to the mountain village of Sonvillier, where he met the watchmaker, Adhemar Schwitzguebel, who was later to become one of his close associates. Through this man, himself a friend of Bakunin, Kropotkin became closely acquainted with the Jura mountaineers, talking to them as they engraved watchlids in the tiny family workshops and attending their informal village meetings, to which as many as fifty people would come from the surrounding hills, often walking through blizzards.

Here he encountered the same devotion as he had found in Geneva, but there was one real difference. In the Jura existed no division between leaders and masses; all the Internationalists were craftsmen, and the nature of their work gave them an independence of thought which Kropotkin had not encountered elsewhere. Out of this attitude, and guided rather than led by such friends as Bakunin, they were evolving a philosophy towards which Kropotkin found himself irresistibly attracted. It was the end of his conversion, the experience that completed the pattern of ideas on which the rest of his life and thought would be based.

"The theoretical aspects of anarchism, as they were then beginning to be expressed in the Jura federation, especially by Bakunin; the criticism of State socialism—the fear of an economic despotism, far more dangerous than the merely political despotism—which I heard formulated there; and the revolutionary character of the agitation appealed strongly to my mind. But the equalitarian relations which I found in the Jura mountains; the independence of thought and expression which I saw developing in the workers, and their unlimited devotion to the cause appealed even more strongly to my feelings; and when I came away from the mountains, after a week's stay with the watchmakers, my views upon socialism were settled. I was an anarchist."

Kropotkin was so impressed by what he had seen that he thought this was perhaps the place where he could best devote himself to the cause he had decided to adopt. Returning to Neuchâtel, he suggested to Guillaume that, instead of returning to Russia, he should remain in Switzerland and earn his living by a manual trade while devoting his spare time to propaganda.

"I dissuaded him", says Guillaume. "I represented to him that he would have much difficulty in making himself, a Russian prince, accepted by the Swiss workers as a real comrade; that his propaganda would be much more effective if it were carried on in Russia among his own fellow countrymen, whose needs he knew well and to whom he could speak the language most fitted to their particular situation; that in his country the harvest was immense and the workers much too few for even a single man to be diverted, unless absolutely necessary, from his task, while in the West, and particularly in Switzerland, with the reinforcements which had been brought to us by the proscriptions in France, we had plenty of militants. He recognised that I was right, and we took farewell of each other, wondering if we should ever meet again."

But before returning to Russia Kropotkin paid a hasty visit to Belgium, where he found once again a "centralised political agitation" in the cities like Brussels; and among the rural craftsmen, the cloth workers of the Verviers area, an independence and a libertarian philosophy which made him regard them as "one of the most sympathetic populations I have ever met in Western Europe".

He then returned to Switzerland, passing again through Zurich, where he found Ross had departed to stir up unrest in the Balkans; he left a message for him: "I am with you and always yours." Early in May he set out on his return to St Petersburg, travelling by Vienna and Warsaw and carrying, besides his new ideas, a more tangible baggage of books and magazines, all likely to be forbidden in Russia, and therefore doubly valuable as material for his brother and friends in St Petersburg.

He was satisfied with his journey. It had given him "definite sociological conceptions", a clear aim, and an example of practical activity which inspired him with confidence. Moreover, it had clarified the ideas he had learnt from the currents of thought in Russia; nihilism and populism were vague conceptions, but in anarchism their emergent tendencies became definite and achieved a meaning in concrete social terms.

Furthermore, what Kropotkin had heard from the Communard veterans and seen in the conflict between Marxists and Bakuninists taught him that it was not only morally more right but even practically more effective to avoid opportunism or indefinite aims. He became, in other words, a political fundamentalist, and, basing his views on the theory that revolutions are inevitable features of the evolutionary process, he considered that they would only succeed if the oppressed portion of society "should obtain the closest conception of what they intend to achieve and how, and that they should be imbued with the enthusiasm which is necessary for that achievement". Since social upheavals, in Kropotkin's view, happened independently of the will of individuals, every effort should be made to see that the conflicts they involved were fought on general and comprehensive issues.

"...The conflict itself will depend much less upon the efficiency of firearms and guns than upon the force of the creative genius which will be brought into action in the work of reconstruction of society. It will depend chiefly upon the constructive forces of society taking for the moment a free course; upon the inspirations being of a higher standard, and so winning more sympathy even from those who, as a class, are opposed to the change. The conflict, being thus engaged in on larger issues, will purify the social atmosphere itself; and the numbers of victims on both sides will certainly be smaller than they would have been in case the fight had been fought upon matters of secondary importance in which the lower instincts of men find a free play."

Kropotkin's only real regret was that he did not meet Bakunin in Switzerland. In his *Memoirs* he merely records that Bakunin was at Locarno, and passes the matter over as if this were the only reason why they did not meet. But an enthusiastic young man who travelled from Switzerland to Belgium and back to gain information about the anarchist groups in that country is certainly not likely to have found too troublesome the comparatively short journey necessary to see the man who was at once the great spokesman of libertarian philosophy and, since Herzen's death, the most distinguished Russian exile. Max Nettlau, the historian of the anarchist movement, collected from Kropotkin and Guillaume two illuminating accounts of this incident. Kropotkin himself told Nettlau that he did not visit Bakunin in Locarno because Guillaume had told him that Bakunin was too old and overwrought to be troubled with visitors. Guillaume, on the other hand, said that it was Bakunin who did not wish to see Kropotkin, of whose presence in Switzerland he was aware. He seems to have suspected Kropotkin of being too moderate in his opinions, because of his brother's friendship for Peter Lavrov; and to have attached exaggerated significance to the fact that in Geneva Kropotkin spent five weeks with Utin and only one with Zhukovsky. It was unfortunate that the two great Russians never met, and Bakunin must perhaps be blamed for too hasty conclusions. But we should remember that he had only recently undergone a bad experience with Nechaev, and in 1872 was being subjected by Marx to the most calumnious accusations over transactions in which he had been involved by that other young enthusiast from Russia. There is little wonder that he was somewhat cautious about commencing another relationship which, for all he knew, might end in the same way. Therefore, behaving for once with excessive prudence, he refused to see Kropotkin.

Kropotkin crossed into Russia on the 3rd May 1872, having arranged in Cracow for a Jewish smuggling organisation to bring his books across the frontier, and in due course he arrived in St Petersburg with his intellectual contraband.

III

His return to St Petersburg was followed in a few days by a formal resignation from the civil service. He now had two tasks before him—to fulfil his obligations to the Russian Geographical Society by completing his report on the Finnish expedition and to find a means of commencing the revolutionary work he wished to pursue.

The first was a matter of time and hard work; the second was fulfilled easily and soon. His establishment of contact with the International Workingmen's Association, of which he spoke freely among his friends, gave him a reputation as a progressive, and it was not long before he was approached by a fellow student, Dmitri Klemens, with an invitation to join a group known as the Chaikovsky Circle.

Klemens was a man of fine character who devoted many years to the struggle against the Tsars, working at home and abroad, and earning his share of prison and exile. He was also an able geographer, and carried out a number of expeditions in Central Asia in which he showed great ingenuity at overcoming inadequate means. His revolutionary youth had given him good training in a voluntarily hard life, and Kropotkin in his *Memoirs* presents a portrait of this friend which describes not merely Klemens himself but a whole class of intellectuals in his day.

"He was very intelligent, had read a great deal, and had seriously thought out what he had read. He loved science and deeply respected it, but, like many of us, he soon came to the conclusion that to follow the career of a scientific man meant to join the camp of the Philistines, and that there was plenty of other and more urgent work that he could do. He attended the university lectures for two years and then abandoned them, giving himself entirely to social work. He lived anyhow; I even doubt if he had a permanent lodging. Sometimes he would come to me and ask, 'Have you some paper?' and, having taken a supply of it, he would sit at the corner of a table for an hour or two, diligently making a translation. The little that he earned in this way was more than sufficient to satisfy all his limited wants. Then he would hurry to a distant part of the town, to see a comrade or to help a needy friend; or he would cross St Petersburg on foot to a remote suburb in order to obtain free admission to a college for some boy in whom the comrades were interested. He was undoubtedly a gifted man. In Western Europe a man far less gifted would have worked his way to a position of political or socialist leadership. No such thought ever entered the brain of Kelnitz [Klemens.] To lead men was by no means his ambition, and there was no work too insignificant for him to do."

The circle to which Klemens introduced Kropotkin has some importance in the history of the Russian radical movement, and for years it was the most considerable progressive organisation. It was essentially propagandist and educational rather than conspiratorial. In later years, when the persecutions of Alexander II and his successor forced the Russian revolutionaries to more direct methods, it was from among young men and women trained in this circle that the first heroes of the People's Will movement were recruited. But in its inception the circle had, to use Kropotkin's words, "nothing revolutionary about it", and it had disappeared as a movement before the revolutionaries turned to the terrorist policy of the *Narodnaya Volya*.

The circle was founded in 1869 by Nicholas Chaikovsky, a student in chemistry, who afterwards called himself an anarchist for some years, and then became a leading Russian co-operator. His first efforts were educational; in collaboration with Sophia Perovskaya, then a girl of sixteen and later to play a tragic role in the terrorist movement, and Madame Korba, he organised classes for children too poor to attend the ordinary schools.

Shortly afterwards he started his first circle, of five, for the purpose of bringing together the advanced students and making a collective study of the best means of reaching the workers and creating the elements of an "intelligent democracy", as he called it. The circle was augmented by a group of women, headed by Perovskaya, and during the next three years spread its activities very widely. An account by Chaikovsky, quoted by G. H. Perris in *Russia in Revolution*, gives a clear idea of the way in which its work was developed.

> "Our method was to create a series of small circles in various parts of the country for common studies and for supplying books and other information from the centres like St Petersburg and Moscow. . . . In Russia co-operative house-keeping was and is common, especially among students and workmen, and these local communes were our best recruiting grounds. Through them our circles could be conveniently connected with provincial groups of a preparatory nature to whom we undertook to supply the best books at that time in circulation. . . . We found this a strong practical method of keeping a large number of groups of the most intelligent and energetic men throughout the country in touch and co-operation. . . . The carrying on of this systematic work on a prearranged plan led to the organisation of secret students' congresses and to tours of visitation in the provinces. Summer settlements served us very well."

The circle did not, however, confine itself merely to distributing books. It found very soon that much desirable literature was not available in Russian; translations had to be made and the books published by the circle itself. Nor did its members fail to be conscious of the need to make contact with the workers and peasants, for, after all, it was the era of "To the People", and the Chaikovtsi were very self-conscious *narodniks*. At the time of Kropotkin's entry into the group they were discussing the direction to be given to their activity; some at first held out for a further period of socialist propaganda among the educated youth, but the more active members thought that the time had come to devote their energies to establishing contact with the lower classes, and, by the necessity of their situation, they were inevitably impelled into the latter course, which Kropotkin supported. Chaikovsky describes him at the first meeting he attended speaking "in favour of an immediate concentration of all the forces of the organisation in working-class circles without waiting for the perfecting of the propaganda groups recruited from the students".

At this time there were some twenty or thirty members in the central group. They were a closely knit circle, connected rather by personal respect and common general aims than by uniformity of opinion. Kropotkin says that they "accepted as members only persons who were well known and had been tested in various circumstances, and of whom it was felt that they could be trusted absolutely". The consequence was that the circle recruited a unique assemblage of pioneers in the Russian underground movement, including, besides Chaikovsky, Klemens, Sophie Perovskaya and Kropotkin, such men and women as Stepniak and Volkhovsky (later celebrated exiles in England), Charashin, Lopatin, the Kornilov sisters, and Tikhomirov. In the provinces they were connected with groups comprising in all between two and three thousand members, situated not only in Moscow but also in towns as far apart as Odessa, Vilna, Perm, Saratov, and Rostov. But there was no attempt at centralised control; all the local circles worked independently, and the function of the circle in St Petersburg, at least during its early years, was to provide them with material for propaganda.

When Klemens first proposed Kropotkin for membership his suggestion met with some hostility. Kropotkin's rank and his known connection with the court were against him. Chaikovsky tells us that their first reaction was to remark, "What sort of a prince have you now? Perhaps at present he desires to amuse himself under the pretence of democracy, but later he will become a dignitary and have us hanged." However, the spirited defence of Klemens, a man of known astuteness, convinced the circle, and Kropotkin was duly invited to join. His fellow members immediately found him a congenial and reliable companion, with whom they could work in complete harmony.

The circle respected Kropotkin's "experience of life, the clarity and maturity of his views, and his scientific knowledge". On his side there was an exaggerated humility, and Chaikovsky says that "he considered us as authorised specialists in the practical work of secret propaganda", and "believed himself as a whole inferior to the group", this feeling being increased both by natural modesty and a feeling of guilt over his princely origin. "For Kropotkin there were no limits as to what he was ready to sacrifice in our favour. He was willing to sacrifice to the cause his scientific discoveries and his merits as a scholar, so deep was his devotion to the popular cause. . . ."

Although he felt a certain obligation to complete the work he had undertaken for the Russian Geographical Society, Kropotkin actually offered to abandon it immediately in order to devote himself entirely to revolutionary work. But his comrades agreed that he should fulfil his promises, and suggested that for the time being at least he should remain outside their secret organisation. "This was done", Chaikovsky tells us, "for purely utilitarian reasons; we wished to maintain his connections for the good of our cause, and to keep him at liberty so that he might continue our revolutionary activity in the event of our arrest." They had good cause to make provision for such an eventuality, since Chaikovsky and other members of the circle had already been arrested for short periods and then released because the Third Section found nothing definite against them; they knew that very soon, as their work became more openly subversive, they could not rely on escaping so easily.

Kropotkin himself says of the circle, "Never did I meet elsewhere such a collection of morally superior men and women as the score of persons whose acquaintance I made at the first meeting of the circle of Chaikovsky. I still feel proud of having been received into that family". This cordiality of relationship is all the more surprising in view of the fact that in theoretical matters he was in a minority of one. For this we have not only his own evidence but that of all the members who have since spoken of him, Chaikovsky, Stepniak and Charashin, who remarked that "there were no followers of the Bakuninist tendency among us except for Kropotkin".

The majority of the members were, according to Klemens when he introduced Kropotkin, "constitutionalists . . . with minds open to any honest idea", while Chaikovsky termed them "Populist Socialists", aiming at the eventual social revolution. Kropotkin himself, speaking to Nettlau in 1901, referred disparagingly to their ideas, contending that they were essentially "social-democrats", and that, apart from himself, the only real revolutionaries were Klemens, Stepniak, Charashin, and Perovskaya. These four were, incidentally, the members for whom he felt the closest personal admiration.

At this time the movement of the *narodniks* was divided into two main currents—the followers of Bakunin and those of Lavrov. Kropotkin was a Bakuninist, the remainder of the Chaikovtsi tended towards Lavrov, but within Russia the differences between these two factions did not then assume the bitterness engendered among the exiles of Zurich, where the divergences were exacerbated by questions of personality. And fundamentally the two ways of thought had much in common. Both Lavrov and Bakunin believed in "going to the people" and, while Lavrov was not a complete anarchist, he certainly looked to an eventual disappearance of the State and to the reorganisation of society on a communal basis; nor did he, like the Marxists, place any faith in dictatorship, even of the proletariat. He held that power must always rest with the people, but that during the period of transition they should voluntarily follow the lead of the gifted and experienced few. Sir John Maynard, in his *Russia in Flux*, further elucidates the differences between the two schools:

"Lavrov was from the beginning a revolutionist, but he stood for preparatory propaganda and the gradual ripening of ideas, as opposed to the abrupt methods of the insurrectionary school of Bakunin. . . . The distinction between the two schools is not between revolution and terrorism on the one hand and peaceful persuasion on the other. . . .

"The contrast is between propaganda for ultimate revolution on one side and agitation for insurrection, whenever possible, on the other. The Lavrovist held that the revolution must come from the instruction of the plain folk by the intelligentsia; the Bakuninist, that the revolutionist is not to teach the people, who already know better than he, and have an instinctive appreciation of the methods of Socialism: he is to combine isolated protests into united action and find occasions for action, and the people will join him spontaneously. The one expected delay in the revolution: the other thought it might come at any time with luck and courage."

The reason for the ability in the moderates of the Chaikovsky circle to work with Kropotkin lies partly in the fact that on both sides their ideas were not yet fully worked out, and that they were not in a situation where a revolution on any basis seemed likely in a proximate future. Consequently, although Kropotkin believed that the political attitude to the revolution towards which most of his friends tended would lead to constitutional monarchy, and although in time, as Chaikovsky says, "the divergence of views between Kropotkin and the majority of our members, in purely political questions particularly, became more and more apparent", they still found agreement in the immediate tasks to be done. Indeed, so much confidence did Kropotkin inspire among his comrades that when they eventually decided that the circle needed a programme it was to Kropotkin that, with great courtesy, the majority delegated this task.

Kropotkin on his side believed that if the group as a whole reached a decision it was for him, as an individual, to "put aside personal feeling and give all his strength to the task". This does not seem a wholly logical attitude for an anarchist; nevertheless, Kropotkin acted upon it to such an extent that when the question of agitation for a constitution arose and it seemed clear that the circle as a whole was in favour of this policy, he even offered to form an organisation of courtiers and higher functionaries who would use all their influence to attain this end. His comrades, however, did not accept the suggestion.

It must also be remembered that Kropotkin was personally tolerant of people who diverged from him on political issues, as was shown by his later friendship with socialists like Hyndman and Morris. Moreover, there is reason to suppose that to some extent at least his own attitude was influenced by Lavrov's moderation. Certainly in later years he was on cordial terms with Lavrov, and Professor James Mavor, who knew them both well, goes so far as to suggest that on some issues Kropotkin was nearer to Lavrov than to Bakunin. Certainly, while Kropotkin maintained a perpetually optimistic belief in the near outbreak of the social revolution, he did in practice devote most of his energy to trying to convince people of all classes by "sweet reasonableness", while in his book on Russian literature he spoke very highly of Lavrov's work and personal character. Nevertheless, as we shall show, there were always considerable differences between the two men.

Although Kropotkin enjoyed the confidence of the circle, he

does not appear to have influenced them greatly by his ideas. Among the known titles of books distributed by them appear the names of Chernyshevsky, Pisarev, Dobrolukov, and Lavrov, of Marx, Owen, Darwin, Herbert Spencer, Lassalle, and Louis Blanc, but there is no trace of any work of either Bakunin or Proudhon having been distributed. Moreover, when the dispute arose between the Bakuninists and the Lavrovists in Zurich over the Russian library in that town and the publication of a magazine in Switzerland, Kropotkin suggested that the group should send Klemens, who held a fairly impartial attitude, to satisfy himself of the actual merits of the case. This was at first agreed to, and Kropotkin gave Klemens his passport for the journey. Eventually, however, the moderates sent Kuprianov, who was already prejudiced against Bakunin and immediately gave his support to Lavrov. This dispute was not so important as may appear at first sight, since Kropotkin, and probably others of the group, tended to depreciate the value of emigré activity and held that the policy should be chosen by men who were actually carrying on the work of propaganda within Russia, an attitude he continued to hold when himself in exile. When Lavrov's magazine, *VPered* (Future) arrived, the circle was disappointed by its detachment from actual Russian affairs, for Lavrov still maintained the attitude of concentrating on the intellectuals which the Chaikovtsi had abandoned.

Kropotkin's work for the circle was unbroken for the two years until his arrest in 1874. It brought him great satisfaction, and he tells us that during this period of high-pressure work and "broadly and delicately humane" relationships, he felt "that exuberance of life when one feels at every moment the full throbbing of all the fibres of the inner self, and when life is really worth living". He never missed the frequent meetings of the circle, which were held in a small suburban house inhabited by Sophie Perovskaya in the guise of a working-class woman, and he portrays the simplicity and enthusiasm with which the group carried on its work.

"The utmost cordiality always prevailed at our meetings. Chairmen and all sorts of formalism are so utterly repugnant to the Russian mind that we had none; and although our debates were sometimes hot, especially when 'programme questions' were under discussion, we always managed very well without resorting to

Western formalities. An absolute sincerity, a general desire to settle the difficulties for the best, and a frankly expressed contempt for all that in the least degree approached theatrical affectation were quite sufficient. If any one of us had ventured to attempt oratorical effects by a speech, friendly jokes would have shown him at once that speech-making was out of place. Often we had to take our meals during these meetings, and they invariably consisted of rye bread, with cucumbers, a bit of cheese, and plenty of weak tea to quench the thirst. Not that money was lacking; there was always enough, and yet there was never too much to cover the steadily growing expenses for printing, transportation of books, concealing friends from the police, and starting new enterprises."

The group soon discovered that the books they could distribute with the approval of the censorship were neither outspoken enough nor sufficiently simply written for their new policy of trying to work among the peasants and artisans. Accordingly, they arranged for a printing press to be started on their behalf in Switzerland, run by Alexandrov and independent of both Bakuninist and Lavrovist factions. They also made elaborate arrangements for smuggling their literature across the frontier, and here the Jewish contrabandists whom Kropotkin had encountered on his return from Western Europe proved extremely helpful. They had to write pamphlets suited to local needs, and a literature committee was formed, of which Kropotkin was a member; its productions included a brochure entitled *The Clever Mechanic* (a fairy-tale exposition of socialism), an adaptation of Erkmann-Chatrian's *A French Peasant*, an account of the Pugachev rising, and a few revolutionary songs. In addition to the actual writing and production, distribution was very laborious owing to the necessity of evading police observation, which involved much travelling and a vast cipher correspondence, and also because of the comparative lack of experience in underground technique among the members of the circle.

Kropotkin's sole literary production at this time seems to have been a pamphlet entitled *Should We Occupy Ourselves with Examining the Ideals of a Future Society?* According to the Russian police report already quoted, this was actually published, but it was produced *in manuscript* at the trial of the 193 contacts of the Chaikovsky circle in 1878, and, with its gaps and its controversial nature, seems rather a memorandum for discussion within the circle than for publication outside. However, it is an important document for the biographer, since it gives the only contemporary account of Kropotkin's ideas during this early part of his revolutionary life, and we are therefore paraphrasing it briefly.

He begins by advocating, in the Bakuninist manner, the possession of the land and factories by the producers themselves. There are to be no privileged categories of workers, and manual work should be regarded as a duty for all men. Education should be universal, and in the schools intellectual teaching should be combined with an apprenticeship to a manual trade. There follows a rejection of the State, and a suggestion of labour cheques instead of money.

In order to attain these ends Kropotkin advocates the complete social revolution. Partial insurrections must be encouraged, but Kropotkin explicitly rejects Nechaev's conspiratorial ideas. Revolutionaries cannot make revolutions, but they can link and guide into one productive channel the scattered efforts of the dissatisfied elements. For the present the circles must spread their ideas, collect adherents and unite into a common organisation. All their activity should be based on going to the people. Direct personal propaganda is important and it should be reinforced by popular literature and a journal that can be understood by peasants and workers. Equally important is the practical propaganda of founding co-operatives of consumers and producers, while movements against local tyrants in factories and villages must be encouraged.

Until a fairly strong movement has been built up among peasants and urban workers, Kropotkin sees little object in the movement in Russia establishing contact with the International Workingmen's Association. He shows his own sympathy for the Federalists (Bakuninists) within the International, but maintains that it would be unwise for the revolutionaries within Russia to become involved in the disputes of the various factions abroad, since the differences are largely personal and are therefore difficult for the revolutionaries at home to consider objectively.

As will become evident when we consider Kropotkin's later works, already at this period he held most of the ideas on which his anarchist communist theory was based, and only in a few points, such as the substitution of labour cheques for money instead of the complete elimination of the principle of financial exchange, would this early statement have been repudiated by him in his more mature days as a social theoretician.

The activities of the Chaikovsky circle among the workers did not end in the distribution of pamphlets. The more capable of them, and particularly Serdukov, Klemens, Stepniak, Perovskaya, Charashin and Kropotkin, set about organising discussion circles among the workers of the capital, particularly the engineers, the building workers, and the badly exploited textile operatives in the Vyborg district. They succeeded in rousing considerable interest and in organising frequent well-attended secret meetings. Even the police admitted that this propaganda had "a certain success" among the workers.

Kropotkin, who was still busy with geographical work and took a fairly large part in the general labour of distributing literature, was not among the initiators of these circles, first started among the engineers by Serdukov. But once the work had begun he entered into it with enthusiasm, disguising himself as a peasant and passing under the name of Borodin. He lived a strange double existence in these days, for he tells us that:

> "Often, after a dinner in a rich mansion, or even in the Winter Palace, where I went frequently to see a friend, I took a cab, hurried to a poor student's lodging in a remote suburb, exchanged my fine clothes for a cotton shirt, peasant's top-boots, and a sheepskin, and, joking with peasants on the way, went to meet my worker friends in some slum. . . . Amongst them I passed my happiest hours. . . ."

He usually chose as his subject the labour movement in Western Europe, and his lectures seem to have been appreciated, for a Bolshevik writer has since said that "as an agitator and a propagandist he won the love and respect of the Petersburg workers", while Stepniak, one of his companions in this venture, pays a tribute to the value of his work.

> "These lectures, which to depth of thought united a clearness and a simplicity that rendered them intelligible to the most uncultivated minds, excited the deepest interest among the working men of the Alexander-Nevsky district. They talked about them to their fellow

workmen, and the news quickly spread through all the workshops of the neighbourhood, and naturally reached the police, who determined at all hazards to find out the famous Borodin."

So well, however, did Kropotkin carry off his assumed role of a peasant that it was long before the police could find any clue to his real identity. Meanwhile, the successive arrests began to eat deeply into the circle, the tempo of persecution growing steadily from the end of 1873. By 1874 it became evident that full activity could not be carried on. Many members had been arrested, several settlements were raided, and some of the more active workers, such as Chaikovsky, Klemens, and Stepniak, had become so well known to the police that their comrades insisted on their departure from the capital. Only five or six members of the original circle remained, of whom one was Kropotkin, obliged to stay in St Petersburg until he had presented his report to the Geographical Society. Then, in March, the circle of engineers was discovered, and shortly afterwards a number of weavers were arrested. As a consequence new information was collected by the police, and within a week only Kropotkin and Serdukov were at large.

They decided that their only way to avoid arrest was to leave St Petersburg. Accordingly, they recruited new members to whom they taught the details of their smuggling and printing organisation and the network of settlements with which they were connected.

When this was all done, Kropotkin intended to depart for southern Russia, where he hoped to form a land league similar to that which was doing such formidable work in Ireland, and to incite groups of peasants to revolutionary action against landlords. But owing to a desire of the Geographical Society that full attention should be given to his highly controversial theories regarding the glaciation of northern Russia, his report was postponed a week—just long enough for the police to make sure that he was the agitator Borodin.

IV

The meeting passed without incident, and Kropotkin went home and spent the next day destroying his papers and preparing for departure at dusk. There was no raid, although his apartment was watched, and in the evening he slipped down the service staircase and boarded a cab. It was not until he had reached the Nevsky Prospect that he was arrested by a detective accompanied by a weaver who had turned informer.

He was immediately taken to the offices of the secret Third Section. The arrest caused a great sensation in St Petersburg; the Emperor was extremely annoyed that a man who had been for a long period his close personal attendant should become implicated in a revolutionary circle, and even insulted Kropotkin's cousin, the eminently loyal Prince Dmitri who was later assassinated in Kharkov by the People's Will.

Kropotkin was kept for some days in the prison of the secret police, being examined at intervals by the procurator. He consistently refused to reveal any information, and according to Stepniak, only admitted to his own name after his landlady had been brought in to identify him. In due course he was informed that his examination was ended, and that he would be transferred elsewhere.

He was placed in a cab with an officer of the gendarmes, who refused to answer his questions, and it was not until they were riding over the Palace Bridge that he realised he was entering the dreaded fortress of Peter-and-Paul, where since the days of Peter the Great successive generations of enemies of the Tsars had been immured, including the Decembrists and, during the past decade, many men personally admired by Kropotkin—Chernyshevsky and Pisarev, Karakazov and Bakunin.

He was received by the governor, his clothes were taken away and replaced by an ugly dressing-gown and slippers, and he was locked in the gloomy cell where he was to spend the next two years.

"This room of mine was a casemate designed for a big gun, and the window was an embrasure. The rays of the sun could never penetrate it; even in summer they are lost in the thickness of the wall. The room held an iron bed, a small oak table, and an oak stool. The floor was covered with painted felt and the walls with yellow paper. However, in order to deaden sounds, the paper was not put on the wall itself; it was pasted upon canvas, and behind the canvas I discovered a wire grating, back of which was a layer of felt; only beyond the felt could I reach the stone wall. At the inner side of the room there was a washstand, and a thick iron door in which I made out a locked opening, for passing food through, and a little slit protected by glass and by a shutter from the outside; this was the 'Judas' through which the prisoner could be spied upon at every moment. The sentry who stood in the passage frequently lifted the shutter and looked inside—his boots squeaking as he crept towards the door. I tried to speak to him; then the eye which I could see through the slit assumed an expression of terror and the shutter was immediately let down, only to be furtively opened a minute or two later; but I could never get a word of response from the sentry."

It was the dead silence, broken only by the striking of the fortress clock, the absolute loneliness, interrupted by the occasional entry of officials who did not dare to exhibit a sign of human feeling, the deadly monotony of day after day spent for an unpredictable future in this dreary room, that oppressed Kropotkin, and he tells how, while at first he sang passages from his favourite operas to relieve the silence, he soon found that he had lost the zest even for singing.

But he resolved not to be broken down by the influence of his environment. At least the food was reasonably good, and from the beginning he was allowed books and tobacco. Once a day he was taken out to walk for half an hour in the prison yard, where occasionally he saw the daughter or son of the governor, and where:

"I always kept my eyes fixed on the gilt spire of the fortress cathedral. This was the only thing in my surroundings which changed its aspect, and I liked to see it glittering like pure gold when the sun shone from a clear blue sky, or assuming a fairy aspect when a light-bluish haze lay upon the town, or becoming steel-grey when dark clouds began to gather."

And as in the traditional tales of prisoners, the pigeons came morning and evening to settle at his window and receive scraps through the grating.

He decided on a regimen of daily exercises to maintain his mental and physical health; daily he paced his cell a set number of times so that he walked five miles, and every morning he performed exercises with his heavy stool.

And then, when he had resigned himself to composing romances in his mind to pass the time, there came the gratifying news that through the intercession of his friends, supported by the learned societies of Russia, the Emperor had agreed to allow him books and writing materials to complete his report on the glaciation of Europe. To work once again delighted him and, despite the loneliness and the damp, which brought on acute rheumatism, he "was cheerful, continuing to write and to draw maps in the darkness, sharpening my lead pencils with a broken piece of glass which I had managed to get hold of in the yard".

But he was not allowed to remain in this relative happiness, and an event happened which he admits nearly broke him down. It was the arrest of his brother Alexander, to whom he was still extremely devoted.

Alexander, excited by the news Peter had brought from Switzerland, had settled in Zurich late in 1872, being further impelled to this decision by the fact that two of his children had died in the unhealthy climate of St Petersburg. Here he became a close friend of Peter Lavrov, but his interests were rather philosophical than political, and he devoted himself to the preparation of a large work which would provide a summary of the knowledge of the age. But the bond uniting the brothers was still so strong that, although they had long drifted apart in ideas, the news of Peter's arrest caused Alexander to leave everything, "the work of his life, the life itself of freedom which was as necessary to him as free air is necessary for a bird", and hasten to St Petersburg in order to do all he could to help Peter through his imprisonment.

Their first interview took place at the offices of the Third Section. Peter says that "the sight of him [Alexander] at St Petersburg filled me with the most dismal apprehensions. I was happy to see his honest face, his eyes full of love, and to hear that I should see them once a month; and yet I wished him hundreds of miles away from that place to which he came free that day, but to which he would inevitably be brought some night under an escort of gendarmes".

It was Alexander who was chiefly instrumental in obtaining permission for Peter to carry on his scientific work. He visited him as often as possible, together with their sister Helen, who also remained loyal. Then early in 1875 he was arrested for a letter to Lavrov in which he talked of the state of Russia, and, having shown contempt for the gendarmes, was exiled, without trial, to the little Siberian town of Minusinsk, from which he never returned. This is what Peter tells of his arrest, but George Kennan, the English journalist who knew him well in Siberia, adds that after his return from Switzerland Alexander worked in the Ministry of the Interior and fell into the bad graces of the Minister for refusing to reveal certain information regarding a third person, and that as a result of this incident he resigned his post. This, says Kennan, was a contributory factor to his being exiled on the alleged grounds of "political untrustworthiness". Peter's first intimation of Alexander's arrest was when his friend Poliakov took over the correspondence regarding his geographical work, but months of anxiety followed before he received any definite news.

To make matters worse the fortress began to fill with prisoners, and he realised that the authorities must have succeeded in making widespread discoveries regarding the activities of the Chaikovtsi and their friends throughout Russia. The break-up of the circles in the big cities had produced another wave of "going to the people" in which "several hundred young men and women, disregarding all precautions hitherto taken, rushed to the country, and, travelling through the towns and villages, incited the masses to revolution, almost openly distributing pamphlets, songs and proclamations". Hundreds of young people were arrested that summer, filling the prisons and bringing up the total of those detained, according to the police reports, to nearly 2,000. Many were later released because no evidence could be found against them, but 900 were kept for a longer period, and of these the most clearly active were involved in the famous trial of the 193 which lasted from October 1877 to January 1878. These police figures have been substantially confirmed from other sources.

The psychological effect of his brother's arrest and of the further break-up of the revolutionary circles brought Kropotkin to a state of physical collapse which had already been prepared by the conditions of the fortress. During the second year he began to be affected by scurvy, and gradually became so weak that the physical exercises he had previously enjoyed were painfully burdensome.

His condition was not improved when, in March 1876, he and his fellow *narodniks* were transferred to the care of the judicial authorities in the St Petersburg House of Detention. This was a show prison and it had its advantages, since there was more opportunity for visits from relatives, for mutual intercourse among the prisoners, and for receiving food from outside. But it was even more unhealthy than the fortress. In *French and Russian Prisons*, Kropotkin remarks of it:

"The three upper stories receive all the exhalations from the floors below, and the ventilation is so bad that in the evenings, when all the doors are shut, the place is literally suffocating. . . . The cells are ten feet long and five feet wide; and at one time the prison rules obliged us to keep open the traps in our doors to the end that we might not be asphyxiated where we sat. Afterwards the rule was cancelled and the traps were shut, and we were compelled to face as best we could the effects of a temperature that was sometimes stiflingly hot and sometimes freezing. But for the greater activity and life of the place I should have regretted, all dark and dripping as it was, my casemate in the fortress of Peter-and-Paul. . . ."

In this atmosphere Kropotkin found his strength failing. He lost his appetite and became steadily more feeble, so that everybody except the prison doctor thought he would die shortly. At last, after great efforts, his sister obtained permission for him to be examined by a military physician of high standing. This man decided that Kropotkin's only real trouble was a lack of oxidation in the blood, and he immediately set to work on his behalf, so that within ten days he was transferred to the small prison attached to the St Petersburg military hospital.

Here, where he could sit before an open window all day, he immediately began to recover. He returned to his geographical work and, more important, decided that his new situation offered opportunities for escape which had not existed in his previous places of confinement. He contrived to get in touch with his friends and in a series of cipher letters various more or less fantastic plots were elaborated. None, however, seemed workable, and it was not until he had received permission to walk in the prison yard to hasten his convalescence that a really practicable plan occurred to him.

"I shall never forget my first walk. When I was taken out I saw before me a yard fully three hundred paces long and more than two hundred paces wide, all covered with grass. The gate was open and through it I could see the street, the immense hospital opposite, and the people who passed by. I stopped on the door-steps of the prison, unable for a moment to move when I saw that yard and that gate.

"At one end of the yard stood the prison—a narrow building about one hundred and fifty paces long—at each end of which was a sentry box. The two sentries paced up and down in front of the building, and had tramped out a footpath in the green. Along this footpath I was told to walk, and the two sentries continued to walk up and down—so that I was never more than ten or fifteen paces from the one or the other. . . .

"At the opposite end of this spacious yard wood for fuel was being unloaded from a dozen carts and piled up along the wall by a dozen peasants. The whole yard was enclosed by a high fence made of thick boards. Its gate was open to let the carts in and out.

"This open gate fascinated me. 'I must not stare at it', I said to myself; and yet I looked at it all the time."

It was through the gate that Kropotkin decided to make his escape. He transmitted to his friends the bare outline of a plan by which he would evade his guard and run out through the gate, to be picked up by a waiting carriage.

Such an audacious plan involved an elaborate arrangement of signals and helpers to assure that the chance of interference was reduced to a minimum. More than twenty people were involved, and at least eleven played major roles. Today it is impossible to identify all the participants, but it is known that Stepniak and Madame Lavrov took part, while the most active organiser outside was Dr Orestes Weimar, a distinguished young physician who was a personal attendant on the Empress and who later died in Siberia in 1885 after having been convicted of complicity in terrorist conspiracies. It was Weimar who provided the carriage and the black horse Barbara, which later figured in other revolutionary episodes and enabled the assassins of General Mezentlov to escape in 1878.

Gradually, with the help of fresh air and renewed hopes Kropotkin grew stronger, and at the same time his plans matured. There followed a period of several days on which action was frustrated either by untoward occurrences outside or by his own indisposition. On the 29th June the plans of the conspirators were completely negated by the failure of the prearranged signal, the releasing of a red toy balloon. As Kropotkin tells us:

"The impossible had happened that day. Hundreds of children's balloons are always on sale in St Petersburg, near the Gostinoi Dvor. That morning there were none; not a single balloon was to be found. One was discovered at last in the possession of a child, but it was old and would not fly. My friends rushed then to an optician's shop, bought an apparatus for making hydrogen and filled the balloon with it; but it would not fly any better: the hydrogen had not been dried. Time pressed. Then a lady attached the balloon to her umbrella, and, holding the latter high above her head, walked up and down in the street alongside the high wall of our yard; but I saw nothing of it; the wall being too high and the lady too short."

To make matters worse the authorities had evidently grown suspicious, for on the night before the actual escape he heard an officer instructing the sentry below his window to have ball cartridges ready for an emergency. He knew then that it would be unsafe to delay beyond the next day, the 30th June.

The exciting events of that day have often been told, and at times the story has been unduly embellished, as when the American editor of a book of Russian memoirs asserted in a footnote that Kropotkin rode away astride a white racehorse, while several other authors have claimed inaccurately that the escape was made from the Peter-and-Paul fortress itself. But there are three accounts which have special claims to authenticity; one is that which Stepniak wrote in 1881; the second is that recorded by Kropotkin himself in 1897; and the third is that taken by George Kennan from one of the conspirators and written down in the commonplace book of Spence Watson, the founder of the Friends of Russian Freedom. All these accounts agree in the main details, and we have therefore used their common facts in the narrative of events.

At two o'clock on the chosen day a woman, possibly Madame Lavrov, came to the prison with a watch which she asked should be transmitted to the prisoner. Her audacity was successful, for the prison authorities did not examine such an apparently innocent gift. It was brought straight to Kropotkin, who found therein a minute piece of paper on which the whole details of the plan had been written in a tiny cipher. The woman, who was herself sought by the police for political reasons, walked calmly out of sight down the boulevard.

Meanwhile, Kropotkin's friends began to take up their positions. A series of sentries was posted for a couple of miles, to see that the streets were clear of peasant carts and any other obstacles. "One was to walk up and down with a handkerchief in his hand; another was to sit on a stone and eat cherries, stopping when the carts came near, and so on. All these signals, transmitted along the streets, were finally to reach the carriage."

In order to inform Kropotkin himself the conspirators had rented a small bungalow which could be seen from the prison yard, and at an open window of this house a violinist would stand ready to play when the street was clear. Finally, a comrade had been deputed to converse with the sentry at the gate in order to prevent him from intercepting the prisoner as he ran out.

At four o'clock Kropotkin emerged for his walk and gave a prearranged signal to show that he was ready. Then he heard the carriage draw up, and a few minutes later the violin began to play. At this time he was on the part of his walk farthest from the gate, and when he was back in a favourable position the playing ceased abruptly. After an apprehensive quarter of an hour a string of carts drew into the yard.

"Immediately the violinist—a good one, I must say—began a wildly exciting mazurka from Kontsky, as if to say, 'Straight on now—this is your time!' I moved slowly to the nearer end of the footpath, trembling at the thought that the mazurka might stop before I reached it.

"When I was there I turned round. The sentry had stopped five or six paces behind me; he was looking the other way. 'Now or never!' I remember that thought flashing through my head. I flung off my green flannel dressing-gown and began to run.

"For many days in succession I had practised how to get rid of that immeasurably long and cumbrous garment. It was so long that I carried the lower part on my left arm, as ladies carry the trains of their riding habits. Do what I might, it would not come off in one movement. I cut the seams under the armpits, but that did not help. Then I decided to learn to throw it off in two movements: one, casting the end from my arm, the other dropping the gown on the floor. I practised patiently in my room until I could do it as neatly as soldiers handle their rifles. 'One, two', and it was on the ground.

"I did not trust much to my vigour and began to run rather slowly, to economise my strength. But no sooner had I taken a few steps than the peasants who were piling the wood at the other end shouted, 'He runs! Stop him! Catch him!' and they hastened to intercept me at the gate. Then I flew for my life. I thought of nothing but running—not even of the pit which the carts had dug out at the gate. Run! run! full speed!

"The sentry, I was told later by the friends who witnessed the scene from the grey house, ran after me, followed by three soldiers who had been sitting on the doorsteps. The sentry was so near to me that he felt sure of catching me. Several times he flung his rifle forward, trying to give me a blow in the back with the bayonet. One moment my friends in the window thought he had me. He was so convinced that he could stop me in this way that he did not fire. But I kept my distance, and he had to give up at the gate.

"Safe out of the gate I perceived, to my terror, that the carriage was occupied by a civilian who wore a military cap. He sat without turning his head to me. 'Sold!' was my first thought. The comrades had written in their last letter, 'Once in the street, don't give yourself up: there will be friends to defend you in case of need', and I did not want to jump into the carriage if it was occupied by an enemy. However, as I got nearer to the carriage I noticed that the man in it had sandy whiskers which seemed to be those of a warm friend of mine. He did not belong to our circle but we were personal friends, and on more than one occasion I had learned to know his admirable, daring courage, and how his strength suddenly became herculean when there was danger at hand. 'Why should he be there? Is it possible?' I reflected, and was going to shout out his name when I caught myself in good time, and instead clapped my hands, while still running, to attract his attention. He turned his face to me—and I knew who it was.

"'Jump in, quick, quick!' he shouted in a terrible voice, calling me and the coachman all sorts of names, a revolver in his hand and ready to shoot. 'Gallop! gallop! I will kill you!' he cried to the coachman. The horse—a beautiful racing trotter, which had been bought on purpose—started at full gallop. Scores of voices yelling, 'Hold them! Get them!' resounded behind us, my friend meanwhile helping me to put on an elegant overcoat and an opera hat. But the real danger was not so much in the pursuers as in a soldier who was posted at the gate of the hospital, about opposite to the spot where the carriage had to wait. He could have prevented my jumping into the carriage or could have stopped the horse by simply rushing a few steps forward. A friend was consequently commissioned to divert this soldier by talking. He did this most successfully. The soldier having been employed at one time in the laboratory of the hospital, my friend gave a scientific turn to their chat, speaking about the microscope and the wonderful things one sees through it. Referring to a certain parasite of the human body, he asked, 'Did you ever see what a formidable tail it has?' 'What, man, a tail?' 'Yes it has; under the microscope it is as big as that.' 'Don't tell me any of your tales!' retorted the soldier. 'I know better. It was the first thing I looked at under the microscope.' This animated discussion took place just as I ran past them and sprang into the carriage. It sounds like fable, but it is fact.

"The carriage turned sharply into a narrow lane, past the same wall of the yard where the peasants had been piling wood and which all of them had now deserted in their run after me. The turn was so sharp that the carriage was nearly upset when I flung myself inward, dragging towards me my friend; this sudden movement righted the carriage.

"We trotted through the narrow lane and then turned to the left. Two gendarmes were standing there at the door of a public-house, and gave to the military cap of my companion the military salute. 'Hush! hush!' I said to him, for he was still terribly excited. 'All goes well; the gendarmes salute us!' The coachman thereupon turned his face towards me and I recognised in him another friend, who smiled with happiness."

There was no immediate pursuit, since the incident had thrown the guard into utter confusion, and all the cabs had been engaged for a mile around by people privy to the plot. In a few minutes the fugitives reached the Nevsky Prospect and alighted in a house in a side street, where they sent away the carriage and Kropotkin met his sister-in-law. Then he and his friend, probably Weimar, took a cab and drove to a remote suburb, where they entered a barber's shop for Kropotkin to have his beard shaved. Then they drove to the Islands, which were a fashionable promenade and where they could reasonably hope not to be interrupted. Finally, as a crowning audacity, they went to one of the most frequented St Petersburg restaurants, "passed the halls flooded with light and crowded with visitors at the dinner hour, and took a separate room, where we spent the evening".

As they had expected, nobody in the Third Section thought of searching such a place. But elsewhere the hue and cry was intense. The news of an escape in broad daylight had created a sensation, and the Tsar himself was so angry that he issued categorical orders "He *must* be found". Almost immediately the first house at which Kropotkin had halted was searched, and afterwards the homes of all his friends. Even houses in St Petersburg which the conspirators had regarded as safe hiding-places were under observation. "Moreover, my portrait had been printed by the Third Section, and hundreds of copies had been distributed to policemen and watchmen. All the detectives who knew me by sight were looking for me in the streets; while those who did not were accompanied by soldiers and warders who had seen me during my imprisonment."

In order to evade this intensive search Kropotkin went in the company of a few friends to a village on the outskirts. Clearly he could not stay in Russia. But the Third Section had posted agents at all the frontier stations and ports in the Baltic provinces and southern Finland. So he decided to take a direction in which he would not be expected. With a friend's passport and an officer's uniform he went north through Finland to the little port of Vasa on the gulf of Bothnia, and thence sailed to Sweden. Crossing into Norway, he took a British ship to Hull. After his recent experiences it was pleasant to find himself under the flag of a country which, in those unhappily past days, offered an asylum for the political refugees of all lands and all opinions.

Two incidents remain to be told. The Tsarist authorities, having failed to locate Kropotkin or the principal participants in his escape, took what mean revenge they could on his relatives, imprisoning his sister Helen for a fortnight and his sister-in-law for two months, until it became clear that nothing could be proved against them.

A more comic aspect is given by the rumour that began to spread among the soldiers of St Petersburg until it assumed the proportions of a legend. The sandy-whiskered Grand Duke Nicholas had visited Kropotkin in prison; the man who drove him away on the day of his escape had sandy whiskers. On this scanty similarity was built up a whole story of how the brother of the Emperor had himself conducted the escape of the anarchist prince from the clutches of the secret police!

CHAPTER IV

THE AGITATOR

I

EARLY in August, 1876, Kropotkin landed at Hull under the assumed name of Alexis Levashov. He did not at first intend to remain in Western Europe longer than was necessary to re-establish his health and allow the excitement over his escape to die down in Russia, when he hoped to return and resume his activity. But he had gained too much notoriety for this to be possible and soon realised that, for some time, he would be forced to accept the life of an exile.

He was very anxious to renew contact with the Jura federation, which had influenced him so much on his last visit to Western Europe, and, apart from a few Russian friends, the only person he seems to have informed of his appearance in the West was his Swiss friend Guillaume, to whom he wrote immediately from Hull.

He entered England freely and for the time being was unmolested by the Russian police, whose agents were searching for him in Eastern Germany, where they were assisted by Prussian police officers. However, as he still envisaged a return, he decided not to go to London, where the spies might well look for him, and instead travelled to Edinburgh, taking a small room in an inconspicuous suburb. Here he found life not without complications, for though he could read and even translate English efficiently, he had no practical experience in the colloquial speech of a Scottish city:

"... I had the greatest difficulty in making myself understood by my Scotch landlady; her daughter and I used to write on scraps of paper what we had to say to each other; and as I had no idea of idiomatic English, I must have made the most amusing mistakes.

I remember, at any rate, protesting once to her, in writing, that it was not a 'cup of tea' that I expected at tea time but many cups. I am afraid my landlady took me for a glutton, but I must say, by way of apology, that neither in the geological books I had read in English nor in Spencer's *Biology* was there any allusion to such an important matter as tea-drinking."

But there were more serious problems than those of mutual understanding, for Kropotkin was soon under the necessity of earning a living, not merely because he thought a socialist should do this on principle, but also because his slight funds were running low and his letters to Russia had been intercepted, so that he could receive no money from his friends or relatives. Accordingly, with his usual adaptability he decided to try living by his pen.

On the ship to England he had encountered a Norwegian scientist, to whom he spoke what he imagined to be Swedish but what his acquaintance assured him was much nearer to Norwegian. The scientist gave him a paper containing a report of a North Atlantic deep-sea expedition; when he reached Edinburgh Kropotkin wrote a short note of this and sent it to the British scientific journal *Nature*. "The sub-editor acknowledged the note with thanks, remarking, with an extreme leniency which I have often met with since in England, that my English was 'all right' and only required to be a 'little more idiomatic'." With this encouragement, he sent *The Times* some paragraphs on Prjevalsky's expedition in Central Asia, which were also printed.

But he found that it was difficult to earn enough by working from the provinces; besides, life in Edinburgh, where he had yet few friends, was lonely and monotonous. During September he therefore moved to London, risking the attentions of Russian agents. Indeed, they had still not located him, for a police report of the time, quoted in 1921 in the Russian magazine *Byloe*, remarks from hearsay that " . . . the socialists of all countries are now meeting at Philadelphia to discuss certain problems, and therefore Prince Kropotkin is most likely in America. With the coming of autumn it is likely that he will arrive in Switzerland, where, it is said, there will also be in November a congress of socialists at Geneva, Zurich, or some other Swiss town."

In London he made a number of friends. One was James Scott Keltie, the assistant editor of *Nature*, whom he visited as soon as he arrived. Keltie received him very cordially, and immediately invited him to write regular notes of scientific events recorded in the foreign press. Kropotkin attended the office every Monday, looked over the reviews in many languages which were set aside for him, and either made notes on articles that seemed interesting or arranged for them to be sent to specialists. With some difficulty he now managed to earn his living.

"Mr. Keltie did not know, of course, that I used to rewrite each note three or four times before I dared to submit my English to him; but taking the scientific reviews home, I soon managed very nicely, with my *Nature* notes and my *Times* paragraphs, to get a living. I found that the weekly payment, on Thursday, of the paragraph contributors to the *Times* was an excellent institution. To be sure, there were weeks when there was no interesting news from Prjevalsky, and news from other parts of Russia was not found interesting; in such cases my fare was bread and tea only."

His friendship with Keltie was sealed by a coincidence which forced him to reveal his identity. One day Keltie handed him a batch of Russian books and asked him to review them. Kropotkin found, to his consternation, that they were his own books on the Glacial Period and the Orography of Asia. He took them home and asked himself in perplexity: "What shall I do with them? I cannot praise them, because they are mine; and I cannot be too sharp on the author, as I hold the views expressed in them."

He decided that the only honest course was to explain the situation. Nearly forty years later Keltie recalled that:

"He called to see me with the books and asked if I read Russian, and alas, I had to admit that I could not. Pointing to the title page he told me it was a treatise on the geology and glaciation of Finland, by P. Kropotkin. He told me briefly his story, and naturally I was intensely interested. I told him we had no one in a position to review the book, and he might write an article stating briefly its main features and conclusions, which I am glad to say he did."

Meanwhile Kropotkin was developing a lively correspondence with Guillaume in Switzerland, and in September sent a note for the *Jura Bulletin* on the Serbo-Turkish war, which had caused a wave of Pan-Slavist enthusiasm among the Russian revolutionaries and had led many old comrades, including Klemens, Ross, and Stepniak, to join the Serbian insurgents in Bosnia. Kropotkin said:

"I understand that impulse. It is impossible to read daily the stories of massacres and to know that the massacred people counted on Russian support and not to be carried away."

But he was also fully alive to the way in which popular indignation at the atrocities of the Turkish government was being exploited in British politics, and, discussing the public meetings held at this time, he wrote:

"It is with real disgust that I daily read the accounts of them. There is nothing more revolting than to see the way in which a movement, born of the purest and most humane sentiments of the working class, is exploited in its own egotistical interests by the Liberal Party."

It was through Guillaume that he established contact with another supporter of the Bakuninists, Paul Robin, who was then teaching French at the Woolwich Military Academy. Robin was an ardent libertarian, but gained more celebrity as a sexual reformer, and particularly for his advocacy of birth control as a factor in the liberation of the workers from economic misery. He also experimented in progressive education, while his most original enterprise was a campaign to secure the liberation of prostitutes from the social stigma and personal disabilities attached to a calling he regarded as necessary in a sexually disequilibrated society. He tried to start a society, *La Ligue anti-esclaviste pour l'affranchissement des Filles*, and a magazine, *Le Cri des Filles*. But the French police intervened, the prostitutes took fright, and Robin's well-meant efforts came to nothing.

This man made a great impression on Kropotkin at their first meeting, and they had lively discussions on what had been happening in Western Europe since 1872, which inflamed more than ever Kropotkin's desire to return to the Continent. Robin's sexual ideas seem to have had little influence on his friend, but they must have formed part of the discussions even at this early date, and it is significant of Kropotkin's essential puritanism that even after he met Robin he allowed little consciousness of the need for a sexual as well as a social revolution to appear in his writings. It was only when Robin accepted, with reservations, the Malthusian theory of the increase of population at a rate too great to allow mankind to benefit by increasing production that Kropotkin was affected, and then only in opposition. This reaction was fruitful, since it led him to take up the constructive consideration of ways and means by which rational production could substantially increase the world output of food and raw materials. These researches will later be considered on their own merits, but here it is interesting to speculate how far, as Robin's biographer Gabriel Giroud has suggested, Kropotkin's opposition to Robin's ideas sprang originally from a puritanical mentality. It is at least significant that in his generally capable refutation of Malthusianism, Kropotkin did not, as Godwin had done in the *Essay on Population* which formed his answer to the original controversy, even attempt to consider the question of how far the limitation of families was desirable or possible. Yet it must be conceded to Robin that, while Kropotkin's arguments of a vastly increased production *after* a fundamental change in the social structure may be valid, the workers in a scarcity economy are made poorer by large families and therefore birth control has its justification as a temporary expedient. So far as we have been able to discover Kropotkin never made any adequate consideration of this point, and we cannot help observing the connection which seems to exist between this omission and his rather romantic attitude towards women in general and their maternal function in particular.

For the present, however, the Malthusian controversy had not attained sufficient acrimony to drive the friends apart, and for some years they remained on intimate terms, exchanging a lengthy correspondence in which Kropotkin's surviving letters form one of the best records of his interests and activities.

After his arrival in London, Kropotkin at first remained aloof from the Russian emigré colony. Peter Lavrov was in the capital, where he continued *Vpered*, of which Kropotkin bought a copy on the King's Cross bookstall when he reached London. But he did not go immediately to see Lavrov; in his *Memoirs* he attributed this omission to the fact that "the editorial office of the Russian paper must have been closely watched by spies", but in an article written during the last months of his life he admitted that his abstention was also partly due to the fact that, after Bakunin's death on the 1st July 1876, Lavrov had printed an obituary which Kropotkin regarded insufficiently appreciative.

However, a few weeks later a notice appeared in *Vpered* inviting "X" to call at the office to receive a letter from Russia, and Kropotkin went there. Although he had shaven his beard and assumed a top hat, the young Russian woman who opened the door and who had never met him recognised the visitor and ran upstairs to announce him. "I knew you immediately", she told him, "by your eyes, which reminded me of those of your brother." He established a friendly relationship with Lavrov which, despite their differing outlooks, lasted until the latter's death. Through Lavrov and his paper Kropotkin encountered a number of younger Russians, and for the first time met Cherkesov, who had likewise escaped from Russia, making his way from exile in Tomsk, through Moscow and St Petersburg to Western Europe, about the middle of 1876.

In London life was thus more interesting than it had been in Edinburgh. But there was hardly any agitational activity in England, and having decided that there was little reason for him to return to Russia, Kropotkin felt drawn towards the Continent, and particularly Switzerland and France. In November he decided to visit the Jura, and towards the end of the month wrote to Robin that he would depart in a few days, remarking, "I am now writing unceasingly in order to put an end to the heap of reviews which I received from *Nature*".

He reached Neuchâtel early in December, where he was welcomed cordially by Guillaume and the Swiss workers he had met four years previously. His record in Russia had inspired them with respect for his abilities, and he was immediately taken into their confidence. He also met Carlo Cafiero and Errico Malatesta, the two leading propagandists of the International in Italy, who were planning an Italian insurrection for the following year. Both had been close friends and disciples of Bakunin. Cafiero was in a very few years to die tragically in an insane asylum, but Malatesta remained for long an internationally famous revolutionary. He was a kind of anarchist knight errant, working for the cause in almost every part of the world, without blemish or inconsistency on his long record. Among many Italians he came to be regarded as almost a saint, so that even Mussolini did not dare to imprison or murder him, but kept him under house arrest until his death in 1932, when his place of burial was kept secret lest it should become a symbolic rallying-point for the enemies of fascism.

With both these men Kropotkin later became friendly, but at this first meeting and for some time afterwards they did not reach any intimacy; indeed, for a time the relationship seems to have been almost hostile. But Kropotkin reinforced his friendship with Guillaume and also established a close bond with Paul Brousse, a young French doctor with whom he soon worked closely, and whom he described as "full of mental activity, uproarious, sharp, lively, ready to develop any idea with a geometrical logic to its utmost consequences; powerful in his criticisms of the State and State organisation . . . constantly active in organising men, with the subtle mind of a true 'southerner'." Brousse afterwards became a reformist, but at this time he was one of the most active anarchists.

This short visit finally decided Kropotkin to leave England and join whole-heartedly in the Jura federation. He returned to London, but it was only for a brief period, during which he obtained through Keltie some work in connection with a geographical dictionary which he could carry on outside England.

In the meantime he was in correspondence with his Swiss friends, and it seems to have been decided that Brousse should go to Belgium to try and increase the propaganda of the anarchist groups in Verviers, and that Kropotkin should precede him to "spy out the land". His departure was delayed owing to the need to fulfil his obligations towards *Nature*, but on the 23rd January he finally left for Ostend, writing to Robin, "I go away regretting that our acquaintance was so short, but I would like very much to renew it some day . . .".

He went straight to Verviers, where he found a strong parliamentary tendency which he did not, however, regard as fundamental, and he expressed the opinion that a popular working-class paper would do a great deal to bring Belgians back to the libertarian idea. But he felt that there was little he himself could do, and decided that unless he stayed for a whole year it was no use remaining. He expected great things of Brousse, but, possibly because he had just made an encouraging trip to France, the latter decided not to visit Belgium after all, and on the 4th February Kropotkin departed for Geneva. A few weeks later he commented:

> "Belgium will remain as it is; and the Jura federation will occupy itself little or not at all with this country. The hope of wielding influence from here [Switzerland] would be an illusion, and to send a man there—well, there is none."

From this abortive effort until Elisée Reclus arrived in 1890, Belgium became unfertile soil for libertarian ideas.

From Verviers Kropotkin travelled directly to Geneva, without touching Paris. There he found his friend Dmitri Klemens, who had left Russia with Stepniak in 1874 and, after fighting in the Balkans, was living in Switzerland under the name of Lenz. At Geneva the two friends took part in discussions with Zhukovsky and Ralli regarding a proposed Russian emigré paper to replace *Rabotnik*, which had expired in 1876. At this time there was some coolness between the French and Russian exiles in Geneva and the Jura federation. Guillaume asserts that when Kropotkin arrived Zhukovsky, Ralli, and the other Russians "sought to keep him, and warned him against the socialists of the mountains. His perspicacity soon enabled him to realise the true causes of certain grievances; but, with his good-humoured character, he first tried to play the part of conciliator."

The differences appear to have been personal rather than theoretical, and from correspondence between Kropotkin and various Jura members, such as Brousse and Guillaume, it seems as though the latter resented the independent activity of the Geneva men and regarded their proposals of a new magazine as a deliberate threat to the *Jura Bulletin*. All this now seems petty, but it was accentuated by the fact that the Geneva group was more heterogeneous and included not only pure anarchists like Reclus, Zhukovsky and Ralli, but also latter-day Blanquists like Gambon, and men like Lefrançais who were suspected of supporting the Belgian De Paepe's idea of a "public service" State.

Kropotkin was eventually persuaded by Guillaume and Brousse; in April, when the Geneva group brought out *Le Travailleur* he refused to write for it, and went so far as to say:

"As far as I am concerned, I openly connect myself with the northern Jurassians, the party of pure anarchism, agitation among the workers, and action. Even if the southern Jurassians were successful in building a Federation du Leman, it would die from internal conflict. The Jurassians of the north are intimately bound to each other and represent a compact party with a clearly defined programme."

He showed a narrowness of outlook in strange contrast to his tolerance in the Chaikovsky circle, and this can only be attributed to the sectarian influence of Guillaume, whom Max Nettlau has blamed for the lack of sympathy which the Jura federation in those days showed not only towards people who differed slightly in theory but also towards other races—Italians, Spaniards, and particularly Germans, for whom Guillaume had an almost pathological dislike, due no doubt to his experience at the hands of Marx in the International. Kropotkin eventually recovered to a great extent from this influence, and in later years worked on close terms with some of the people he had originally rejected.

At Geneva he and Klemens conceived the idea of compiling a socialist dictionary, which the local group offered to publish, but in the subsequent differences the plan was abandoned. After a few days they went on to Vevey in order to meet Elisée Reclus, whom Kropotkin had not yet encountered. Reclus was a celebrated geographer, who had become a close friend of Bakunin and an anarchist nearly ten years before. He had fought among the ranks of the Paris Commune, and for this was forced to live in exile in Switzerland. He welcomed the two Russians cordially and the three geographers found much in common, Reclus offering to secure for Kropotkin the patronage of the Swiss Geographical Society. But it was some years yet before this friendship became intimate, and Kropotkin hurried on to Neuchâtel, where he found Guillaume tired out from over-work, and where Brousse, just returned from a secret trip to France, gave him encouraging news of the situation there, so that he wrote to Robin:

"The awakening is increasing (the Paris students take part in it with enthusiasm) and the tendency purely anarchist. France France, is the refrain everywhere, in Belgium as well as here."

On the 16th February he went, still with Klemens, to Chaux-de-Fonds, the central town of the Jura watchmaking industry, which he describes as "the least attractive" town in Switzerland, situated "on a high plateau entirely devoid of any vegetation, open to bitterly cold winds in the winter, when the snow lies as deep as at Moscow and melts and falls again as often as at St Petersburg".

It was, however, the town in which most of the militants lived, including the watchmaker Spichiger, an early disciple of Bakunin whom Kropotkin described as a "philosopher . . . always trying to get at the full meaning of every fact, and impressing all of us by the justness of the conclusions he reached while he was pondering over all sorts of subjects during his work of scooping out watch lids", and Pindy, a French refugee who had been a leader of the Commune, escaping almost miraculously from the Versaillese troops, and who was now an assayer, "spending his days by the side of his red-hot stove and at night devoting himself passionately to propaganda work, in which he admirably combined the passion of a revolutionist with the good sense and the organising powers characteristic of the Parisian worker". Albarracin, the Spaniard, was also here, and in the neighbouring valley of St Imier lived the "jovial, lively, clear-sighted" Schwitzguebel, whom Kropotkin had met in 1872.

At this time the Jura federation was the ideological centre of European anarchism. This arose from a number of circumstances, of which two were particularly important. Firstly, the Jura had from the beginning been in the van of the struggle against Marxist centralism, and it was the group in and with which Bakunin had developed the fullest expression of his philosophy. Even now, despite some sectarianism, it probably contained the largest proportion of capable theoreticians and propagandists. Secondly, when the International broke up after the split between the Marxists and the Bakuninists, the Latin countries alone remained solidly libertarian. But in France, Italy, and Spain alike there was during the 1870's a heavy governmental repression, and the only country in which open theoretical development could continue was French Switzerland. Consequently there gravitated to the Jura, at various times, French, Spanish, Italian, and Russian militants, while its local congresses took on an international character. Its influence was particularly strong in France; this can be attributed partly to the number of Communard refugees in Switzerland, but it was also due to the fact that the two men most active in external propaganda, Brousse and Guillaume, were far more concerned with France than any other country. The French movement was beginning to grow again from the waste created by the fall of the Commune, and the newly formed anarchist groups, while retaining some Proudhonian traditions, looked mostly to Switzerland for support. Clearly there was much to be done, and Kropotkin, finally rejecting the idea of returning to Russia, where a more rigidly conspiratorial tendency prevailed, settled down to work for an international movement which would be based, like populism in Russia, on a wide appeal to the working class, to the people.

> "A life full of work that I liked began now for me. We held many meetings, distributing ourselves our announcements in the cafés and workshops. Once a week we held our section meetings, at which the most animated discussions took place, and we went also to preach anarchism at the gatherings convoked by the political parties. I travelled a great deal, visiting other sections and helping them."

But although a certain amount of sympathy was aroused by these activities the work was hampered by many factors, and particularly the crisis in the watch trade, which caused much unemployment, depleted the funds of the group, and made it difficult to maintain the co-operative workshop the anarchists had set up in La Chaux-de-Fonds. Many of the poorer people were sympathetic, but at this time of distress were disinclined to show their feelings for fear of discrimination.

Indeed, the anarchists were already feeling a new isolation from the masses. Guillaume seemed to blame the groups, for in February he wrote, "Our friends lead too isolated a life; they are too cut off from the rest of the population". But Kropotkin, in a letter to Robin, appeared to find the cause in external political circumstances.

"The situation of the Federation here is everything but good. All sections have been reduced to few members. Here, for instance, there are only ten, or rather eight, who come to the meetings. . . . That would be nothing. The number does not matter *if* the masses are with them. But this is not the case. They have *no* connections with the masses. More than that, they are divided from them as if by a wall. And my endeavours, or rather my wishes, to penetrate into other circles than that of the ten have been without success. Among the masses the radicals are the gods of the day, and the socialists are not trusted. A few years of prosperity, with the leanings towards bourgeois luxury which have made themselves felt (on Sundays people like you and I would be taken for dirty workers), the habit of lounging about in cafés, to gossip about the theatre and bourgeois weddings—all this estranges the people from minorities like ourselves."

But as so often happens in such situations, the authorities by their very stupidity helped to resurrect support for the rebels. A wholly unjustified panic among the Berne police induced them to forbid the carrying of the red flag in that city, an act held to be in contravention of guaranteed civil liberties. The anarchists therefore decided to go to Berne on 18th March, anniversary of the Paris Commune, in order to defy the ban. Kropotkin went with a contingent of forty from the St Imier valley; they resolved to fight if necessary, but did not carry firearms.

There was a scuffle with the police, but the demonstrators succeeded in carrying their flag to the town hall where, exceeding all expectations, a crowd of two thousand gathered, and many citizens declared their adhesion to the International. Thirty demonstrators, not including Kropotkin, were prosecuted, but the trial aroused yet wider sympathy and the sentences were light.

However, in April the International received a great setback in the failure of the Benevento rising in Italy. The Italians had been working out for some time the theory, famous in anarchist and terrorist history, of "propaganda by deed". Later this term was applied chiefly to individual acts of violence, but in Italy at this time, with its insurrectional traditions, the conception was applied to the technique of local revolts. Already in 1876 it had been expressed thus by Malatesta and Cafiero:

"The Italian Federation believes that the *insurrectionary deed*, intended to affirm socialist principles by actions, is the most efficient means of propaganda, the only one which neither cheating nor depraving the masses is able to make its way effectively into the lowermost social strata, and to direct the living forces of mankind into the support of the international struggle."

The rising in the hills of Benevento was prepared by Malatesta, Cafiero and Stepniak, who could always be found where there was talk of an insurrection. Having aroused the suspicions of the *carabinieri*, the conspirators had to make a start before preparations were fully organised. They entered a few villages, burnt public records, distributed the cash in the treasuries, proclaimed the social revolution, and incited the villagers to rise. The priests of two villages declared them true apostles of God, and marched at the head of the column, shouting "Long live the Social Revolution". But eventually the conspirators, wet through, starved and dispirited, were surrounded and surrendered without a fight.

This failure marked the virtual end of insurrectionism as an important revolutionary technique in Italy. The news was heard with consternation in the Jura, and Kropotkin wrote to Robin:

"You can imagine how furious we are with the Italians. I suggest, if they let themselves be surprised and did not defend themselves, to vote for their exclusion from the International. The republic of '93 knew well how to guillotine its generals when they gave proof of incapacity."

This self-righteous and doubtfully libertarian tone was mitigated when Kropotkin saw the letters which Malatesta wrote to Guillaume about the affair, and a few weeks later he wrote that he now believed the Italians to be blameless.

New activities soon began to draw his attentions away from the local affairs of the Jura, and in this he was particularly influenced by the dynamic urge of Brousse, who was anxious to make effective propaganda in France, and who also, lacking Guillaume's prejudices, hoped to use eastern Switzerland as a base for work in Germany.

It was still impossible to publish a libertarian paper in France, and Brousse therefore decided to start one in Switzerland with an international character. During April he invited

Kropotkin to collaborate, but the first issue of *L'Avant Garde* did not actually appear until the 2nd June. Most of it was written by Brousse, but Kropotkin provided international notes, and while the paper continued, until December of the following year, the two friends carried on the main work, assisted by various French refugees, of whom Pindy was the most active. Publication was prepared by a series of hurried congresses and clandestine crossings of the frontier to confer with Savoyard peasants, who helped to smuggle the paper into France.

Kropotkin's collaboration in German propaganda began at conferences with a number of Zurich anarchists, of whom the most active were Otto Rinke and Emil Werner, as well as a Fräulein Landsberg, who was in love with Brousse and provided most of the funds. In order to expand the work it was decided to start a new German organisation completely separate from the Social Democrats, and Kropotkin was invited to elaborate its statutes. This he did at the end of April, and next month the tiny group assumed the status of the German-speaking Anarchist Communist Party, affiliated to the International Workingmen's Association, and possessing a correspondence bureau of three members. The Berne *Arbeiterzeitung*, which had been started by Brousse, Werner, and Rinke in 1876, became the organ of the new "party", the articles being for the most part written in French by Brousse and Kropotkin and translated by Werner. It is not surprising that a journal edited by men out of touch with conditions in Germany, and already busy in other directions, should have been unsuccessful, and the *Arbeiterzeitung* eventually expired in October 1877.

Long before this time Kropotkin had become absorbed in other activities. It was a restless period, and he seems to have been attracted to a new project every other week, so wide were the possibilities of action.

Early in June Albarracin returned to Spain, to take part in the insurrectionary struggles that seemed likely. Kropotkin was fired by the idea of action, and told Guillaume of his plan to accompany the Spaniard. Guillaume dissuaded him, saying:

"I think that, not speaking Spanish, you could only render service as a combatant; but they are not likely to be in need of just one additional rifle, and, if that is not the case, it would not be worth the trouble of starting. My advice, then, is that you should not go. France is the only country where foreign revolutionary elements can really render any service. In remaining here you will help us in the struggle against an enemy as dangerous, but in quite a different way, as the Spanish government—against Marxist intrigue.

"Naturally, you must make your decision; but my idea is that, while you remain in the West, you should occupy yourself essentially with propaganda and organisation. If you wish to fight, you have a field of battle more appropriate than Spain; go back to Russia and form a band there."

Kropotkin accepted Guillaume's advice not to go to Spain, but he did not go to Russia either, for he felt that his health would not withstand the privations of an underground life or endure a return to the rigours of a Russian fortress. He was still much weakened by the scurvy contracted in the prisons from which he had escaped a year before.

For the time being he was occupied on various revolutionary papers, and in the latter part of June wrote two articles in the *Jura Bulletin* on the Russo-Turkish war, which had broken out a short time before, nominally to give Russian protection to the Slavs under Ottoman rule. Kropotkin, while supporting the uprisings of the Balkan peoples, categorically dissociated himself from both Russian and Turkish governments. Nettlau, in *Probuzhdenie* (1931), suggests that Kropotkin supported Russia, but the following quotation seems to indicate that all he supported was the actual struggle of the peoples seeking liberation, an attitude fundamentally different from that which he adopted in 1914. He said in 1877:

"We can sympathise neither with the Turkish armies nor with the Russian armies; both are slaughtered in the interests of their despots. But we desire the complete emancipation of the Slav and Greek provinces, and we have, consequently, every sympathy for their insurrections, so long as they remain popular. We also believe that the social revolution will not be possible until the various nationalities of the peninsula are liberated from every external yoke. That is why we would like to see the whole peninsula take fire, rise up without waiting for the arrival of the Russian armies, the population grouping themselves freely, without allowing the laws of their saviours to be imposed on them, and finish once for all with this necessary preamble to the social revolution in the peninsula—the dismemberment of the Ottoman Empire."

Early in July Kropotkin was so filled with enthusiasm by Brousse's reports from France, and by his own brief experience of smuggling the *Avant Garde* across the frontier at Delle, that he decided to visit Paris. On the 3rd July he wrote to Robin: "I have a fixed idea to go to Paris, to cultivate connections there with Paul's friends and to establish new ones. This journey gives me an almost childish joy." He was waiting for money to come from *Nature*, for which he still worked.

But before setting out he received a warning from Ralli in Geneva that the French police would certainly arrest him if he crossed the frontier. Brousse, with his quick suspicion, regarded this as a trick of the Geneva group, but both Kropotkin and Guillaume believed Ralli, and Kropotkin stayed in the mountains, he and Brousse editing the *Bulletin* while Guillaume went to France. On the 22nd and 29th July he published his earliest theoretical articles. The first was an exposure of the use of falsehoods in politics, and an attack in particular on the social-democrats. The second is much more interesting, since he expanded his ideas on "the constructive elements of revolutionary socialism". He proclaimed the orthodox collective idea of distribution, saying that "each should enjoy the integral product of his toil", and stated his conviction that the existing unjust order "cannot continue to live, that it is possible to abolish it and replace it by another". Finally, he declared the need for "the feeling of revulsion against injustice, the spirit of revolt", which would not be developed by parliamentary gradualism but by "energetic protests against tyranny, by the habit of following words by deeds".

He ended in good *narodnik* spirit by proclaiming his faith in the wisdom of the people.

"They will understand that one only gets what one aims at and furthermore that it is not reached by a single step. . . . They will understand that it is not the rights of the citizen but the rights of the worker that we have to proclaim. They will understand that once the conviction has been acquired that without economic liberty there is no political liberty, that conviction should not remain a mere word. It merely remains, then, for us to . . . say that, apart from the expropriation and suppression of the bourgeoisie, the demolition of the State and all bourgeois institutions, there is no salvation. We must seize every opportunity to make that programme real, be it only for a day."

Here is no evidence of the influence of communist ideas of economic organisation or of the scientific attitude which was later to be Kropotkin's personal contribution to the anarchist idea. He was merely repeating the propaganda which Bakunin and the Jura federation had already elaborated.

Nor, in the conference of the federation, held in August at St Imier, was there any departure from the existing attitude. Indeed, from the point of view of the biographer this congress is interesting principally because it was attended by a further demonstration against the arbitrary actions of the Berne authorities, who had now banned the red flag in the whole canton. Kropotkin tells us that:

"This time most of us were armed, and ready to defend our banner to the last extremity. A body of police was placed in a square to stop our column, a detachment of the militia was kept in readiness in an adjoining field, under the pretext of target practice—we distinctly heard their shots as we marched through the town. But when our column appeared in the square, and it was judged from its aspect that aggression would result in serious bloodshed, the mayor let us continue our march undisturbed to the hall where the meeting was to be held. None of us desired a fight; but the strain of that march in fighting order, to the sound of a military band, was such that I do not know what feeling prevailed in most of us during the first moments after we reached the hall—relief at having been spared an undesired fight or regret that the fight did not take place. Man is a very complex being."

This was the nearest Kropotkin ever came to revolutionary street-fighting, and he certainly seems to have shown a spirit rather different from that of the gentle scholar he has so often appeared.

Within a month Kropotkin had attended three further important congresses. Late in August there was a meeting of the Swiss members of the confidential group which continued Bakunin's secret Alliance, in its turn the heir of the International Brotherhood. This was attended, among others, by Malatesta, Brousse, the Spaniard Viñas, and Kropotkin, who was elected secretary of the international correspondence bureau to be set up in Switzerland. The congress decided on the formation of a French federation of the International, and took *L'Avant Garde* under its patronage.

Then the delegates proceeded to Belgium, where at Verviers was held the last international congress of the Bakuninist section of the First International. Kropotkin went under the name of Levashov; the Belgian police records state that he registered thus at the hotel where he stayed, and, having no passport or other official papers, produced as evidence of his identity a letter addressed to him from Norwich. According to Max Nettlau and also the Belgian police spies, Kropotkin held a mandate for the Russian emigré groups, but the Bolshevik G. M. Steklov, in his *History of the First International*, asserts that he had only a consultative voice. However, he was voted to the important function of taking the minutes of the congress.

Apart from a number of resolutions affirming the need for international revolutionary solidarity, for opposition to parliamentary parties, for expropriation of the means of production, the main discussion centred round the distribution of the product of labour. A number of varying solutions were put forward, and the eventual compromise resolution was that, after taking over the means of production, each group must find its own means of distributing the work product. Already, however, the signs of a tendency towards anarchist communism, or sharing the pool of goods on a basis of need, were becoming evident.

From Verviers most of the anarchists went on to the International Socialist Congress at Ghent, which started on the 9th September and where they hoped to prevent the German social-democrats from re-establishing a centralised Marxist control over the whole European socialist movement. With the help of the centrist followers of De Paepe, they succeeded in frustrating this danger. But Kropotkin was unable to stay to the end. And the incident which caused his departure has been given so many different interpretations that it may be well to record them. Kropotkin himself related it thus:

"The Ghent Congress ended for me in an unexpected way. Three or four days after it had begun, the Belgian police learned who Levashov was, and received the order to arrest me for a breach of police regulations which I had committed in giving at the hotel an assumed name. My Belgian friends warned me. They maintained that the clerical ministry which was in power was capable of giving me up to Russia, and insisted upon my leaving the congress at once. They would not let me return to the hotel; Guillaume barred the way, telling me that I should have to use force against him if I insisted upon returning thither. I had to go with some Ghent comrades, and as soon as I joined them, muffled calls and whistlings came from all corners of a dark square over which groups of workers were scattered. At last, after much whispering and subdued whistling, a group of comrades took me under escort to a social-democratic worker, with whom I had to spend the night, and who received me, anarchist though I was, in the most touching way as a brother."

This version is confirmed by Guillaume; Max Nettlau, who collected information from both Kropotkin and Guillaume, says that the warning came from a socialist, Denichère, who also spoke of the activities of Russian spies.

But a wholly different version exists in the Belgian police records, and the General Archivist of that country has sent us a report of these dossiers, in which he says:

". . . He (Kropotkin) went to Ghent, to the International Socialist Congress, and was present at the first sitting. But on the 11th he left in haste for Antwerp, and thence for London. His companion, Anna Ivanov, was abandoned by him in Ghent.

"He had received from his wife, staying in Neuchâtel, the information that the Russian government was pursuing him for forgery [of passports] and had asked his extradition of the Swiss government. So he feared to be arrested in Belgium and asked a Ghent socialist to be allowed to pass the night of the 10th–11th September in his house, before fleeing."

The report adds that no orders had been given for his arrest.

Political police spies are notoriously inexact in their information, and the assertion that Kropotkin fled because of the warning from his wife seems untrue, since he was not married until October of the following year and appears, from the evidence of his own letters, to have met his wife only a short time beforehand.

It seems fairly certain, however, that the fear of being arrested immediately by the Belgian police was unfounded, and a Belgian writer, Mr Hem Day, has told us that he was informed by a contemporary of the Ghent Congress that the social-democrats were not wholly innocent of ulterior motives in warning Kropotkin, who held a number of mandates and thus might swing the voting. This certainly seems possible, and it may well be that all the whistling and whispering in the dark was merely an elaborate deception of a man who, after his experiences, was naturally inclined to imagine himself under police observation.

The question of his "companion", Anna Ivanov, remains to be solved. We have found elsewhere no record of any person of this name at the congress; on the other hand there was present, without any mandate, a Russian friend of Kropotkin named Anna Kulichov, a woman of many aliases, who had already gone under the names of Anna Rosenstein and Anna Makarievich, and who therefore may well have chosen a new pseudonym for this occasion. Anna was a beautiful young woman, and already a veteran in revolutionary activity, since she had been converted to Bakunin's ideas in 1872 at Zurich, and had taken part in Armand Ross's activities in southern Russia. She was well known to the members of the Jura federation, and several of them appear to have been in love with her, so that, in Nettlau's opinion, she may have contributed to their personal differences. Kropotkin was certainly on friendly terms with her, since, when he proposed to visit Paris earlier in the year, he gave her address as that to which letters for him should be sent. He may have met her in Zurich during his first visit to Western Europe in 1872, and certainly encountered her early in 1877 when he came to the Jura. The exact nature of their relationship is difficult to determine; she may have gone to Verviers independently or with another delegate, particularly as Costa, whose companion she became in later years, was present. A fairly close friendship between her and Kropotkin, based on common interests, seems the most we are entitled to assume.

Sailing from Antwerp, Kropotkin proceeded to London, "provoking a number of good-natured smiles from the British custom-house officers, who wanted me to show them my luggage, while I had nothing to show but a small hand-bag", and seeking once again the hospitality of Paul Robin, whom he had seen the previous month at the Jura congress.

II

In London he began to visit the Reading Room of the British Museum, where he commenced his first studies of the French

Revolution, in order to gain an insight into the ways in which revolutions begin. He was already going beyond mere agitation and attempting to give a scientific basis to his ideas; of this period he tells us:

> ". . . I gradually began to realise that anarchism represents more than a mere mode of action and a mere conception of a free society; that it is part of a philosophy, natural and social, which must be developed in a quite different way from the metaphysical or dialectic methods which have been employed in sciences dealing with men. I saw it must be treated by the same methods as natural sciences; not, however, on the slippery ground of mere analogies, such as Herbert Spencer accepts, but on the solid basis of induction applied to human institutions."

But the opportunities for research in London did not then compensate for lack of action, and in a very few weeks he departed for Paris, where there were some open stirrings of discontent against the reaction which had ruled since 1871. Here he found Andrea Costa and Jules Guesde, the latter of whom became the founder of a Marxist party, but was at this time an anti-parliamentarian who co-operated in forming the first libertarian socialist groups in Paris.

Kropotkin continued, at the Bibliothéque Nationale, his studies of the French Revolution, but his main interest was in propaganda. It was difficult work, for he tells us that:

> "Our beginnings were ridiculously small. Half a dozen of us used to meet in cafés, and when we had an audience of a hundred persons at a meeting we felt happy. . . . There were not twenty of us to carry on the movement, not two hundred openly to support it. At the first commemoration of the Commune, in March 1878, we surely were not two hundred."

But such clandestine work could not go long unobserved, and early in 1878 the Paris police began an active search for those responsible for the agitation. In April they arrested Costa; he was imprisoned for eighteen months. They were also looking for Kropotkin, whom, through their spies, they knew as Levashov. Fortunately he had on this occasion registered under his own name, and the detectives arrested a student with a name similar to Levashov, whom they had to release. Kropotkin stayed on for another month, but had to be so cautious that his work was of little use, and at the end of April he travelled to Geneva. He spent some weeks in Switzerland, discussing the French question with Brousse and others, then decided to fulfil his earlier desire to visit Spain.

Spain was then, as it remains today, the only country in which anarchism had a great mass following. The International had 80,000 members there, and in Catalonia alone a hundred thousand workers were grouped in trade unions entirely under libertarian influence. It was the first time Kropotkin had encountered anything of the kind, and he was impressed by the resolve and stamina displayed by these men who held their belief with an almost apocalyptic enthusiasm. There was a certain inflexibility of theory among them, and this had led to disunity between the Madrid group, under the influence of Morago, who inclined towards terrorism, and the movement in Barcelona, led by Viñas, which concentrated on trade-union work and was already developing in a rudimentary form those theories of revolutionary syndicalism to become widely popular in Western Europe during the next two decades. Kropotkin, who spent six weeks in Spain and visited both great cities, acted as a mediator and succeeded in promoting a reconciliation.

But he did not confine his time wholly to the anarchists. We also find him visiting the Prado in Madrid, where he "deeply enjoyed" the paintings of Murillo, of whose *Madonna* he says that "every detail—her hands, her hair, down to the folds of her garments, harmonise with the fundamental idea of the picture: the ecstasy of pure love". The appreciation of these works, with their somewhat sentimentalised and adolescent feminine figures, is an interesting manifestation of the almost reverent attitude which Kropotkin adopted towards women in his writing and which it is difficult to think he did not hold in real life. This æsthetic experience, if it can strictly be called so, involved him in the question: "Why does the beautiful live for centuries?", to which Elisée Reclus gave him years later the answer, that "The beautiful . . . is an idea thought out in detail"—from which it seems that Kropotkin's view of art may have been concerned with ideas rather than with æsthetic values. He himself dabbled in painting and drawing, and could produce a vivid thumb-nail sketch or a brisk caricature. But his more deliberate works, particularly his landscapes in water colours of the Alpine lakes and mountains, were rather flat, naturalistic and sentimental in feeling—the kind of painting which visitors to southern Europe produced in bulk during the Victorian era. He did this work purely for his own amusement, and his friends were quite astonished when they discovered the paintings among the papers he left after his death. Some, like Emma Goldman, were enthusiastic, but it seems from the reproductions we have seen that Kropotkin's modesty was more fitting.

Early in August he returned to Geneva, where he found Russian friends awaiting him. One was his Siberian comrade Poliakov, with whom he went on a trip to the Aletsch Glacier. Another was Vera Zasulich, the young Russian *narodnik* who had gained international fame that year for her attempt on the life of General Trepov and for the trial in which she was acquitted and afterwards saved, by a crowd of students, from the police who tried to re-arrest her. Her action was historic, for it marked the inauguration of a new period in the Russian revolutionary movement, the replacement of the peaceful propaganda of the *narodniks* by the terrorism of the *Narodnaya Volya*. Vera Zasulich came to Switzerland after her acquittal, and Kropotkin went with her on "an excursion into the mountains" near Zurich, as he told Robin.

He found conditions in the Jura federation very disappointing. Guillaume had retired from activity, the *Bulletin* had been abandoned in March owing to a great fall in subscriptions. The congress of the Swiss groups took place at Fribourg on the 3rd–5th August, and Kropotkin wrote to Robin:

"Here things have gone rather badly. Most sections are disorganised—all tired. . . . There are some signs of life. The Congress is not numerous (eight delegates), but new questions are being thrown up and, in accordance with my suggestion, we may participate in agitation in the communes. . . . As far as I am concerned, I feel, after my return from Spain, morally completely rehabilitated and also physically stronger."

The Jura federation, indeed, was clearly declining, and it was not long before the enthusiastic movement which Bakunin had built up in the mountains dwindled to a tiny core. The reason can be found partly in the economic conditions which had made many formerly active supporters withdraw for fear of discrimination. But it may also be attributed partly to the actions of various militants. Guillaume, even before his retirement from activity, had been showing difficulty in personal relationships. Brousse and Kropotkin were concentrating on international affairs. And such working-class militants as Spichiger and Schwitzguebel, besides being less eloquent or accomplished than Kropotkin, Guillaume or Brousse, were also more exposed to economic distress.

Kropotkin's speech to the congress was based on the significance of the commune, or local unit of administration, in social life. He thought that the end of the nineteenth century was marked by a disintegration of the State, but that a fundamental social change could only happen through a spontaneous appropriation of the means of life by communes and productive groups. The independence of town and country communes, he suggested, would be the aim of future revolutions, and therefore the best practical field for the realisation of ideas would lie among the innumerable questions of communal and municipal interest. Through strikes, tax resistance, etc., the commune could be made a focal point for those risings which "go in advance of every great revolution and prepare the people's ideas and feelings". It is evident from these remarks that Kropotkin, while retaining the traditional Bakuninist idea of the spontaneous popular origin of revolutions, was already applying to it the historical lessons he had learnt from his inquiries into the French Revolution and from the facts he had gathered in Spain regarding the insurrectionary movement of 1873.

From Fribourg he went to Geneva, where he joined Cherkesov. Neither at this time nor at any later date, we have been told by the cantonal archivist, did he obtain from the local police the required permit to live in Geneva, and it seems likely that he arrived clandestinely, though his public activity must soon have made his presence known. At first he intended to stay for only two months, but he found that Geneva rather than the mountains had become the centre from which propaganda could be conducted most effectively. When, shortly, he began to lecture in the principal towns of Switzerland, he found that in the Jura the attendances were slight, but that in the south interest was much more lively. Now began his most active period as an agitator. Since the termination of the *Bulletin*, *L'Avant Garde* had become the local as well as the international organ, and, collaborating with Brousse, he succeeded in increasing its circulation. He began to work on the organisation of groups, travelling to all the small towns around Lake Leman in the hope of finding, through local discontent, the means of re-establishing the International.

An excellent portrait of the devoted agitator of this period has been given by his old friend, Serghei Stepniak, in *Underground Russia*, which was published shortly afterwards:

"His great gifts specially qualify him for activity in the vast public arena, and not in the underground regions of the secret societies. He is wanting in the flexibility of mind, and that faculty of adapting himself to the conditions of the moment, and of practical life, which are indispensable to a conspirator. He is an ardent searcher after truth, a founder of a school and not a practical man. He endeavours to make certain ideas prevail, at all cost, and not to attain a practical end, by turning everything tending to it to account. . . .

"He is an incomparable agitator. Gifted with a ready and eager eloquence, he becomes all passion when he mounts the platform. . . . His speeches, although he cannot be called an orator of the first rank, produce an immense impression; for when feeling is so intense it is communicative, and electrifies an audience. . . .

"He is very effective in private discussions, and can convince and gain over to his opinion as few can. Being thoroughly versed in historical science, especially in everything relating to popular movements, he draws with marvellous effect from the vast stores of his erudition, in order to support and strengthen his assertions with examples and analogies, very original and unexpected. His words thus acquire an extraordinary power of persuasion, which is increased by the simplicity and clearness of his explanations, due, perhaps, to his profound mathematical studies.

". . . He is an excellent journalist, ardent, spirited, eager. Even in his writings he is still the agitator. To these talents he adds a surprising activity, and such dexterity in his labours that it has astonished even a worker like Elisée Reclus.

"He is one of the most sincere and frank of men. He always says the truth, pure and simple, without any regard for the *amour propre* of his hearers, or for any consideration whatever. This is the most striking and sympathetic feature of his character. Every word he says may be absolutely believed. His sincerity is such, that sometimes in the ardour of discussion an entirely fresh consideration presents itself to his mind, and sets him thinking. He immediately stops, remains quite absorbed for a moment, and then begins to think aloud, speaking as though he were an opponent. At other times he carries on this discussion mentally, and after some moments of silence, turning to his astonished adversary, smilingly says, 'You are right'."

It will be seen that in the Kropotkin shown here, and also portrayed in the feverishly active work of the next three years, there appears an aspect very different from the self-conscious neophyte of the Chaikovsky circle or the mature scholar of the later London years. Yet there was no fundamental change, no real emergence, as sometimes happens with schizoid characters, of a hitherto concealed side of the personality. The capacity for toil had already been developed in exploration and clandestine propaganda, while the scientific tendency was merely undergoing that process of adaptation which changed the geographer into the sociologist and gave to the study of human society those talents which had before been concentrated on the structure of the earth. What Stepniak tells us of Kropotkin's powers as an orator and his manifest sincerity in private discussion has been confirmed by many observers at all periods. But perhaps the most interesting point of this description is the suggestion that Kropotkin did not show himself well adapted for conspiratorial work, because he held his principles too rigidly to allow him to use any means in order to attain the end he desired. Kropotkin held, quite correctly, that methods incompatible with the objective desired would certainly hinder its attainment and corrupt the revolutionary attitude. Later conspiratorial groups fell once more under the influence of Nechaevist doctrines of expediency, and this led them to the cynical opportunism of the Bolsheviks and a society that merely travestied what successive generations of Russian revolutionaries sacrificed so much to achieve.

Here it is necessary to record an important personal event which is almost submerged in the sweep of political activity, and which Kropotkin even omitted from his *Memoirs*. During the last month of 1878 he met, among the Russian emigrés, a young girl, Sophie Ananiev, to whom he was immediately attracted. Not long afterwards he said to Robin:

"I met in Geneva a Russian girl, quiet, kind, very gentle, with one of those wonderful dispositions which, after an austere youth, grow still better."

Sophie was born in 1856 at Kiev, of Jewish descent, though her features showed considerable Slav blood. Her family seems to have been prosperous, and when she was five years old they moved to Tomsk in Siberia, where her father operated a gold mine. Of her own departure from that life she told the Cobden-Sandersons:

"At seventeen, revolting against the hard lives of the miners, she refused to live on the money won by their labour, and left her home to gain her own living. She became 'one of the people', and a *sage femme*. Her health gave way after some few years of labour and hardship . . . and she was sent by her friends to Switzerland to rest."

No doubt the common experience of Siberia gave her and Kropotkin an added sympathy.

They were married on the 8th October, 1878, but lived for some time what Kropotkin called a "gypsy" existence, owing to the fact that, while his work kept him in Geneva, Sophie was forced to carry on her studies in biology at Berne, because Geneva University would not accept Russians without a gymnasium diploma. For the time being, they could only be together on the occasional weeks when Sophie was able to leave her studies.

Kropotkin was clearly much in love, in that rather chivalrous way which characterised his attitude towards women, and particularly towards the liberated women of Russia. One has the impression that his sexual development had been relatively slow, so that a kind of "innocence" still characterised this otherwise experienced man of nearly forty. Certainly there is little record of sexual adventures in his life up to this time. Apart from the doubtful incident of Anna Kulichov, we have encountered only one such instance, and that of a clearly romantic and unrealised nature. In a diary he kept during July 1862 there are references to a girl named Lydia, whom he had met on his family estate and who "was no more than the first girl who, it seems, felt some sympathy for me". However, it seems that she made more than a superficial impression, for in December he still recalls sadly "her lovely, gay voice, her smile, and her brows, which at times knit very nicely". A few weeks later, in the self-conscious rejection of a shy youth, he remarks: "In general I would say I am not made for women, nor women for me." The shadowy Lydia fades, and nobody seems to have taken her place in Kropotkin's emotions until the advent of Sophie sixteen years later. With other women, like Sophia Perovskaya and Vera Zasulich, he could have comradely relationships of a high order, but there is no sign of his having fallen in love with them.

Sophie was an attractive girl and a photograph taken at this time shows a melancholy, intelligent face, with a wide brow, large and rather slanting eyes, high cheeks and fullish lips. She was sharp-witted and strong-willed, but intellectually decidedly inferior to Kropotkin. Her attitude towards him seems to have been one of admiring devotion. Her one real fault may have been a lingering snobbery, for Solomon Mendelsohn, the Polish revolutionary who was in Switzerland at the time of her marriage, used to recall that she was delighted at the idea of having become a Princess. (Roger Baldwin, who met her in Moscow during the 1920's, still found her exhibiting the same pride of rank.) Against this it must be remembered that, but for her consistent loyalty and care, Kropotkin would not have lived so long as he did or have completed so much important work.

Kropotkin did not allow marriage to interfere with his agitational work, which he continued assiduously; but not without moments of doubt, for in November he wrote to Robin:

> "But with what shall we occupy the people—that is the greatest of all questions. Discussion and again discussion at last becomes boring, and what practical things can one do? . . .
>
> "You say that the workers must become accustomed to acting for themselves. Themselves they will do nothing. . . . A section only lives if a more or less earnest and interesting man is there. Because—unfortunately it is so—the International has been until now and is at present particularly only a study association. It has no practical field of activity. Where can this be found? . . .
>
> "Please do not think that these sad reflections discourage me. Sometimes I think in that way, but usually I say that old women lament thus."

It was the old story of the revolutionary movement which, in periods of political stagnation, finds itself deserted by the masses and forced to carry on in a pervading atmosphere of apathy.

On the 10th December the Swiss authorities intervened and suppressed *L'Avant Garde* for articles praising terrorist attempts on European rulers; Brousse, although he did not agree with these articles, took the responsibility and early next year was imprisoned for a short period. The question of starting a new paper arose, but the prosecution had caused a panic, and early in 1879 Kropotkin wrote, "We still do not know anything as regards the paper. Paul's arrest... caused a certain demoralisation. For three weeks I have been unable to get an answer from anyone."

Eventually it was found possible to begin anew, and on the 22nd February appeared the first issue of *Le Revolté*. For various personal reasons, none of the leading Swiss anarchists was willing to accept responsibility in this work, Brousse leaving the movement for good shortly afterwards, and Kropotkin had to assume the editorship.

> "I had to write most of it myself. It was moderate in tone but revolutionary in substance, and I did my best to write it in such a style that complicated historical and economical questions should be comprehensible to every intelligent worker."

Le Revolté was started on a fantastically slight amount of money. *L'Avant Garde* had thirteen francs left in its funds, and a gift of ten francs made the total up to twenty-three francs. Up to that time, none of the Jura papers had sold more than 600 copies. Kropotkin and his associates, full of confidence, decided to print a first run of 2,000; by hard begging they collected the necessary 65 francs, and in due course the paper appeared. To everybody's astonishment, it sold out in a few days.

Kropotkin found himself almost deserted by his old colleagues. Reclus and Malatesta, then in Geneva, were sympathetic but inactive, though later Reclus began to write articles for *Le Revolté*, while Cherkesov came to assist in office work and in folding the printed sheets. But Kropotkin was only able to carry on by the active help of two Geneva working men, François Dumartheray and George Herzig; these remarkable men he has portrayed vividly in his *Memoirs*:

"Dumartheray was born in one of the poorest peasant families in Savoy. His schooling had not gone beyond the first rudiments of a primary school. Yet he was one of the most intelligent men I ever met. His appreciations of current events and men were so remarkable for their uncommon good sense that they were often prophetic. He was also one of the finest critics of the current socialist literature, and was never taken in by the mere display of fine words or would-be science. Herzig was a young clerk, born at Geneva; a man of suppressed emotions, shy, who would blush like a girl when he expressed an original thought, and who, after I was arrested, when he became responsible for the continuance of the journal, by sheer force of will learned to write very well. . . .

"To the judgment of these two friends I could trust implicitly. If Herzig frowned, muttering, 'Yes—well—it may go', I knew that it would not do. And when Dumartheray, who always complained of the bad state of his spectacles when he had to read a not quite legibly written manuscript, and therefore generally read proofs only, interrupted his reading by exclaiming, 'Non, ça ne va pas!' I felt at once that it was not the proper thing, and tried to guess what thought or expression provoked his disapproval. I knew there was no use asking him, 'Why will it not do?' He would have answered: 'Ah, that is not my affair; that's yours. It won't do; that is all I can say.' But I felt he was right, and I simply sat down to rewrite the passage, or, taking the composing stick, set up in type a new passage instead."

If Dumartheray and Herzig were conscientious critics, all who knew him then say that Kropotkin was even more severe towards his own work, and would rewrite a passage several times before he felt it suitable for *Le Revolté*. It was thus, by sheer hard work, that he evolved the excellent journalistic style of this period, conveying knowledge and judgment in a manner simple and clear enough to appeal to uneducated people, yet—most difficult of all in such work—without a trace of condescension.

The unusual vigour of *Le Revolté* was quickly recognised, and its success was immediate. By April it had 550 subscribers, and its reputation had spread so far that very soon the printer approached Kropotkin to say that, while he himself liked the paper, he dared not continue to produce it because he would lose all his government contracts. And when Kropotkin toured the printing offices of French-speaking Switzerland, he was given everywhere the same answer.

The young paper seemed doomed. But Dumartheray's enterprise saved the situation, for he put forward the daring suggestion of buying their own plant on credit. Upon Kropotkin objecting that there was no money, he shouted, "Money? Nonsense! We *shall* have it! Let us only order our type at once and immediately issue our next number and money will come!" His confidence was justified, for, as soon as the first issue of *Le Revolté* had come from the new *Imprimerie Jurassienne*, money flowed in and enabled them to pay off their debts.

The paper was composed in a tiny room, by a Little Russian who worked for sixty francs a month. He knew no French, but somehow, with vigilant correction, they managed quite well, and in time Kropotkin also learned to compose type. Dumartheray has, indeed, remarked on the great activity which he showed in producing as well as writing the paper.

"He never wasted a moment at the printing establishment, either working as a compositor or handling a little hand-press for the printing of our small pamphlets.

"When the formes of the journal had to be carried to the printing house, he was the first to seize the shafts of the cart. When the printed sheets were returned to the shop, he set an example of great agility to his comrades in folding and dispatching copies."

Kropotkin's early articles were concerned mainly with contemporary issues, prophesying, in the optimistic mood of those days, the rapid dissolution of the massive States which already threatened the peace of Europe. On the 1st November, however, appeared an item which has considerably more interest, since it marked the beginning of his career as the most celebrated protagonist of anarchist communism. It was entitled "The Anarchist Idea from the Point of View of its Practical Realisation", and consisted of the report which he had read, under the name of Levashov, at the Jura Congress on the 12th October. The report itself is a long document of several clauses dealing mainly with propaganda and revolutionary techniques in the international uprising which he regarded as imminent. It stresses the need for the revolution to be based on local communes, which should carry out expropriation and collectivisation of the means of production. Then, he foretells, "a new form of organisation and manner of exchange will be formed unavoidably, first in a limited way, then extending, after a certain amount of trial and error. This form will correspond more with the people's aspirations, the demands of life and mutual relations than with any kind of theory, however beautiful . . . Yet we believe we are not mistaken, if we foresee already today that the foundations of the new organisation, at least in Latin countries, will be the federation of communes and independent groups." Although in the report he did not mention the communist theory of distribution, in his speech to the congress Kropotkin quite clearly stated that he envisaged the evolution passing through collectivism to communism. The nature of his ideas on this subject and the fundamental difference between anarchist communism and the misnamed communism of the present day will be discussed more fully in Chapter VII.

During 1880 Sophie had come to live in Geneva, but the cold winds of that city proved detrimental to her health, and the doctors suggested removal to a more sheltered place. Elisée Reclus was living in Clarens, and, as he had invited Kropotkin to collaborate in the *Geographie Universelle*, they decided to move there.

"We settled above Clarens, in a small cottage overlooking the blue waters of the lake, with the pure snow of the Dent du Midi in the background. A streamlet that thundered like a mighty torrent after rains, carrying away immense rocks in its narrow bed, ran under our windows, and on the slope of the hill opposite rose the old Castle of Châtelard. . . . Here, aided by my wife, with whom I used to discuss every event and every proposed paper, and who was a severe literary critic of my writings, I produced the best things that I wrote for *Le Revolté*, among them the address 'To the Young'. . . . In fact, I worked out here the foundation of nearly all that I have written later on. Contact with educated men of similar ways of thinking is what we anarchist writers, scattered by proscriptions all over the world, miss, perhaps more than anything else. At Clarens I had that contact with Elisée Reclus and Lefrançais, in addition to permanent contact with the workers, which I continued to maintain; and although I worked much for the geography, I was able to produce even more than usually for the anarchist propaganda."

The *Appeal to the Young* was certainly one of the most moving exhortations of its kind ever written, and it had the widest circulation among Kropotkin's writings and a greater influence than any other of his brief pamphlets. It first appeared in *Le Revolté*, running from June to August. It was reprinted in 1881 as a brochure. During the next twelve years, besides appearing in France, it was translated into fourteen European languages, and appeared in the United States and South America. Later, clandestine Russian editions were printed, as well as translations in Chinese and Japanese.

The peaceful pattern of life begun in 1880 did not last; in the early spring of 1881 it was broken by the news that the youth of Russia, exasperated by continued repression and broken promises, had finally made its great act of protest in the slaying of the Emperor by the People's Will.

III

Kropotkin heard the news on the 13th March from Stepniak, who had shortly before arrived in Geneva. He immediately printed a special edition of *Le Revolté* and was the first to make the fact public in the streets of the Swiss city. And, while he recognised the immense possibilities which were opened by this event, he could not fail to see the tragedy of this death of an old hero.

"To me, who had the chance of witnessing the first reactionary steps of Alexander II and his gradual deterioration, who had caught a glimpse of his complex personality and seen in him a born autocrat, whose violence was but partially mitigated by education, a man possessed of military gallantry but devoid of the courage of the statesman, a man of strong passions and weak will—it seemed that the tragedy developed with the unavoidable fatality of one of Shakespeare's dramas. Its last act was already written for me on the day when I heard him address us, the promoted officers, on 13th June, 1862, immediately after he had ordered the first executions in Poland."

On the 15th April came the further news that a number of Russians implicated in the assassination had been executed, under particularly brutal conditions. One of the victims was Kropotkin's comrade of the Chaikovsky circle, Sophia Perovskaya, and this moved him to extreme grief and indignation.

Immediately he printed a small pamphlet, *La Verité sur les Executions en Russie*, and prepared and posted up a placard, denouncing boldly the barbarity of the executions. The police made difficulties over the various drafts submitted to them, and eventually, in exasperation, Kropotkin posted up the final version on his own responsibility, an act which was later to be used against him. On the 21st April he was the principal speaker at a protest meeting, in which, without justifying the assassination, he described the circumstances from which it sprang, and pointed out that he had nothing personally against the Tsar, who really had liberated the peasants, but had got into the hands of a conservative clique. After the meeting he was questioned by the Geneva police, whom he told that if anyone had actually attacked the assassination he would have felt obliged to defend it, but that the occasion had not arisen. For the time being nothing was done against him.

All this time he remained much excited by news from Russia, and soon he and Sophie volunteered to place themselves at the disposal of the *Narodnaya Volya* for work there, since this seemed the only way in which to share the perils of revolutionaries at home. However, Stepniak refused to accept this sacrifice, and Cherkesov provided a diversion by persuading Kropotkin that it was imperative for him to go as a delegate to the International Revolutionary Socialist Congress to be held in London during July.

The main difficulty here was that Kropotkin was at this time very poor. Early in June he had written to Malatesta, saying that he no longer received cash from Russia and detailing his difficult financial position:

"... I am obliged to live on my work only. The *Revolté* and all the rest take usually a week [the paper appeared twice a month], so that I am left with two weeks every month during which I am obliged to earn from 150 to 200 francs for two of us, and 50 francs for Robert,* another 40 francs for the Russians, and 30 francs for correspondence, as well as 10 to 15 francs for the paper, etc.; in short, more than 350 francs."

In the same letter he complained that in order to earn this money and to keep up his work for *Le Revolté* he had to toil until

* Fritz Robert, a young man from Neuchâtel who helped to produce *Le Revolté*.

four in the morning. But Cherkesov and his other friends made sure that he went to London by raising a collection for his fare.

On the 10th July he went to Paris, where he felt pessimistically that the situation was falling into the hands of the followers of Guesde, who were adopting an increasingly Marxist attitude, and he proceeded to London three days afterwards.

The congress began on the 14th July, in the club rooms of a public house off Euston Road. It had been called by a small conference in Brussels the previous year, and its main aim was to explore the possibilities of founding a new International to include all revolutionaries opposed to State socialism. Forty-five delegates arrived. Besides Kropotkin, who represented the Geneva group and also the six anarchist sections of Lyons, they included Chaikovsky, who had now reached Western Europe, Malatesta, representing many groups in Italy and the Levant, Dr F. S. Merlino, Emile Gautier, a leading French anarchist, Louise Michel, the famous Communarde, Herzig, and a number of English revolutionary socialists, of whom Frank Kitz and Joseph Lane later became well known as anarchists. The two tendencies in German anarchism, collectivist and communist, were represented by Johann Neve and Joseph Peukert, there were two Spanish delegates, the Mexican Federation of Workers sent Dr Edward Nathan-Ganz and Miss M. P. Le Compte, an elderly New England lady, carried the mandate of the Boston Revolutionists.

Finally, the French police were represented by Serreaux, alias Spilleux, a creature of the Paris Préfect of Police, who had embarked on a campaign of provocation and actually financed an "anarchist" paper, *La Revolution Sociale*, edited by Serreaux, which talked in irresponsibly violent terms of "burning, assassination, dynamite bombs". Serreaux regarded the London congress as a fine opportunity for his disruptive work. But he was unsuccessful. Kropotkin and others immediately detected him: "At the congress, during which he introduced all sorts of terrible resolutions, the delegates kept aloof from him; and when he insisted upon having the addresses of anarchists all over the world, the refusal was made in anything but a flattering manner."

The conference was not very successful, for although there

was much high-flown talk, very little practical work was done. This was due largely to the atmosphere of mistrust caused by Serreaux and one or two other delegates under his influence. But it can also be attributed partly to the preoccupation with bomb-throwing due to the assassination of Alexander II that year. After this sensational act, many of the delegates seem to have believed that by dynamite alone they would blast their way to Utopia. In the case of Ganz of Mexico, the concern for what he called "education in chemistry" amounted to an obsession, and he kept interrupting the proceedings to draw attention to his pet theme. He seems to have been quite sincere, but his enthusiasm was used for more doubtful purposes by Serreaux and his friends. Most of the delegates were concerned with more fundamental social issues, but the vocal minority certainly had a disproportionate influence on proceedings and even resolutions.

Kropotkin sought to bring a sense of proportion into the congress when he deprecated, as a scientist, the light talk about chemistry. He warned his friends:

> "The study of chemistry is not so easy. First, one must gain technical ability, a process which would cost us many men in view of the difficulties and dangers. . . . Do not let us spread the disastrous illusion that some hours of study are enough to become a chemist or an electrician. . . . Chemistry and pyrotechnics are beautiful things, but they will not be a universal panacea."

He recommended them to turn their attentions to the much more important question of secret presses in countries where open publishing was impossible.

Much discussion centred round the point of revolutionary morality. Many delegates tended to dismiss morality out of hand, others considered the question unimportant, but Kropotkin was insistent that a moral attitude was the prime necessity for a revolutionary movement, and in the end this point of view was adopted, on the basis that morality was not "to be understood in the sense given to that word by the bourgeoisie; but in the sense that since extant society is founded upon immorality, its abolition, by any means that are possible, will inaugurate morality".

It was decided to found a new International, and a correspondence committee was formed. Finally, a blanket resolution was adopted, affirming the proximity of great revolutionary struggles and the need for propaganda by deed, for unconstitutional methods, for secret presses, and for agitation among the rural workers; in deference to the persistent appeals of Ganz, special attention was drawn to "the technical and chemical sciences".

Kropotkin was disappointed with the congress, which he considered had left the future of the International undecided. In discussions with Malatesta, recounted by the latter to Nettlau, he reverted to Bakunin's ideas of founding both public and secret organisations, the latter to specialise in infiltration, the leading of strikes, etc. But he also realised that there were few people to carry on this work.

In the end neither a secret nor a public organisation materialised, and the conference may be regarded as abortive. However, the ferocity of its deliberations had given it an importance out of all proportion to reality in the eyes of European governments—based on their ignorance of the real forces the revolutionaries could command. The St Petersburg government, in particular, was greatly scared, and during August the British Ambassador, reporting an interview with the Russian Foreign Minister, said that the latter " . . . had received fearful details of what had passed at the meeting of socialists recently held in London at which he said the Russians, Spaniards and personalities of other nationalities had been present, the speeches of the Russians surpassing in expressions of wicked designs those of any other of the socialists who had attended it". The Tsarist agents had evidently spiced their reports, for the three Russians, Kropotkin, Chaikovsky and Goldenberg, were among the most moderate in their declarations. But it was enough to make the Minister feel "much alarm" at "the proceedings of these miscreants".

Kropotkin stayed in England for a month after the congress, making the acquaintance of the Radical M.P., Joseph Cowen, and writing for his *Newcastle Chronicle* on Russian affairs. Then he travelled back to Switzerland via Paris, rejoining his wife in the mountains.

He had hardly returned when, on the 23rd August, the Swiss Federal Council, at the insistence of the Russian government, issued an order for his expulsion. The ostensible reasons were his allegedly illegal poster regarding the executions in Russia, and the "terrible" speeches he was reported to have made in London. However, the influence of St Petersburg was clear enough, and the Russian government openly expressed satisfaction. The British Ambassador reported, in September, having been told by the Russian Foreign Minister that the incident had been mentioned by the latter in conversation with Bismarck, as an example of the kind of co-operation against socialism that might exist even without treaties, and that the Iron Chancellor had cautioned him "that the string must not be drawn too tight". No doubt Bismarck, having to deal with an orderly social democratic movement, could afford to counsel caution to his neighbours, who at this period had been driven into a state of panic by the activity of the terrorists.

A protest meeting against the expulsion was fruitless, and Kropotkin and Sophie left their Swiss home, walking to Aigle and "enjoying for the last time the sight of the mountains that we loved so much". On the 30th August he left Geneva for the French side of the lake; Kropotkin's Swiss comrades bade him farewell at the boat and he left his work in Geneva for good, Herzig and Dumartheray carrying on *Le Revolté*, for which he continued to write regularly.

At the time of the expulsion Sophie had not yet taken her degree of Bachelor of Science, and they settled in the little French town of Thonon, on the Savoy shore of Lake Leman, from which she could travel back to the Swiss city until her work was completed. They stayed there for two months.

The period was not without excitement. A reactionary organisation, the Holy League, had recently been formed in Russia to combat revolutionary activities; it was secretly supported by the Tsar and the police, and its members were largely recruited from the officer class. Besides spying, it intended to specialise in kidnapping and murder. Kropotkin was soon chosen as a potential victim, and, at the instigation of the Grand Duke Vladimir, an old comrade at the Corps of Pages was deputed to carry out the assassination. But in good time a certain Dr Bechterev sent a warning which was transmitted to Kropotkin by Lavrov, then in Paris. He was not greatly perturbed.

"I simply communicated the fact to the Geneva correspondent of *The Times*, asking him to publish the information if anything should happen, and I put a note to this effect in *Le Revolté*. After that I did not trouble myself much about it. My wife did not take it so lightly, and the good peasant woman, Madame Sensaux, who gave us board and lodgings at Thonon, and who had learned of the plot in a different way (through her sister, who was a nurse in the family of a Russian agent), bestowed the most touching care upon me. Her cottage was out of town, and whenever I went to town at night—sometimes to meet my wife at the railway station—she always found a pretext to have me accompanied by her husband with a lantern. 'Wait only a moment, Monsieur Kropotkin', she would say; 'my husband is going that way for purchases, and you know he always carries a lantern.' Or else she would send her brother to follow me at a distance, without my noticing it."

The plans of the Holy League were effectively frustrated, and in November Kropotkin and his wife left Thonon for England. On the way he stopped at various towns in the Midi, to address groups with which he had established contact through *L'Avant Garde* and *Le Revolté*. They included Vienne, St Etienne, where he spoke to an audience of 250 people on the principles of anarchism, and Lyons, where he addressed a group of 150 in a café. Then he proceeded to Paris and called on Jean Grave, a young anarchist who had sent him articles for *Le Revolté*, and with whom he had established a correspondence. Grave, a shoemaker by trade and a completely self-educated man, later emerged as a capable writer and one of the leaders of the French anarchist movement, and after 1886 his friendship and collaboration with Kropotkin was to become steadily closer. At this first meeting he was much impressed by the Russian's "simplicity, kindness and enthusiasm".

In London the Kropotkins went to Myddleton Square, a seedy district in Islington, where they stayed with the Russian terrorist, Leo Hartmann. The foggy weather and the complete apathy of England at this time of social quiescence weighed down so much on Kropotkin that he described the year he spent there as a time of "real exile".

"For one who held advanced socialist opinions, there was no atmosphere to breathe in. There was no sign of that animated socialist movement which I found so largely developed on my return in 1886. Burns, Champion, Hardie, and the other Labour leaders were not yet heard of; the Fabians did not exist; Morris had not declared himself a socialist; and the trade unions, limited in London to a few privileged trades only, were hostile to socialism. The only active and outspoken representatives of the socialist movement were Mr and Mrs Hyndman, with a very few workers grouped round them."

If no real English socialist movement existed, still less was there any anarchist movement. A few working men were revolutionary socialists, opposed to the State; these included Kitz and Lane, whom Kropotkin had met at the London Congress, and Ambrose Barker. But not even the beginnings of an English anarchist group existed.

The German emigrés were better off, since when Kropotkin arrived *Freiheit* was still being published. But Most was in prison, and would remain there until October 1882, for an article in praise of the assassination of Alexander II, and *Freiheit* itself was finally suppressed in May 1882, when, on the shooting of Lord Cavendish in Dublin, the editors expressed sympathy with the Irish Nationalists. In any case, Kropotkin was on distant terms with the *Freiheit* group who, following Most's lead, had not yet adopted free communism. The only anarchists with whom he had close contact were those transients who made fleeting visits when their affairs brought them to England—Malatesta, Cafiero, Reclus.

The winter under these conditions was hard, and in the spring of 1882 he wrote to Robin:

"I work much and as I have to write everything in English it tires me much. At the end of the winter I was almost finished, but now after a walking tour in Surrey, I feel much better."

At this time he made a number of short journeys in the English countryside. Once he went to Brighton and spent much time observing the habits of fishes and crabs in the Aquarium. Another walk in Surrey later in the year was taken in the company of the English Marxist, Ernest Belfort Bax, who has left in his own *Reminiscences and Reflections of a Mid and Late Victorian* an interesting recollection of their conversation:

"I well remember a long walk I had with him in the early summer of 1882 from Croydon to Leatherhead, during which he expounded his views on the Social Revolution and had much to say against Marx and the other leaders of the main social-democratic movement. . . . As regards economics, he insisted on the theory that concentration in industrial processes was only a passing phase in industrial revolution which had reached its greatest intensity during the period in which steam was the main motive power in production, but that the full development of the era of electricity would show a return, in a large measure, to the old small industry of individual production, owing to the fact that, unlike steam power, electricity can be split up without losing its efficiency."

It is significant that Kropotkin already held in 1882 the ideas of industrial decentralisation which were to form one of the main bases of his sociological theories, and that he was putting forward a suggestion on the role of electricity in breaking down large concentrations of industry which has become almost a commonplace among sociologists today.

Kropotkin met Belfort Bax through the German socialist, Hermann Jung. It was through Joseph Cowen that he met H. M. Hyndman, the dean of English Marxists, who writes of him at this period:

"He was overflowing with enthusiasm and vigour. When he came to our house, I was at once captivated by the charm of his manner and the unaffected sincerity of his tone. His appearance was to me what I then thought was typically Russian, a bright engaging face, in spite of its irregular features and nose of the Kalmuck type, lightly brushed long hair, and heavy beard and moustache. At first I tried to argue with him about his anarchist opinions, which seemed to me entirely out of accord with his intelligence and naturally charming disposition. I found this was quite hopeless. You could pin him to nothing, and his capacity for genial misrepresentation of social-democratic thought and principle transcended belief."

Kropotkin thought much the same, from his point of view, of the perversity of Hyndman's views, but they continued good friends for the rest of Kropotkin's life, and when he died, Hyndman still felt strongly enough to remark, after so many theoretical polemics, "In my whole life I have never met a personality whom I admired more than he".

Hyndman introduced Kropotkin to James Knowles, the enterprising editor of *The Nineteenth Century*, who immediately recognised the value of Kropotkin's judgment and experience, and commissioned from him a series of articles on the Russian prison system, of which the first was published in January 1882. It was the beginning of an association with this review which lasted for more than thirty years.

For the rest, Kropotkin continued to write for *Nature* and *The Times*, and contributed to *The Fortnightly Review* a long article on the Russian revolutionary movement. He also began his work for the *Encyclopædia Britannica*, and still wrote for *Le Revolté*, contributing during this period two important social studies, *Law and Authority* and *Revolutionary Government*.

Another article, although of less permanent interest, shows how even at this period he was beginning to see Germany as the country likely to precipitate a war in Europe, and to identify himself with the Latin races, particularly France, in the struggle he foresaw as early as January 1882.

"Bismarck knows that on the day on which the alliance of the peoples of Latin race takes place, German supremacy will be at an end. He understands that the principle of the almighty State will also be done away with, whose faithful expression and final vanguard at this moment is Germany—the monarchist as well as the republican, and the republican as well as the social-democrat. An almighty State, even if it wore the republican colours, can satisfy neither France nor Italy, and even less Spain. . . . Therefore the alliance of the Latin peoples is the nightmare which presses on Germany and against which Bismarck works. . . . If the German Empire fails to come out victorious from a war, this will not only be the defeat of European reaction; it will also be the defeat of the principle of the State."

Kropotkin was already thinking along those lines of anti-Germanism and Francophilism which were to lead him eventually to the support of the 1914 war. A more scientific theme appears in an article on Darwin and his evolutionary theories (April 1882); here Kropotkin foreshadowed the main outline of his mutual-aid theory by contending that "solidarity and communal work—these strengthen the species in the fight for the maintenance of their existence against adverse powers of nature".

From England Kropotkin continued to maintain his interest in the Continental events, and when the annual congress of the Jura federation assembled in June he sent a letter in which he set forth his ideas of the possible character of future revolutions, and emphasised the need for a thorough rectification of grievances and a swift progress towards important goals (appropriation of houses, food and better places of work), if the people as a whole are to give active support. Drawing from the defeats which the revolution of 1789 and the Commune of 1871 suffered because of their failure to recognise this fact, he declares:

". . . Never will there be such intensive work in the workshops as on the day when the worker knows that he works for himself, for the community, and for nothing else. Houses and useful objects will be created as in fairy tales. The spirit of invention will be at work as never before, to make work easier for the people and to make it fit the new conditions."

It is a vision that sounds Utopian, yet Barcelona, in the early days after the rising of 1936, saw something very like it in the industry and enterprise which for a time inspired the communalised workshops.

But Kropotkin's letter was not all encouraging prophecy. He realised well enough the stagnation that existed, particularly in Switzerland, and declared roundly:

"Our inactivity is not the outcome (as the social-democrats declare) either of our principles or of our programme; it depends upon our indolence. So long as this indolence persists, no change of programme will bring about any change in our conduct."

He was voicing, perhaps unconsciously, one aspect of the dilemma which faces many revolutionaries. A disciplined party destroys that sense of freedom and responsibility which alone can build a liberated society. But a movement without discipline tends, except in times of crisis, to decline into the condition where only a minority is active and the vast mass of adherents sink into "indolence".

During this period much of Kropotkin's time was spent on Russian propaganda. Lavrov and Chaikovsky were both in London, and with the latter Kropotkin organised meetings in workmen's clubs in which they combined a description of conditions in Russia with discussions on the anarchist point of view. The audiences were tiny, "seldom consisting of more than a dozen men", but Kropotkin had more success later in the year when he went to the north, addressing the Durham miners at their annual gathering, and then speaking at Newcastle, Glasgow and Edinburgh, where he "was received with enthusiasm, a crowd of workers giving hearty cheers for the nihilists". At these meetings Kropotkin and Chaikovsky, according to the Russian police spies, collected small sums of money for "the Red Cross of the People's Will".

But by this time the loneliness and apathy of London were more than he and Sophie could endure. In the autumn they decided to return to France, where activity in the south was increasing so rapidly that there were said to be three thousand anarchists in Lyons alone. "We were sure that in France I should be arrested; but we often said to each other, 'Better a French prison than this grave'." On 26th October they returned to Thonon, and took the same lodgings, Kropotkin resuming his literary work and alternating it with occasional gardening and sawing wood. They were joined here by one of Sophie's brothers, who was dying of consumption.

Soon Kropotkin found himself the object of attention not only from the local gendarmes, who persistently questioned his landlady about his movements, but also from Russian spies, of whom he claims that "flocks, literally flocks of Russian spies besieged the house, seeking admission under all possible pretexts, or simply tramping in pairs, trios and quartets in front of the house".

All this boded no good, and it was made worse by the panic into which the French authorities were thrown by the disorders caused by the crisis in the Lyons silk industry. Finally, the miners at Monceau-les-Mines went on strike and carried out a series of small dynamite explosions, while in Lyons the hatred felt by the workers for the factory owners and the priesthood began to take on more and more violent forms. In all this Kropotkin had no part at all, since he had lost touch with the French movement during his residence in England. But his close connection with the principal anarchist paper, his already international reputation as a revolutionary theoretician, and the fact that his return to France coincided with the worst series of outbreaks, gave the newspapers an excuse to hold him responsible. The campaign grew, and after sixty anarchists had been arrested, it became evident that Kropotkin's free days were numbered.

Reporters added themselves to the spies, and when they could gain no replies, inserted fanciful interviews in their papers. Provocateurs of all kinds became active:

> "Almost every day I received letters, evidently written by spies of the international police, mentioning some dynamite plot, or mysteriously announcing that consignments of dynamite had been shipped to me."

Then, during December, the house was searched by gendarmes, who threw Kropotkin's sick brother-in-law out of bed, an act which, according to Reclus, shortened his life by some weeks. The young man died on the 21st December, in Kropotkin's arms, and he and Sophie were deeply affected by the event. A few hours afterwards the police came to arrest the anarchist. He asked to remain with his distressed wife until after the funeral, but this was refused, and the same night he was taken to Lyons.

IV

This added brutality did the authorities little good, for not only did Reclus and many people come from Geneva to accompany Sophie at her brother's burial, but the peasants of the vicinity attended *en masse*, and afterwards followed Kropotkin's trial with great interest.

He was installed at Lyons in the St Paul Prison, a modern building in which he was given a large cell with a clean bed and a coke-stove, "a tolerably comfortable dwelling place, provided the incarceration does not last too long". He was only allowed to see his wife in a noisy common meeting hall, where they gazed at each other through a wire grill and found it impossible to converse. It was therefore with some surprise that one day he received in his cell an English friend, who had come with a message from another Englishman (probably Cowen) offering to go bail for him, and suggesting that he should then leave France. But he did not wish to evade the issue in this way, and maintained his intention to stand trial.

The proceedings began on the 8th January, 1883, before the Lyons Police Correctional Court, and lasted until the 19th January. Since the prosecution had no evidence at all on which to accuse the prisoners of complicity in the recent explosions, they were tried under a law proscribing the International, which had been decreed at the time of the Commune. The fifty-four prisoners, as well as fourteen men who were in hiding, were accused of affiliation to the International and of having carried out functions in connection therewith.

Since the International had died in 1877 and all attempts to resuscitate it had been in vain, this seemed a rather untenable indictment, but it was the best the prosecution could do, and the trial proceeded.

Both sides strove to gain the maximum publicity. Gautier, Bernard, and Kropotkin made long propaganda speeches, and all the accused signed a statement of their principles, drawn up by Kropotkin, in which they declared:

"We desire freedom, that is to say, we demand for every human being the right and the means of doing whatever pleases him, and of not doing what does not please him; of satisfying integrally all his needs, with no limit except natural impossibilities or the needs of his neighbours, respected equally.

"We desire freedom, and we believe its existence incompatible with the existence of any power, whatever may be its origin or shape, whether elected or imposed, monarchist or republican, inspired by divine right or popular right. . . .

"History teaches us that all governments are alike and equal. . . . Evil, in the eyes of anarchists, does not reside in one form of government more than in another. It is in the governmental idea itself, it is in the principle of authority.

"The substitution, in human relationships, of a free contract, perpetually revisable, for administration and legal tutelage, for imposed discipline, is our ideal. . . .

"We believe that capital, the common patrimony of humanity, since it is the fruit of the collaboration of past and present generations, should be at the disposal of all, so that none should be excluded from it. . . .

"We desire equality, actual equality, as a corollary or rather as a primordial condition of freedom. From each according to his abilities, to each according to his needs. . . .

"Scoundrels that we are, we demand bread for all; for all equally independence and justice."

The examination of Kropotkin aroused particular interest. To the prosecuting counsel he replied firmly and uncompromisingly, refusing to answer any question relating to his activity outside France, but admitting his editorship of *Le Revolté* and affirming very emphatically his anarchist faith. He denied the charges on which he and his friends were accused, and himself cross-examined the chief of the Lyons secret police. The latter admitted that in fact the International did not exist in France and that it had not been re-established. Finally, Kropotkin made a long speech in which he told his own revolutionary history, analysing the indictment and evidence of the prosecution with devastating thoroughness, and ended by warning the court that a condemnation would merely result in spreading anarchist ideas, and by appealing to the magistrates not to perpetuate class hatred, but to join in the task of establishing a society from which want and strife would alike be abolished.

But the result of the trial was a foregone conclusion; neither Kropotkin's appeal nor the evident nullity of the prosecution's evidence could change its course. On the 19th January the sentences were announced; Kropotkin, with three others, being condemned to five years' imprisonment, a fine of a thousand francs, ten years' police supervision, and loss of civil rights for five years, and the rest of the prisoners to shorter sentences.

A significant feature of the latter days of the trial was the number of threats of death received by the members of the court. On one day alone the chairman read out nineteen such letters. One is moved to ask whether they in fact came from anarchists, or whether they were merely another police precaution to ensure the continuance of a prejudiced attitude towards the prisoners. The forces behind the trial were revealed somewhat tactlessly when, shortly afterwards, the prosecuting counsel and one of the magistrates were presented with the Tsarist Cross of St Anne.

But if the Russians were pleased many people were shocked by the proceedings, and most of the French press, even the moderate *Journal des Economistes*, wrote in condemnation of it. A resolution for an amnesty, brought forward immediately in the Chamber of Deputies by Clemenceau, received a hundred votes. The mountaineers of the Savoy demonstrated outside Kropotkin's house at Thonon, firing rifle shots in his honour, while in Lyons a great impetus was given to the anarchist movement. The very turnkeys in the prison, said Reclus, "have the pretension of being anarchist and confine themselves to posing timidly the question of practical means"

Most of the defendants lodged an appeal in the higher court, but Kropotkin refused to do so. For another two months, while the appeal was pending, all the prisoners remained at Lyons, where they enjoyed remand conditions, staying in their *pistoles*, which were more comfortable than the ordinary cells, retaining their own clothes and obtaining food from outside. Kropotkin took advantage of this to continue his work for the *Encyclopædia Britannica* and the *Geographie Universelle*; now, and later at Clairvaux, he wrote on Russian subjects for *The Nineteenth Century*, and also an interesting dissertation on *What Geography Ought To Be*, subjecting to strong criticism the academic methods of teaching and practising that science.

During this period the Reclus brothers and a number of English friends did their best to get Kropotkin transferred to the Paris prison of Saint Pelagie, where he could work in comfort. But he had no desire for preferential treatment, and in due course was moved with his comrades to the Clairvaux prison, situated in the old abbey of St Bernard, where they were allowed to continue in their status of political prisoners. The prison authorities, in fact, treated them with great consideration. "The governor and the warders were most polite to us", and the day after arrival they were assigned a suite of three large rooms in the hospital wing, as well as a smaller room in which Kropotkin and Gautier would write. The rooms gave a view on the surrounding countryside; under the windows was a little garden where the prisoners played ninepins and *boule*. They could also cultivate a vegetable bed, on which Kropotkin gained his first experience of intensive gardening. "One would suspect me of exaggeration if I enumerated all the crops of vegetables we made in our little kitchen garden", he remarked.

They also tried other manual trades, and bookbinding became a favourite occupation. Besides this, Kropotkin was very active in the organisation of classes, so that his comrades should gain at least some profit from their enforced leisure. He gave them lessons in cosmography, physics and geometry, and helped them to study languages. He was amazed at the results.

"I was glad to find at Clairvaux a practical proof of what I formerly maintained on scientific grounds—namely, that the Russians are not the only people who easily learn foreign languages.

SOPHIE
AT THE TIME OF HER FIRST MEETING
WITH PETER KROPOTKIN

My French comrades learned, with great ease, English, German, Italian and Spanish; some of them mastered two languages during a two years' stay at Clairvaux."

He himself continued his writing, adding to his labours work for the Paris *Revue Scientifique*, and thinking over "the bases of what I consider a new system of philosophy—the bases of Anarchy".

But although their days were filled with various occupations, the prisoners found life very monotonous. No doubt, this was partly due to the supervision by which their apparent freedom of action was negated. They could write and receive as many letters as they wished, but a strict censorship was imposed. They could obtain books, but no newspapers. A concession was made for scientific journals and illustrated papers, the arrival of which formed a great event in the prisoners' lives. Any kind of socialist publication was forbidden, and during the whole period Kropotkin never saw a copy of his "child", as he called *Le Revolté*, the editorship of which had been taken over by Grave, at Sophie's suggestion, towards the end of 1883. And there were warders always present whenever the prisoners left their closely locked rooms.

These conditions produced lassitude, and Kropotkin found that his mind functioned with much less activity than in normal circumstances. Nevertheless, he clearly indulged in much serious thinking, and there is no doubt that from this period dates the beginning of his change from a pamphleteer and an agitator to a scholar concerned in a scientific way with the problems of sociology.

Meanwhile, his situation was arousing a great deal of sympathy, both in France and abroad. In Paris the French Academy of Sciences offered to send him any books he needed for research, and Ernest Renan wrote to Sophie, laying his own library at the prisoner's disposal. In England indignation at the trial, and disquiet aroused by reports of his ill health, caused an impressive list of scholars and men of letters to sign a petition stressing the importance of his contribution to science and asking for his early release so that he might continue his work, which seemed to them of undoubted value to humanity in general.

The signatories represented a fair cross-section of the world of learning in Victorian England. There were fifteen professors of Cambridge, London, Edinburgh and St Andrews Universities, as well as a number of Oxford Fellows; all the leading officials of the British Museum and the Royal School of Mines, the secretary of the Geographical Society, and the editors of the *Encyclopædia Britannica* and nine important newspapers and periodicals, including the *Athenæum*, the *Pall Mall Gazette*, and the *Cornhill*. A number of independent writers lawyers and scientists completed the list. Personally, they included William Morris, A. C. Swinburne, Theodore Watts-Dunton, Edward Burne-Jones, Leslie Stephen, H. W. Bates, Frederick Harrison, Stopford A. Brooke, Alphonse Legros, Sidney Colvin and Patrick Geddes. Liberal opinion was represented by John Morley and James Runciman, while Joseph Cowen represented the Radicals. Alfred Russel Wallace, the great evolutionist, also added his name, and thus compensated for the churlish refusal of T. H. Huxley. In his *Memoirs* Kropotkin says that Herbert Spencer was a signatory, but our examination of the original document in the French National Archives showed that his name was not appended.

The petition was presented to the French Minister of Justice by Victor Hugo, who added a few words in support. It was sent to the Procureur-General, who in April returned a report in which, describing Kropotkin as a *rentier*, he admitted that his habitual conduct and morality, as well as his conduct since imprisonment, were unimpeachable, but told once again the story which had formed the basis of the prosecution. The papers then seem to have gathered dust for two months, for it was not until the 6th June that the Minister of Justice wrote to Victor Hugo regretting that, owing to the active part played by Kropotkin in a "prohibited association" and the recent date of his sentence, it was impossible to accede to the request.

Meanwhile, his friends did what they could to alleviate his conditions. Many, including Dumartheray, Reclus and Keltie, wrote regularly and sent presents when they could. In November 1883, for instance, he replied to Dumartheray:

"The comrades have asked me to thank you for the apples which we received yesterday in a very good condition. They were delightful, and we had a general holiday when we got them. Is it necessary, dear friend, to tell you how often I think of you and how often I mention you when we speak of Geneva and everything that is dear to us?"

And early in 1884 he wrote to Keltie, thanking him for a batch of Russian pamphlets and English illustrated magazines, which contained "more news than any French review", and describing the geologist Tyndall as "a humbug".

Towards the end of 1883 the effect of prison life began to make itself felt, and Kropotkin was seized with the malaria which was endemic around Clairvaux. This illness was complicated by a return of scurvy. For a time he was very ill, and in the beginning of March 1884, *Justice,* the social-democratic paper edited by Hyndman, printed a report that "the health of this vigorous agitator and friend of the people had suffered so severely from imprisonment that his death approaches".

Sophie, who on her husband's transfer to Clairvaux had gone to Paris to stay in the house of Elie Reclus (Elisée's elder brother, the celebrated anthropologist) and study for her Doctorate of Science, hurried to the tiny village beside the prison. There, despite the dullness of life in this isolated corner of France, she stayed until his final release. During the first year she had been allowed to see him only once every two months.

"But when she settled at Clairvaux, declaring her firm intention to remain there, she was soon permitted to see me every day, in one of the small guard-houses of the warders, within the prison walls, and food was brought me from the inn where she stayed. Later, we were even allowed to take a walk in the governor's garden, closely watched all the time, and usually one of my comrades joined us in the walk."

His health improved slowly and irregularly, so that in June Reclus wrote, full of concern, "These alternations in your health distress me. Obviously, your organism does not react sufficiently against the causes of enfeeblement, and you will need to be helped by the weather in securing a definite cure." Reclus was working hard to get Kropotkin's work published; to the English journalist Richard Heath he talked of publishing the letters on anarchism which Kropotkin had written to the French author Lavelaye during his imprisonment at Lyons, and he also collected the principal articles from *Le Revolté* into a volume which he called *Paroles d'un Revolté,* and which was published in Paris by Flammarion in November 1885. It carried an introduction by Reclus, in which he made a long and eloquent tribute to his friend, ending in the often quoted passage:

"Public opinion is unanimous in respecting this man, and yet it is not astonished to see the gates of the prison remain obstinately shut upon him, so natural it seems that superiority should pay dearly and that devotion should be accompanied by suffering. It is impossible to see Kropotkin in the yard of the gaol and to exchange a greeting with him without asking oneself: 'Why am I free? Is it perhaps because I am worth nothing more?' "

In the meantime the demands for Kropotkin's release had become so insistent, both in the Press and in the Chamber of Deputies, that as early as June 1884, *Justice* claimed "Peter Kropotkin will, it is almost certain, be released shortly, and it is possible that he may come to England". But the hope was premature, though the campaign for release grew steadily, and was increased by the fact that Louise Michel had, at about the same time, been sentenced to nine years' imprisonment for highway robbery; the real offence being that she had marched at the head of a column of starving unemployed and distributed a few loaves from a baker's shop. Louise, who had served a term of transportation in New Caledonia for her part in the Commune, was a woman of the highest personal integrity, and enjoyed an immense popularity in Paris, the workers and students alike regarding her as a heroine.

Soon the demand for the release of Kropotkin and the "Red Virgin" became a rallying cry for all opponents of the government, and in the autumn of 1885 the President tried to placate public opinion by releasing all the lesser-known anarchists. This only increased the clamour for a complete amnesty, and de Freycinet, the Premier, hard pressed by Clemenceau, was one day forced to admit that "diplomatic reasons stood in the way of Kropotkin's release", meaning that the French government was allowing itself to be influenced by the demands of the Tsar. This resulted in a final outburst of such a breadth that the President was left with no alternative but to pardon the remaining prisoners and release them on the 15th January, 1886. On the eve of Kropotkin's release a procureur arrived at Clairvaux, with the intention of re-imprisoning him at Bar-sur-Aube for non-payment of the fine which had been imposed. This, however, was too much even for the prison governor, who refused to hand over Kropotkin until it was conceded that he should go completely free. The release aroused much rejoicing in radical circles, even Marx's daughter, Eleanor, writing in *The Commonweal* to welcome the liberation and to expose the insult by which the prisoners had been *pardoned* for offences which all the world knew they had not committed.

Kropotkin and Sophie went immediately to Paris, where they stayed at the house of Elie Reclus. They were almost destitute, and it was only a draft of 300 francs for royalties on *Paroles d'un Revolté* that enabled him to pay for the journey. In Paris, however, they found means to gain a little more cash, for Henri Rochefort accepted for publication in *L'Intransigeant* a novelette, *Woman No. 4237*, which Sophie had written about the Russian terrorists, while Kropotkin himself wrote for *The Nineteenth Century* on his recent experiences in French prisons.

From this and the earlier essays on Russian prisons, he compiled during the next few months a book entitled *In Russian and French Prisons*, in which he not only gave a very objective account of his own wide experiences of gaols, both as an investigator in Siberia and as a prisoner in several establishments, but also expressed his conviction that no reform could take away the intrinsic mental and spiritual harm of incarceration, and that the only real solution was the abolition of prisons and a humane understanding of criminals. This opinion is diffused throughout the book, and is supported formidably by the uncomfortable facts which he presents to the reader, but perhaps a better summary of his general views can be gained from his *Memoirs* relating to this period, in which he says:

"Incarceration in a prison necessarily, fatally, destroys the energy of a man, and still more kills his will. In prison life there is no room to exercise one's will. To possess one's own will in prison means surely to get into trouble. The will of the prisoner *must* be killed, and it is killed. Still less is there room for exercising one's natural sympathies, everything being done to destroy free contact with those outside the prison, and within it with whom the prisoner may have feelings of sympathy. Physically and mentally he is rendered less and less prepared for sustained effort; and if he had formerly a dislike for regular work, this dislike is only the more increased during his prison years. If, before he first came to prison, he soon felt tired by monotonous work, which he could not do properly, or had a grudge against underpaid overwork, his dislike now becomes hatred. If he doubted about the social utility of current rules of morality, now, after having cast a critical glance upon the official defenders of these rules, and learned his comrades' opinions of them, he openly casts the rules overboard. And if he has got into trouble in consequence of a morbid development of the passionate sensual side of his nature, now after having spent a number of years in prison, this morbid character is still more developed—in many cases to an appalling extent. In this last direction—the most dangerous of all—prison education is most effective."

In Russian and French Prisons had a curious history. It was first published in March 1887, and immediately disappeared from the market, almost the whole edition having been bought up and destroyed by the agents of the Russian government. Indeed, the holocaust was so thorough that when Kropotkin tried to obtain a copy for himself shortly afterwards, he found this completely impossible. However, it was eventually reissued by another publisher, and sufficient precautions were taken this time to prevent a recurrence of the previous incident.

In Paris Kropotkin found a great deal of enthusiastic activity. Grave had transferred *Le Revolté* there, so as to have a more central position for his work, and had opened, in the shabby Rue Mouffetard, behind the Pantheon, a printing office which for many years produced a great mass of literature. Louise Michel was addressing well-attended meetings in all parts of Paris, and everywhere there was such a ferment of activity that when Herzig wrote from the quiet atmosphere of Geneva, expressing feelings of disillusionment, Kropotkin sent an indignant rebuke.

"You speak . . . about disillusionment. With what right do you dare to talk about that? When you started to work, what did you think to find—the revolution after two years' effort, like Brousse? Because you have not reached it quickly, does this make you sulk, like a little aristocrat? Or did you think to find only ideal people, entirely devoted to the cause, entirely without low personal passions?"

Kropotkin goes on to say that "man is an extremely complicated animal", but that the task is to encourage the "beautiful" passions, "so that when the exercise of these beautiful attributes becomes a habit the race will better itself". The dumb masses are infinitely better than the "intelligent blackguards who speak from the platforms", and "there exists an honest core in politics and in personal relationships—the young", who, if they become corrupt in their turn, are ever renewed by the rising generation. And finally, after having rated Herzig so soundly for having expected results too quickly, he suggests that they might have to wait even ten years for the revolution—the hardest of realism, no doubt, in those hopeful days.

It soon became clear to Kropotkin that, even though the Republican authorities had been forced to liberate him, they were by no means content to see him moving about freely in France, particularly at a time when his greatly enhanced reputation, both as a martyr and a theoretician, made him a rallying-point for the vast social discontent which manifested itself in those years. Any excuse, he knew, might be used to enforce a deportation, and, having heard that England had at last awakened, and that there was much for him to do, he decided to leave France as quickly as possible, hoping in this way to leave the door open for a return. But before he departed he spent some time on visits to the market gardeners of Paris, reinforcing by conversation and observation of practical methods the ideas on intensive culture which had been suggested to him by the unexpectedly good results obtained in the prison garden at Clairvaux. Finally, on 28th February, the eve of his departure, he delivered in Paris, to an audience of several thousands, a farewell lecture on "Anarchism and Its Place in Socialist Evolution". The difference between this large and enthusiastic meeting and the tiny groups to whom he had spoken only nine years ago filled him with happiness in the realisation that his own fearless expression of convictions and dignified endurance of injustice had not been in vain.

CHAPTER V

"THE WHITE JESUS"

I

KROPOTKIN's fourth arrival in England, at the beginning of March 1886, marked the commencement of a long and relatively stable epoch of his life. From that date until 1917, his existence was quite different from that of the explorer up to 1872 or the conspirator, agitator, and prisoner of the active and troubled years from 1872 until his release from Clairvaux.

Now began the period of the saintly scholar, the retired theoretician who saw his social ideal advancing, not so much in the revolutionary endeavours of a restricted movement as in the broad forward progress of society towards a libertarian way of life. His outlook was still coloured by hope, but, towards the end, a consciousness of threatening war flecked his vision with pessimism, with a foreboding that events might delay unavoidably the realisation of his ideal. During this period he returned to scientific work, elaborating his sociological writings and taking his place as a respected figure in international learning. Many circumstances, his failing health, the character of the English labour movement, the atmosphere of mutual tolerance and legality in which its work was carried on, perhaps even the half-submerged feeling that his early agitational efforts had not brought the rapid results he had anticipated, led him to retreat more and more from the work of day-to-day propaganda.

For years he lived in virtual retirement in the outer suburbs of London and, at the end, as far away as Brighton, only returning to the capital for brief periods of research or to deliver occasional lectures. When he went abroad in the years after 1896, it was either as a popular lecturer or as an invalid seeking to escape the English winter, which had become harmful to a constitution weakened by six years of imprisonment. His scientific and literary work and his continually growing correspondence made heavy demands on his time, and, from 1903, events in his own country led him to turn away from immediate English problems towards those of the Russian revolutionary movement, in which, as the most distinguished emigré in Western Europe, he played a significant role. And again, particularly from 1912, we find an increasing preoccupation in power politics, which arose largely out of his concern with Russian affairs and which led to his support of the First Great War and a never fully healed break with the main stream of the libertarian movement whose apostle he had been for so long.

In addition to the varied pattern of these activities and developments, it is necessary for us to give at least brief attention to the wide circle of men and women of literary, scientific and political importance with whom Kropotkin was on cordial and often intimate terms during his residence in England. For it is always necessary to remember that, while in Russia, Switzerland and France he had been one of a persecuted minority, in the Victorian England that had fêted Garibaldi and Kossuth and given tolerant hospitality to political refugees of every land and creed, he appeared as a romantic figure, half saint and half hero—an image enhanced, although he himself would have been the last to take conscious advantage of the fact, by his aristocratic origin. Many undoubtedly valued him for his amiable personality and wide culture, but some at least of those who sought his acquaintance were drawn by the sensational story of the anarchist prince.

While this period forms a broadly homogeneous part of Kropotkin's life, it is impossible to discuss its various aspects and activities within one chapter of the present book. The present chapter will therefore give the main outline of his residence in England, his social and scientific work, his contact with the British labour movement, his friendships and the general background of his personal life. A second chapter will discuss the journeys to America and the Continent between 1886 and 1914, and Kropotkin's links with international movements. It will be followed by an exposition of the ideas put forward in his main sociological and scientific writings; and a fourth chapter will describe his attitude towards Russian affairs during the whole period from his escape in 1876 until the eve of his return to his own country after the February Revolution of 1917, and will deal also with his related attitude towards the Great War. Afterwards, the story of the unhappy years from his return to Russia until his death in 1921 will be told as a single unified narrative.

II

After Kropotkin left prison in January 1886, England seemed his natural choice for at least a temporary home. Russia and Switzerland were definitely closed to him, the attitude of the Belgian authorities was doubtful, and it seemed certain that if he stayed in France the government would issue an expulsion order that would prevent a return. Germany he regarded with disfavour, because of its authoritarian tendencies, not only in the governmental structure but also in the social-democratic movement which at that time had almost complete control of the workers' organisations. Italy and Spain, after the disturbances of the 1870's, were going through periods of reaction and the only major European country in which he was likely to find freedom from direct interference was England, which, since he left it in 1882, had shown a great resurgence of activity and thought. The Democratic Federation, founded as a radical body in 1881, had in 1884 gone over to socialism and changed to the Social Democratic Federation. It was led by Kropotkin's friend, H. M. Hyndman, but its policy was Marxist throughout. In the same year was formed the Fabian Society. This reformist body, which later championed the cause of State socialism, included in its early days a number of members holding libertarian views. And in the following year the more revolutionary members of the S.D.F. split away from Hyndman and formed the Socialist League, led by William Morris. These three bodies were in the van of an awakening movement of great breadth and vitality, and from this period dates the rise of modern British socialism.

As yet there was no English-speaking anarchist movement, but a leavening of individual anarchists permeated the various socialist groups. In the Fabian Society was Mrs Charlotte Wilson, later to become a close collaborator of Kropotkin. She was a Girton graduate and the wife of a London stockbroker;

contemporary reports described her as an intelligent and capable woman on the "right side" of middle age, with an appearance influenced by the æsthetic modes of the 1880's. She lived in Hampstead, but on her conversion to socialism assumed a simpler way of life in a cottage at the edge of the Heath. She was a founder member of the Fabian Society, and in December 1884 was elected, with Bernard Shaw and three others, to its first executive committee. She had been interested in anarchism through the reports of the Lyons trials, and a few months later became a convinced devotee of Kropotkin's ideas. In these early days, before the bitterness of Continental struggles among socialist factions had reached England, there was much mutual tolerance, and Mrs Wilson was thus able to publish two of the earliest English articles on anarchist communism in *Justice*, the organ of the S.D.F., and also to devote the fourth Fabian tract to this subject. Indeed, the interest in anarchism was so widespread that in 1885 even the respectable *Contemporary Review* commissioned Elisée Reclus to write on the idea. A strong anarchist current existed within the Socialist League, led by Mainwaring, Kitz and Lane. The last two had attended the Revolutionary Socialist Congress of 1881, and Lane, an elderly man who remembered the enclosure of the commons in the early part of the century, issued in 1887 his *Anti-Statist, Collectivist and Revolutionary Manifesto*, the first English anarchist pamphlet since Godwin and his immediate disciples.

Outside the main stream of the socialist movement was Henry Seymour, an individualist who supported the neo-Proudhonist ideas of the American Benjamin Tucker, editor of the periodical *Liberty* and protagonist of a form of economic organisation based on individual property, as distinct from accumulated property, and bearing a close resemblance to the distributist ideas later put forward by such writers as G. K. Chesterton. Seymour, who afterwards became an enthusiastic Baconian, published from Tunbridge Wells in 1883 the first English translation of Bakunin's *God and the State*, and in 1885 launched an individualist periodical called *The Anarchist*.

In addition to these English pioneers, there was a considerable body of Continental refugees who upheld libertarian socialism. These included a number of Germans, survivors of the group which had gathered round Johann Most, the stormy

German social-democratic deputy who turned anarchist, published *Freiheit* as an emigré paper in London, and later transferred his activities and his paper to New York, where he had a large influence on the immigrant workers. These Germans, together with some Frenchmen and a scattering of other nationalities, gathered in a number of clubs in the West End, of which the most celebrated were the International Club, later to become the Communist Club, in Rose Street, Soho and the Autonomie Club, in Windmill Street, off Tottenham Court Road. The French were at first mostly exiles from the Commune, but during the 1890's there came a second wave of refugees from police persecution. Half a dozen ephemeral French anarchist sheets appeared in London between 1890 and 1893, and in 1894 *Le Pere Peinard* was published there for some months. In the East End there was a growing movement among the Jewish immigrants from eastern Europe, who up to 1914 formed the most numerically strong nucleus of libertarian socialism in Britain. Their activities centred round the International Club in Berners Street, which was founded in 1885; in the same year they began to publish a Yiddish anarchist paper, *Der Arbeiterfreund*.

With all this activity, Kropotkin felt there was an encouraging prospect in England. Moreover, he had already been assured a means of expression, for on the 20th January, 1886, he told his Geneva friend, Herzig: "I am called to London to found an anarchist (English) paper; the means are existent and I will get to work busily". It is not certain from whom the "call" came, but it was very probably from Charlotte Wilson.

Kropotkin delayed his departure until after his lecture in Paris on "Anarchy in Socialist Evolution", and then, in the early days of March, left immediately for London. Here he was welcomed by many friends, and went first to stay for about six weeks, until he and his wife could find their own house, with Stepniak, who was now living in Alma Square, St John's Wood.

The founding of an anarchist periodical was one of Kropotkin's first concerns, and it seems certain that the original Freedom Group began in March, or at the latest in the first half of April. The first members seem to have been Kropotkin and his wife, Charlotte Wilson, Dr Burns Gibson, and one or two others. It was never intended as anything but a working group, for the purpose of publishing written propaganda and organising lectures. Its membership was always limited and confidential, and this was due, not to a desire for the inverted sensationalism of secret societies, but merely to the fact that, in this last refuge from arbitrary authority, Kropotkin had no desire for his activities to become known unnecessarily.

The new group did not immediately publish its own magazine. Henry Seymour, who had been in correspondence with Kropotkin at Clairvaux, offered the hospitality of his paper, and for a while the Freedom Group worked through *The Anarchist.* The invitation does not appear to have been wholly disinterested, since Seymour was in difficulties and the funds which the Freedom Group already possessed enabled them to contribute towards his costs. He abruptly declared himself converted to Kropotkin's ideas, and the magazine assumed a sub-title declaring its adherence to anarchist communism.

Meanwhile, it was not only anarchists who welcomed Kropotkin. The Socialist League invited him to speak at its first Commune anniversary meeting on 18th March. According to the *Commonweal,* he prophesied hopefully that "the social revolution . . . was approaching rapidly, and it was being brought about by giant strides, not so much by us as by the bungling and avarice of the ruling classes", adding, "while they have no clothes to wear sufficient to keep out the weather, it is not the pleasure of the working classes to manufacture fine robes for Indian rajahs or Russian princes". On this occasion he met William Morris for the first time, and they soon became cordial friends.

There followed the first of those illnesses which were to grow steadily more frequent and severe during his residence in England. On the 11th April he wrote to Morris, still from St John's Wood, apologising for the fact that a week's bronchitis had prevented him from replying to an invitation to write for the *Commonweal.* The invitation he declined, saying, in fluent but not yet idiomatically perfect English:

"All my time is so taken that I have not even the necessary hours of rest—necessary for the health, of course. So even with the best will I could do nothing. Even for my child, the *Revolté,* I see with some anxiousness that we shall soon be compelled to make it appear weekly, and that I shall be bound to give it some two days, or more, every week, instead of every fortnight. Moreover, I have already promised to our London friends to help them a little in giving a new start to *The Anarchist*.

"And besides, or rather above the newspaper work, there is so much work to do for elaborating the principles of our anarchist philosophy which, like each new system of thought, require sound labour."

During April he succeeded in finding a house at Harrow, and moved there on the 18th. A correspondent, who was a boy at the time of Kropotkin's arrival in Harrow and who used to deliver fruit to his house, remarks that it was "a cheap, newly built cottage near the foot of the hill, just off the Pinner Road, in a new road—Boxborough Road—that had not been made up, in a district then called 'New-found-out'." There was not much money for furniture, about which Kropotkin cared little, and the same writer tells us that, by English standards, the cottage had an appearance of "pitiful poverty"—"there was no carpet and no table-cloth, everything being bare". However, by this time Chaikovsky had arrived in England from America and settled near Harrow. In his travels he had learnt carpentry, and with his help Kropotkin built a great deal of the simpler furniture for the cottage, and particularly for the study, enjoying himself in this manual work.

Despite the hurried activity of the past weeks, he had not recovered from the psychological effects of his imprisonment, and his first reaction after the move to Harrow was to withdraw into his work. Early in May he wrote to the German revolutionary, Victor Dave, also exiled in London:

"You know what it means to come out of prison, when work has fallen behind, when it is necessary to work persistently, when one has to hurry. Still worse when the release comes suddenly. This is why I did not go anywhere and have not walked farther than two miles from our home for the past eighteen days we have spent here. I shall remain at home for another fifteen or twenty days or a month, except to go out for a few hours to make notes at the British Museum."

However, there was one relaxation he and Sophie enjoyed, and that was cultivating their garden, "a small plot of heavy London clay". They continued the experiments in intensive cultivation begun at Clairvaux, and, besides growing vegetables, erected a crude greenhouse in which a single vine brought them every year fifty pounds of grapes for half an hour's pruning and a barrow of manure, as Kropotkin says with pride.

In addition, he began to take extended walks in the neighbourhood of Harrow, then a small town completely detached from London, and in one of his later books he describes the distress he felt at seeing the badly tended meadows, stretching as far as he could look, which should have been covered with well-cultivated market gardens to feed the people of London.

The Kropotkins had hardly settled in Harrow when Sophie was seized with a violent attack of typhoid fever, which for a fortnight kept Peter in acute anxiety. However, by the 6th June he was writing to Dave that her recovery had already begun, and her convalescence was assisted, he says in his *Memoirs*, by a course of work in the garden which proved "more completely restorative than a stay in the very best sanatorium".

Indeed, they could hardly have afforded even a poor sanatorium, for next month Kropotkin had to refuse writing for Most's *Freiheit* because, with his articles for *Le Revolté* and "the work which gives me means of existence", he could not find time to add to his commitments. At this time he resumed his notes for *Nature* and commenced the articles which began to appear in *The Nineteenth Century* early in the following year; the first of these was "The Scientific Bases of Anarchy", followed later in 1887 by "The Coming Anarchy". He also re-established contact with *The Times*, and, besides his small scientific items, sent a number of letters to that paper.

In the summer of 1886 occurred one of the most tragic incidents in Kropotkin's life. His brother Alexander had vegetated in Siberia for twelve years after his arrest in 1874, successive committees having increased the term of his exile. At last, October 1886 seemed a definite date of release, and in anticipation Alexander sent his family back to Russia. As soon, however, as he was alone, he seemed overcome with despair for the future; his estates had been sequestrated, and, according to a Russian paper, *The Eastern Review*, he had only about £30 left, while he could not look forward with confidence to earning a living, since he would probably be forced to live in some wretched provincial town, cut off entirely from the contacts necessary for scientific work. On the 6th August he shot himself. To Peter, who had retained all these years his attachment for Alexander, the event came as "a heavy stroke", and he tells us that "a dark cloud hung upon our cottage for many months".

Nevertheless, towards the end of 1886 he began to move into a wider circle of activity. The association of the Freedom Group with Seymour had not succeeded; the latter evidently wished to keep a close control over the contents of *The Anarchist*, and a number of references in later issues of the paper, which continued until 1888, suggest personal friction with Mrs Wilson and a feeling that Kropotkin held his anarchist communist doctrines too much to the exclusion of the individualism from which Seymour was not wholly converted.

Kropotkin and his friends decided to withdraw from *The Anarchist*, and in October 1886 appeared the first issue of *Freedom*. Most of the work had been done by Kropotkin and Mrs Wilson, the latter becoming editor. The launching of the paper was assisted by friends outside the group; until June 1888 the type was composed at the printing office of the Socialist League, an arrangement made by William Morris, while Annie Besant lent the hospitality of the Freethought Publishing Company for office headquarters.

The first number of *Freedom* is a four-page sheet, with articles, foreign news, brief notes and a poem, all unsigned, as well as a manifesto representing the views of Kropotkin and his friends at this time.

It opens with some generalisations upon human slavery, and identifies slavery with the institution of property in our own time.

"Therefore, we are Socialists, disbelievers in Property, advocates of the equal claims of each man and woman to work for the community as seems good to him or her—calling no man master—and of the equal claim of each to satisfy, as seems to good him, his natural needs from the stock of social wealth he has laboured to produce. We look for this socialisation of wealth not to restraints imposed by authority upon property, but to the removal, by the direct personal action of the people themselves, of all the restraints which serve property against the claims of popular justice."

ELISÉE RECLUS

There follows a condemnation of laws as the means of upholding anti-social authority, and a statement that "social feeling, and the social habits formed and corrected by common experience, are the actual cement of associated life". Hence the editors look to the abolition of all arbitrary restraints and declare that:

". . . We are Anarchists, disbelievers in the government of man by man in any shape and under any pretext. The human freedom to which our eyes are raised is no negative abstraction of licence for individual egotism, whether it be massed collectively as majority rule or isolated as personal tyranny. We dream of the positive freedom which is essentially one with social feeling; of free scope for the social impulses, now distorted and compressed by Property, and its guardian the Law; of free scope for that individual sense of responsibility, of respect for self and for others, which is vitiated by every form of collective interference, from the enforcing of contracts to the hanging of criminals; of free scope for the spontaneity and individuality of each human being, such as is impossible when one hard-and-fast line is fitted to all conduct. . . .

"We believe each sane adult human being to possess an equal and indefeasible claim to direct his life from within by the light of his own consciousness, to the sole responsibility of guiding his own action as well as forming his own opinions. . . . We deprecate as a wrong to human nature, individually, and therefore collectively, all use of force for the purpose of coercing others; but we assert the social duty of each to defend, by force if need be, his dignity as a free human being, and the like dignity in others, from every form of insult and oppression. . . ."

This statement was declared to be "the touchstone" by which *Freedom* purposed "to try the current ideas and modes of action of existing society", and it certainly gives a fair idea of the general attitude of this paper with which Kropotkin was associated for the next twenty-eight years. He willingly added to his already heavy commitments the writing of at least one fairly long article a month for *Freedom*—unsigned in the early days—and during the next three years contributed a whole series in which the social question is examined from many angles, dealing, from an especially English point of view, with similar problems to those discussed in *The Conquest of Bread.*

About the same time he began to deliver a series of lectures in London and various provincial towns. The preparatory work of the socialist societies had created a public interest in social reconstruction, and the novelty of anarchist communism, combined with the glamour of Kropotkin's personal fame, provided attentive and even enthusiastic audiences. In this way he visited "nearly every large town of England and Scotland", and he tells us that:

"As I had, as a rule, accepted the first invitation I received to stay the night after the lecture, it consequently happened that I stayed one night in a rich man's mansion, and the next night in the narrow abode of a working-class family. Every night I saw considerable numbers of people of all classes; and whether it was in the worker's small parlour or in the reception-rooms of the wealthy, the most animated discussions went on about socialism and anarchism till a late hour of the night—with hope in the workman's home, with apprehension in the mansion, but everywhere with the same earnestness."

Among the rich, he says, he "seldom heard the justice of the socialist contention merely denied, or described as sheer nonsense"; on the other hand there existed the strong conviction that England was not a revolutionary country and that the workers here would be content with the gradual amelioration of their standard of living. Similarly, among the workers, he found less concern for broad principles than for details of constructive realisation in those industrial fields which they seem to have regarded the State as incapable of administering.

Early in November he went to Newcastle, where he met once again his friend Joseph Cowen and R. Spence Watson, founder of The Friends of Russian Freedom. But his most important trip this year was to Scotland, where he lectured, among other places, at Glasgow, Edinburgh and Falkirk. At Glasgow, where he spoke under the auspices of the Socialist League on the 27th November, he was received with enthusiasm, and an audience of two thousand people heard him lecture on "Socialism, Its Growing Force and Final Aim". In Edinburgh he stayed with John Stuart Blackie, the classical scholar and translator of Aeschylus, and on this occasion he made the acquaintance of a number of men who were later to be among his closest scientific friends. One was James Mavor, another was Patrick Geddes, the biologist, who later shared Kropotkin's views on many sociological matters. At the house of Geddes Kropotkin also met Nansen, the Polar explorer, then a young man studying at Edinburgh.

Remembering this meeting, Mavor has given the best portrait we have of Kropotkin at this period, when he was forty-two and still at the height of his vigour.

"He was short, not more than five and a half feet, slight in build, with unusually small feet, a slender waist and broad shoulders. He had a short neck and a large head. He wore a full brown beard, seldom trimmed and never lacking its distinctive character. The top of his head was destitute of hair, but on the sides and back of it his dark-brown hair was ample. His eyes sparkled with genius, and when he was roused became almost incandescent. His manner had about it the air of a court; but with his friends his affectionate solicitude was the outcome of a sincere and warm heart. He wrote in English with accuracy and distinct sense of style, and he wrote in French with equal facility and distinction, but in speaking the languages his accent was by no means perfect."

In these early years Kropotkin was liable to commit some odd lapses of pronunciation, but later his English became very fluent, although in writing it often needed polishing by his friends. He was indeed a very accomplished linguist, for he could speak German and Italian, had a working knowledge of the Scandinavian tongues, besides Dutch and Finnish, and during his period in Siberia had picked up an acquaintance with Mongol, Manchu, and other Far Eastern languages.

During this period of intense activity, at the end of 1886, Alexander Kropotkin's wife came from Russia to stay for some months at Harrow. Her health had been broken by the trials of Siberian life and the shock of her husband's suicide, but under the care of Sophie she recovered quickly. It is to this visit that we are indebted for one of our few accounts of Kropotkin's domestic life in this early period of his residence in England, for his nephew, Nicholas Alexeivich, then a small boy, was in later years to contribute to the Detroit Russian paper *Probuzhdenie* (in 1931) a brief account of his memories of this and a later visit to England.

He tells us what we have already learnt from Kropotkin himself of the fascination which manual work then held for him. He also says that the family at this time lived very modestly, in a house that was plainly furnished and looked very empty, which no doubt explains the impression of poverty gained by other observers. However, Kropotkin was sufficiently well-off to afford the services of an English maid, who was later replaced by the nurse of his brother's children. At this time, according to Nicholas, there were comparatively few visitors to the Harrow house, and the most regular were Russians—Chaikovsky, Serghei and Fanny Stepniak, and an engineer named Linev.

In spite of his occasional periods of ill health, Kropotkin was very vigorous, and his nephew remarks, "I remember that our uncle astonished us with his adroitness in physical exercises, in bicycling, when that was still new in England". Kropotkin rode some kind of "penny-farthing", for "the wheel in front was enormous and the rear one very small". He entered freely into the play of the children, particularly when it was of a belligerent nature, for he himself was still in the stage of being fascinated by barricades and street battles.

> "He taught us all the rules of fortification (a science to which he referred with great respect, regarding it indispensable for a revolutionary) and made fortifications in the snow. We arranged desperate battles with our comrades, little English boys, with my uncle's benevolent assistance."

Kropotkin's sister-in-law was at this time completely destitute, for despite the efforts of friends within Russia, she had been unable to obtain restitution of the property sequestrated at the time of Alexander's arrest. So Peter added to his already heavy responsibilities by undertaking to help her with money from his own earnings. Nicholas says that he kept the family wholly during their residence in England, and Mavor records that the assistance continued afterwards.

It was not, however, merely a sense of family responsibility that prompted Kropotkin. He was naturally generous, and whenever possible would help friends who were in need and give to groups in which he was interested. Nor was his generosity confined to friends or comrades. The indignation over injustice which had brought him to anarchism was no merely abstract affair; he was touched by the sufferings of strangers as much as by those of friends. Louise Michel, who knew him well during her own exile in London, said that he "could not see others suffer" and that to hear of "the least misfortune brought tears to his eyes". He was well known to tramps and beggars, some of whom came every day to his home. "Kropotkin gave something to all of them. He also tried to spread his beautiful doctrine in the minds of these unfortunate ones." Perhaps the gift accompanied by an anarchist homily seems less meritorious, but all those who knew him well say that Kropotkin would have helped an enemy in want.

This generosity did not spring from any carelessness about money, for he was always extremely scrupulous in financial dealings. He had seen too often, in cases like that of Bakunin, how the merest suggestion of living parasitically had been used to discredit revolutionaries. He never borrowed or accepted gifts of money, nor would he take payment for work he did on behalf of anarchist papers or groups. All he needed was earned by writing for scientific publications or from royalties on books, which source was slight in the early years.

In 1887 Kropotkin continued to give frequent lectures, and began to work closely with the Socialist League. In January we find him writing to May Morris about talks at Hammersmith, where meetings took place in Kelmscott House, and in the spring he made another trip north, lecturing at Bradford to an audience of 1,200, several hundred people being turned away from the hall, and at Glasgow influencing the Socialist League so much that Morris remarked, "Kropotkin's visit has turned them a little in the anarchist direction, which gives them an agreeable air of toleration, and they are at present quite innocent of any parliamentary designs". Indeed, he was growing steadily in Morris's estimation, for after the Commune meeting of this year the latter noted in his diary, "Kropotkin spoke in English, and very well".

During April, however, his activity was interrupted by an event which gave him much joy and removed the heavy melancholy into which he had fallen at the death of his brother. On the 15th of that month his wife bore their first and only child. The little girl, he wrote to Mrs Blackie two days later, "came to life with some difficulties". He named her Alexandra, or Sasha, after his brother.

Kropotkin was delighted with the child; years later he said that after her birth he "overheard in my heart new chords vibrating", and he was certainly an enthusiastic and indulgent father. Five months later he was still expatiating to May Morris on the troubles of his wife, refusing on her behalf an invitation to stay at Kelmscott because, "It is so difficult to do so with a baby. A baby! Never one would imagine, without experience, how difficult it is to move for a mother who nurses her first baby." He thought he himself might visit his friends, but a few days later found the pressure of work too great, and was forced to write to William Morris, who had repeated the invitation, "I shall not be able at all to leave Harrow before I do not know how many weeks or months. Much work comes—always pressing. Probably no holiday at all will be possible this year."

The latter end of 1887 was marked by the agitation over the death sentences on a number of Chicago anarchists for alleged complicity in the throwing of a bomb which had killed some policemen at an Eight Hours' Day demonstration. To this day it has not been ascertained who actually threw the bomb, but the accused men had been responsible for a paper, *The Alarm*, in which they published a few articles on the use of explosives—the kind of talk that had gone on at the 1881 conference, had since been elaborated by Most in *Freiheit*, and had formed the stock comic relief of Irish Nationalist sheets for thirty years. Apart from these articles, which show almost no technical knowledge of explosives, there was no evidence against the men, but scapegoats had to be found, and in the panic they were tried and condemned; several of them were hanged, while others were sentenced to long terms of imprisonment. Some years later, when the storm had abated, the Governor of Illinois reviewed the case and found it a gross miscarriage of justice.

The news of the trial caused great indignation in those countries where free expression remained. Radicals, liberals, socialists, anarchists, freethinkers, all united in protest meetings, and on the 14th October a great gathering was held in London, addressed by William Morris, Bernard Shaw, Annie Besant, Henry George (the Land Reformer), Stepniak, and Kropotkin, while Oscar Wilde and some other writers associated themselves with the movement. However, these activities were of no avail, and on the 11th November 1887 the men were hanged.

Two days later discontent over conditions in London itself reached a sensational climax. The years 1886 and 1887 were characterised by acute economic distress and great unemployment, and the position of the workless, forced to live on the scanty parish relief or the assistance of charitable bodies, was desperate. Half-starvation was frequent, deaths from privation were not uncommon. The contemporary novels on slum life and the reports of coroners' inquests tell their own story. During these years, partly because of the preachings of the socialists and partly because of the resentment bred by their worsening position, the destitute Londoners began to invade the West End in a series of demonstrations intended to draw attention to the extremity of their need. Trafalgar Square was the centre of these activities; it was here that Morris, Cunninghame Graham, Burns, Champion, Hyndman and many lesser-known orators spoke from the plinths, and on occasion the demonstrators swarmed out to startle the wealthy with stones through the club windows of St James.

Instead of trying to remove the evident grievances, the government attempted to cure the disease by removing the symptom, and they accordingly forbade the use, sanctioned by custom, of Trafalgar Square as a public-meeting place. Sir Charles Warren, Commissioner of Police, issued an order that there should be no further meetings; the progressive groups immediately took up the challenge. On the 13th November, led by Morris, Cunninghame Graham and Burns, several large columns converged on the Square. Kropotkin marched in the ranks, and many other foreign exiles took part. A series of police charges and scuffles ensued, in a more or less indecisive battle. Burns and Cunninghame Graham, then a M.P., were arrested for inflammatory speeches, and received light sentences. But on the whole, with the generally hostile reaction to the police and the sympathy aroused at the trial of Burns and Graham, a victory had been gained for the cause of free speech and interference became less intensive. Kropotkin's part in this incident was slight, but that he should have gone at all, in his insecure position as an alien in the one country that offered a free refuge, showed the depth of his concern for such concrete issues.

At this time a number of circumstances led to an increased anarchist influence within the labour movement. Among these were the attention created by the Chicago trials, the general disillusionment with the "benefits" of parliamentary democracy, the personal unpopularity of Hyndman, and the good impression which Kropotkin had made among socialists and radicals. The Freedom Group expanded, and some of its recruits came from among the active members of other movements. But perhaps the most rapid spread of anarchist ideas was within the Socialist League, where a struggle arose during 1887 between parliamentarians and libertarians, with Morris trying to hold the balance.

Morris's position still leaves room for speculation. He dissociated himself clearly from the parliamentarians, saying to Bruce Glasier, the Scottish socialist:

"We should treat Parliament as a representative of the enemy. We might for some definite purpose be forced to send members to Parliament as *rebels*. But under no circumstances to help to carry on their government of the country. And therefore we ought not to put forward palliative measures to be carried through Parliament, for that would be helping them to govern us."

The kind of society he envisaged in his Utopian romance, *News from Nowhere*, differs in no essential from the free society sketched by anarchist theoreticians. But he refused to take the final step of calling himself anarchist, and, while in discussion with Kropotkin he admitted the latter's criticism of parliamentary institutions, he still thought that tactically they might be used, with caution, to facilitate the transition to a revolutionary order. On the general issue he said:

". . . What I aim at is communism or socialism, not anarchism. Anarchism and communism, notwithstanding our friend Kropotkin, are incompatible in principle. Anarchism means, as I understand it, the doing away with, and doing without, laws and rules of all kinds, and in each person being allowed to do just as he pleases. I don't want people to do just as they please; I want them to consider and act for the good of their fellows—for the commonweal, in fact. Now what constitutes the commonweal, or common notion of what is for the common good, will and always must be expressed in the form of laws of some kind—either political laws, instituted by the citizens in public assembly, as of old by folkmoots, or if you will by real councils or parliaments of the people, or by social customs growing up from the experience of society. . . . I am not going to quibble over the question as to the difference between laws and customs. I don't want either laws or customs to be too rigid, and certainly not oppressive at all. Whenever they become so, then I become a rebel against them, as I am against many of the laws and customs today. But I don't think a socialist community will require many governmental laws; though each citizen will require to conform as far as possible to the general understanding of how we are to live and work harmoniously together."

This is a very muddled statement. Morris attacks individualist anarchism and blandly asserts that no other kind can exist. But Kropotkin and all the great anarchists since Godwin have shown that the greatest level of individual freedom can exist only when men are responsibly conscious of the social good. Kropotkin was even reconciled to the idea that moral pressure might be necessary to deal with the irresponsible. The theory of mutual aid would probably have answered Morris's objections, but it was fully elaborated only after his death.

However, the anarchists within the Socialist League were not all followers of Kropotkin, and their attitude tended towards negative destructionism. In 1888 the parliamentarians, led by Eleanor Marx and Belfort Bax, left the League, Morris remaining with the anarchist faction. In 1890 Morris was ousted from the editorship of *Commonweal*, and the paper, which later described itself as a 'journal of anarchist communism', declined into badly written demagogy.

The experience dismayed Morris, but it did not lower his respect for Kropotkin. May Morris says their friendship was "undisturbed by this difference of outlook", and it seems clear that Kropotkin held aloof from the conflict. Indeed, relationships between him and the League deteriorated after the triumph of the anarchists within it. After 1888 the Freedom Group co-operated less with the Socialist League in lectures and meetings, and Nettlau, who knew many of the active people of this time, expressed the opinion that:

> "There was a latent lack of sympathy between the anarchists of the League and those of the Freedom Group in those early years; the latter were believed by the former to display some sense of superiority, being in possession of definitely elaborated communist anarchist theories."

Despite this division, there is no doubt that in those days the anarchists appeared to the State socialists as important rivals.

Admittedly, Hyndman and his followers did their best to minimise the claims of the libertarians, speaking disparagingly of Kropotkin's opinions and particularly of his objections to social-democratic methods. Yet Hyndman himself translated *An Appeal to the Young* and admitted: "The thing is a masterpiece, alike in conception and execution. Nothing ever written so completely combined the scientific with the popular, the revolutionary with the ethical. Anarchist in sentiment, here and there, it may be; but all sectional differences are merged and carried away in the broad sweep of its universal sympathy...."

The Fabians, perhaps because they then claimed to stand above the struggle of parties, were more honest than the social-democrats in admitting the relatively strong influence of anarchism in the late 1880's. Sidney Webb, writing in 1890 on *Socialism in England*, said that, although the anarchist movement was "infinitesimal in numbers, . . . the high personal character and intellectual attainments of its leaders enable it to command a respect which neither its strength nor its doctrines would otherwise permit". He was speaking specifically of Kropotkin and Mrs Wilson and their work on *Freedom*. And Edward Pease, in his history of the Fabian Society, remarks that:

> "In the 'eighties the rebels were communist anarchists, and to us at any rate they seemed more portentous than the mixed crowd of suffragettes and gentlemen from Oxford who before the war seemed to be leading the syndicalist rebels. Anarchist communism was at any rate a consistent and almost sublime doctrine. Its leaders, such as Prince Kropotkin and Nicholas Chaikovsky, were men of outstanding ability and unimpeachable character, and the rank and file, mostly refugees from European oppression, had direct relations with similar parties abroad, the exact extent and the significance of which we could not calculate."

In those halcyon days before 1890 there was a certain co-operation between the sections of the progressive movement in England. The various groups shared platforms at public meetings, worked together in the campaign for the Chicago anarchists and the yearly Commune celebrations, and even invited speakers of rival viewpoints to address their own groups. Thus, though Kropotkin's connection with the social-democrats and the Fabians was not so close as with the Socialist League during Morris's ascendance, he did occasionally address their branches or take part in meetings organised by them, and was soon widely respected throughout the socialist movement.

III

During 1887 Kropotkin settled down to a pattern of life which can be associated with his residence in Harrow until 1892. In it agitation and the retired life of a scholar were combined, but the latter became more and more predominant.

Even now, agitation had ceased to be the main purpose of his activity. For the first time since boyhood he was enjoying a more or less settled domestic existence, and, while he never set any great store by physical comforts, there is no doubt that he appreciated the comparative tranquillity of a retired family life, devoted in fairly balanced proportions to study and manual work. To this must be added the fact that England was his last place of refuge, and he was not anxious to play unnecessarily a role that might embroil him with the authorities. He did not for this reason mitigate his revolutionary theories. But he no longer entered the day-to-day work of any group, was not among those who printed and sold literature, and confined his propaganda to lecturing, writing, and occasional attendance at the reunions and celebrations organised by anarchist groups and the London working-men's clubs.

Moreover, he still devoted much time to international work, writing regularly for *Le Revolté* and, after its foundation in 1895, for *Temps Nouveaux*, sharing, particularly in later years, in the work of the Russian anarchist movement abroad, and taking an especial interest in the colonies of foreign refugees in England.

His own work was as arduous and continuous as his health permitted. He wrote regularly for three anarchist papers, occasionally for several others, continued his work on the scientific papers and other publications already mentioned, and between times elaborated the sociological treatises which he had begun to prepare. In later years he also wrote occasionally in such periodicals as *The Speaker*, *The Forum*, and several American magazines, including *The Atlantic Monthly*, *The North American Review*, and *The Outlook*.

His lectures represented a heavy additional toil. In 1889, for instance, besides speaking on various occasions in London, his tours took him to Glasgow, Aberdeen, Dundee, Edinburgh and the Manchester area; the next year he visited Darlington, Leicester, Plymouth, Bristol, Manchester, Walsall and other towns. His subjects were various, ranging from prison experiences and Russian affairs to anarchism, from industrial organisation to the first tentative exposition of mutual aid. Always they showed breadth of learning and appreciation, and when he took an unusual subject, such as "The Poetry of Nature", delivered in London during 1892, he showed a wide literary knowledge, illustrating a rather pantheistic theme by the study of the Greek poets, and of Byron, Shelley, Goethe and Whitman.

Sometimes these lectures were given freely to assist organisations in which Kropotkin was interested; on other occasions he was paid by some local scientific or cultural society. But he was inclined to be touchy on this question. During 1889 illness had prevented him from doing his usual quota of writing for payment. A group of friends, including May Morris and Cobden-Sanderson, arranged for him to deliver a series of lectures at Kensington Town Hall. They solicited the support of a number of celebrities; some agreed, others refused, like Frederic Harrison, who said that, while he respected Kropotkin personally, he spent much time "in trying to show how futile and mischievous I think such teaching can be".

Meanwhile, Kropotkin set about industriously preparing a list of six lectures, dealing with the social problems of the nineteenth century. He was filled with doubts as to success, but said that, for himself, he would be happy to address the smallest audience, "be it but half a dozen persons or a score. . . ."

Unfortunately, when all the arrangements were complete, some tactless individual showed Kropotkin one of the letters which had been written to ask for support. He immediately smelt charity, felt his dignity attacked, and cancelled the lectures. However, it is characteristic of his sense of fairness that he suggested his bad health should be made the *public* reason for the cancellation, and even offered to pay from his scanty means the expenses already incurred.

It was during correspondence with May Morris over this

project that he talked of the hard work and strain which lecturing involved, saying:

> "It will take me two months, I suppose, before I could write down these lectures, and I must write them in full, because I cannot trust to my speaking in English before having couched the lecture on paper almost entirely, and I cannot reckon to do much work between the lectures, as each lecture fatigues me so much."

He turned his provincial tours to good purpose, for, with the habit of observation gained in his youth, he neglected no opportunity to inspect factories, workshops and coal mines in the towns he visited, while he always kept an acute eye on the state of agriculture in the counties through which he passed.

Although Kropotkin was not an habitual frequenter of the haunts of socialists or literary men, his friends were always welcome in his home, where Sunday afternoons became a recognised time of gathering. Even at other times intimates found an open welcome, though strangers had to undergo a fairly thorough screening by Sophie.

This was due partly to past experiences which had made the Kropotkins fearful of Russian agents—not wholly without reason, for Ford Madox Ford, who used at times to travel home from London in the company of Stepniak and Kropotkin, tells how spies would sometimes follow them as far as Hammersmith, where Stepniak occasionally dismissed them with the price of a drink. Spies and *agents provocateurs* were, indeed, a permanent cause of anxiety to Kropotkin. As late as 1911 he wrote to an anarchist friend warning him against a correspondent whom he suspected of seeking an excuse for a prosecution. He had also a rooted objection to reporters, from whose misrepresentations he had suffered, and Charles Malato tells the story of a French journalist from *Figaro*, who travelled out to Harrow, and, on the door being opened by Madame Kropotkin, said, "I have come to interview Prince Kropotkin". "Prince Kropotkin does not wish to be interviewed" was the determined reply, and the door was slammed. The journalist revenged himself by writing of Kropotkin as an "old idiot".

Perhaps because Kropotkin was so often away, Harrow was not the place of pilgrimage his later homes became, and we have not so many portraits of his domestic life as in the periods at Bromley and Brighton. But another child's-eye view has been sent us by Miss E. M. Heath, who later painted the excellent portrait now in the possession of the Royal Geographical Society.

"I used to stay with them at Harrow and though I think they were very poor then, they always had friends staying or visiting them—amongst others Stepniak and Chaikovsky. . . . It was a delightful experience to stay with them. . . . Madame Kropotkin was kindness itself, but was of a somewhat melancholy temperament and even as a child I was conscious of it, whereas Kropotkin was gay and brimming over with life and interest in everything—very warm and affectionate. His vast knowledge, his vast experience and his great powers of thought, I was quite oblivious of them. It was enough for me to listen to his stories and play the delightful game he taught me, where he was a bull-fighter and I the bull, hurling myself in vain on him."

A more serious Kropotkin at home is revealed in the diary of Cobden-Sanderson, who visited him at Harrow in March 1891, and noted:

"We were most affectionately welcomed. The little room was crowded with Russians and Swedes of both sexes. I had a long talk with Kropotkin. He was very animated. He hoped that all the necessaries of life would come to be made by machinery, so that they might be abundant and cheap. At present machinery was in the hands of capitalists, and was misapplied, and the 'hands' were enslaved. In the better times to come machinery would be the property of the commune or community, be directed to social ends, keep always going, and be worked by frequent and short shifts of all classes. The necessary wants of all being so satisfied, all could betake themselves in security to such additional labours of love as might please them, whether of hand, or brain, or both."

At this time he was hard at work preparing *Fields, Factories and Workshops*, his major work on economic organisation, and was naturally inclined to talk much of the subject.

It was during these years at Harrow that Kropotkin first made many of the friendships that were to continue through his life. And the circles in which he moved were certainly much more varied than in France or Switzerland. England was more like Russia in the sense that social consciousness was spread among individuals of all classes, and even those intellectuals who were not socialist or radical were tolerant of able men, no matter what opinions they might hold. The friends whom Kropotkin made in these years included some of the most talented men of the time, and they were to be found among scholars and literary men as well as among social rebels.

We have already referred to his friendship with Morris. He was a frequent visitor at Kelmscott House, and he was present, with Elisée Reclus, at the first private performance of Morris's farce, *Nupkins Awakened*, being delighted at the poet's "bonhomie and simplicity of manner". Of another evening, in 1889, Morris himself has left a vivid picture in a letter to his daughter Jenny:

"Kropotkin was very pleasant last Wednesday, though he was far from well: sitting with us in the dining-room after the lecture, he told us many interesting though sad things about our comrade in Siberia and the prisons, and how good and self-sacrificing the nihilists are out there. Also he told us this anecdote. . . . There was a little colony of Russians in the far west of America right among the Redskins; one day the Redskins fell on them and burnt their fields and lifted their cattle: now if they had been Yankees they would have shouldered their rifles and gone after the Indians, and shot as many as they could; and so have established a regular deadly feud between them. But the Russians bided their time and, watching an opportunity, got hold of all the women of the tribe and brought them home to their own block-house, where they kept them fast but treated them well. Then the Indians came to them, and said, 'Have you got our women?' 'Yes.' 'How are they?' 'Oh, pretty well, thank you.' 'Well, give them back to us.' 'Wait a bit.' 'If you don't we will fall on and kill you.' 'No, you won't, because then we will kill *them* first.' 'Well, give them back to us.' 'Presently, but you must do something first.' 'What?' 'Why, you must till our land again that you burned.' 'We don't know how.' 'Never mind, we'll teach you.' So the Indians turned to, and as they worked between the plough-stilts and otherwise, the Russians stood by and encouraged them, crying out: 'There! good fellow, how well he works! How clever he is!' And so on. Then the work done, they got their women again and they had a feast together, and were very good friends ever after. Isn't this a pretty little picture?"

It was at Morris's house that Kropotkin met W. B. Yeats, who agreed with him about the French Revolution, and it seems most likely that it was also through Morris that he encountered Wilde, who was later, in *De Profundis*, to describe Kropotkin as one of the two men he had met who had lived perfectly fulfilled lives. Other members of the Morris circle with whom he was on very intimate terms was the book designer, T. J. Cobden-Sanderson, whom he saw frequently up to the end of his residence in England, and whom he first met at a Hyde Park demonstration in 1889, Sydney Cockerell, the printer, and Ernest Rhys, then a poet.

On the outskirts of the pre-Raphaelite circle were other friends. William Rossetti knew and admired Kropotkin, but the anarchist was probably on more cordial terms with the critic's two children, who in their 'teens were devoted anarchist propagandists and ran their own paper, *The Torch*, which despite its juvenile staff acquired the contributions of Zola, Mirbeau, and Lucien Pissaro. It was through these young admirers that Ford Madox Ford, as a young man, first met Kropotkin.

During his very early years in England Kropotkin became acquainted with the painter, G. F. Watts, who immediately recognised a sympathetic spirit, remarking that such "extreme people" had an instinctive feeling about art which was ignored by the *dilettanti*. Another painter, celebrated in his time, who became intimate with him was Felix Moscheles, formerly the close friend of Mazzini, while a third, Walter Crane, was associated with him through Morris and the Socialist League. Crane mentions having encountered Kropotkin at Weddes' Hotel, in Soho, then a favourite resort for progressive intellectuals, and says that he "won universal respect and sympathy . . . charming all who have had the pleasure of his acquaintance by his genial manners, his disinterested enthusiasm for the cause of humanity, and his peaceful but earnest propaganda. . . . "

In the borderland of literature and politics he won the friendship of two other deservedly celebrated men—Cunninghame Graham and Bernard Shaw. Graham also was a nobleman who had abandoned his title to devote himself to the workers; he was, besides, a colourful character and a great short-story writer. He was much impressed by Kropotkin and the sufferings he had undergone; once, when he emerged from a short prison term in consequence of his political activities, he pointed out that he had endured far less than his Russian friend. He often spoke with Kropotkin at public meetings, in these early days in favour of the Chicago martyrs and nearly twenty years later to protest against the illegal execution of the educationalist Ferrer in Barcelona, and once in 1889, when Kropotkin delivered one of his popular addresses in Glasgow, Graham rode on horseback thirty miles through the rain from his home at Gartmore to take the chair.

Shaw was even more closely acquainted, and he has since remarked more than once that with Kropotkin he felt as he did with none of the early socialists, except Morris and the Webbs. From the beginning the two men differed in opinions, and Shaw would sometimes claim that Kropotkin's anarchism was in fact only what Englishmen and Americans called 'Free Democracy'. But there was a close personal sympathy, which Shaw expressed to one of the authors of this book, when he wrote:

> "Personally Kropotkin was amiable to the point of saintliness, and with his red full beard and lovable expression might have been a shepherd from the Delectable Mountains.
>
> "His only weakness was a habit of prophesying war within the next fortnight. And it came true in the end."

The remark about Kropotkin's prophecies of war is hardly an exaggeration. Even at the beginning of 1887 he was quite convinced of the proximity of a major European war, and declared in *Le Revolté*, "The European war is at the point of breaking out". He believed that not later than the spring of that year the German armies would attack France, and that Belgium had actually become an accomplice of the German imperialists by allowing passage through its territory to avoid attacking the fortified Vosges gaps. He recommended the declaration of revolutionary communes as a means of resistance. And after this, war became a continually recurring nightmare that haunted the next thirty years of his life, until, as Shaw said, it came true.

Among progressive political leaders Kropotkin enjoyed a considerable *personal* prestige, although he had little ideological influence over them. We have already mentioned his friendships with the leaders of the Social Democratic Federation, the

Socialist League, and the Fabian Society. Very shortly the limelight of the left was to fall on a new and more clearly political organisation, the Independent Labour Party, led by Keir Hardie, a Scot who preserved a singular personal integrity throughout his political career. Hardie became a close friend of Kropotkin, who would spend many hours trying to convince him of the dangers of parliamentary tactics. Hardie remained unconverted, claiming to the end of his days that political and economic methods could complement each other. But he would also say: "Were we all Kropotkins, anarchism would be the only possible system, since government and restraint would be unnecessary."

Another leader of the I.L.P. and the Labour Party, who received his first introduction to socialism from Kropotkin, was Philip Snowden. When Kropotkin went to Aberdeen in 1889, Snowden was working there. He says that he had then little interest in socialism, but that, one idle evening, he strolled into a hall where a meeting was being held.

> "The speaker was a short, burly man with a big bushy beard, who spoke with a foreign accent. I learnt afterwards that he was Prince Kropotkin, a Russian exile, though at the time the name conveyed nothing to me. His address was on the philosophical basis of anarchism, and so far as I can remember it advocated the arguments which he elaborated later in his great work *Mutual Aid*."

Snowden, indeed, did not take Kropotkin's lessons to heart, for *his* conversion to socialism led him to parliamentary methods and to a destination in the House of Lords.

Lastly, we must mention one socialist who was as individual a personality as Kropotkin himself. This was Edward Carpenter, who spent much of his life trying to bring about a more liberal attitude towards crime, and a better understanding of sexual deviations. (In the latter respect he was ahead of most other socialists—including Kropotkin.) In these early days Carpenter was carrying on propaganda in Sheffield, and Kropotkin would sometimes speak to the groups there, staying at the Commonwealth Café, which was run by the local comrades. Like Morris, Carpenter stood between the anarchists and the social-democrats, and in later years he contributed many articles to *Freedom*. He regarded as too naïve Kropotkin's tendency to find government at the root of all human evils, but agreed on the fundamental importance of his positive principles—individual liberty and free association. He himself might perhaps be described as an anarchist who did not imagine all problems would be solved when governments ceased to exist, and who realised that it was necessary to carry on the struggle against prejudice in other fields than the political. Personally he liked Kropotkin, respecting his "vigour, sincerity, ability and devotion", and he assisted him greatly in collecting information on the organisation of industry.

Carpenter, who had many interests beyond the merely social, can serve as a bridge to that other world of science and culture in which Kropotkin also moved.

With the geographers Kropotkin was on terms of particular familiarity, and Keltie, who later became secretary of the Geographical Society, tells how he quickly made himself at home in that institution, writing articles for the *Geographical Journal*, a work which he continued regularly from 1893 to 1905, and intermittently before and after this date. Apart from the British Association, at whose congresses at Nottingham in 1893 and Toronto in 1897 he spoke, he seems to have had little connection with other learned societies, and even from the Royal Geographical Society he refused to accept a Fellowship. His reason was that he could not join an organisation under royal patronage, and in this connection Georg Brandes, the Danish writer, recounts a characteristic tale. The Danes in London were giving a banquet to celebrate some national event, and Kropotkin was invited. He refused, explaining to Brandes:

> "I cannot come. Doubtless they will toast the King of England. In conformity with my convictions, I could not rise and this would scandalise the assembly. A month ago I was invited to a banquet of the Royal Geographical Society of London. The chairman proposed, 'The King'! Everybody rose and I alone remained seated. It was a painful moment. And I was thunderstruck when immediately afterwards the same chairman cried, 'Long live Prince Kropotkin!' And everybody, without exception, rose."

The tale is a token of Kropotkin's consistency, but even more a tribute to the courtesy and tolerance of English geographers.

When Kropotkin arrived in England the secretary of the

Royal Geographical Society was H. W. Bates, the great field naturalist who had spent ten years of pioneer work on the rich fauna of the Amazons, which he made the subject of one of the greatest nineteenth-century travel books, *A Naturalist on the Amazons*. Bates became much interested in his Russian friend's experiences and ideas; similar experiences as travellers gave them much common ground, and Bates was also one of the few scientists who was attracted towards the idea of mutual aid as soon as he heard it explained. This was probably due to his vast practical experience of field work, for his own masterpiece was full of instances of co-operation among animals and primitive man. Bates actually offered to write a preface to Kropotkin's book, endorsing its main contentions and its attack on Huxley's distortion of Darwinism. But he was dead before the first edition was ready.

Keltie, who succeeded Bates at the Geographical Society, was still, in 1886, assistant editor of *Nature*, and in this capacity provided Kropotkin with much remunerative work. Their friendship assumed a great cordiality during Kropotkin's remaining years in England, and Keltie was probably his closest friend apart from his old Russian comrades and a few English and European anarchists.

Keltie was a Scot, and so were three other scholar friends, Patrick Geddes, James Mavor and Robertson Smith. Geddes he saw frequently, though the actual records of this acquaintance are scanty. Mavor we have already noticed elsewhere as a close and constant friend. Robertson Smith was a Christian of independent spirit who created a great stir in the Scots kirk by defying its institutional authority, and afterwards became Professor of Arabic at Cambridge and an editor of the *Encyclopædia Britannica*.

Robertson Smith is connected with the somewhat shadowy affair of Kropotkin and the Cambridge Professorship of Geography. Boris Lebedev has asserted that Kropotkin was offered this Professorship but declined it because the authorities made a condition that he should abandon anarchist propaganda, and in this form the incident has been recounted by such writers as Roger Baldwin and Fernand Planche. Even on the face of it this version seems suspect, since it is very unlikely that an academic institution would openly impose such conditions, and we are much more inclined to accept a rather different account given by Mavor. According to this it was Robertson Smith who first thought of securing the chair of Geography for Kropotkin. But the latter, although he "felt very pleased that Robertson Smith's friendship had prompted him to so generous a project", decided that "he did not care to compromise his freedom by accepting such a position". It seems from this account, which Mavor had from Kropotkin himself, that the question never developed beyond conversations with Robertson Smith, and that no actual offer was ever made by the University.

Kropotkin's other most valued friend in the cultural world was Sir James Knowles, whom also he had met on his previous visit to England, and who, as editor of *The Nineteenth Century*, gave him a great deal of assistance. Knowles was the first man, apart from Bates and Geddes and outside socialist circles, to see immediately the point of Kropotkin's evolutionary ideas and to give a willing encouragement by commissioning the first articles on mutual aid. Kropotkin, according to Mavor, considered Knowles "one of the best-informed men in Europe", and in his company made the acquaintance, often fleeting, of many distinguished literary men of that day. On one of these occasions he met the declining Tennyson, and was not impressed. He thought the old poet reactionary, and considered he had no real grip on contemporary problems. Nor did he think much of Tennyson's vague pretensions to scientific ideas.

With this *memento mori* we will end this brief survey of the more important men whom Kropotkin encountered in these early days. There are many lesser-known people, almost anonymous workers in the intellectual and social struggle, whom it has not been possible to mention, but other names will appear as our narrative expands, and it will become evident that despite his adherence to a relatively unpopular and insignificant revolutionary sect, as well as the retirement into which he withdrew in ensuing years, he had, as much for his personality as his ideas, a recognised position in the pattern of English intellectual life for at least two decades, from 1890 to 1910, and perhaps even longer, as well as a very wide influence abroad. But for the present, having drawn the background of the first phase of Kropotkin's period in England, it is necessary to return to our narrative of events.

IV

During 1888 Kropotkin applied himself more than ever before to writing, and began the sociological work on which his reputation outside the anarchist or even the wider socialist movement was to rest. He set to work on elaborating the information he had collected on industrial organisation, relating it to the tendency for the centralisation of the Industrial Revolutionary period to give way to self-sufficiency among former colonial and industrially dependent countries. The first result of this work was a series of three articles in *The Nineteenth Century*. "The Breakdown of Our Industrial System", appearing in June, dealt with the effects of economic decentralisation on existing British production. "The Coming Reign of Plenty" and "The Industrial Village of the Future" discussed the kind of society that might be attained with the replacement of capitalist centralisation and monopoly production by economic regionalism, integrating industry and agriculture so as to provide a balance of intellectual and manual work, as well as the full use of intensive farming and scientific methods to lessen the burden of toil and at the same time increase its productivity. These were massive essays involving great research, and, after revision, much of their material was eventually embodied in *Fields, Factories and Workshops*.

During the same period Kropotkin delivered on 13th July, at the Socialist League Hall in Farringdon Road, his lecture on "The Wage System", in which he advocated the application in practice of the principle of free distribution and voluntary work—"From each according to his means, to each according to his needs". Among the audience was John Burns, then still a fiery trade-union agitator, who remarked that it was "a good lecture . . . full of interest to all", and said that he was "much impressed with his [Kropotkin's] earnestness and his impersonal way of dealing with his subject". Burns added, with the usual vanity of this future Liberal Minister, "Joined in the discussion, much to his delight!"

This lecture formed one of the best of those brisk and concise expositions at which Kropotkin was an adept. It was published later as a series of articles in *Le Revolté*, and then began to appear as a pamphlet in many languages; within seven years it had been published not only in English and French, but also in Italian, Portuguese, Spanish, German, Dutch, Norwegian, Czech and Bulgarian, while South American editions had appeared in Argentina, Uruguay and Brazil. This gives some idea of the wide popularity of Kropotkin's pamphlets and the rapidity with which they attained international currency.

The end of 1888 was marked by a resurgence of the campaign concerning the Chicago anarchists, with the difference that now the men were dead and already in the process of receiving sanctification as martyrs in the revolutionary pantheon. The wave of emotion which was evoked by their memory reached its height in 1888, when Mrs Lulu Parsons, wife of one of the executed men, came to England to deliver a series of speeches on the situation in America. Morris found her ". . . a curious-looking woman: no signs of European blood in her, Indian with a touch of Negro; but she speaks pure Yankee", and says that he was "much tickled by her indignation at the barbarous and backward means of communication in London".

Several meetings were held to welcome her, and these took on a tone of almost religious revival, all the main leaders of the Left, including Morris, Cunninghame Graham and Kropotkin, taking part, and the speeches being interspersed with the choral singing of revolutionary songs, as well as "Annie Laurie", the favourite song of Parsons, and, a more morbid choice, "Down among the Dead Men".

The organisers of these gatherings seem to have been sublimely unconscious of the comic side to such manifestations, and in reporting the meeting to bid farewell to Lulu on the 27th November, *Commonweal* actually included the following incongruous juxtaposition:

> "Kropotkin dealt with the decentralisation of social life and the increased scope for development of the individual that socialism would bring about, and insisted on the elevation of character that would result. The choir then sang 'Down among the Dead Men'."

In fact, on this particular evening Kropotkin's was much the best speech, since he did make an effort to lead the thoughts of the audience away from negative feelings of revenge to a more constructive attitude.

During 1888 and 1889 the discontent of the working class in

London ran high, and in July 1888 a wave of industrial disturbances began with the strike of the girls at the Bryant and May match factory. The conditions under which these girls worked, for tiny wages, were appallingly unhealthy, and Annie Besant wrote an indignant article of exposure. The mere realisation that even one middle-class person was conscious of their grievances was sufficient to propel the girls into action. They were completely unorganised, with no trade union, no experienced leaders, no funds and no ideas of socialism, but the public sympathy aroused by Annie Besant's revelations forced the employers to retreat, and the girls won their claims.

This was only a prelude to the greater events of 1889, and in the summer of that year a veritable industrial storm burst. About the middle of August a small dispute arose in the West India Docks. The dock company remained obdurate, but the only result was that in a few days all the docks for twenty miles, down to Tilbury, were idle. The most amazing feature of this dockers' strike was perhaps not the solidarity of the men, unexpected though this was, but the sympathy they received from all sides. In Australia a fund of £30,000 was subscribed in a few days. In England the dock companies found themselves almost completely isolated. Through Cardinal Manning the prestige of the Roman Catholic Church was thrown on the side of the strikers; the Lord Mayor pressed the dock magnates to enter into negotiations; even the police would not be provoked into attacking the men. But while this generous wave of middle-class sympathy provided a dramatic element, it was the solidarity and tenacity of the dockers themselves that brought a success few can really have anticipated.

Kropotkin was greatly excited by these events. Like Morris, Shaw and Cunninghame Graham, he went down among the dockers to inspire them with his speeches, and he made at this time a friendship with Tillett and Mann which lasted until his eventual departure from England. On Mann he had even some influence, for while Burns and Tillett both took the road that led to political power and a high place in the rapidly growing hierarchy of the trade unions, Mann remained very much a rebel and soon followed Kropotkin's example in doubting the value of political action. His later adhesion to revolutionary syndicalism, when he founded the Syndicalist Education

League, was undoubtedly due in great part to the influence of his anarchist friends.

Kropotkin had little direct influence in the Dock Strike. It was well started before he appeared on the scene, and whatever he may have said or done during its course had certainly less importance at the time than the actions of John Burns or even Cardinal Manning. He found the great lesson of the strike not in its adherence to any particular theory, but in the practical instinct with which the men set about organising their own affairs in a rational and efficient way. All his militant optimism revived, and he saw visions of a proximate revolution. Undoubtedly the great daily processions in which Burns marched at the head of eighty or a hundred thousand strikers through the City and the West End formed a spectacle eminently fitted to arouse the spirits of those who were naturally hopeful, and Kropotkin placed the blame for the lack of revolutionary action on the leaders; writing to Cunninghame Graham at the height of the struggle, he declared that Burns, with all these men behind him, could start a revolution, but was too cowardly to take the chance. However, while Burns admittedly showed a tendency to keep too much on the right side of the police, there is no real evidence that the dockers wanted anything more revolutionary than increased wages and better conditions. And these they gained very satisfactorily by the methods which Burns followed.

Kropotkin was on much more secure ground when he praised the constructive achievements of the strike. In *The Conquest of Bread* he instanced the way in which the dockers organised the distribution of food as a fine example of popular powers of organisation, and later, in 1907, he said in *Freedom* that:

> "The strike was a wonderful lesson in many respects. It demonstrated to us the practical possibility of a General Strike. Once the life of the Port of London had been paralysed, the strike spread wider and wider, bringing all sorts of industries to a standstill, and threatening to paralyse the whole of life of the five million of Londoners.
>
> "Another lesson of this strike was—in showing the powers of working men for organising the supply and distribution of food for a large population of strikers. The demonstration was quite conclusive."

At first it seemed as though the Great Dock Strike had brought added unity to the Left, as though a common sympathy for the strikers had welded the tiny sects into one stream of progressive activity that might assume a revolutionary character. A leading article in *Freedom* for October 1889, which if not actually written by Kropotkin can be taken as representing his views, talked at length of this apparent gain.

"Political humbug disappeared from the socialist programme as soon as our comrades in the various societies found themselves face to face with a live workers' movement. Evidently socialism has passed out of the select circle period, has become too strong, too widespread, to be managed by two or three groups with high-sounding names, and is penetrating the mass of the people. Federations, leagues, associations and unions, so organised as to restrict the initiative of action to an elected few, have been overshadowed in this strike movement by the individual action of their own members, and the common bond of union which the members of all the bodies seek has been found in the common cause."

The writer went on to discuss the foundation of a number of new unions, and expressed the opinion that: "These unions will all be useful in bringing the workers into line for the Social Revolution, and it is hoped that they will not be spoiled by centralisation." He concluded by suggesting that the workers were beginning to understand the inefficiency of State assistance, and that the strikes were teaching them to rely on their own strength in the struggle for emancipation.

Such a happy picture was not wholly unreasonable at the time. Then and for a while afterwards there did survive a genuine solidarity among the members of various socialist groups, so that even during the spring of the following year Kropotkin himself spoke at the Commune meeting organised by the S.D.F.

But in a comparatively short time it became evident that the Dock Strike really marked the beginning of an irreconcilable split in the socialist ranks, and a tendency for the main labour movement to aim at political success and, in following this aim, to assume a hierarchical structure. This was partly because the new unions justified anarchist fears by becoming centralised bodies instead of maintaining a diffused organisation based on the places of work, and partly because the strike itself showed to certain individuals the possibilities of attaining popularity and personal power through manipulation of working-class demands. Kropotkin summed up this development admirably in his 1907 article:

> "This was the beginning of the decay of the whole socialist movement in this country. . . . Petty electoral considerations took the place of the outspoken revolutionary language of the previous years. To preach revolution became a crime. To speak of socialism pure and simple was to indulge in Utopias. A reduction of the hours of labour and 'labour legislation' became quite sufficient topics of discussion. Social Democracy—that is, a compromise with the middle classes for sharing political power with them in a middle-class State—took the place of socialism."

Personal circumstances, and particularly his steadily declining health, as well as the change in the character of the labour movement, were soon to drive Kropotkin out of the main stream of progressive agitation. But for the brief halcyon days after the Dock Strike he continued his active lecture tours all over the country, and frequently appeared in London, at the Autonomie Club, the Berner Street Club in the East End, the South Place Hall and the Athenæum in Tottenham Court Road, then used for lectures by the various socialist groups.

It was about this period that the journalist, H. W. Nevinson, who soon became one of Kropotkin's close friends and admirers, first heard him at the Autonomie Club. Nevinson was then associated with the International Sunday School, which Louise Michel started in 1890 for training children in good anarchist principles, and his work brought him to the Charlotte Street area in which the Autonomie Club was situated. He tells us that it was held in a cellar, and was crowded with the various foreign refugees and English enthusiasts for anarchism who at that period frequented or inhabited this part of London. He then gives some interesting comments on Kropotkin's appearance and his way of speaking:

> "Anarchists do not have a chairman, but when enough of us had assembled a man stood up and began to speak. His pronunciation was queer until one grew accustomed to it ('own' rhymed with 'town', 'law' with 'low', and 'the sluffter fields of Europe' became a kindly joke among us). He began with the sentence, 'Our first

step must be the abolition of all low'. I was a little startled. I had no exaggerated devotion to the law, but, as a first step, its abolition seemed rather a bound. Without a pause the speaker continued speaking, with rapidity, but with the difficulties of a foreigner who has to translate rushing thoughts as he goes along. . . .

"Comrade Kropotkin was then about fifty, but he looked more. He was already bald. His face was battered and crinkled into a kind of softness, perhaps owing to loss of teeth through prison scurvy. His unrestrained and bushy beard was already touched with the white that soon overcame its reddish brown. But eternal youth diffused his speech and stature. His mind was always full gallop, like a horse that sometimes stumbles in its eagerness. Behind his spectacles his grey eyes gleamed with invincible benevolence. Like Carlyle's hero, he seemed longing to take all mankind to his bosom and keep it warm. . . . And yet there lived a contradiction in the figure of the man, for there was nothing soft or tender about that."

But in these years Kropotkin did not, and indeed could not, neglect his scientific and scholastic work. During 1889, his main interest was concentrated on the French Revolution, and he wrote a series of articles on this subject in *Le Revolté* and also a long essay, "The Great French Revolution and Its Lessons" in *The Nineteenth Century*. These were the preliminary sketches for the major work which he completed nearly two decades later.

Nor did he abandon the subject of integrated work, for in March 1890 appeared his essay on *Brain Work and Manual Work*, and during the same year he was gathering information to support his contentions regarding intensive agriculture and the possibility of increasing the output of the soil of Britain so as to support its present population. A trip to South Devon, where he stayed in the vicinity of Linton, gave him an insight into the wastefulness of the extensive cultivation (or rather non-cultivation) then in use in Britain, and little altered since, and he gave a dismal picture of the desolation he saw there as a result of the nineteenth-century neglect of home farming in favour of imported foodstuffs.

"Field after field is covered with nothing but grass, three inches high, and thistles in profusion. Twenty, thirty such fields can be seen at one glance from the top of every hill; and thousands of acres are in that state, notwithstanding that the grandfathers of the present generation have devoted a formidable amount of labour to the clearing of that land from the stones, to fencing it, roughly draining it and the like. In every direction I saw abandoned cottages and orchards going to ruin. A whole population has disappeared, and even its last vestiges must disappear if things continue to go on as they have gone. And this takes place in a part of the country endowed with a most fertile soil and possessed of a climate which is certainly more congenial than the climate of Jersey in spring and early summer—a land upon which even the poorest cottagers occasionally raised potatoes as early as the first half of May. But how can that land be cultivated when there is nobody to cultivate it? 'We have fields; men go by, but never go in', an old labourer said to me; and so it is in reality."

In contrast to this waste of the most fertile land in England, Kropotkin found in the Channel Islands an inspiring display of careful cultivation, by means of which an infertile soil was made to produce an abundance of fruit and vegetables far exceeding anything obtained on the ordinary farms of England, as well as to support large herds of milking cattle. The sight of the greenhouses on Guernsey moved him to almost lyrical admiration.

"All over the island, especially in the north, you see greenhouses. They rise amid the fields and from behind the trees; they are piled upon one another on the steep crags facing the harbour of St Peter; and with them a whole generation of practical gardeners has grown up. Every farmer is more or less a gardener, and he gives free scope to his inventive powers for devising some cheap type of greenhouse. . . ."

He spent his time inspecting gardens, interviewing growers, taking down information regarding methods and their results, all of which was later used in *Fields, Factories and Workshops* to reinforce his contentions on food production. He was so impressed that he returned twice, in 1896 and in 1903, to see what developments had been made in the meantime, and also to gain up-to-date information which, with true scientific spirit, he always endeavoured to gather personally.

He also turned his attention more seriously to biology and anthropology, and to elaborating his theory of the role of mutual aid in human and animal life as a factor in evolution. The seeds of this theory had been sown during his Asiatic travels, when he looked in vain for evidence of that intense struggle for existence between members of the same species which Darwin had postulated as the principal factor in natural selection, and saw instead a high development of co-operation. Then, during his imprisonment in Clairvaux, he had read the account of Kessler's Moscow lecture in 1883, when the latter indicated, in very general terms, the importance of co-operation as a factor in evolution. Kessler's arguments struck Kropotkin as providing an important contradiction to the conclusions of unreserved competition which the neo-Malthusian school had drawn in applying Darwinism to political thought. He therefore began to collect information from the accounts of field naturalists, and, as he had anticipated, found that while the scientists of the classroom and laboratory glibly followed Huxley in declaring the perpetual war of "each against all", the observations of practical zoologists indicated a prevalence of co-operation, at least within each species, and furthermore, showed that social species had a greater tendency to survival than solitary kinds.

The event which prompted him to elaborate these observations was the publication, in 1888, of Huxley's paper on "The Struggle for Existence and Its Bearing Upon Man", in which he compared the animal world to a gladiators' show, where:

> "The creatures are fairly well treated and set to fight; whereby the strongest, the swiftest, and the cunningest live to fight another day. The spectator has no need to turn his thumb down, as no quarter is given."

Huxley went on to apply his theory to primitive man:

> "Life was a continuous free fight, and beyond the limited and temporary relaxations of the family, the Hobbesian war of each against all was the normal state of existence."

Even in Huxley's own day the observations of anthropologists were showing abundantly that his view was far from reality, and that primitive man actually practised a highly organised tribal co-operation.

Encouraged by Bates and Knowles, Kropotkin set about systematising his information, and by 1890 he was ready with the first essay, a copious survey of "Mutual Aid Among Animals" (*The Nineteenth Century*, September and November). It was followed in the next year by "Mutual Aid Among Savages". Kropotkin intended to expand the series and embrace the incidence of mutual aid in later stages of human society, but he was unable yet to complete the extensive research, and the final essays were held over for some years.

This interruption was due partly to the fact that during 1892 he was preparing for publication the French edition of *The Conquest of Bread*, based largely on articles from *Le Revolté*. But in the latter part of 1892 he also undertook new work on scientific subjects in order to help him to earn a living. In September 1893, he wrote to his Swiss friend Dumartheray:

> "Already for one year and three months I have been writing for a salary on scientific matters, which are frightfully boring to me, and are absorbing my time and annoying me."

He then expressed a wish that this work would soon be finished, so that he might resume the studies in which he was interested—mutual aid and "the economic order of anarchy".

It seems likely that Kropotkin is referring here to the articles on "Recent Science", which he wrote for *The Nineteenth Century*. The first appeared in August 1892, and others followed at fairly regular intervals until 1901, comprising seventeen essays in all, in which were discussed with virtuosity a wide range of issues of contemporary scientific interest, including not only geological and biological subjects but also complicated chemical and physical questions, such as the liquefaction of gases, Röntgen rays, and the transmission of energy. Apart from their display of knowledge and understanding, these essays have the merits of a clarity and ease of expression which help the uninitiated reader to understand quite abstruse scientific problems. Taken in all, they represent some of the best "popular" scientific writing in Kropotkin's day. In spite of an appearance of moving familiarly in his varied subjects, he had to carry out much painstaking research, and his preparations would sometimes involve lengthy sojourns in London to be near the libraries, although, after having read the essays, one is obliged to dismiss as an exaggeration the statement of Cherkesov's wife that they "kept him busy for several months".

During 1892, while Peter was in the midst of this period of intensive scientific writing, the Kropotkins left Harrow and moved to Woodhurst Road, Acton. Although the reason for the move is not known, it had clearly been contemplated for some time, since in March 1892 Kropotkin wrote to Mrs Sparling, asking whether she could help him to find a house at Worthing, and saying that he had already been searching in Surrey but had found nothing he could afford.

The choice of Acton for a temporary abode was probably motivated by the fact that there was already a small colony of Russians living there. Indeed, Kropotkin's immediate circle had recently been augmented by the arrival of the Georgian anarchist Cherkesov, who now settled in England, and who, with his wife Freda, became very active in the Freedom Group. Malatesta, who had paid a brief visit in 1889, also returned in 1891, but while Kropotkin was much involved with science, his Italian friend was engaged on absorbing conspiratorial preparations and they saw little of each other. Kropotkin was also visited by a number of friends from abroad, including Elisée Reclus and Gustav Steffen, the Swedish chemist, as well as some students from Russia and the Balkans, one of whom, the Armenian Alexander Atabekian, devoted his life to introducing anarchist literature into Russia and later, in 1917, became the leader of those Russian anarchists who adhered most faithfully to the teachings of Kropotkin. During 1893 he was also visited by the Scottish socialist and friend of William Morris, J. Bruce Glasier.

Of the Acton days little record remains. There do not appear to have been many visitors, and this home seems to have been regarded as a makeshift until a house in the country more suitable for Kropotkin's health could be found. As before, the house was small and unpretentious, and it was at Acton that Sasha, Kropotkin's daughter, growing into a dark, lively, and, according to Bernard Shaw, "most lovely girl", first started her education at a local private school.

The year 1893 marked a turning-point, both in Kropotkin's career and in that of English anarchism. From this time the anarchist movement began to lose its contact with the main stream of socialism and declined into a neglected sect. Conversely, from the same period Kropotkin became more universally respected and more successful with the general public as a writer. As a symptom of this new "respectability" can be taken the fact that in April 1893 he was invited to address the conference of the Teachers' Guild, where he delivered an address on "The Teaching of Physiography", and that later in the same year he spoke at the Nottingham congress of the British Association. According to Ford Madox Ford, he also delivered at this period a number of evening lectures in biology at London University. And in 1894 the *Contemporary Review* contributed towards his sanctification in public opinion by publishing a long article devoted solely to Kropotkin as "Our Most Distinguished Refugee".

The decline of anarchism in England can be attributed to several causes. Firstly, the general tendency of the labour movement had by now swung definitely towards parliamentary activity. When Burns, Hardie and Tillett accepted the idea of a Labour Party and an eventual Labour government, their lead was followed with hardly any dissent. Outside the anarchists, the only important socialist who regarded this change with open distrust was Morris, and he was already a dying man. The disagreement over means of struggle drove a chasm between state socialists and libertarians. The logic of their position made the former devote all their energies to tasks associated with winning elections. The libertarians, disliking a socialist as much as a bourgeois State, and foreseeing the inevitable compromises that political life would involve, refused to share in such activity and denounced it publicly and privately. With such fundamental divisions on day-to-day policy it became impossible for the two factions to collaborate any longer.

In 1893 the Independent Labour Party was formed, with Hardie as its figurehead and Tom Mann as secretary. Although the Fabians, the S.D.F. and Blatchford, the influential editor of *The Clarion*, kept aloof, it was clear that they also approved *in principle* the adoption of parliamentary action, and only stood aside because of minor disagreements of procedure.

The split became obvious. On one side stood the Socialist League, the Freedom Group, and the various small English and emigré anarchist groups in London and the large towns. Their membership it is impossible to estimate, but the total circulation of all their papers, in English, Yiddish and German, was probably a good deal less than 10,000. On the other side were the remaining socialist organisations, including all the leading personalities except Morris and Kropotkin, and having a vast prestige among the growing trade unions. In the same year the Marxist majority at the Zurich congress of the Socialist International treated the anti-parliamentarian delegates cavalierly and voted that they should not be admitted to the next conference, to take place at London in 1896.

The anarchists had a difficult position to defend, and it was not improved by the continued split in their ranks. The Freedom Group and the Socialist League held apart until their final fusion in 1895. In the meantime, from 1892 onwards, there had been continued prosecutions, particularly of members of the League. The Staffordshire police faked a bomb plot in Walsall. Then *Commonweal* was suspended owing to its violent language, and further persecutions ended in its final collapse in the summer of 1894.

Early in 1895 Mrs Wilson resigned the editorship of *Freedom*, and after three months during which the anarchists had no means of propaganda, the fusion that had long seemed desirable was achieved, the rump of the Socialist League joined the Freedom Group, and *Freedom* was re-started, under a combined editorial board, with Alfred Marsh as editor. For the rest, the movement remained organised in scattered autonomous groups in London and the larger towns. But this unity came too late. Had a consolidated libertarian movement existed in 1891, it might have done much to enhance that free tradition which had been part of English socialism from its early Owenite days, but even then this would have been difficult. As it was, although the anarchists actually increased in numbers and activity after the reorganisation of *Freedom*, their strength in relation to the general labour movement became less and their influence was neutralised by isolation.

Another factor in the increasing unpopularity of the anarchists was the extension among Continental groups of individual terrorist acts. Terrorism in Russia had always been regarded as a special case, for the autocratic government seemed so atrocious that even liberals would admit extreme means of attack. But the assassinations which began to take place in France and Italy during the 1890's only aroused alarm, and while some of the acts against individuals might find excuse, it is difficult for an impartial person to justify deeds like that of Vaillant, who threw a bomb into a crowded middle-class café. This killing of innocent people only antagonised public opinion and induced many to regard anarchism as a doctrine of mere destruction with which the teachings of men like Kropotkin had little in common.

The English anarchists grouped around *Freedom* did not approve of these acts, and, while pointing out that the men who committed them were often placed in intolerable circumstances by the injustices they had to see and endure, left no doubt that they themselves did not advocate such methods. But there were individuals among the *Commonweal* group who spoke in a more violent way, and the police were only too glad to make use of this fact when they could discredit the anarchists in general. Nor was the state of affairs improved by such foreign visitors as the Spanish anarchist who shocked a *Times* correspondent at a meeting by giving, instead of a speech, an exhibition of target shooting with a revolver over the heads of his audience.

Even in the 1890's only a minority of working men were interested in any kind of socialist activity, and most of these were scared by extreme measures, so that the popular Keir Hardie lost his seat in Parliament for an outburst against the Royal family. If this happened to a celebrated socialist leader, there is little wonder that the members of the League, with their talk of an immediate bloody revolution which they could not hope to achieve, failed to make any substantial impression.

If, on the other hand, Kropotkin's prestige increased at this time, it was at least partly because in the minds of the wider public he was no longer regarded as a militant anarchist. And indeed, from about 1890 he began to withdraw from the closer work of the movement. Although he contributed regular articles to *Freedom*, he abandoned editorial duties, and never played the same active part in producing literature as in his Geneva days. When he spoke at anarchist meetings it was as a guest rather than as a member of a group. From 1890 to some degree, and almost completely from his removal to Bromley in 1894, he ceased to be the agitator and pamphleteer of the 1870's–1880's, and became rather the savant, living in retirement, to be visited occasionally, to be asked for advice and articles, to be welcomed when he made a rare appearance at some meeting or reunion.

If Kropotkin appeared thus to the anarchists, he seemed even more a scholarly recluse to the public outside the socialist movement, who knew him mostly as a writer of books and a contributor to *The Times* and learned periodicals. Until 1906 he published in England no book on anarchism. *Paroles d'un Revolté* has never been translated as a whole, and, although *The Conquest of Bread* appeared in France in 1892, it was not published in England for another fourteen years, by which time Kropotkin was already known as the author of an absorbing book of adventure, four very serious volumes on sociological and literary subjects, and as a Continental revolutionary. Even by the early 1890's the assiduous assistance of editors like Knowles had presented him as an important scholar, while the benignity and earnestness of his personal appearance at lectures made it impossible for his most bitter enemy to present him as the monster of sadistic destruction which the average Englishman expected when he heard the word "anarchist". So the natural tendency was for those of the public who knew and respected Kropotkin to dissociate him in their minds from the violent anarchists and to regard him as a genial idealist aiming at some pleasant but distant Utopia.

There was at least some substance in this opinion. Kropotkin never regarded his anarchism as Utopian, and always contended that it represented a method of social organisation which could be put into practice at any given moment. But, while he continued to believe that anarchism was ready for the world, he became less convinced that the world was ready for anarchism. As the 1890's advance, the note of extreme optimism begins to fade from his writings. The revolution, instead of taking place next year, or in ten years, will probably be far ahead, and even when it comes may only give a partial realisation of anarchy. In the meantime, a long work of preparation will be necessary before people become disillusioned with the fallacies of social-democracy, before they cease to be led away by patriotic appeals, before they realise that government under any form will be just the same and that they must rely on their own powers to achieve freedom, economic prosperity and social justice.

There are intervals of renewed optimism—the rise of syndicalism and the Russian revolution of 1905 provide examples in later years—but Kropotkin's tendency is henceforward towards increasing fear of disaster in the near future, though, indeed, he always remained confident of the *ultimate* triumph of liberty. And as he became more uncertain of an immediate realisation of the free society, his thoughts were less preoccupied with ideas of revolutionary action, less tinged with violence. In compensation, he became more concerned with inquiry into social construction and the scientific and ethical problems aroused by the search for freedom.

As early as 1891, in a speech at Leicester, he suggested that anarchy might come "by the ripening of public opinion and with the least possible amount of disturbance", and put forward the contention that anarchists should try to apply their principles in the organisation of social life here and now, since everything that tends to limit the functions of government and promotes the growth of community feeling is an advance in real progress. From this time he began to realise that the role of the anarchist must for a long time be one of permeation, of providing an alternative idea to State socialism.

The reasons for this new attitude are not obscure. The betrayal in the labour movement of the fine hopes of 1889–91, the steady progress of Continental reaction, the gathering threat of war, all helped to remove, for a man of Kropotkin's mental calibre, the basis on which any social revolutionary change might operate in the near future. He might say, as in December 1892, at a meeting to celebrate the Chicago anarchists, "After having had our period of isolation, during which period we have elaborated and strengthened our principles, let us now enter the 'wide, wide world' and propagate among the masses the ideas which we consider as the bases of the coming development". But at other times he showed himself aware that anarchism had become a current against the general trend of the left towards parliamentarism. It was perhaps for this reason that he retired more and more into the intellectual world where his ideas might play a useful preparatory role.

Personal circumstances, increasing illness, the desire for a more settled life as he grew older, all played their subsidiary part in changing his attitude. And a great deal can be attributed to the general influence of English society, where he found a tolerance in political matters which he had encountered in no other country, an atmosphere in which, like Marx, he began to think that here at least the social revolution might be achieved without violent disturbance. In 1899, speaking in a tone of unusual gravity and admitting that "Europe is traversing now a very bad phase with the development of the military spirit", he ended thus the *Memoirs of a Revolutionist*:

> "And now, in my fifty-seventh year, I am even more deeply convinced than I was twenty-five years ago, that a chance combination of accidental circumstances may bring about in Europe a revolution far more important and as widely spread as that of 1848; not in the sense of mere fighting between different parties, but in the sense of a deep and rapid social reconstruction; and I am convinced that whatever character such movements may take in different countries, there will be displayed in all of them a far deeper comprehension of the required changes than has ever been displayed within the last six centuries; while the resistance which such movements will meet in the privileged classes will hardly have the character of obtuse obstinacy which made revolutions assume the violent character they took in times past."

These words were written at the end of the 1890's, but they represent the conclusion of a development he had been undergoing throughout the decade. Optimism remained, but it was transferred from the idea of heroic revolutions on the pattern of 1789, 1848 and 1871 to the conception of mutation in society, analogous to the Industrial Revolution rather than to the French Revolution. And, indeed, for one who believed that the essence of revolution lay not in political changes but in the alteration of social forms and economic organisation, it was not an illogical view.

During these years the problems of violence preoccupied Kropotkin greatly. His own naturally gentle character had always been repelled by concrete acts of destruction, even though at times, and particularly in the years immediately following 1881, he had felt that there were certain circumstances in which they became the only possible means of protest. In his early days of the Chaikovsky circle he had helped to dissuade a young man who came to St Petersburg for the purpose of killing Alexander II. But later, when the People's Will actually assassinated that Emperor, he had found himself unable to condemn the act. When the wave of assassinations spread to Western Europe in the 1890's, and when he was faced by some of the pointedly brutal outrages committed in France, he felt less sure of his position. By this time he had passed to regarding violence, except when used in strict self-defence during a revolution, as harmful. It was an attitude Bakunin had also reached in old age. Ford Madox Ford, who saw much of Kropotkin during these years, is very insistent on this point, and even recounts one incident which deserves to be quoted, since, although it may not be accurately told, it clearly conveys a vivid impression.

During the coal strike of 1893, Charles Rowley invited Ford to a lunch at the Holborn Restaurant, to which also came Ben Tillett, Tom Mann and Kropotkin.

"As long as the discussion remained on general lines of the relief of suffering or even of strikes these leaders of advanced thought got on very well together, and that stage lasted for the greater part of the meal. But the moment it came to the discussion of remedies, Kropotkin's quietism acted like a bomb at the table, the Labour representatives being all for strong measures against authority. Kropotkin was all for non-resistance, mediation and propaganda, so that eventually we broke up in disorder after a deadlock in which Mr Mann . . . had gone on for a long time . . . exclaiming over and over again: 'We must destroy! We must pull down! We must be rid of tyrants!'

"But always in the pauses came the quiet, foreign accent of the Prince, who, with the eyes of a German scientist behind his gleaming spectacles fixed intently on his interlocutors, exclaimed gently and unceasingly: 'No; there must be no destruction. We must build. We must build the hearts of men. We must establish a kingdom of God.' "

We need not take all this very literally. Ford Madox Ford admits that he had never a good head for politics, and he was no doubt under a misapprehension when he talked of Kropotkin's "quietism" and his advocacy of "non-resistance", both of which ideas were opposed to his lifelong teachings. But the general impression of Kropotkin seeking to draw the conversation into constructive consideration of the kind of world at which the social struggle should aim is no doubt accurate.

At this period he was certainly much perturbed by the question of terrorism, and his attitude is well summarised in a letter to his friend Mrs Dryhurst at the end of 1893. After discussing the atrocities committed by the reactionaries in Europe, he continues, with regard to the revolutionary terrorists:

"There is a limit to human patience as well. Men are driven to despair, so they make desperate acts. . . .

"We may say that revenge is no aim in itself. Surely it is not. But it is *human* and all revolts have borne and for a long time will bear that character.

"In fact, *we* who have not suffered from the persecutions as they, the workers, suffer; we who, in our homes, seclude ourselves from the cry and sight of human sufferings, *we are no judges* for those who live in the midst of all this hell of suffering. . . .

"Personally, I hate these explosions, but I cannot stand as a judge to condemn those who are driven to despair. . . .

"*Force* will certainly have to be used to get rid of the *force* which maintains the present. But—this is a quite separate thing and many who condemn any explosion will take the rifle to fight against force."

He goes on to discuss the question of revenge, claiming that while it is in no way an anarchist principle, it is a human impulse which cannot be finally dismissed.

"One single thing—that revenge must not be erected in a *theory*. That no one had the right to incite others to it; but that if he keenly feels all that hell and does a desperate act, let him be judged by those only who are his peers, his equals in bearing those pariah's sufferings."

The reasoning of this letter is confused, but it is clear that Kropotkin had a strong personal dislike for violence, and sought to evade condemnation mostly out of a feeling of solidarity with the terrorists. They were outcasts, and he was not going to join the cry against them. It was an understandable human attitude, but it contributed little to the main discussion and either a terrorist or a Tolstoyan could have demolished with ease the reasoning behind this refusal to take a clear stand. Yet it must be granted that Kropotkin was in a really difficult position; the actions of these few terrorists, a tiny minority among the anarchists, discredited the movement in England

and elsewhere, and he found himself continually forced to defend anarchism against the accusation of being a creed based primarily on destruction. But he could on occasion put a good case against the accusers on this count, and these paragraphs from his speech at the Commune celebration of 1893 act as a permanent rebuttal of the perennial legend of the anarchist as the man with the pockets full of bombs:

"Anarchism is represented as *the* party of violence. But when I look back to the acts of violence which I have lived through during the last twenty years, I see the 35,000 Paris workers exterminated by the French property owners in May 1871; the attempt of the Social-Democrat Hoedel and the Republican Nobiling against the German Emperor, the attempt of the Socialist Otero in Spain, and in Italy that of Passanante, who was a Mazzinian more than anything else; thirty-two gallows in Russia, and upon them not one Anarchist; the Irish Nationalists' violence; and the Anarchists' acts of violence during the last few years; and I maintain that violence belongs to *all* parties, and that they all have recourse to it when they lose confidence in other means and are brought to despair.

"Of all parties I now see only one party—the Anarchist—which respects human life, and loudly insists upon the abolition of capital punishment, prison torture and punishment of man by man altogether. All other parties teach every day their utter disrespect of human life. Killing the foe, torturing him to death in prison, is their principle. For the interest of bondholders they will massacre the miners in the mine, kill passengers in a train, or bombard Alexandria, slaughtering women and children in the streets. They only ripen the fruit of their own teachings. The sacredness of human life! Yes, by all means; but society itself must first learn to recognise the sacredness of human life, and not teach the opposite."

V

It was in the late summer of 1894 that Kropotkin moved to Bromley, then a small Kentish town sufficiently removed from the spreading houses of London to be regarded as "in the country". His new home, called Viola, lay in Crescent Road, on the outskirts. It was, like his other dwellings, a small cottage —Ford Madox Ford has called it "troglodytic". Vines covered the outer walls, and there was a fairly large and, as always, well-cultivated garden.

In the house itself the visitor entered first a living-room, furnished scantily but neatly. A friend who went there towards the end of the 'nineties described the miscellany of scientific curios which formed its decoration.

"Opposite from where I sat was a tall glass case containing a variety of specimens of flies, butterflies, and other larger insects, all held on pins stuck in the back of the case. On the shelves in the same case there was a large assortment of small mineral stones of various sizes and colours; on the bottom shelves were a small bee-hive, an assortment of small pieces of metal, and a piece of tree with a root."

The casual visitor would be given tea with lemon and sugar in this living-room—sometimes by Sophie, occasionally by Peter himself; and it was here that his friends gathered on Sunday afternoons, a custom which became even more established than in the Harrow days—in 1897 he wrote to an acquaintance, refusing an invitation because: "Unhappily Sunday is a day when I must stay at home. It is the day when London friends may drop in, being sure to find us home, either at lunch-time or in the afternoon."

Close friends were admitted to the study, where they would find, like Rudolf Rocker when he called in 1896, that "the walls of his simple but comfortable room were filled with books to the ceiling, while the great work-table was covered with papers and documents". There would also be piles of newspapers on the floor, arranged, as H. N. Brailsford found, in an order which was disorder to all but Kropotkin, and there were home-made boxes and portfolios, full of papers and cuttings. The table, the work-bench and the shelves had all been carpentered by Kropotkin himself, and he had also bound many of the books.

His hospitality was wide, and in these Bromley days the list of visitors was extended far beyond the group of Russians who were the regular attendants at Harrow. Malatesta, Louise Michel, the Spaniard Torrida del Marmol and revolutionaries of almost every European and American country mingled with Fabians like Shaw and Pease, trade unionists like Tom Mann, Guy Bowman and Ben Tillett, artists like Moscheles, craftsmen like Cobden-Sanderson, writers like Nevinson and Ford, and odd figures of the literary half-world like Frank Harris.

The last has a tale of Bromley hospitality which is amusing, but need not be taken too literally:

> "Though the Kropotkins were in straitened circumstances, they always kept open house. There is an amusing story to tell of their hospitality. Madame Kropotkin would be preparing dinner for her small family of three persons. An unexpected visitor arriving, Peter would rush into the kitchen, saying, 'Sophie, add a little water to the soup.' A little later another visitor would appear and again Peter would hurry to the kitchen: 'Sophie, add some more water to the soup'. Often this process was repeated several times, and when the meal was served it was usually six or seven people Sophie had to feed instead of three."

When he describes Peter as a host, Harris expresses an observation made by all who visited him:

> "Peter's graciousness as a host was among his most lovable traits. He had the rare gift of making even a stranger feel at home in his presence. He was always deeply concerned in the personal life and struggle of the people who came to him. Knowing no fear for himself, he was ever anxious for the safety of others."

Sometimes, at these Sunday gatherings, Kropotkin would play the upright piano which stood in the living-room. On these occasions he usually chose revolutionary songs, because he probably thought his visitors preferred them, but sometimes he would play for his own amusement, and then indulged in the classical music he had learnt to love in his youth. But he had a live interest in modern music, and in his old age was still sufficiently aware of the new currents to show an active appreciation of Scriabin, then a very revolutionary young composer. As for the quality of his playing, opinions differ widely, and almost ideologically, for while many anarchists claim that he was an excellent pianist, G. D. H. Cole, who heard him in Hampstead when he was a boy, remembers the playing as "atrocious".

In addition to those who formed the regular group at Kropotkin's Sunday parties, there were others who came from abroad and called in for longer visits. Sometimes Georg Brandes would arrive from Denmark, and there were always Russians, like the philologist Stassov and Kropotkin's old friend Klemens, who came to stay in 1900. Both the Reclus brothers appeared occasionally on geographical missions, and sometimes "the grandmother of the Russian revolution", Brechkovskaya, would come to stay, dressed in the poor clothes of a Russian peasant woman.

Apart from the visitors, Kropotkin was on very friendly terms with his neighbours in Bromley. In appearance he was highly conventional, for he wore always the customary black frock-coat of the Victorian era and, although he spent little on dress, his clothes were neat and his spreading white beard was that of a savant rather than a Bohemian. Most of the neighbours knew vaguely that he was a "writer", and for those who were a little better informed and who watched with astonishment the odd-looking visitors he entertained, the fact that he was a prince compensated for any possible short-comings. The English middle class have long regarded the "eccentricities" of aristocrats with a tolerant veneration. For the rest, he seemed a hard-working, mild old gentleman, who was always willing to give hints about gardening and whose own achievements in that field were much envied.

The move to Bromley coincided with a return, after two or three years of more ephemeral work, to the studies which Kropotkin regarded as necessary for providing a sound theoretical basis to his social ideas, and very shortly afterwards he published the remaining articles in his series on mutual aid.

The years 1895 and 1896 were still largely concerned with affairs of the anarchist movement. In the first came the internal crisis, when *Freedom* was suspended for three months, but finally reappeared in May after the union with the *Commonweal* group. And in August there was a congress in London to discuss participation in the Socialist Conference of 1896. It was agreed that the findings of the Zurich Congress should be ignored, and that anarchists should present themselves as if nothing had happened. It was in the same month that the Cobden-Sandersons encountered Kropotkin in London," revelling in the affection of the Reclus brothers and living with them quite a 'dissolute' life—at the Geographical Congress and the British Museum".

At this period there came to Bromley the celebrated Russian-American anarchist, Emma Goldman, who had been speaking in the English towns, and who records a discussion regarding conditions in Britain. Kropotkin's remarks throw some light on his attitude at the time. "He said that England was a nation of shopkeepers engaged in buying and selling instead of producing the necessaries required to keep her people from starvation. 'The British bourgeoisie had good reason to fear the spread of discontent, and political liberties are the best security against it. . . . The average Britisher loves to think he is free; it helps him to forget his misery. That is the irony and pathos of the English working class.' " He seemed already to be losing hope in the British workers as a revolutionary force.

And this feeling was only reinforced by the disappointing events of 1896. It is true that in March of that year, when he was ill, with "fever every second day", he sent a confident message to the Commune meeting, in which he said:

> "A young generation of workers, fully conscious of the great task incombing [*sic*] upon them and fully aware of the great problems they have to solve, has grown since the Paris workers, twenty-five years ago, made a first attempt at solving the social problem in one free city. The next attempt will certainly be a real advance towards the solution of the great problem."

He was talking of the French workers, who were showing considerable activity in the early syndicalist movement. But even here the phraseology had undergone a significant change. He no longer expected the social revolution itself in the near future, but only an "advance" towards what was so indefinable that he had to call it "the solution of the great problem". The old sureness was fast fading.

The demands of a literary life were also causing him much discontent, and in July he wrote to his old friend Robin about his desire to give up the drudgery of intellectual labour.

> "I cannot continue any longer living entirely by my pen, I sink under the load, whereas if I went over to market gardening and the planting of corn I could give real teaching."

And it was perhaps because of this feeling that his own work was out of touch with the practical realisation of his ideas that he sent an encouraging letter to a Tyneside group who contemplated founding an agricultural community. He warned them of all the pitfalls they were likely to encounter—the internal friction of small groups, the difficulties of town workers embarking on landwork, the dangers of inadequate capital, and the deceptive path of asceticism. But he concluded by exhorting them:

> "Follow that path if it attracts you. You have a chance of succeeding better than your predecessors. In any case, you will not find sympathy lacking, and mine will go with you."

He had realised that the ways to freedom were many and diverse, and that none could be despised.

In July 1896 took place the London Congress of the Socialist (Second) International. As they had threatened, the social-democrats succeeded in keeping out the anarchists and thus making quite definite the division that had already existed *de facto* for some years between parliamentary and libertarian socialists. But it was no easy victory. Although the Germans and the English S.D.F. were in favour of the exclusion, the Dutch and French delegates and a number of Englishmen opposed it, and several anarchists actually gained admission on Dutch and French mandates.

This incident caused a temporary enhancement of anarchist prestige in socialist circles, since at a protest meeting on the 28th July there appeared not only the great international figures of anarchism, Kropotkin, Malatesta, Domela Niewenhuis, Gustav Landauer, Pietro Gori, Louise Michel, Elisée Reclus and Tortelier, but also the socialists Keir Hardie and Tom Mann, while Morris, Walter Crane and Robert Blatchford sent messages of support. There followed an anarchist congress at which Kropotkin took no active part, since, although in London during the congress, he was in rather bad health.

A few weeks later he summed up the result of the Socialist Congress as "the separation of the economic working-class movement from the semi-bourgeois political movement which, under the name of social-democracy or of parliamentary socialism, threatens to absorb the socialist movement of our country". He called on the socialists to reconsider their ideas, and to declare openly for the abolition of servitude and exploitation in all forms. It was a call in vain, as Kropotkin probably expected.

The year was further saddened by the death of two close

friends. During the autumn William Morris died. In the past two or three years he had retired from active participation in the socialist movement, and he and Kropotkin had seen little of each other. But mutual affection remained, and when Morris died Kropotkin felt that a good friend and a great supporter of the libertarian ideal had gone. In the obituary article for *Freedom* he declared that Morris's influence had played an immense part in preventing the labour movement in England from following the authoritarian course which social-democracy had taken in Germany.

An even harder blow came in December, when Stepniak, the comrade who had been with him right from the beginning, was killed at a railway crossing in Surrey. Kropotkin insisted on speaking at the funeral of his beloved friend; his words had a depth of personal feeling which he rarely allowed to appear:

> "It is hard for me to speak at the grave of my friend Stepniak, who was so young, so full of energy and hope, and so ready to work for the common cause—to continue the work which he had done for all his life since his very earliest youth. . . . He could not live in the narrow feeling of party worship—he stood much above that. And when it came to him to discuss with anybody whose opinions he did not agree with, he never abandoned his opinions, but in those beautiful, gentle and soft loving eyes of his you could see the very depths of his heart; he understood your emotions and warm-hearted feelings, which he was always ready to share with you. Only the great poets are gifted with such pure sympathy. . . ."

For many months he remained saddened by Stepniak's pointless death.

The next year began with the agitation over the tortures committed by the Spanish government on 400 republicans and socialists in the Montjuich prison at Barcelona, and Kropotkin spoke at the protest meetings during January. But in March he was again ill, and Sophie lectured in his place at Spitalfields. It was the first time she had appeared on a public platform and her subject was the women's movement in Russia. This was the beginning of a custom which assisted the family in its straitened circumstances, for a little later, with the assistance of Mrs Wilson and others, Sophie began to give lectures on chemistry and botany in Surrey and afterwards in Hampstead, besides writing occasional articles for such papers as *The Contemporary Review*.

During 1897 Kropotkin worked on the final draft of his first major sociological book, *Fields, Factories and Workshops*, which involved not merely the revision and bringing up to date of his articles on industrial organisation, but also the writing of the elaborate chapters dealing with intensive cultivation. This book appeared in 1898. But its publication meant no respite in the succession of hard work, for during his American tour of 1897 he had received a commission to write his memoirs as a series of articles in the *Atlantic Monthly*. These appeared during 1898, and then followed an offer to publish the autobiography in book form, which involved Kropotkin during 1899 in the enlarging of the original material to make the long and extremely fascinating book which was published early in 1900.

Indeed, the work on this book absorbed so much time that in December 1899 he wrote to Edward Clodd, the popular scientific writer, declining an invitation because of the arrears of work owing to the need to get the *Memoirs* ready. This letter, incidentally, contained some interesting reflections on nineteenth-century education, arising out of a conversation with Grant Allen in Clodd's house in which Kropotkin had defended the destruction of ancient monuments by the Communards. Now he said:

"Alas! demolition alone would not help and could only increase the 'poetical regret'. So long as *scientific methods of thinking* remain a closed letter, not only with the millions and millions, but even with the immense mass of men imagining themselves to be scientific (historians, economists, students of law, etc., etc.), so long the inculcation of these methods in school will be kept in horror, and the unscientific methods of thinking will be inculcated by all possible means. So long as three-quarters of the education of this country is in the hands of men who have no suspicion of there being such a thing as *scientific* (inductive and deductive) thinking, and so long as science herself will do everything in her power to preach most absurd and unethical conclusions, such as *woe to the weak*, then all will remain as it is. Belief in mysterious agencies, and the unreasonable need of man for ethical-political conceptions, will rebuild cathedrals and worship in one way at the altar."

The outbreak of the Boer War in 1899 distressed Kropotkin greatly, for he saw it as a further setback to his hopes for social progress, and he wrote to Elisée Reclus:

"Here we are experiencing a very difficult time. How passions are swamping all circles! I cannot speak for two minutes with an Englishman without being exasperated. . . . Worse than all this is that this war can very easily cause immediately another war with Russia and France; in any case, compulsory military service has already been decided."

His more pessimistic prophecies remained unfulfilled; the Boer War resulted neither in a European conflagration nor in conscription in England. Nevertheless, its effects were bad enough, and to stand against it was to court extreme unpopularity. However, Kropotkin was definitely in opposition, and in the following spring he stigmatised it as "the most unjust war ever fought", "the most scandalous slaughtering of human beings in the interest of a handful of capitalists, and the most terrible illustration of the crimes which even such a freedom-loving nation as England is capable of committing once it endeavours to base its well-being upon the exploitation of serfs in Africa". He declared that, although this war had not yet ended, "guns and rifles are already prepared for new wars and new conquests", and spoke again in fear of a war between England and France.

The conflict dragged on, and a year later in June, 1901, he again felt bound not only to denounce the barbarities which had been committed by the English army, but also to make the bitter admission that the blame lay at the door of the British working men, who had the power to end it, but who allowed themselves to be deceived by jingoist propaganda. He had a premonition that the workers of other countries would alike be led away when *their* masters incited them to war. (Ironically, when that time came, Kropotkin also was among the led.)

During the Boer War he received a second visit from Emma Goldman, who talked of organising anti-war meetings in England. Kropotkin dissuaded her, because her status as a Russian might endanger emigrés who were faced with death or Siberia if they were expelled from England, the one country in Europe which still offered a safe asylum.

On the same occasion Emma and Kropotkin discussed the emphasis which she placed on sexual emancipation in her paper *Mother Earth*. Kropotkin thought that this propaganda should not be over-emphasised, since he contended that feminine equality was an intellectual rather than a biological question. "When she is man's equal intellectually and shares in his social ideals, she will be as free as he." After a heated argument Emma became personal. "All right, dear comrade," she shouted, "when I have reached your age, the sex question may no longer be of importance to me. But it is now, and it is a tremendous factor for thousands, millions even, of young people." Kropotkin was amused rather than offended. "I didn't think of that", he admitted. "Perhaps you are right, after all." This talk is interesting because it is almost the only occasion on which we find Kropotkin discussing the subject of sex. Indeed, the whole province of sexual psychology, and of psychology in general, was a field of science which he neglected, to the detriment of a balanced sociological approach.

In April 1901 occurred the second lecture trip to the United States, and for some time before this Kropotkin was engaged in collecting the material for the lectures on Russian literature which he was to deliver at the Lowell Institute in Boston. Then, on his return, there was his final work on shaping and expanding his essays on *Mutual Aid* into the book of that title, which appeared in 1902 and finally established his reputation as a scientific thinker.

The years following the Boer War were marked by increasing illness. He was now suffering from an incurable enlargement of the bronchi, which made him the victim of any unfavourable change of weather and which badly affected his heart. Frequently in the newspapers of this period we find notices of his having been unable to attend meetings through ill health, and from 1901 his appearances in public were rare, for the excitement of oratory had become dangerous. It was only on occasions which specially touched his feelings, like the Ferrer agitation of 1909, that he would insist on speaking from a platform, to the great anxiety of his wife and friends.

In 1903 and 1904 he delivered important addresses on his geological theories to the Geographical Society (already discussed in Chapter II), but these probably involved little emotional effort and were therefore fairly harmless. On the other hand, a speech at the anniversary celebration of the Decembrists, given in the East End in 1905, nearly had fatal results. Rudolf Rocker was present, and has described the incident and the peculiar appeal of Kropotkin's oratory even on this occasion.

"To prevent overcrowding, the meeting was not publicly announced, since Kropotkin's wife urgently appealed to us to take care of the 'old man'. Nevertheless, the news spread like lightning, and in the evening the great hall and the gallery were overcrowded, and hundreds could not be admitted and had to turn back. His voice faltered slightly at the beginning of his speech. An invisible charm seemed to issue from this man and enter into the inmost hearts of the audience. I had heard him speak many times, but only once before this had I noticed such a tremendous impression as that evening. Kropotkin was no orator of rhetorical gifts; sometimes even his words were uttered with some hesitation; but the manner of his speaking, this undertone of deepest conviction underlying each word, penetrated the minds of the audience with elementary force and put them completely under his spell. But Kropotkin, also, was mightily impressed by this audience which listened to his words with breathless attention, and when he had returned home he suffered from a grave heart attack which put his life in danger and tied him down for several weeks to a sick-bed."

During the intervals between illnesses, he worked continuously on a great variety of subjects and a correspondence that increased from year to year. His life at this time formed a pattern in which, as Nettlau has said, "work, overwork, breakdown and enforced rest succeeded each other automatically". Yet he endured his troubles patiently and "was cheerful and gay and loved to joke and to laugh". Sophie cared for him conscientiously; to his friends she may sometimes have seemed too officious, and Ford Madox Ford has left a slightly malicious picture of her solicitude:

". . . Suddenly the Princess would descend upon him when he had thought out something really crushing to say, but before he had had time to formulate it. She would drape his plaid about him, he would be led off, spitting fiery sentences at me over his shoulder."

It is easy to jeer at Sophie in this way for her anxious wish to prevent Peter from endangering his health, but her attitude can be largely excused by the evident devotion which motivated it.

The recurrent illnesses involved more care, and much more expense, than had been required for the simple family existence of earlier years. Kropotkin began to take more frequent holidays for his health. In 1901–2, for instance, nearly two months of the winter were spent at Hove, and in the summer of 1902 he was at Eastbourne. The following year he visited the Channel Islands and Eastbourne again, while later he found it necessary to spend whole winters out of England.

But the books which he was publishing now, and which appeared in both England and America, expanded his income considerably, so that, in addition to these extensive holidays, he was even able to employ a maid. When his nephew Nicholas returned to visit him from Russia in 1904, he found a French girl, Marie, living with them, whom Kropotkin treated with great consideration, as if she were a member of the family.

Meanwhile, Sasha had grown into an attractive, lively and from all accounts flirtatious girl. From their arrival at Bromley until 1904, when she was seventeen, she attended the Bromley High School for Girls. Her cousin, meeting her again in that year, remarked that she seemed very English in her behaviour, and there is certainly nothing Continental in the round handwriting of her letters. She did not speak Russian very fluently, although her father and mother used persistently to address her in that language. Kropotkin's attitude towards her had always been indulgent, but not in any negative way. He believed that children had the same right to freedom of development as everybody else; for this reason he held that parents should not make their children the subjects of experiments which might unfit them for facing the realities of adult society, but he believed in inculcating at an early age a sense of responsibility by drawing the child into the family life as an equal partner.

He was always very anxious for Sasha to go to Russia, and in 1903 it was planned to send her there. However, this project was frustrated by the usual difficulties which haunt emigrés, for in July he wrote to his friend Dr G. B. Clark, the Radical M.P. for Inverness:

"We have quite a busy time, as we met with the refusal of the Russian consul to visa the passport of our daughter and, after endeavours to obtain it, had to give up entirely her proposed journey, and improvise on the spot some other holiday for my wife and daughter.

"It appears that the Russian government absolutely refuses to recognise that children of Russian subjects born in England should be British subjects; and the British government does not insist on this; the moment they are on Russian territory it does not claim them as British—in such conditions the journey was impossible."

His wife and Sasha went to Germany instead, but in 1909, when the regulations seem to have been easier, Sasha went to Russia, staying for several months with her cousin Nicholas and travelling a great deal.

To resume our narrative, the middle of 1902 saw Kropotkin in a mood of renewed optimism. For some years he had been watching with interest the rise of revolutionary syndicalism in France and the new direction it had given to the anarchist movement. This will be discussed later in more detail, but here it is not inappropriate to remark that the appearance of syndicalist ideas among the English trade unionists, reinforced by the Barcelona general strike of that year, had caused him once more to expect international action on a large scale, and in July he wrote to Guillaume, who had now emerged from twenty years of inactivity, suggesting a new International Workingmen's Alliance, with a more intimate inner organisation of revolutionaries who were known and trusted by each other. It was a resurrection of the old Bakuninist idea, but he did not cherish it for long.

Early in the following year he was filled with enthusiasm by certain discoveries of Cherkesov regarding the borrowings which Marx and Engels had made from earlier socialists in the Communist Manifesto, and in their theories regarding the accumulation of capital. Besides a number of French revolutionary thinkers, the writers from whom ideas had been taken under the pretence of originality included early Godwinians such as William Thompson. Kropotkin wrote to Guillaume, with whom he had resumed a regular correspondence, describing *Das Kapital* as "a huge revolutionary pamphlet", and adding:

"For Germany it was necessary. But its scientific significance—zero. It created for itself such a fame only thanks to our ignorance of French and English socialism before 1848."

Meanwhile, Kropotkin's ideas were already beginning to turn towards the need for libertarian ethics, which had also preoccupied Bakunin in his old age. He began a wide plan of reading during 1903, and in 1904 published his essay on *The Ethical Need of the Present Day,* followed in 1905 by *The Morality of Nature.* These, together with his pamphlet on *Anarchist Morality,* published somewhat earlier, represent the first sketches of that massive general survey of ethics which he was so anxious to complete. It was continually put aside because matters that seemed more pressing were always intruding themselves, but he was ever conscious of its importance, and in 1912 wrote to Luigi Bertoni, the Genevan editor of *Le Reveil,* talking of his *Ethics* as if the book were fully planned. But it was not until his final years of quiet at Dmitrov, after 1918, that he resumed full work on it, and then too late for completion.

The events of 1905 diverted much of Kropotkin's attention to Russia, and, indeed, from that time onwards his concern with English affairs and his connection with English society became steadily more tenuous. Russian interests, and the foreign visits which took up an increasing amount of time from 1904 onwards, belong to subsequent chapters, and the aspect of his career with which we are here concerned dwindles gradually to a shadow of that rich participation in English life which had characterised the 1880's and 1890's. For this reason we shall deal here more briefly with the remaining years up to 1914, and treat amply in subsequent chapters the problems that mainly dominated the period.

In the autumn of 1907 he moved from Bromley to Highgate, where he took a small villa in Muswell Hill Road. Besides continuing his articles for anarchist papers and much work for the Russian cause, he was now engaged in collecting and arranging the vast mass of material he had accumulated for *The Great French Revolution,* his most monumental work, which finally appeared in 1909. In the same year appeared also *The Terror in Russia,* in which he was assisted by H. N. Brailsford and Nevinson, and in connection with which the latter has given a disturbing picture of Kropotkin's manner of working at this penultimate period of his life.

"His method of work was peculiar and, to an orderly Englishman, embarrassing. . . . Order was his difficulty. He knew so much, thought so much, felt so much, it seemed impossible for him to keep within limits. Writing at great speed, he produced sheets of straggling manuscript. Then omissions occurred to him—omissions by the dozen. With strange devices of flying lines, loops, brackets and circles he struggled to get them in. He was constantly altering his arrangement, never sure in what sequence the statements or reflections ought to come. Loose leaves would be scribbled over, and they had to be tucked into the manuscript somehow.

"Unaccustomed to work in this manner, I felt as though floundering in a bottomless bog upon an unlimited steppe. All appeared uncertainty, confusion, and chaos. But Kropotkin never for a moment lost his temper or his genial exuberance. I suppose his was the Russian way of doing things, for he never thought it in the least perplexing or strange. And in the end the chaos worked itself out, as definite and well-arranged as the starry heavens. No one reading that book could imagine what a turmoil of confusion it went through before it emerged perfectly clear and clean and trim as it stands. In reading his other books . . . always so well-ordered and easy to understand, I often wonder whether they too had passed through this process of dishevelled undress."

No sooner was his work on the French Revolution completed than Kropotkin was afoot on another new trail. The consideration of ethics had set him thinking again on the general question of evolution. He saw more clearly certain errors of Darwinism, and felt that in some respects Lamarck had been unjustly passed over, particularly in the matter of the direct action of environment on the development of plants and animals. Accordingly he set to work on this question, and in the process produced a whole series of neatly argued articles which were published in *The Nineteenth Century* during the next five years. "Evolution and Mutual Aid", "The Direct Action of Environment on Plants", and a double essay on "The Response of Animals to their Environment" appeared in 1910. In 1912 came "The Inheritance of Acquired Characteristics", in 1914 "Inherited Variations in Plants", and in 1915 the conclusion on "Inherited Variations in Animals". These essays were of a highly controversial nature, involving an attack on Weissmann's theory of the germ plasm, and endeavouring to prove the inheritance of characteristics acquired through the direct action of environment. Kropotkin, as usual, massed a great deal of evidence to support his arguments, and certainly put forward an impressive case, though it was by no means the last word on this still open and fiercely disputed question.

His health continued to decline, and in the autumn of 1911 he moved to Brighton, taking a house in Kemp Town which was to be his last home in England. It represented a virtual retirement from English activities. Half the year he spent abroad, and the rest of the time his health was so poor that he rarely went to London. However, in 1912 he attended the International Eugenics Congress at the University of London, and delivered a warning against considering as a science what was "simply a few ideas, generalities and desires that had been expressed by a certain number of people", and deprecated the undiscriminating propaganda for sterilisation advanced by many eugenicists. As an alternative to such ideas he put forward his own contention that sociability was the strongest factor in "the survival of any species, in the struggle against natural causes". Here he was encountered for the first time by the great Italian sociologist Robert Michels, who was very much impressed by his character and his idealism.

In the same year he took part in a further campaign against victimisation. Malatesta had accused a certain Belleli of being a spy of the Italian police. Scotland Yard, who had a grudge against Malatesta because he had evaded their attempt to implicate him in the Sidney Street affair* of the preceding year, persuaded Belleli to bring a libel action, and Malatesta was sentenced to three months' imprisonment and recommended for deportation. A great agitation was aroused in the Labour movement, and Kropotkin went personally to see his former friend, John Burns, now a Liberal cabinet minister. A rather heated altercation took place, in which Kropotkin reminded Burns of his own past, when he led the processions of striking dockers through the London streets. Burns remarked that he had long seen the stupidity of such acts, and then Kropotkin heatedly answered that it was a good thing there were still people willing to indulge in "stupidities" for the good of their fellows, though by such means one could not grasp at a

* This was an incident in which a number of Russian revolutionaries, including the celebrated Peter the Painter, barricaded themselves into a house in the East End and withstood for a long time a siege from the London police and a squad of Guardsmen, the operations against them being directed by Winston Churchill, then a Liberal Minister. As all the men involved were either killed in the house or escaped, their identity was never fully established, and it has often been claimed that they were anarchists; there is, however, very strong evidence pointing to the probability of their having been a group of Baltic social-democrats.

ministerial chair. Burns then laughed, and Malatesta finally escaped deportation.

In December of the same year Kropotkin's seventieth birthday took place, and he was overwhelmed by congratulations from all sides; newspapers like *The Times* treated it as almost a national event, and at the meetings of celebration many prominent people spoke. One such crowded gathering was held at the Palace Theatre in London. It was addressed not only by the leading anarchists, but also by Bernard Shaw, George Lansbury, H. M. Hyndman and Josiah Wedgwood, then a Radical M.P., a friend of Kropotkin and a descendant of the Thomas Wedgwood who had been Godwin's benefactor. Shaw went so far in his praise as to say that he was beginning at last to wonder whether Kropotkin had not been all these years in the right and he and his friends in the wrong.

Kropotkin was too ill to attend this meeting, and a week later he was seized with double pneumonia, from which he recovered only with difficulty. Indeed, the only meeting of importance he seems to have attended in England after this date was that of the British Medical Association at Brighton in July 1913, when he appeared on the platform as "an old jail bird", to plead for a more humane attitude towards prisoners. And here, with Kropotkin remembering his own former privations in prison and speaking up for those who still underwent them, we will draw in the threads of this chapter and allow the remaining years until his departure in 1917 to emerge in the sections to which they more strictly belong.

CHAPTER VI

THE TRAVELLER

WHEN Kropotkin left France in the early months of 1886, he had no intention of retiring into an insularity of attitude corresponding to the physical insularity he adopted for some years in England. While from the first days of his arrival he did his best, as always, to participate effectively in the progressive movements immediately around him, he never lost his cosmopolitan outlook. Allowing for certain distorting prejudices, he retained a sound understanding of world affairs, and contributed a not inconsiderable influence to international thought.

In the years immediately following his departure from the Continent, he kept in close touch with friends abroad. Before departing he had spent much time with Jean Grave, and had promised to send material regularly for *Le Revolté*. This he did, writing for each issue, even when the paper became a weekly in the early summer of 1886, and continuing for *La Revolte*, the new journal which followed the suppression of *Le Revolté* in September 1887. Almost the whole of *The Conquest of Bread*, as well as *Anarchist Morality*, appeared in serial form in these two papers, the various articles being reprinted as pamphlets before they were compiled into books.

It must be emphasised that the circulation of these works in France was not restricted to anarchists or even to the socialist movement as a whole. When *The Conquest of Bread* appeared in 1892, it was hailed by Zola as a "true poem", while the critic, Maurice Barrés, writing in *Figaro* during 1891, said that Kropotkin's pamphlets sprang from a "beautiful logic and a strong generosity". Apart from these elder writers very many of the young poets and critics were impressed by Kropotkin's clear writing and sincerity. Not only did the less reputable writers like Stuart Merrill, Octave Mirbeau, and Laurent Tailhade adopt him with enthusiasm, but he also made a profound and lasting impression on some of the greatest modern French writers. Henri Barbusse said years later:

"Kropotkin represents and always will represent the symbol of him who rises in his righteousness and honesty, and who thus becomes a magnificent destroyer of the badly-conceived laws that surround him and the things that hem him in. The unity of that long, vast and precious existence, its impeccable harmony, the power of its anger and its rebellion against all abuse and all injustice . . . confers that superior intelligence and genius which only morality can create."

And Romain Rolland, a great admirer of Tolstoy, said of Kropotkin:

"Simply, naturally, he has realised in his own life the ideal of moral purity, of serene abnegation, of perfect love of humanity that the tormented genius of Tolstoy desired all his life, only achieving it in his art (save during happy and rare moments, by flights, powerful and broken)."

As for Kropotkin's influence as an anarchist in other Continental countries, it is sufficient to remark that while *The Conquest of Bread* was not published in England until 1906, it was translated into Italian in 1894, into Spanish and Portuguese in 1895, and into German in 1896 (being published in Zurich).

With these wide international interests and contacts it was natural that Kropotkin should not wish to remain always in England, and in the winter of 1887 he returned to Paris, delivering a lecture on "The Moral Influence of Prisons on Prisoners" to a large audience in the Salle de Rivoli on the 20th December. In this address he raised the arguments against the prison system which we have already noticed in connection with *In Russian and French Prisons*. Except for the lecture itself, we have no record of the circumstances under which the visit was made, but it may be indicative of unpleasant attentions from the French police that Kropotkin did not again attempt to cross the Channel for another nine years.

Instead, his attentions turned towards America, where since

the days of the Chicago anarchists the libertarian movement had spread rapidly among the immigrant workers, assuming a quite different character from the native individualist anarchism of Benjamin Tucker, derived from Thoreau, Josiah Warren and Proudhon. At first this immigrant movement fell under the collectivist influence of Most and his *Freiheit*. But later there had been a growing tendency towards adoption of Kropotkin's point of view; Most had been impelled in that direction by his readers and associates, and the younger leaders of anarchism in America, like Emma Goldman and Alexander Berkman, regarded Kropotkin as their prophet.

During 1890 Berkman belonged to a group which was holding meetings in a small hall in the Jewish quarter of New York. Their influence was steadily increasing, but they felt that they would be helped greatly if they could enjoy, even only for a short time, the presence and advice of such a teacher as Kropotkin.

"We decided to reduce our living expenses to the minimum and devote our earnings to defray the expense involved in our invitation to Kropotkin to visit America. Enthusiastically the matter was discussed in the group meetings of our most active and devoted comrades; all were unanimous in the great plan. A long letter was sent to our teacher, asking him to come on a lecture tour to America and emphasising our need of him.

"His negative reply gave us a shock: we were so sure of his acceptance, so convinced of the necessity of his coming. But the admiration we felt for him was even increased when we learnt the motives of his refusal. He would very much like to come—Kropotkin wrote—and he deeply appreciated the spirit of our invitation. He hoped to visit the United States some time in the future, and it would give him great joy to be among such good comrades. But just now he could not afford to come at his own expense, and he would not use the money of the movement even for such a purpose."

This invitation, however, awakened in Kropotkin a desire to see for himself the new social developments emerging in this hardly formed nation. He realised that it contained much that would interest him, particularly as a sociologist, and when in the following year a lecture agent offered to arrange a tour in the United States, he accepted gladly. The trip was conceived on an ambitious scale. Kropotkin was to leave at the beginning of October and to spend ten weeks travelling in the eastern States, giving four lectures each week. His tour would extend as far west as Chicago, and he hoped to reach that city on the 11th November, so as to speak on that anniversary day at the graves of the Chicago martyrs.

On 26th September a farewell party was held by the London anarchists in the Athenæum Hall, Tottenham Court Road. Several hundred people arrived, and the usual programme of dancing, choruses, revolutionary songs and speeches ensued. A number of groups expressed their desire for Kropotkin to transmit greetings to the American anarchists, and then he himself rose to deliver a rousing attack on American society:

> "America is just the country that shows how all the written guarantees in the world for freedom are no protection against tyranny and oppression of the worst kind. There the politician has come to be looked upon as the very scum of society. The peoples of the world are becoming profoundly dissatisfied and are not appeased by the promises of the social-democrats to patch up the State into a new engine of oppression. . . . Our Chicago comrades have shown us how to hold high the banner of anarchy amid death and imprisonment, but we must not spend precious time in looking for an American revolution; we must actively prepare here in Europe by our own efforts for the historical moment which will surely come."

But the celebrations were in vain, for on the very eve of departure the agency informed Kropotkin that they had been unable to make the arrangements anticipated, and that the tour must be abandoned. The reason for this sudden withdrawal has not become evident, but it seems probable that Kropotkin's uncomplimentary references to American civilisation had led his potential employers to retire hastily before the responsibility of sponsoring a revolutionary with such uncompromising views. Cobden-Sanderson records that Kropotkin was greatly "put out" by the failure of this tour, since he had made no plans for earning his living over the winter of 1891–2.

Meanwhile, his attention began to turn back to the Continent, where terrorism was causing much controversy in the Latin countries, and bringing new dangers to the anarchist movement. In 1892 a bomb was thrown in the Liceo theatre at Barcelona, killing many innocent people, and Kropotkin, whose kind heart was stirred by the thought of this unnecessary suffering, immediately sent an article to *La Revolte*, disowning the act and its perpetrators. Grave, agreeing that terrorism of this kind was not an "efficacious means of proclaiming brotherhood, solidarity and justice", pointed out to Kropotkin the provocations Spanish people had undergone from an oppressive and obscurantist government, which did not stop short at torturing its enemies. Kropotkin agreed to withdraw the article, and Grave's arguments seem to have impressed him, for, as we have seen, he afterwards adopted the attitude that, while he himself disliked terrorist acts and would not willingly commit violence, he could not stand in judgment over those who performed them in sheer desperation.

The struggle between the anarchists and the authorities grew steadily more bitter. Figures like the Russian terrorists began to appear in France. Such men as Ravachol and Vaillant, gentle in their daily lives and in their dealings with people around them, were yet moved by their outraged sense of justice to commit, like Dostoevsky's Raskolnikov, acts of repellent violence. Their motives were of the highest kind, but it was, as with Nechaev, a question of whether the end justifies the means or whether in reality the means conditions the end. For in the long run the acts of these devoted assassins, instead of drawing attention to the undisputed social injustices of the time, merely surrounded anarchism with an aura of brutality, foreign to the basic humanity of its philosophy, which it has taken half a century to dispel.

Eventually, in March 1894, the police decided to strike at the principal organ of anarchist opinion; *La Revolte* was suppressed under one of those charges which can always be found to destroy a revolutionary sheet, and Grave was imprisoned. He was taken to Clairvaux, where, although it was nearly ten years after Kropotkin's release, he found his memory among the prison officials "as fresh as if he had been there only the day before, so impressed were they by his personality".

The next year Grave was released under an amnesty, and decided to found a new paper to replace *La Revolte*. He wrote immediately to Reclus and Kropotkin, asking if he could count on their help. Reclus invited him to Brussels, and there told him that Kropotkin's advice and support were absolutely necessary. So Grave made a brisk trip to London. "Our business was quickly settled. Kropotkin was enchanted that the paper would reappear. We could rely absolutely on him. He would send articles whenever they were needed." And so, in May 1895, the first number of *Les Temps Nouveaux* was published.

Kropotkin's contribution began with a long series of articles, lasting until the end of the year, in which he analysed the crises socialism was undergoing during the 1890's. He saw it was passing away from the simple ideal of the early days—the transfer of the means of production to the producers themselves and the abolition of political power. Under the influence of Marx and the social-democrats had arisen a new conception for everyday activity: "The conquest of powers in the existing State, legislation to protect the wage slave against the too-brutal faults of exploitation, and a certain amelioration of the fate of some categories of privileged workers." It will be seen how prophetic this was of what has happened where parliamentary socialists have gained their share of power, as in England. Kropotkin went on to examine the various phases of this tendency in the 1890's, and showed how the scramble for petty expedients diverted attention from the greater social transformations which the workers would in the end have to accomplish themselves, with their own strength. He declared, once again, that in the choice before the people in those vital days, the old ideal of a wholly free society, still advocated by the anarchists, should take the place of the attempts of the social-democrats to engage the workers in political competition or collaboration with the bourgeois parties. In particular, he counselled distrust of the free gifts of the State, which, like the bread and circuses of classical antiquity, were intended to consolidate the power of the rulers. Freedom, he concluded, could only be won by unremitting struggle against the State and authority.

Early in 1896, Grave decided to hold a series of lectures in Paris in connection with his paper, and Kropotkin was invited to speak at the Milles Colonnes Hall, one of the largest meeting-places in Paris. It was to be his first visit to the French capital since 1887, and an audience of five thousand people was expected.

Kropotkin wrote his lecture on the State, one of his most important short works of social analysis, and the reading was advertised for the 7th March. These arrangements might have gone undisturbed had not the heir to the Russian throne announced his intention to visit Nice, where he would be welcomed in state by the representatives of the Republic. On such an occasion the arrival of Kropotkin was an evident embarrassment. The authorities cannot have imagined that he would take part in any terrorist attempt, but they recognised that he was sufficiently respected in Paris to receive a great ovation, and that his presence might serve as an excuse for all those, Russian and French alike, who wished to show in a vocal way their disapproval of Tsarism. In those days when the Franco-Russian military alliance was of paramount importance to the Third Republic, they could clearly not risk such an implied insult, particularly as ten years before, on Kropotkin's release from Clairvaux, Alexander III had been so rude to the French ambassador that the latter had resigned his post. So orders were sent out to stop Kropotkin from entering France. What happened is told by him in a letter to Guillaume, shortly after the resumption of their friendship in 1902.

"I arrived, suspecting nothing, on the daily boat from Newhaven to Dieppe. A police officer approached me. 'Mr. Kropotkin, I have a few words to say to you; I am a police officer.' 'Very well.' He introduced himself as Monsieur Merdes ('of Spanish descent', he added every time he repeated his name).

"He read me the telegram from Bourgeois,* which was composed roughly on the following lines. 'In case Kropotkin disembarks, inform him that he is expelled, and that he must return with the first boat. In case he resists, take him into administrative custody.'

" 'All right,' I replied, 'I shall send telegrams to Grave and my wife.' This I did.

"As regards my return, I had arrived with the second daily boat; the sea was rough—so bad that I, who had never suffered from sea sickness, had to lie down (I was beginning to recover so well after the influenza). 'I shall return tomorrow morning,' I said, 'by the same boat.'

* Léon Bourgeois, a French Minister who, ironically, published in 1896 a book on *Solidarisme*, a similar theory to mutual aid.

" 'No,' answered Monsieur Merdes, of Spanish origin, with a grimace. 'You must return immediately by the night boat—otherwise I shall have to send you to prison. Your cell is already prepared.'

" 'Very well,' I replied, 'I shall go to prison. But you must realise what the Press will say of it.'

"From then . . . they telegraphed all over France . . . to find out whether I could spend the night in the neighbouring hotel (with two policemen in the next room) or whether I had to be taken to prison. The Deputy Prefect did not dare to take upon himself this terrible responsibility. Nor did the Prefect. They even telegraphed and telephoned to Nice.

"At ten o'clock Monsieur Merdes approached, beaming. 'The Minister will permit you to spend the night in the hotel.'

" 'Is the weather good?' I asked. 'Then . . . telegraph to the Minister that I am leaving by the night boat.' And that is what I did."

Kropotkin evidently intended to extend to the full his principle of accepting nothing from the State, even when he had won it by his own tenacity.

He hoped that the French Press would give publicity to his case. But by this time the social-democrats like Jaurés and Millerand were well advanced in their careers as politicians, and, particularly now that the split in the international socialist ranks was clearly defined, had no desire to make themselves unpopular by protesting because an anarchist had not been allowed to enter the country to expound his doctrine. French politics had reached a level of corruption in which the principle of civil liberty no longer meant a great deal to the leaders of any camp. Even the ex-Communard, Henri Rochefort, who had in the past been friendly towards Kropotkin and had printed his letters on Russian affairs in *L'Intransigeant*, acted like the rest. When Kropotkin wrote describing the incident, Rochefort did not even publish the letter, but contented himself with remarking fatuously, "Our friend Kropotkin understands, no doubt, that there are situations in which personal interest suffers".

At last, in 1897, came the opportunity to visit North America which he had long desired. In September the British Association held its annual meeting in the Canadian city of Toronto, and, largely through the persuasions of his friend James Mavor, now

Professor of Economics at Toronto University, Kropotkin decided to participate. He delivered two papers, one on the glacial deposits in Finland, and the other on his theory of the structure of Asia.

He received a good welcome, and stayed for some weeks with Mavor. Then he travelled across Canada, to the Pacific coast, taking advantage of an excursion which the Canadian Pacific Railway had organised on behalf of the visiting scientists. It was a tour full of interest to a geographer and a sociologist, and Kropotkin wrote in *The Nineteenth Century* an account which gives a very interesting picture, not only of the physical nature of Canada, but also of its vigorous pioneer society.

The journey out to the coast was made in the company of two Canadian geologists and was devoted mostly to observing the physical formation of the country, which, as we have seen, reminded Kropotkin greatly of Russia. In Manitoba, particularly, he recalled the Russian steppes. The journey led across the Rockies to Victoria, the capital of British Columbia, and then Kropotkin returned alone, devoting his attention to agriculture and the conditions of the settlers. He visited the principal towns—Brandon, Regina, Calgary, Edmonton, all pioneer shack settlements which were growing rapidly.

But what interested him most was the life of the settlers, and particularly of the Mennonites, a sect of Dutch Protestants who, after having settled in Russia, had left in 1874-8, to avoid military service. In Russia the Mennonites had adopted the village community, even improving it to fit their radical Christian principles, and had brought their communal ideas to Canada. Kropotkin found that, while they had not adopted complete communism, they had extended it to many aspects of village life. Land was held in common, each family receiving a portion in accordance with its working capacities, while pasturage took the form of common meadows. There were communal funds for purchasing land, communal mills and schools, but as yet no common cultivation or distribution. Nevertheless, and in spite of the obscurantism of some of the older Mennonites, the communities had set an example of good farming which was envied by their neighbours, and which Kropotkin regarded as due to their communistic tendencies.

He was impressed by the agricultural activity throughout Canada; it showed him "how rich mankind could be if social obstacles did not stand everywhere in the way of utilising the gifts of nature", and he felt that the expansion of human endeavour and civilisation all over the earth "has widened the circle of ideas, it has opened to thought newer horizons, it has shattered many traditions of old".

But he was also moved to the reflection that, if the social conditions had been right, the energy used in breaking new land would have been turned in Europe to raising the productivity of its soil and cultivating its waste lands so that none need want.

> "I understand the Icelander who exchanges his polar island for a settlement in Manitoba, or the Norwegian who moves from his subpolar fjord to a fjord in British Columbia. But what has driven the Mennonite from his South Russian steppe to the Manitoba steppe, where he sighs after the blossom and the fruit of his apple and cherry trees? What drives the Galician to Saskatchewan, the Swede to Alberta, and the Scotsman to Ontario? The social conditions alone drive them from lands which badly want the work of their hands, but which they are not allowed to give it. If only Canada could avoid creating the same conditions! But I am afraid she also is making rapid strides towards the building up of the same land monopolies which now drive the European peasants out of Europe."

These melancholy forebodings were to be largely fulfilled in the ensuing years.

From Canada Kropotkin entered the United States, where he made a brief tour of Chicago, Philadelphia, New York, Boston and Washington. The meetings in Boston were held at the Lowell Institute, where he gave three lectures on mutual aid, supported by Professor Charles Eliot Norton and other Harvard dignitaries. In the remaining towns he spoke mostly on anarchism and usually at the request of anarchist groups. The lecture at Philadelphia, held in the Oddfellows' Hall, was devoted to a survey of history from the sociological point of view; some 2,000 people attended, and one of them has told us that the audience was extremely attentive and sympathetic.

In New York the first lecture was given at Chickering Hall, in Fifth Avenue, a fashionable concert hall. Kropotkin's theme was Russian literature, and the chair was taken by Ernest Crosby, the friend of Tolstoy. The hall was packed and the lecture well received, but Kropotkin was worried because an entrance fee of 25 cents made it too expensive for the workers. So another meeting was arranged, this time on the 23rd November at the Cooper Union, a much larger hall. Invitations were sent to the New York trade unions, and the meeting of more than five thousand people was probably the largest Kropotkin ever addressed. He spoke on the general theme of anarchism, and the gathering, chaired by the elderly John Swinton, an associate of Horace Greely and a former editor of the *New York Tribune*, was attended not only by a great mass of working men of all nationalities but also by many men of letters, including Professor Robert Erskine Ely and Walter Hines Page, the editor of the *Atlantic Monthly*. The atmosphere was enthusiastic, and a representative of the New York trade unionists read a message, which was adopted unanimously, for Kropotkin to bring back to the people of Europe.

"Go back, Kropotkin, to the workers of England, of Europe, and tell them that you have fashioned another link in the brotherly bond that binds the toilers of all lands. Tell them that, notwithstanding our Immigration Commissioners, the poorer they are and the more radical they are, the better we love them. . . . Tell them, finally, we recognise the same causes, the same effects, the same despots, and the same workers the world over, and stand ready at all times to render to the latter such assistance as is within our power."

It was a period of bitter industrial struggle in America, for the industrial trusts were fighting with every means in their power, including organised violence, to resist improvements in working conditions and wages. Only a few weeks before had occurred the battle at Hazelton, in which strikers were shot down, and which prompted Kropotkin to say despairingly, in a note to *Les Temps Nouveaux*: "Nothing, nothing but war, war without mercy, will lead to any solution for the United States, and the war will be terrible, for the limit of the workers' patience has long been exceeded."

At this time Alexander Berkman was lying in prison because, in a moment of indignation over attacks on strikers at the Carnegie steel-works, he had shot at H. C. Frick, one of the principal executives. The merits of Berkman's deed need not be discussed; it was the act of a righteous man whose patience was moved beyond endurance by what he had witnessed and who wished, rightly or wrongly, to make an example of the individual he held responsible. Kropotkin travelled to Pittsburg in the hope of seeing Berkman, but the latter was in solitary confinement, and could not be seen. On arriving in New York, Kropotkin found an invitation from Andrew Carnegie, who was beginning to feel uneasy over his ruthless past and to pose as a benefactor of humanity. He wrote a frank and dignified refusal, saying: "Because of your power and influence my Comrade Alexander Berkman was given twenty-two years prison for an act which in the State of Pennsylvania calls for seven years as the highest penalty. I cannot accept the hospitality of a man who has helped to doom a human being to twenty-two years of misery."

In New York he stayed with an anarchist, John Edelman, and handed to him the takings of the two public meetings, which, after deducting expenses, amounted to more than five hundred dollars, and enabled Edelman to start *Solidarity*, the first English-speaking anarchist communist paper in New York. He also encountered the two veteran leaders of libertarian thought in America, Johann Most and the individualist, Benjamin Tucker.

Although they were both in Western Europe from the 1870's until about 1882, Kropotkin had never met Most, a man of strong personality who did not mingle well with the older anarchists. Most's activity was confined to the German-speaking field, and for many years he maintained obstinately the collectivist ideas which most anarchists had abandoned for the free communism advocated by Kropotkin. Even the German movement was split over this issue, and a strong group stood in opposition to Most. Added to this, he enjoyed some unpopularity outside his immediate followers because of the jealousy with which he guarded his personal control of *Freiheit*. Kropotkin, in 1888, took a clear stand with his opponents, and when Otto Rinke founded in London a short-lived anarchist-communist magazine, *Autonomie*, he wrote to him:

> "If I were one of the editors of *Autonomie* I would quietly and pointedly make clear my position to the American and European comrades of *Freiheit*. And that position would be—to recognise the great achievements of *Freiheit*, but to add that the comrades of

Autonomie are not in agreement with the centralist tendencies of *Freiheit*, as they are manifested in Most's manner of writing, and therefore have a separate organ for the purpose of promoting the autonomistic tendencies of anarchism."

Unfortunately this letter, which seems to have been written without malice towards Most, whom Kropotkin admired personally, was used by the warring factions among the German and Austrian anarchists. The bitterness of this conflict was exacerbated in 1887 by the fact that Johann Neve, one of the finest personalities in the history of German socialism, had fallen into the hands of Bismarck's police through an indiscretion of Most's rival, Peukert, so stupid that many suspected him of informing deliberately. When Peukert appealed to Kropotkin for defence, the latter could only tell him that such folly left only one course open—to disappear from the movement.

Eventually, despite the indiscretions of Peukert, the anarchist-communist idea triumphed, and Most himself bowed to the general change. By 1897, the old quarrels had died down and Kropotkin made a point of seeking out Most in order to express personal esteem. It is recorded that the old German fighter, who was very sentimental beneath his outward cynicism, was deeply moved by this gesture of his old opponent. When he was seeking Most's editorial office in Gold Street, Kropotkin encountered another celebrated figure of the American radical movement, for Harry Kelly, the American educationalist, has told us that:

> "By mistake he wandered into the office of *The Weekly*, or *New York People*, edited by Daniel de Leon, head of the Socialist Labour Party. De Leon was an able man, but vituperative and bitter. He was very cordial to Kropotkin, and they had a pleasant conversation. When the paper came out later in the week, de Leon ran true to form and printed a sneering article with disparaging remarks about Peter and his title of 'prince'."

Kropotkin's past connections with Benjamin Tucker had always been slight, and marked by great disparity of views, for Tucker thought that Kropotkin's idea of communal organisation had nothing to do with anarchism, and Kropotkin adopted a similar attitude towards Tucker's individualism.

Tucker had founded in 1881 an individualist anarchist paper called *Liberty*. He advocated absolute freedom and equality for all as the only basis for society, and held that collective ownership of production, *accepted as a principle*, was wrong, since it deprived individuals of the freedom to produce as they thought fit. Three brief quotations will show how, from these premises, he rejected Kropotkin's views as wholly un-anarchist. In 1886, after Kropotkin's Paris lecture on "Anarchism and Its Place in Socialist Evolution", Tucker remarked:

> "Thus Kropotkinian anarchism means the liberty to eat, but not to cook; to drink, but not to brew; to wear, but not to spin; to dwell, but not to build; to give, but not to sell or buy; to think, but not to print; to speak, but not to hire a hall; to dance, but not to pay the fiddler."

In 1887, linking Kropotkin with the Chicago anarchists, who more or less shared his views, Tucker accused them all of denying the right of "individual production and exchange".

> "Kropotkin says, it is true, that he would allow the individual access to the land; but as he proposes to strip him of capital entirely, and as he declares a few pages further on that without capital agriculture is impossible, it follows that such access is an empty privilege not at all equivalent to the liberty of individual production."

Finally, in 1888, criticising what he regarded as the spurious simplicity of anarchist communism, Tucker said:

> "Just as it is easier to rest satisfied with the statement, 'Male and female created He them', than to trace in the geological strata the intricacies in the evolution of species, so it is easier to say that every man shall have whatever he wants than to find the economic law by which every man may get the equivalent of his product. The ways of Faith are direct and easy to follow, but their goal is a quagmire, whereas the ways of Science, however devious and difficult to tread, lead to solid ground at last. Communism belongs to the Age of Faith, Anarchistic Socialism to the Age of Science."

It is unfortunate that the individualist criticism of Kropotkin (and a valid one is possible) should not have been made by someone of higher calibre than Tucker, who, despite his industry and sincerity, was a vain and unconvincing writer. In the passages quoted, which represent the acme of his polemic against Kropotkin, he partly misinterprets his opponent, as when he suggests that the latter's idea of communal organisation would *prevent* the individual from working on his own if he wished (a fact which Kropotkin always explicitly denied, since the basis of his theory was the voluntary principle). Where he faces the actual issues of anarchist communism, he retreats into the arguments of a 'small man' capitalism which had already been superseded by trusts and monopolies, and when he reproaches Kropotkin for not having found "the economic law by which every man may gain the equivalent of his product", he is merely nonsensical, since he himself was unable to find this same "economic law", which it is difficult to imagine could exist in any society where there is the least complexity of production.

From these arguments it is impossible not to grant Kropotkin's claim that such individualists as Tucker "are driven into the liberal individualism of the classical economists". Individualism has its important core of social teaching in the realm of personal relationships; but in the economic field it can only be applied logically in some wholly mythical hypothesis, like Rousseau's conception of the primordial man living his solitary existence devoid of any social tie.

What happened at Kropotkin's meeting with Tucker in 1897 we do not know. But it did not alter his attitude towards individualism, for in 1902 he wrote a long letter to Nettlau in which he outlined his main objections to that theory, particularly in the forms put forward by Nietzsche, by the Decadents, and by certain younger French anarchists of the 1890's. His main argument, briefly, is that individualism "as it has been presented from Mandeville's *Fable of the Bees* up to Nietzsche and the young French anarchists", is merely a form of egoism which lowers the quality of the individual and in its stupidity completely fails to reach its supposed object—"the complete, wide and most perfect attainable development of individuality". He continues:

"Nobody, except Ibsen, has been able, it seems to me, to rise to the conception of true individualism, and even he, having perceived it by a vision of genius, has not succeeded in expressing it in such a manner as to make himself understood. All the same, there is in Ibsen a certain vision of an individualism to come which I can understand and which will be the superior affirmation of individuality—as different from misanthropic bourgeois individualisms as from Christian Communism, and equally hostile to both, since each is an obstacle to the full development of the individuality.

"The individualism which, I believe, will become the ideal of the philosophy shortly to appear will not seek its expression in the appropriation of *more* than the just share for each of the common patrimony of production (the only kind understood by the bourgeoisie); nor in the creation in the name of the world of a crowd of slaves serving the elect nation (*Individualismus* or *Pro sibi Darwinianum*, or rather *Huxleianum*); nor in the sensual individualism and the 'liberation' of good and evil which has been preached to us by some French anarchists—pitiful reflections of our fathers, the 'æsthetes', the 'admirers of beauty', the Byronic and Don-Juanesque poets who also preached this; nor in the oppression of the neighbour (*individualismus Nietzscheanum*) which debases the 'beautiful blond beast' to the status of a bull in a herd of bulls—but in a kind of *individualismus* or *personalismus* or *pro sibi communisticum*, which I see coming and which I would seek to define clearly if I could give the necessary time to it."

What Kropotkin clearly means is that real individualism, in the sense of an enrichment of personality, will only arise from a society where co-operation in the material factors of life has removed those causes of strife and oppression which in any other order relegate individualism to a privilege of the few who live at the expense of the toiling many.

His criticism of the mass of individualist thinkers on this point is manifestly just. He is particularly cutting about Nietzsche, to whom he gives full credit for his iconoclastic virtues, his "superb" demolition of Christianity, but of whose general doctrine he says:

"It is the individualism of the bourgeois who can exist only on condition of the oppression of the masses and of lackeyism, of servility towards tradition, of the obliteration of individuality in the oppressor himself, as well as in the oppressed mass. The 'beautiful blond beast' is, fundamentally, a slave—a slave to his kind, to the priest, to the law, to tradition—a cipher without individuality in the exploiting herd."

These observations anticipate quite remarkably the way in which the unconsidering acceptance of Nietzschean doctrines did in fact affect two generations of German intellectuals. But Kropotkin made perhaps his most devastating reference to Nietzsche on another occasion, when he described him to Cherkesov as a "philosopher in carpet slippers" and "the first Philistine".

If Kropotkin was correct in his attack on the unsure foundations of the theories of most individualists, there is one writer of this school to whom he did not do justice. Some ten years before, Oscar Wilde, in *The Soul of Man Under Socialism*, had put forward the same theory of individualism based on voluntary co-operation in production and distribution as Kropotkin now advocated. Are we to assume that he had not read Wilde's book, which had a wide vogue in anarchist circles? Or was he prejudiced against Wilde because of his extravagant way of living, because he confused the "two individualisms"?

The tour of 1897 had two important results. The first was that Walter Hines Page, persuading the reluctant publishers of the *Atlantic Monthly* by his enthusiastic faith in Kropotkin's abilities, commissioned the anarchist to write his reminiscences as a series of monthly essays during 1898. The result was the *Memoirs of a Revolutionist*, a very lively account of Kropotkin's life up to his last arrival in England. He had shown himself an able polemicist and sociological essayist. Now he appeared as an autobiographer of rare vigour and expressiveness. His book remains a classic in this literary *genre*; it has delighted many readers, from his great contemporary Tolstoy down to writers in our own day like Herbert Read and Lewis Mumford; but since we have used it copiously in the early chapters of the present book, it seems unnecessary to do more than say that our quotations give only a scanty idea of the strength and amplitude of mind shown by the book as a whole. It is not merely a story of Kropotkin's own development, told with a modesty that does not attempt to cast any inflated personal image on the reader's mind, but also a representation of the society in which that development emerged. Apart from the memoirs of Herzen, there has been no better representation of the Russia of the nineteenth-century rebels, nor is Kropotkin any less interesting when he portrays the European labour movement in the 1870's. Many excellent men who would otherwise have had no memorial are remembered in all their individuality, and if the author is not thrust forward unnecessarily, we can nevertheless see in the background of the whole narrative the steady development of personality, leading to that drama of conversion which is the real climax of the book.

The second result of the 1897 trip was that it enabled Kropotkin to repay the debt he owed to those Doukhobor peasant communists who more than thirty years before had influenced his ideas by their practical example. During the 1890's the Doukhobors were subjected to violent attacks for their refusal to be conscripted. They stood firm, and when it seemed clear that the Russian authorities intended to continue persecutions, petitioned the dowager Empress that they might be allowed to emigrate. Tolstoy threw all his influence into supporting their appeal, and eventually it was granted.

Assisted by the Quakers, nearly two thousand Doukhobors went to Cyprus. But the climate proved unsuitable, and the question arose of finding a new home for these emigrants and also for the greater number of their brethren still in Russia. Here Kropotkin intervened. He had seen the fertile and empty plains of north-west Canada, which enjoyed a climate very similar to that of central Russia, and had observed how well the Mennonites, with their semi-communal methods, throve there. It seemed to him an ideal locality for the Doukhobors, who were industrious and good farmers. Accordingly, he went over to Purleigh in Essex, where he discussed the matter with the English committee, and in August 1898 wrote to Mavor in Toronto, suggesting that the Canadian Government should be approached on behalf of the Doukhobors. Mavor acted immediately, and in due course nearly twenty thousand Doukhobors left Russia and settled in the Canadian West, establishing themselves first in Saskatchewan, and later moving to British Columbia, where their descendants still live as an almost autonomous community.

The part played by Kropotkin in this matter is recorded not only by Mavor but also by Aylmer Maude, the friend of Tolstoy, who wrote an account of these settlers (*A Peculiar People*), saying that Mavor "had done more than anyone else" to arouse interest in Canada, and that he had been instigated to this by Kropotkin, "another good friend of theirs". Kropotkin modestly remarked to Guillaume that he had helped them "a little". His interest in the Doukhobors continued; some of those who passed through England visited him at Bromley, where he welcomed them gladly. In 1902 he even contemplated returning in the summer to see how "our Doukhobors" were settling down in their new home, but his ill health prevented him, and he never went.

Kropotkin's next journey, in 1901, was also to North America. He had received from the Lowell Institute of Boston an invitation to deliver a further series of lectures, this time on Russian literature. The American writer Roger Baldwin has described this as "his most memorable visit to the United States", and he was certainly received with even more interest than before, speaking at most of the great centres of learning in the north-eastern United States.

Towards the end of February he sailed to Boston, where he stayed at the Colonial Club, and renewed many friendships of his first visit. He seems at first to have been disturbed about the success of his course, for he wrote to Professor Norton concerning the opening lecture:

> "...To tell the truth, I feel nervous for it. Such as I wrote it, it is too long, and may be too dull. So I rewrite it entirely, and so long as it is not done, I feel quite nervous. So I sit now, and write, and will work till late at night."

However, the series was a great success; according to Baldwin, "he spoke from notes, and in an English strongly accented, in a professorial but very earnest style". The Press reports were friendly, and the audiences large and alertly interested, a feature which characterised the whole of this tour. These lectures eventually formed the basis of the book, *Ideals and Realities in Russian Literature*.

Before leaving Boston he delivered a number of other lectures, speaking at Harvard University and Wellesley College. He even received an invitation from the unconventional clergyman, Edward Everett Hale, to speak in his church. He refused, since he objected to the institution, but, on being pressed, compromised by speaking in the church's lecture hall. Finally, he left Boston for New York on the 29th March, writing on the day before his departure a note to one of Professor Norton's daughters which gives some hint of the net of social visits into which he had been drawn.

"Your note is a great temptation for me—cups of tea included—but unfortunately Mr Ely has taken other engagements for me for this afternoon, and I will be deprived of the very great—verily very great pleasure that I should have had to see your dear father, yourself and your sisters. Tomorrow at one I go to New York and thence to Chicago."

In New York he delivered four major lectures to packed audiences. Two were at the fashionable Chickering Hall, in Fifth Avenue, where he spoke on Russian literature and anarchism. He also addressed the League for Political Education, and finally spoke on anarchism to a vast audience at the Cooper Union, where Ernest Crosby this time took the chair. Here, as in Boston, he was lionised by the fashionable world, and met a number of the ephemeral leaders of New York society. Perhaps the most incongruous of his visits was to Mrs Jefferson Davis, widow of the former Confederate President during the Civil War. Kropotkin had been taken there by Robert Erskine Ely, and during the visit the negro educator, Booker Washington, called at the hotel to ask for Ely. Mrs Davis wished to meet him, and the afternoon ended with the curious spectacle of the negro leader, the anarchist prince, and the widow of the slave-owning President talking together in the friendliest manner. But Kropotkin was not wholly swallowed up in the sensation-hunting of fashionable American society. He also spent much time at little meetings which his anarchist and radical friends organised in the working-class districts.

From New York he travelled to Chicago. On the way he was seized with a severe influenza which incapacitated him for a few days. But he recovered rapidly, and delivered a final group of lectures in this Middle Western city and the surrounding university towns. In Chicago he stayed at Hull House, the social settlement conducted by his friend Jane Addams, and there delivered a lecture on industrial organisation to the Chicago Arts and Crafts Society. Dr Alice Hamilton, who was staying in Hull House at the time, writes that Kropotkin impressed them all by the broad humanity of his attitude.

"More than any man I ever met he impressed me as one who loved his fellow men. No matter how dingy and unattractive a visitor might be—and the Russian revolutionaries in our neighbourhood were mostly both—Kropotkin would meet them with a warm welcome, kissing them on both cheeks. He was absolutely free from bitterness, toward his persecutors, toward the Russian regime of the Tsars, toward even the interviewing reporters of American papers, bent on getting him to defend assassination."

He also lectured to various literary and scientific societies, and to the local anarchist groups. And here, according to Emma Goldman, he at last grew tired of the attentions of fashionable hostesses and dealt with them in his own way:

"In 1901, while in Chicago, Kropotkin had Mrs Potter Palmer and other society ladies constantly at his heels. Once they arranged a luncheon for Peter; it happened to be on the 11th November—the anniversary of the Chicago Anarchists' martyrdom, a day on which the workers *en masse* visit Waldheim, where the murdered anarchists are buried. When Mrs Palmer called on the 'Prince', Peter with his usual charm and a mischievous twinkle in his blue eyes remarked: 'Madame, you can have the Prince, but I shall go with the workers to pay my deep respects to my dead comrades—Spies, Parsons, Lingg and the others'."

It is a story which is apocryphal in detail, since Kropotkin was in Chicago not in November, but in April, 1901, yet it certainly sounds true in substance.

The tour ended with a short trip west of Chicago. On the 22nd April Kropotkin addressed the University of Illinois, at Urbana, on "The Modern Development of Socialism"; in this lecture, after surveying the general field, he ended by expounding his own anarchist views. He was well received, and the student newspaper ended its long report by remarking:

"Prince Kropotkin's lecture was, on the whole, a clear and extremely forcible exposition of the views of the advanced scientific anarchists of the present day. It was of especial value in clearing up the haze of erroneous impressions which surrounds the subject of anarchists and anarchism. The opportunity of hearing him was one which was highly appreciated by those who took advantage of it."

The next day he went on to Madison, where he spoke at the University of Wisconsin on "Turgenev and Tolstoy", the lecture being reported "a success from every point of view". Afterwards he travelled back through Ohio, collecting information on American methods of wheat growing, which he used in the later editions of *Fields, Factories and Workshops*. He also visited Buffalo, where his friend Mavor came down from Toronto to spend two days with him. Then, in May, he sailed back to Europe. It had been an arduous journey, and Kropotkin regarded it as partly responsible for the severe illness he experienced towards the end of the year, for the lectures to audiences of between four and five thousand people had tired him "to death".

It was the last trip he could make to the United States, for in 1901, not long after his departure, Czolgosz assassinated the amiable but ineffectual President McKinley. Czolgosz was a young Polish worker who had acted on his own responsibility; he claimed to be an anarchist, but certainly had no connection with any American group. However, the incident was enough to let loose a campaign of virulent hatred against anarchism of every kind. Most, who had unfortunately been lazy enough that week to reprint in *Freiheit* an old editorial on the use of dynamite, was sent to prison for a year. Anarchists were beaten up in the streets, and Theodore Roosevelt came forward with proposals for drastic repression. The Press carried out one of its most unscrupulous campaigns of invention, and Chicago papers went so far as to suggest that the shooting of the President had been plotted at Hull House between Kropotkin, Emma Goldman and Czolgosz. There was no truth in the story, but Kropotkin was very distressed, more for the trouble it caused his Chicago friends than for the unjust reflections upon himself. The storm gradually died down, but left as its permanent relic the famous clause in the Immigration Laws which still forbids anarchists to enter the United States.

Since 1896, although Kropotkin had not yet paid any visit to the Continent, he had repeatedly contemplated doing so. During 1897, when Elisée Reclus founded his Free University in Brussels, he invited Kropotkin to deliver a course on Natural Science, and Edward Picard, the celebrated jurist, approached the Belgian Department of Justice to gain permission for the journey. The authorities, however, refused, and it appears that, although Kropotkin had departed from Belgium unnecessarily in 1877, a ban on his entry must subsequently have been imposed.

His strong interest in French affairs continued; centred round the question of terrorism within the anarchist movement, and also round the corruption in French politics revealed by the Dreyfus affair, which he associated with the Franco-Russian alliance as symptoms of the same social disease.

We have already indicated his general attitude towards terrorism when the question became acute in the early 1890's. As the decade continued the wave of assassinations mounted to a climax, but Kropotkin retained his own attitude of refusing to stand in judgment, and in 1898, on the occasion of the murder of the Empress of Austria, wrote a particularly impressive letter to his Danish friend, Georg Brandes. He admitted the evil of the act itself, and with his characteristic chivalry declared that "women and children at least ought to be spared in the terrible struggle amidst which we live". But he saw its cause in the general state of society, and analysed the conditions under which the assassin was brought up, the oppressions he witnessed in Italy, the violence which the State itself had taught him by example. And he contended that while society used violence in wars and executions, it could not expect the individual to have a higher moral standard.

> ". . . So long as contempt for human life shall be taught to men, and so long as they are told that it is good to kill for what one believes to be beneficial for mankind—new and newer victims will be added, even though the rulers should guillotine all those who take sides with the poor, who study the psychology of poverty and courageously tell what they have learned of that psychology."

Within the anarchist movement Kropotkin's influence was always against terrorism as a principle. But when at the turn of the century the fashion for assassination declined, it was not because of his disapproval, but because of the general realisation that in Western Europe such methods had merely a negative result and served to rouse public opinion, even among the workers, against the anarchists, while the advent of syndicalism gave a new field into which the activities of the movement, at least in the Latin countries, were largely diverted.

Kropotkin's concern with the Dreyfus affair and its connection with the prevailing tendency towards Cæsarism in France, represented by a whole series of articles written during 1899 in *Les Temps Nouveaux*, is interesting for a number of points which have a bearing on his attitude during the 1914 war. In these articles he made it clear that he regarded England and France as the countries which were socially most advanced and which, to fulfil their past, should have put themselves at the head of the revolutionary movement. That France did not do this, he declared, was due to three principal causes. Firstly, there was the weakness of her own radical leaders, who had allowed themselves to be led away from the revolutionary principles for which France should stand in the minds of men. Secondly, there was the influence of Russia which, by playing on the fear and cupidity of French politicians, led them into the Franco-Russian alliance, with its retarding influence. But the greatest blame of all was placed on Germany, whose imperialist ambitions, according to Kropotkin, were the great menace to peace. Early in 1899 he already declared: "It will be our fault, the fault of our generation, if it still hesitates, for fear of the German cannons, to raise, before the end of the century, its standard of the people in revolt." And here he not only blamed the German rulers, but also the German social-democrats, saying:

"The triumph for Germany was the triumph of militarism in Europe, of military and political despotism, and at the same time the worship of the State, of authority and State socialism, which is in reality nothing but State capitalism, triumphed in the ideas of a whole generation. If these ideas crib and confine the European mind at present, and even the minds of revolutionaries, we owe it in a great measure to the triumph of the military German Empire. On the other hand, if France is inclined to slide down the slope of Cæsarism instead of being the vanguard of the communist-communalist movement towards which her evolution tended, it is also in consequence of the disaster of 1870."

The whole error of Kropotkin's reasoning in these articles seems to arise from the tendency this old internationalist was assuming, to see social progress and retrogression in national terms. He approved of France because it was the country of the Great Revolution, and granted England credit for its traditions of rebellion. Germany he rejected because its philosophy did not appeal to him, and also because of the anti-German feeling among Russian revolutionaries, due to the Prussian associations of the Romanovs. Only towards Russia herself did he adopt the attitude he should have maintained everywhere, dissociating the misdeeds of the rulers from the essential peaceableness of the people, and finding in a system of authority, rather than in national characteristics, the reason for certain faults. If he had applied this standard everywhere, his general attitude would later have been much less confused.

During 1900 an anarchist congress was planned to take place in Paris. Kropotkin did not go, since he was unsure whether the ban on his entry still applied. It was perhaps fortunate that he stayed away, for when the congress began in September it was immediately suppressed by the French police, and his long report on experimental communities and their past failures, which he attributed mostly to authoritarian structure and the lack of leisure, was never read.

Meanwhile, increasing illness had given a new urgency to his desire to leave England. The end of 1901 brought symptoms of an alarming kind; in December he wrote to Guillaume:

> "Today exactly a month ago I nearly died. The heart stopped almost completely. I did not faint—not for a second did I lose consciousness, and told Sophie and Sasha (my little daughter) what to do, but had the sensation that life was coming to an end."

He thought it might have been due to *angina pectoris*, or merely to the overwork of the past seven or eight months. This gradual failure of health began to arouse concern among his family and friends, and for some time the question of his going abroad was discussed continually. He spent most of the winter of 1901–2 on the south coast, but a warmer climate seemed necessary for a complete cure. France was the obvious place, and there appears to have been some possibility that the French authorities might have allowed him entry, if he went only for reasons of health, particularly as the expulsion in 1896 had left his future status indefinite.

A long correspondence took place with Guillaume during January and February 1902, in which Kropotkin maintained consistently that he would insist on unconditional withdrawal of any ban on his entering France. Some efforts seem to have been made by Guillaume, for on the 19th January Kropotkin wrote to him, regarding the leaders of the French socialist and radical parties:

"These gentlemen, who agreed without hesitation to my expulsion (in 1896), when I came with the aim of lecturing on anarchism, would be delighted if they could boast in the streets that they had obtained for me the right to return to France—to be treated at some spa. I do not want to give them all that satisfaction, particularly as, if the doctor actually told me, 'Go to the South', I have the conviction, based on sound facts, that it would be enough for me to ask Clemenceau to persuade the Government that I am proceeding to such and such a place for treatment, to give an order to the police to leave me in peace, provided I do not appear in public.

"In case the radical socialists want to raise in full the question of expulsion in the manner I told you—all is well. This would annul all expulsions. As regards those who come for treatment, the greatest toleration is already being shown now. Indeed, I think I could go through the whole of France and travel to the South without anybody saying anything. Nevertheless, I never meant to avail myself of this toleration."

Guillaume appears to have wanted to get Jaurés to intervene, for in the next letter Kropotkin expressed his opinion of this celebrated leader of the French socialists, whose qualities he valued, but who, he could not forget, did not intervene over the question of his expulsion in 1896. He further referred to an intrigue by which Jaurés and Millerand were admitted to the 1896 International Socialist Congress, on the grounds that they were members of the Chamber of Deputies. "They started a Marxist intrigue, which consisted of abolishing international workers' congresses and replacing them, by fraudulent means, with international congresses of elected socialists." He ended by saying that, although he might wish to dissociate Jaurés from the rest of the socialist intriguers, such incidents were impossible to pass over. All this seems rather exacting, since he had always claimed that political life naturally led to intrigue, and therefore he could not reasonably pick out a politician and blame him for a defect which was the necessary "occupational disease" of his trade. After this correspondence, it appears that the French government would not agree to a complete withdrawal of the expulsion order, and a week later Kropotkin no longer wished to make his visit to France, since "quite understandably I cannot agree to such curtailment of my liberty".

During the next two years there were several unfulfilled plans of trips abroad. In the spring of 1902 an unknown friend proposed a cruise in the Mediterranean, and in the following winter, when Kropotkin had been incapacitated by damp weather for several weeks, he wrote: "Sophie advises me to go somewhere in the south in January. The prospect of the Pyrenees I do not relish greatly. Perhaps Algiers—at least it would be new." He seems to have been alarmed by the severity of his recurrent illnesses, for he added:

> "What, in particular, keeps me back is that I know that I cannot live long, and I want to spend my few remaining years with Sophie and Sasha, who both love me so much. And they are so depressed in my absence."

He was over-pessimistic, and as the years passed he adopted a more resigned attitude towards his bouts of alarming prostration, which his naturally strong constitution enabled him to sustain where they would have killed a weaker man.

The next summer he had more plans for wide travel, which again did not materialise. Trips to Norway or Teneriffe, a quick visit to French Canada, were considered, but the summer was too cold and he settled, as he told Guillaume, "extremely prosaically on the north shores of Devon", which he liked because it reminded him "of the narrow valleys of some parts of the Jura". Guillaume was at this time in Switzerland, and Kropotkin asked him, if he went to Geneva, to "see without fail Herzig and Bertoni".

Meanwhile he had been persistently inviting Guillaume to visit him in England, and his old friend had as persistently evaded acceptance, until at last it transpired that he was too fearful of sea travel even to make the short Channel crossing. In the autumn of 1903 Kropotkin remarked that "I have never yet suffered from sea-sickness", and therefore announced his intention of going to St Malo or some other Breton town. A long correspondence followed in which Guillaume suggested a meeting in Paris, and Kropotkin did not think it safe to go there or even to Boulogne, where his arrival on the sea-coast in the winter might arouse the suspicions of the police. He suggested that Holland remained a possibility, but that it was a country he did not like, although he had visited it without difficulty. When and where this visit was made we cannot say, since this remark is the only trace of it we have been able to find.

In these years Kropotkin's anxiety over trouble with the police of various countries became almost an obsession, no doubt because he felt that his state of health would not allow him to endure imprisonment or bad treatment. As late as May 1904, when invited to speak on mutual aid at the International Philosophical Congress in Switzerland, he refused to go, although his friends there had promised to make sure the Swiss government would not intervene.

But in the next month he finally broke the barrier of mingled apprehension and pride that had kept him away from the Continent for so many years. He had heard that Reclus was seriously ill, and decided that to see his old friend again he would risk any obstacles that might arise. No attempt was in fact made to stop him at Ostend, and he stayed in Brussels for four days without interference. He was greatly distressed by the state in which he found Reclus, and on returning wrote to Mrs Dryhurst:

> "You know he is seriously ill; that is, he is the same, but he has continual attacks of the heart (obstruction of the aorta) and with them a fearful anæmia. I came just in time to find him in Brussels, before he left for the country. He speaks with the same energy as always, but is very weak; fatigue calls forth at once an attack of the heart."

He thought his friend's death might occur at any moment, but Reclus survived for a whole year. When he died, on the 4th July 1905, Kropotkin was moved more deeply than at any time since the death of Stepniak; he wrote long obituary articles for both the *Geographical Journal* and *Freedom*, in which he told of his intense admiration for this man, whom he respected both as an able scientist and as a pure and humble person who, more than anyone else he had met, contrived to live as an anarchist even within the capitalist State.

Two months later the long-projected meeting with Guillaume at last took place, in Brittany. The French authorities did not interfere with Kropotkin, and it seems likely that they decided to consider the matter of expulsion as lapsed, particularly in view of his old age and the great increase in his fame during the past ten years. He stayed at Etables, where, beside Guillaume, he met a number of Russian friends of liberal inclinations. He and Guillaume were equally delighted to renew their former intimacy, even though they had drifted apart a great deal in their attitude since the days of 1877. Their differences were cordially expressed, and resulted in no acrimony. Guillaume's adhesion to anarchist communism had always been reluctant, and now he seemed definitely opposed. He had in the meantime become an enthusiastic syndicalist, and regarded the recently founded Confederation General du Travail, the French trade-union organisation which still exists in a drastically changed form, as the great hope for achieving revolutionary changes in the near future.

Kropotkin's attitude was more cautious. Where Guillaume placed syndicalism in the forefront, Kropotkin regarded it as only one aspect and phase of anarchism. The main object of anarchist activity was, for him, the attainment of the maximum real freedom of the individual by any means that did not tend to destroy the end itself. Thus he regarded syndicalism with a live interest, and thought that if its revolutionary elements came to the surface, it might represent a workers' movement which would re-create the old spirit of the Bakuninist International. But he did not wish to place too much trust in the C.G.T., which already had reformist tendencies and was beginning to show the centralist trend that in his opinion had spoilt the English trade unions. He saw an encouraging tendency in the insistence of revolutionary syndicalists that workers' organisations must be built from below on local autonomy and without an official hierarchy, and thought it natural that all anarchists who worked in a trade should enter the appropriate union and endeavour to prevent it from coming under the control of politicians. Indeed, he went even farther when, in 1907, he declared:

> "Workmen's organisations are the real force capable of accomplishing the social revolution—after the awakening of the proletariat has been accomplished, first by individual action, then by collective action, by strikes and revolts extending more and more;

and where workmen's organisations have not allowed themselves to be dominated by the gentlemen who advocate 'the conquest of political power', but have continued to walk hand in hand with anarchists—as they have done in Spain—they have obtained, on the one hand, immediate results (an eight-hour day in certain trades in Catalonia), and on the other have made good propaganda for the social revolution—the one to come, not from the efforts of those highly-placed gentlemen, but from below, from workmen's organisations."

But, unlike the more sectarian syndicalists, he did not regard trade unions as themselves capable of providing the skeleton of a free society; across the lines of organisation by industry would run those of commune and locality, so that, since any organisation involves a concession of principle, there would be the maximum safeguard for freedom. He expressed this view briefly but clearly in a letter to Luigi Bertoni in March 1914:

"The syndicate is absolutely necessary. It is the only form of working-men's group that permits of maintaining the direct struggle against capital, without falling into parliamentarism. But evidently it does not take that trend mechanically, since we have in Germany, France and England syndicates rallying to parliamentarism, and in Germany orthodox syndicates which are very powerful, etc. The *other* element is necessary, the element of which Malatesta speaks and which Bakunin has always practised."

Among those who visited Kropotkin at Etables was Dr Fritz Brupbacher, a young Swiss scientist whose ideas tended towards anarchism, and who has recorded a number of interesting facts about his conversation with Kropotkin.

"I began by asking his opinion of municipal socialism, as recognised by social-democrats. He thought that only the capitalists, above all the landlords, profited by it. . . .

"Kropotkin spoke in harsh terms of Marx, and still more harshly of Engels; Engels had exercised the worst possible influence upon Marx in his opinion. . . .

"His conversation showed warm interest and natural exuberant charm, suddenly interrupted by dire wrath against Marxists and Russian Social Revolutionaries. This wrath easily propelled him to make unjust remarks. But it was not repulsive and I liked it rather, want of justice and all. It was the want of justice of a living man who hates and loves with equal warmth."

For the rest, conversation turned mainly on Russia, which was already going through the early stages of the 1905 Revolution. Brupbacher says that Kropotkin at first struck him as of a retiring disposition, but the evening ended gaily, with Guillaume playing the piano, while Kropotkin "danced with the girls and did all sorts of nonsense and playful things".

From Brittany Kropotkin went back with Guillaume to Paris, where he spent the latter part of September, staying, it seems probable, in the house of Camille Pissaro. It was his first visit to the French capital for eighteen years. He met many old and new comrades there, spending much time in the company of Grave at the offices of *Les Temps Nouveaux*. Most of the conversations were concerned with questions of propaganda, but they also talked about the question of anti-militarism.

The traditional anarchist position has always been one of opposition to military organisation, on the grounds that the armed forces are the chief buttress of authority and that military service is itself a denial of individual liberty. This attitude does not necessarily imply a rejection of violence, or of all kinds of war; indeed, many anarchists have sided with Bakunin in advocating revolutionary wars based on the uprising of a country against a native or foreign oppressor. But in 1905 Kropotkin stepped right out of this tradition; already in Brittany he had expressed to Brupbacher "his disagreement with the anti-patriotic anti-militarism of syndicalists, since he considered it worth while to defend republican France", and when he went to Paris he continued to maintain this attitude, contending that anarchists should take part in a war against Germany, and even suggesting that opposition to conscription should be dropped. As Nettlau has remarked, "This was not quite unexpected to those who knew him before, but it was a great sensation to some, and a great distress to others". In a later chapter we shall show more thoroughly how this attitude ended finally in an almost complete separation from the international anarchist movement. For the present it is sufficient to record the symptoms of its development.

This journey to France was the beginning of a regular series of trips to the Continent, since it was evident that the French government did not intend to interfere with Kropotkin, and his immunity was probably enhanced by the increase of his international reputation through the publication of *Mutual Aid* in France in 1906.

He went to Brittany again in the summer of 1906, and to Paris during January 1907, meeting many Russian and French friends. He seems to have been in the French capital again with Sophie during the summer of 1907, since Emma Goldman met them when she came to Europe for the international anarchist congress at Amsterdam. Kropotkin himself did not attend this gathering, which was the largest anarchist congress yet held, including eighty delegates from European, American, and Asiatic countries. Why he stayed away is not clear. His health was possibly a reason, but it also seems likely that he realised already that the movement as a whole, and many of his old friends, were sharply hostile to some of his own ideas. This was particularly so on the issue of militarism, for the congress adopted unanimously a strong resolution with which he can hardly have agreed.

"The Anarchists, desiring the integral emancipation of humanity and the absolute liberty of the individual, are naturally the declared enemies of all armed force in the hands of the State—army, navy, or police.

"They urge all comrades, according to circumstances and individual temperament, to revolt and refuse to serve (either individually or collectively), to passively and actively disobey, and to join in a military strike for the destruction of all the instruments of domination.

"They express the hope that the people of all countries affected will reply to a declaration of war by insurrection."

Indeed, reading the minutes of this congress, one has the feeling that, while men like Malatesta were kept by their activity in the main stream of the revolutionary movement, Kropotkin was already thought of as a man to be respected as a theoretician, but to be disregarded on the question of tactics in the daily struggle from which he lived in retirement. This attitude was largely justified, for his increasing tendency towards a kind of mitigated French patriotism was already leading him into that political abstractionism which he had so often condemned in others.

Towards the end of this decade Kropotkin's concern over his health again became acute, and in the early summer of

1908 he made a journey to Ascona, on the shores of Lake Maggiore, to consult an anarchist physician, Dr Raphael Friedberg, who appears to have recommended him to spend his winters away from the damp climate of England which aggravated his periodical attacks of chronic bronchitis. He returned home in July, but was again in Paris in October, this time in connection with the commission over the Azev affair, which will be discussed more fully in the chapter concerning his Russian interests. The protracted hearings wearied him greatly, and when, in his spare hours, he saw James Guillaume, it was to talk for relaxation on trivial subjects.

Finally, at Christmas 1908, he went to Locarno for the first of his long winter sojourns out of England. He had not been in Switzerland since his expulsion in 1881, but the authorities seem to have made no objection to his entry. It was only after nearly three months, towards the end of March, that trouble began when two Swiss newspapers, the *Neue Zuricher Zeitung* and the *Basler Nachrichten*, expressed their astonishment that he should be allowed to stay for so long. He wrote to Luigi Bertoni, who was then editing *Le Reveil* in Geneva, saying that "these articles may compel me to leave suddenly". However, the Ticinese cantonal authorities were not anxious to expel him; the local police inspector called, but behaved with great politeness and there was no further interference. In fact, after hearing of this incident, Guillaume established contact with some old acquaintances who had now become leading figures in the Bundesrat at Berne, and received the assurance that no attempt would be made to interfere with Kropotkin's stay. In Locarno he was visited by many old Swiss friends, such as Herzig and Dumartheray, who had been unable to come to England, and he also spent some time with his English friend, Charles Rowley, the Manchester frame-maker and founder of the Ancoats Brotherhood, who had been one of his admirers for many years. He returned to England in about May 1909.

The next winter he varied his programme, going to Italy, where he could be sure of no interference of the type which, even if it had no definite result, had given a distressing atmosphere to his last stay in Switzerland. He chose as his place of residence the little sea-coast town of Rapallo, and stayed there the whole winter until the end of April, working desultorily on articles for *The Nineteenth Century*. He had a good deal of rest there, with few visitors except for Marsh, the editor of *Freedom*, Rowley, and a few Italian comrades. Sasha and Sophie both accompanied him on this tour, as the family funds seem to have been more abundant, and on leaving Rapallo he went with his daughter to Florence, where they spent some days with the Cobden-Sandersons, going almost daily to the churches and museums of the city. They departed on the last day of April, Sasha for Paris and Peter for Locarno, and the lonely and morbid Cobden-Sanderson recorded in his diary:

"I may be of no account in my own family, but sometimes on some seem to work a strange and wonderful impression. And dear Kropotkin spent an almost sleepless night in 'ecstasy', in consequence of a few words of mine about the Cosmos—spoken as we crossed together the Ponte Vecchio—so he told me. We kissed each other on both cheeks when we parted. How dear and affectionate he is. We are very happy together, the times we meet."

At Locarno Kropotkin spent some weeks, taking elaborate precautions against police interference by giving the address of his physician at Ascona and exhorting his friends on no account to write his name on their letters. Finally, at the end of May, he returned to England, and wrote to a friend that the visit had done him "a lot of good". He added, at the end of the same letter:

"But we ask ourselves—what next? We should not like to abandon England entirely, and to have a house—however small—here, and to spend the winter in Italy—as the doctors advise me to do—is so difficult!"

However, by the end of the year he appears to have solved this problem, for until the outbreak of the Great War in 1914 he contrived to spend all the winters except one abroad. His income from royalties had increased with the appearance of American and Continental editions of his books, and the removal from Highgate to a small house in Brighton was probably an economy. Another change in family arrangements was made by the marriage of Sasha, who had grown into an attractive young woman, to an emigré Social Revolutionary, Boris Lebedev, who is not to be confused with Kropotkin's anarchist disciple, Nicholas Lebedev, the later editor of some of his works. Sasha left home after her marriage, and went to live in Ladbroke Grove, Kensington, but very close relationships continued between her and her parents, so that the closely knit family ties were in no way broken, and when Kropotkin went to London it was at Sasha's flat that he always stayed.

Early in December 1910 he again set off for Rapallo, spending four days at Milan, during which the continual rain forced him to stay indoors with some English friends. From Rapallo he wrote to Marsh:

> "We are now on the other side of Rapallo. Do you remember the little river up the valley, which you reach in passing near the rly. stn. under the bridge? It is in this valley we are, some 8 min. from the rly. stn. Pretty apartment, but the view (backs of poor tenement houses) is not so good, and we cannot yet succeed in getting stove etc. put in order.
>
> "We have had pouring rain—cats and dogs—all these nine days since I came. Today is the first sunny day—and beautiful it is! In the afternoon we had to go to Chiavari, and the view on the sea made us forget all the rainy days. . . .
>
> "Nobody but a few Russian ladies in Rapallo of visitors. Otherwise, before the 'natale' (Christmas) the little town is animated."

He also mentioned the death of Tolstoy and the articles he was writing on this event.

The stay at Rapallo once again lasted to the end of April, and was followed by a further visit to Locarno. In the middle of June he was taken ill, which *The Times* considered sufficiently important to report. Then, at the end of the month, the question of his presence in Switzerland was again raised. For some inexplicable reason the government, which in 1909 had allowed him to stay unmolested, became anxious to get rid of him, and he wrote to a friend that the Federal Police wished the Ticinese to tell him that his banishment still held good. The report of *The Times* correspondent was slightly different, for on the 16th July he wrote:

> "Prince Kropotkin spent eight weeks this summer, for reasons of health, in Locarno without first obtaining the permission of the Swiss government. The authorities of the Canton Ticino, on discovering his presence, informed the government, and, this coming to Prince Kropotkin's knowledge, he left Switzerland to avoid a

second expulsion. The government would, probably, have granted him permission to remain in Switzerland had he applied for it."

What seems likely is that the Swiss Federal authorities wished to attach conditions to their permission, and that Kropotkin had no desire to accept them, particularly as, by June, the need for absence from England was already over.

The winter of 1911–12 was spent in England. It was the first year at Brighton, and Kropotkin may well have found that the coast air rendered it unnecessary for him to leave. At the end of 1912, however, he departed again to Locarno. He seems to have decided to defy the Swiss ban, but his doctor, a Ticinese named Tognola, himself made a request for the decree of expulsion to be withdrawn. The Federal Council replied by granting permission for Kropotkin to stay for three months on account of his health. He outstayed the time, and in due course the interference began again; for he told Tom Keell, the manager of Freedom Press:

> "But now the Fed. Council put the condition that I shall apply for pardon—for the abolition of the decree—which I, of course, refuse to do.
>
> "So they do not reply to the citizens of Locarno, who met once more and repeated this application. Also the Freethinkers of French Switzerland."

He remarked that his health was good, and commented on the suffragettes, who at this time were actively borrowing the anarchist tactic of direct action:

> "I also wish the women get their darling vote. But it will take them fifty years, or more, to realise its futility—and in the meantime their leaders will help the privileged classes to defend their privileges. Why should they be more intelligent than the workers were when they got the universal suffrage?"

In spite of these views he was personally on good terms with many suffragettes, including the Pankhursts and Mrs Despard.

In May 1913 he was visited by Luigi Bertoni, the Ticinese, who was conducting from Geneva the publication of a wide variety of anarchist books and pamphlets which could not be printed in Italy itself. Until his death in 1947, Bertoni ran a bilingual review, *Le Reveil Anarchiste*, and it was he who published the Italian versions of *Paroles d'un Revolté* and *The Great French Revolution.* Ironically, the translator of the greater part of these works was Benito Mussolini, then a young and poor revolutionary socialist. He translated *Paroles d'un Revolté* in 1904 for no payment whatever, and described the book as overflowing "with a great love for oppressed humanity, and with infinite kindness". Kropotkin was delighted with his translation of *The Great French Revolution*, and said to Bertoni, "I am going to write to Benito Mussolini in Forli, to thank him for his brilliant translation. . . . I am delighted by his boldness; how much courage he must have to keep cool during these outbursts of 'patriotism' in connection with Tripoli". The founder of the New Rome was then an ardent opponent of militarism, and not for some years yet was he to begin his progress towards dictatorship.

At this meeting, in 1913, Bertoni and Kropotkin discussed the trend of current events, and Bertoni has left this record of their conversation:

"The last time I saw Kropotkin at Locarno I had a private talk with him, which lasted about six hours, from 4 to 10 in the evening, about the dreadful subject—War. We parted deeply shaken by the diversity of our opinions. Kropotkin felt that the majority of our comrades shared my views, while I was even then inexpressibly grieved about the influence which he would no doubt exercise over some of our comrades, and the great consequences which his trend of thought would have on our movement. Further, it was difficult to be in conflict with a man whom I greatly loved and respected."

It represented a cleavage, not only with Bertoni, but also with older friends in Geneva, Dumartheray and Herzig, for in November 1914, writing to these men after he had made open his position regarding the war, Kropotkin said: "Nothing is more excruciating than the difference between me and you three."

He finally left Locarno in the second week in June, halting on his way for five days in Paris, where he again met his French friends at the offices of *Les Temps Nouveaux* and discussed the likely trends of the immediate future. But his contact with the French movement was now only with individuals, and, although he still wrote for Grave's journal, and in August 1913 sent a letter to the French Anarchist Congress on the essentials of anarchism, he seems to have been regarded already by the younger generation as an old idealist. Sorel, who tried to give syndicalism a seductive mythology, was the fashion of the time. He and Kropotkin never met, and if they had it is unlikely that they would have agreed.*

The journey home on this occasion almost undid the good which this holiday had effected, for there was a high storm in the Channel and Kropotkin was prostrated by sea-sickness. He told Bertoni that he had been in four other bad storms at sea during his life, and been affected by none of them, "but in this I suffered terribly and could not even raise myself to see Sonya". His constitution had become so sensitive to disturbance that it was three weeks before he recovered wholly.

The last visit to Western Europe took place in the winter of 1913–14, and this time the whole six months, up to mid-summer 1914, was spent at the little North Italian sea-coast town of Bordighera. Shortly after arriving, he wrote to Keell in England:

> "Yes, dear Keell, plenty of sunshine here. A very quiet spot, a very primitive road for walking along the sea, a beautiful sea which one is never tired to admire and of which I always think as of the cradle of our civilisation; beautifully ragged mountains, losing themselves in a blue mist, every square yard of which is cultivated for hundreds of years since. And an air quite invigorating now that it has snowed in the mountains. . . . We were happy enough to get a very nice, sunny apartment."

He talked of the progress of *Freedom*, expressed pleasure at the large sale of pamphlets in England, and concern at the health of George Barrett, the brilliant young editor of the Glasgow *Anarchist*, who was dying of consumption.

The trend of world affairs was already clear by the early days of 1914; in January he wrote despairingly to Keell, "When? When shall we see the dawn?" In March he was discussing with Bertoni the possibility of war breaking out within the next two months, and deploring the strife between the ultra-syndicalist Guillaume and the "pure" anarchists, which was

* Kropotkin actually had a bitter dispute with Sorel's leading disciple, Hubert Lagardelle, who many years later justified the anarchist's suspicion by assuming office in the Vichy government during the Second World War.

threatening to immobilise the Continental movement at this critical time.

But his days were not spent wholly in gloomy forebodings. Many old and new friends visited him at Bordighera, often meeting him for the last time, and he received them with his old pleasure and gaiety. He was especially pleased when Madame Lavrov, who had introduced him to anarchism more than forty years ago, came all the way from St Petersburg to see him, travelling by train, at the age of seventy-two, three days and nights. Jean Grave and the English radical, Dr G. B. Clark, also came, and it was here that Max Nettlau saw him for the last time. Grave has portrayed him on this holiday as the same light-hearted and kindly figure, playing Russian music on the piano, and calling the servant girls from the next villa to join in the party.

This last spring in Italy dwindled away, with the threat of war drawing ever nearer, and in the first week in June he returned to England. It was his last visit to those countries to whose awakening he had devoted the most active years of his life, his last meeting with many old comrades in work and struggle, from whom the events of a few weeks ahead were to estrange him permanently.

CHAPTER VII

THE WRITER

I

We have dealt with the principal events of Kropotkin's career in Western Europe, reserving his Russian interests for later chapters, and here we must turn aside to consider the literary productions which form his contribution to political and sociological thought. The object of the present chapter is mainly expository, since the significance of Kropotkin's teachings in that historical perspective which embraces his day and ours will be discussed at the end of the book.

The main works we shall consider are five in number. *Paroles d'un Revolté* and *The Conquest of Bread* are concerned directly with the anarchist theory of revolution and social organisation. *Mutual Aid* is a treatise on evolution which proceeds from biology into anthropology and thence to the sociological realm of human relationships. *Fields, Factories and Workshops* is a more strictly sociological work, embracing such important themes as economic decentralisation, the relationship between industry and agriculture, and the integration of work and education. *The Great French Revolution*, besides being a lively and comprehensive history of a significant period, is also an elaborate inquiry into the origin of revolutions and the reasons why they do not always preserve their original impetus or gain all the aims for which their more clear-sighted actors strive. In addition, we shall consider his pamphlets on *The State* and *Anarchist Morality* which represent the most important short writings during the period before 1917. Three major books do not enter into this pattern and are dealt with elsewhere. They are the *Memoirs of a Revolutionist*, already discussed, *Ideals and Realities in Russian Literature*, which fits most appropriately into the narrative of Russian activities, and *Ethics*, which belongs to the final days after 1917.

In considering these books, one important fact must be borne in mind. With the exception of the major part of *The Great French Revolution*, all appeared originally as articles in anarchist papers or as essays in literary reviews like *The Nineteenth Century*. This fact inevitably affected their style, particularly in the case of *Paroles d'un Revolté* and *The Conquest of Bread*, which were written for working men, and have a simplicity and brevity of expression not usually encountered in political books. Even the more directly scientific writings are executed with a minimum of jargon and in very straightforward terms, for Kropotkin believed that ideas should always be made understandable to the common man, and that technical phraseology could be much diminished when discussing broad scientific issues.

This way of writing had both faults and virtues. It created freshness of expression and ease of understanding. Any of Kropotkin's books is incomparably clearer to the general reader than most Marxist treatises. But it also encouraged a tendency to simplify complex issues and to generalise where particular analysis might have been more appropriate. Kropotkin's scientific view had many gaps; he was, for instance, by no means sufficiently conscious of the young science of psychology, and tended to relegate it too easily to a subordinate branch of physiology. Yet such flaws were more often the faults of the age than of the man, and if Kropotkin's judgments were at times too sweeping or hasty, it must also be said that what Havelock Ellis has called his "many-sided nature" gave him a much more balanced attitude towards human problems seen as a whole than can usually be found among scientific specialists.

Paroles d'un Revolté is a collection of articles written in *Le Revolté* between 1880 and the end of 1882. It shows impressively the maturity and certainty of expression which Kropotkin had attained in the comparatively short period since his arrival in Switzerland in 1877. Three years of active agitation had been sufficient to develop his ideas and to enable him, when circumstances forced him to assume the editorship of *Le Revolté*, to emerge as the most accomplished spokesman of anarchist thought since Proudhon.

The quality of this book is uneven, largely because it was

collected soon after the articles had been written, with the consequence that there are a number of prophetic utterances relating to a revolution which Kropotkin expected in the near future and which never materialised, and these tend to obscure the excellent social judgment of the more analytical essays. But even such ephemeræ show an accurate perception of genuine social disturbances, of symptoms which Kropotkin wrongly interpreted as presaging the final destruction of the State. In fact they foretold the decay of private capitalism and its replacement by a more acute economic and political centralisation. It was an error which many others, including Kropotkin's leading Marxist opponents, made in those optimistic days before the long disillusionment which has paralysed socialist intellectuals in our day.

But, setting aside the four essays written in this vein of inaccurate prophecy, there remains a group of sixteen articles which have a varying degree of interest as illustrations of Kropotkin's general theories of social development. Some, like *An Appeal to the Young*, are little more than eloquent exhortations to activity, and others deal too briefly with their subjects to have lasting value. But the rest illustrate admirably the writer's criticism of political activity, his own theory of revolution, and his conception of the general lines along which a free society might emerge from the vague aspirations of the discontented.

The criticism of political activity, particularly in those countries which boast that their constitution gives them peculiar freedom, is contained in a long analysis of representative government. Kropotkin begins from the assumption that:

> "... The *political* regime to which human societies are submitted is always the expression of the economic regime which exists within that society. Political organisation does not change at the will of legislators; it can, it is true, change its name, it can today be presented in the form of a monarchy, tomorrow in that of a republic, but it does not suffer an equivalent change; it is fashioned and made to fit the economic regime, of which it is always the expression and, at the same time, the consecration and support."

Thence he demonstrates that universal suffrage cannot in itself effect anything, since the system will always act in accordance with the interests of those who control the economy; real gains by the oppressed have only been won by direct action, which has scared property owners and legislators into making concessions.

The natural tendencies of government in general are manifested in the case of representative government by centralism and a unification of functions which clearly leads to practical incompetence, particularly since the typical legislator attempts to deal with a multitude of issues, on all of which he cannot be expected to have real knowledge.

> "A veritable Proteus, omniscient and omnipresent, today a soldier and tomorrow a pigman, successively a banker, an academician, a street-sweeper, doctor, astronomer, drug-manufacturer, tanner, or contractor, according to the orders of the day in Parliament, he never knows a moment's hesitation. Accustomed in his capacity as lawyer, journalist or public orator to speak of things he knows nothing of, he votes for all these and other questions as well with only this difference: while in the newspapers he merely amused with his gossip, and in the court room his voice only awoke the sleeping judges, in Parliament he will make laws for thirty or forty million inhabitants."

Against the passive obedience, waste and bureaucracy of representative government, Kropotkin raises his ideal of a society based on individual and communal responsibility and voluntary agreement, "the formation from the simple to the composite of groups constituted freely for the satisfaction of all the multiple needs of individuals in society".

His attack on government does not, indeed, end with its parliamentary form. He is equally opposed to the so-called revolutionary government, whether elected or dictatorial, by which State socialists claim they will bridge the period of transition to a free society. In the essay entitled *Revolutionary Government* he examines a series of historical instances and shows how the attempt to consecrate a revolution by the establishment of an authority merely halts further development and begins the process of retrogression. This happens because a revolution is a growing movement and cannot be restricted within an institutionalised form.

> "The practical solution will not be found, will not be made clear until the change will have already begun. It will be the product of

the revolution itself, of the people in action, or else it will be nothing, the brains of a few individuals being absolutely incapable of finding solutions which can only spring from the life of the people."

Any government tends to crystallise progress at the point of its own development, and then, in resisting further change, to become the bulwark from which counter-revolution can advance. Nor can it be regarded as an instrument capable of the task of reorganisation which, altering all that is today based on property and exchange, will be "so immense and so profound . . . that it is impossible for one or any individual to elaborate the different social forms which must spring up in the society of the future". This can only be done by the "collective suppleness of mind of the whole people", and any external authority will merely be an obstacle, and a "source of discord and hatred".

While it can be admitted that these contentions show a somewhat extreme *narodnik* faith in the people, it must be stressed in Kropotkin's favour that all his arguments regarding the faults of revolutionary government were thoroughly based on past events, and have been confirmed in our own day by the example of Bolshevik Russia.

If we admit the criticisms of the path followed by State socialists, what is the anarchist alternative? Kropotkin puts forward a theory of revolution and sketches the main features of the kind of society at which he would aim.

We have already seen that in 1872, on his first visit to the Jura, he had come to regard revolution as a phase in social evolution, largely independent of individual initiative and obeying obscure laws of mass impulse. In his essay, *The Spirit of Revolt*, he elaborates this conception. At certain periods the existing social framework, which may in the past have evolved in accordance with economic demands, now becomes incapable of dealing with the cumulative effect of social change. Growing and active elements in society become aware of its inadequacy and move towards revolt. The existing authorities try by repression to halt the rebellious impulses, and thus to economic demands is added a sense of injustice which further inflames opposition to the government. At such times attempts at gradual adjustment are made. But these reforms are of no avail;

they merely show the impossibility of anything short of a complete and immediate reconstruction. "Such periods demand revolution. It becomes a social necessity; the situation in itself is revolutionary."

Revolution itself is the act of the masses, but it is always prepared by minorities conscious of the realities of their situation, who have a clear conception of the necessary remedies, and who pursue a policy of continuous action, on all planes, "in order to keep the spirit alive, to propagate and find expression for dissatisfaction, to excite hatred against exploiters, to ridicule the government and expose its weakness, and above all and always, by actual example, to awaken courage and fan the spirit of revolt".

It is this action which appeals to the masses, and which will one day lead them into casting aside their fears and advancing courageously to the destruction of the old order. And for this reason, says Kropotkin in this persuasive apology for the theory of "propaganda by deed", the greatest influence in a revolutionary situation will adhere to that group which has made itself most respected by the people for its continual activity, even though there may be other groups who have worked out their theories more fully and made more thorough propaganda by speech and writing.

But Kropotkin does not suggest that the revolutionary groups should assume power. Their role would be to awaken the revolutionary consciousness of the people, and to keep it directed towards fundamental goals. But he insists that the revolution will be nothing, if, after overthrowing the authority to which it is opposed, it does not immediately proceed to the satisfaction of real grievances.

> "If on the morrow of the revolution the masses of the people have only phrases at their service, if they do not recognise, by clear and blinding facts, that the situation has been transformed to their advantage, if the overthrow ends only in a change of persons and formulæ, nothing will have been achieved. . . .
>
> "In order that the revolution should be something more than a word, in order that the reaction should not lead us back tomorrow to the situation of yesterday, the conquest of today must be worth the trouble of defending; the poor of yesterday must not be poor today."

In our age, says Kropotkin, there is only one way of achieving this clear satisfaction of popular needs, and that is by means of a full expropriation by the oppressed of social goods and means of production. He recognises that a total change of attitude cannot be expected immediately, but the breakdowns of authority in which revolutions occur make it possible to lay the foundations of such a change. Moreover, all the various manifestations of social and economic life are interconnected so intimately that only a complete transformation can ensure against a retrogression such as has followed every revolution in the past.

> ". . . When these days shall come—and it is for you to hasten their coming—when a whole region, when great towns with their suburbs shall shake off their rulers, our work is clear; all equipment must return to the community, the social means held by individuals must be restored to their true owners—everybody, so that each may have his full share in consumption, that production may continue in everything that is necessary and useful, and that social life, far from being interrupted, may be resumed with the greatest energy."

Farms, stores, workshops, railways, all are necessary if a complete and lasting social change is to be effected, if the people are not to find themselves once again under the heel of the oppressor.

The method of administering the social amenities which have been expropriated, and of replacing the government of men by the administration of things and services, Kropotkin finds in the commune. By this he means the local association of individuals linked by residential ties, or other bonds of interest, for the satisfaction of common needs. By a clear analysis of the functioning of urban and rural communes in the Middle Ages he shows, not only that this is practicable, but also that it provides an insurance against both economic want and political oppression that cannot exist in the centralised State. But he also shows that, while the mediæval commune was often a little isolated "State", the technological progress of modern society makes such a clear division impossible. Communes, urban and rural, composed alike of peasants and industrial workers, will be the centres of life and production in town and country, but they will also be points of intersection in a whole network of federal associations for various purposes, while each commune itself will be a federation of smaller groups of individuals.

> "For us, 'Commune' is no longer a territorial agglomeration; it is rather a generic name, a synonym for the grouping of equals, knowing neither frontiers nor walls. The social commune will soon cease to be a clearly defined whole. Each group of the commune will necessarily be drawn towards other similar groups in other communes; it will be grouped and federated with them by links as solid as those which attach it to its fellow citizens, and will constitute a commune of interests whose members are scattered in a thousand towns and villages."

He sees already a tendency in this direction in the many scientific, literary, and sports organisations which link thousands of people in all countries. The universal application of this principle will constitute the pattern of future society. "It is by free groupings that the social commune will be organised, and these groupings themselves will overthrow walls and frontiers."

Each commune will itself consist of associated groups of producers, and for the satisfaction of regional needs there will be spontaneous associations between communes and their component groups. Of course, it is possible that the various communes may become jealous of each other, may even be drawn into physical conflict. But Kropotkin does not regard this as a very formidable danger, for there will be common interests as well as grievances, and the existence of bonds between individuals and groups outside the communes will tend to prevent the emergence of territorial strife.

In *Paroles d'un Revolté* this communal conception of society is necessarily sketched out roughly, yet Kropotkin manages to make his picture very convincing and at the same time he discusses many important related subjects. Here we have room to pay special attention only to the study of *Law and Authority*, in which he discusses one essential feature of the anarchist case—the contention that law and authority are unnecessary for human relationships—more than this, that they are positively harmful and evil.

He begins by tracing the development of law, through primitive superstitions, exploited by certain classes in order to ensure their domination, and afterwards through the decrees of conquerors. These laws, he says, have little social significance, except in a few cases where such a rule of sociability as "thou shalt not kill" has been incorporated with reservations into the written law. But the greater proportion of the normal intercourse of men is carried on, even in authoritarian societies, by custom and free agreement, with the law interfering only in exceptional cases.

Most laws, in fact, have one of two objects. They are intended either to protect property or to maintain the machinery of government, which is in its turn an institution for protecting property. If property, in itself an immoral exploitation of the labour and needs of others, were abolished, most so-called crime would cease, for even offences against the person are usually caused by the existence of property or by the psychological disorders produced by want or superfluity. Genuine crimes of passion are very few, and not likely to increase because of the lack of punishment.

If law is of little use, except as means of protecting property, it creates a great deal of harm by the brutalising effect of physical punishment, the degradation produced by the encouragement of informing, and the wholesale evils of prison life.

> "Finally, consider what corruption, what depravity of mind is kept up among men by the idea of obedience, the very essence of law; of chastisement; of authority having the right to punish, to judge irrespective of our conscience and the esteem of our friends; of the necessity for executioners, jailers and informers—in a word, by all the attributes of law and authority. Consider all this, and you will assuredly agree with us in saying that a law inflicting penalties is an abomination which should cease to exist. . . . The main supports of crime are idleness, law and authority; laws about property, laws about government, laws about penalties and misdemeanours; and authority, which takes upon itself to manufacture these laws and to apply them."

In place of law, Kropotkin sets the network of custom and free contract which unites men and regulates their daily life together, and which in a society of free communes would naturally extend to all features of social life. One of the first duties of a revolution must be to abolish law and its penal instruments, and thus clear the ground for goodwill to abolish the incentives to crime.

II

The Conquest of Bread, although it covers the same ground as Kropotkin's first book—the anarchist idea of revolution and the resultant free society—is markedly different both in style and emphasis. It also is a collection of essays, written originally for *Le Revolté* and *La Revolte*, but conceived as a series to fit into a broad general plan. Moreover, these essays were not produced under the stress of editorial responsibility, and were eventually collected by their author himself, who was able to smooth out irregularities and fit them more happily into an integrated whole. And they were all written five or more years after the Geneva articles; during the intervening time Kropotkin had gone through the period of reflection at Clairvaux, and had since settled in the relatively moderate atmosphere of England. As a result, the emphasis was very largely shifted from revolutionary tactics to a discussion of the reasons why a life of "well-being for all" is scientifically possible, and a somewhat elaborate sketch of the free society of the future and the anarchist answer to various social problems. It is Kropotkin's nearest approach to a Utopia, yet it can hardly be called Utopian, since he does not actually construct an imaginary society. Like most anarchists he regards an exhaustive plan of the future as both absurd and harmful, since it attempts to interfere with the liberty of those who may at some time create a society based on free agreement; instead, he begins always from a problem which vexes people at the present time and moves on to a rational discussion of how it might be solved within the framework of a society which would depend, unlike our own, on production for use and not for profit, and which had for its real aim the discovery of a means or a variety of means by which the needs of all may be reconciled and satisfied.

The whole basic theme of *The Conquest of Bread* is to be found in the contention that the heritage of humanity—the means of production as well as the product—is a collective one, in which it is impossible to distinguish the contribution of various individuals, and that therefore it should be enjoyed collectively.

"Individual appropriation is neither just nor serviceable. All belongs to all. All things are for all men, since all men have need of them, since all men have worked in the measure of their strength to produce them, and since it is not possible to evaluate everyone's part in the production of the world's wealth. . . . All is for all! If the man and the woman bear their fair share of the work, they have a right to their fair share of all that is produced by all, and that share is enough to secure them well-being."

Hence it arises that social life should be based neither on the ruthless competition of capitalist individualism nor on the restrictive regulation of State socialism, but on solidarity between individuals, on voluntary co-operation, which alone provides the atmosphere where justice can be done to all. Capitalists and rulers, he points out, have found the virtue of free agreement in their international railway and postal conventions, which work smoothly without any coercive threat, and the same principle has been found workable in communal societies of many kinds in past history. There is no really valid reason why these principles, which have been applied widely in the past, and are still applied partially, should not become universal in a rational society, so that the need for the State or any authority will vanish and be replaced by the federative structure of libertarian communes.

Anarchist communism, it should here be stressed, has nothing to do with the economic or political theories put forward by communist parties in the twentieth century. Present-day "Communism" is what the communists of sixty years ago would have called State socialism. The communism of Kropotkin was a theory that envisaged the ownership of means of production by associations or communes of producers, organised on a voluntary basis and connected federally, in which each man would do whatever work he could and receive from the common pool of goods sufficient to provide for his needs without exchange or money. This would prevent the return of the wages system and the accumulation of capital in individual hands, while avoiding the somewhat absurd attempt of earlier theoreticians to ensure that each man should enjoy the exact product of his own labour.

It represented the culmination of a long period of development in economic ideas. Godwin, the father of anarchism, had been less concerned with economic than with moral considerations, but he had already claimed that accumulated property is the basis of all tyranny and injustice and that need is the only fair standard by which we can assess who should use a given article or commodity. On the other hand, Godwin's conception cannot truly be called communist, since he distrusted co-operation and seems to have envisaged a society of individual craftsmen and farmers living by the exchange of necessities. It is difficult to determine how much influence Godwin's ideas actually had on the early Continental anarchists; certainly he was not mentioned among them until the later days of Kropotkin's career, but it is possible that his ideas permeated indirectly, via Benjamin Constant and Robert Owen, to the men of 1848, and thence to the International.

Proudhon, the first Continental anarchist, shared Godwin's distrust of close co-operation in production, and also envisaged an end to accumulated property and interest, which he regarded as the principal means of operating capitalism. Associations he admitted to be necessary for carrying out certain work, but he clearly wished them to be reduced to a minimum, and saw society as a network of mutual contracts between individual producers. He still regarded exchange and remuneration as essential, and, while he did not insist on the eventual continuance of money, suggested a scheme of labour cheques which would take its place. Exchanges of goods between individual producers would operate through a Bank of the People, and by this means work would be paid for by labour cheques equivalent to the hours expended. Proudhon always declared himself opposed to communism, which was then associated with the authoritarian social ideas put forward by the Babeuvists and later by the Blanquists and Marx, the founder of "scientific socialism".

Bakunin, the third great anarchist thinker, did not elaborate very thoroughly his ideas on economics. He was a man of action concerned primarily with the overthrow of the State, and seems to have considered that the actual form of the free society must be left to shape itself spontaneously. Unlike Proudhon, he believed in the need for co-operation, and foresaw a society more in accordance with large-scale industrial production, in which the workers would be organised in associations for productive purposes. He envisaged what he called a collective system, by which the means of production would become the common property of society, vested in the groups of producers. But he did not work out fully the question of the distribution of products and still held that the worker was entitled to the equivalent value of his actual labour. This view was originally shared by Guillaume and the earlier anarchists of the International.

The emergence of anarchist communism, by which the product as well as the means of production would be held in common and distributed according to need, can be traced to the middle of the 1870's, and with some certainty to the year 1876. It seems highly probable that in part it was due to the arrival in Switzerland of the refugees from the Paris Commune, many of whom had been associated with various communist and Utopian groups during and after 1848. Reclus, in particular, had been an active propagater of the ideas of Fourier, who foresaw a society of phalansteries practising a mitigated community of goods.

It has often been suggested that Kropotkin was the originator of anarchist communism. This was not so, and he never claimed it. Nor, as Max Nettlau has pointed out, is there any truth in the legend of his "stormy urge" towards it. By the time he became an open and convinced exponent, the idea had been circulating for some years, and Cherkesov was probably right when in 1895 he said that since 1877 everybody had accepted the idea of anarchist communism and only shied away from the name. The earlier brief reference appears in a tiny pamphlet, *Aux travailleurs manuels partisans de l'Action politique*, which Kropotkin's friend Dumartheray published in Geneva in 1876, and from which it appears that the group there, probably under the influence of Reclus, was already well advanced in its discussion of anarchist communism. From that year also the Italian groups were discussing this more logical idea of economic organisation. But it was not until the Jura Congress of 1880 that Kropotkin actually pressed the question in an urgent manner, and then not alone, as is shown by a letter to Guillaume in 1903, where he said:

"Thus, without knowing that the Italians had done this already at their last congress, I worked for the Jura federation to call itself *communist* at its Congress of 1880. Elisée, Cafiero, and I got in touch over this; it was accepted, and from then onwards our paper, *Le Revolté*, became communist anarchist. From that moment onwards dated the successes of anarchism in France. . . ."

But if Kropotkin was not the sole originator of anarchist communism, he was perhaps the most active among its initiators, and certainly the theoretician who gave it a reasoned and scientific basis, particularly in *The Conquest of Bread.*

Many important questions relating to anarchist economics are raised in the latter part of this book, in which Kropotkin attacks the ideas of production and consumption maintained by the orthodox economists, whether liberal or Marxist, denounces the wages system and the current theories of "division of labour", and advocates industrial decentralisation, the better integration of urban and rural activities, and the use of intensive scientific methods of food production, which last point he regarded as the practical keystone of success for the revolution and the free society. He attacks the economists because they proceed from a consideration of production as it exists in their time and thence discuss the means by which the consumption needs can be satisfied. Kropotkin contends that this attitude is wholly fallacious, and that a rational consideration of the problem would begin with needs and proceed to their satisfaction, since it is need that originally urges man to produce. A further assumption of orthodox capitalist and Marxist economists which he sets out to disprove is the theory of over-production. He shows clearly that the troubles of a capitalist society are due, not to over-production, but to under-consumption. It is merely a question of the consumers being debarred by the financial system from ever satisfying the full extent of their needs; if this barrier were dissolved we should find that the present is in fact a period of under-production. The theory of over-production is one which makes its perennial appearance whenever economic crises occur, and it may therefore not be unprofitable to give the gist of Kropotkin's simple but effective refutation:

"Is there a single economist, academician, or candidate for academical honours, who has not supported arguments proving that economic crises are due to over-production—that at a given moment more cotton, more cloth, more watches are produced than are needed? Have we not, all of us, thundered against the rapacity of the capitalists who are obstinately bent on producing more than can possibly be consumed?

"However, on careful examination, all these reasonings prove unsound. In fact, is there one single commodity among those in universal use which is produced in greater quantity than need be? Examine one by one all commodities sent out by countries exporting on a large scale, and you will see that nearly all are produced in *insufficient* quantities for the inhabitants of the countries exporting them. . . .

"As a rule it is not a surplus that is exported, though it may have been so originally. The fable of the barefooted shoemaker is as true of nations as it was formerly of individual artisans. We export the *necessary* commodities. And we do so because the workmen cannot buy with their wages what they have produced, *and pay besides the rent and interest to the capitalist and the banker.*

"Not only does the ever-growing need of comfort remain unsatisfied, but the strict necessities of life are often wanting. Therefore, 'surplus production' does *not* exist, at least not in the sense given to it by the theorists of Political Economy."

He begins his own investigation by considering the elementary needs of men—food, clothing and shelter, and comes to the conclusion that if all men worked on the basic requirements instead of producing luxuries or indulging in the socially useless employments of the capitalist State, it would be possible to produce enough of the basic necessities in a relatively short period of work, and leave a high proportion of leisure in which each man could satisfy his desires for individually creative activity. He goes into the question of production in some detail, and arrives after very reasonable calculations, at the conclusion that the basic necessities for each family could be produced in 150 days a year of five hours each, with another 150 days for the secondary necessities, such as wine, furniture, transport, etc. Here he falls into almost Utopian language as he describes the result of his calculations:

"After studying all these facts together we may arrive, then, at the following conclusion: Imagine a society, comprising a few million inhabitants, engaged in agriculture and a great variety of industries —Paris, for example, with the Department of Seine-et-Oise. Suppose that in this society all children learn to work with their hands as well as with their brains. Admit that all adults, save women, engaged in the education of their children, bind themselves to work *five hours a day* from the age of twenty or twenty-two to forty-five or fifty, and that they follow occupations they have chosen themselves in any one of those branches of human work which in this city are considered necessary. Such a society could in return guarantee well-being to all its members, a well-being more substantial than that enjoyed today by the middle classes."

It is a vision which is in no way unreasonable, even if one considers only the standard of productivity of a country like the United States, and the increase of useful goods that would ensue if the artificial restraints of the capitalist market and the demands of the organs of the State were removed.

Kropotkin, unlike many of the Utopians, demanded no Spartan sacrifices from the members of his communes; on the contrary, he devoted a whole chapter to "the need for luxury", and contended that:

"Man is not a being whose exclusive purpose in life is eating, drinking and providing a shelter for himself. As soon as his material wants are satisfied, other needs, which, generally speaking, may be described as of an artistic character, will thrust themselves forward. These needs are of the greatest variety; they vary in each and every individual; and the more society is civilised, the more will individuality be developed, and the more will desires be varied. . . . Would life, with all its inevitable drudge and sorrows, be worth living if, besides daily work, man could never obtain a single pleasure according to his individual tastes?"

The first task of the revolution is indeed the rectification of existing social iniquities and the assurance to all men of bread and the prime necessities. But a society that destroys all artistic tastes, all love of pleasure, will destroy also individual feeling, and therefore Kropotkin declares that, "After bread has been secured, leisure is the chief aim". And by leisure he means the facilities for each man to follow, in the time free from essential work, all those individual inclinations which produce art, literature, and science. He sees this achieved by a great extension of mutual-interest associations, similar to the existing learned societies, but embracing all amateurs of each particular activity. Thus science and the arts will be freed from the domination of money and, "exclusively cultivated by those who love them,

With Acknowledgments to "Freedom Press"

ERRICO MALATESTA

and for those who love them", will take "their proper place in the work of human development". The fact that all writers and scientists will also do their share of chosen manual work Kropotkin sees as an advantage, since it will give strength and balance to the work they produce in the study or laboratory.

Allied to these questions are those of agreeable work and division of labour. Here Kropotkin has much to say in anticipation of those who are trying to change the industrial system of our own day. A great deal of the unpleasantness of manual work, he contends, lies in the remediable conditions under which it is normally conducted. There is no reason why work in a factory should not be as healthy and devoid of nervous strain as that in a laboratory. When men are free and all do their share of manual work, these conditions will certainly change, for those who labour voluntarily will not endure as much as those who work under the duress of want or more direct coercion. And this will in turn affect the efficiency of industry, for, Kropotkin remarks wisely, "the most important economy, the only reasonable one, is to make life pleasant for all, because the man who is satisfied with his life produces infinitely more than the man who curses his surroundings".

Similarly, women will at last be truly emancipated through the elimination of household drudgery by new mechanical devices and communal domestic services. Kropotkin states emphatically that he does not necessarily envisage phalansteries or the communal dining-rooms and living-quarters so often regarded as essential by Utopian communities. People must make what domestic arrangements they choose, for privacy is essential to many, and "isolation, alternating with time spent in society, is the normal desire of human nature".

All these contentions are mere good sense, and have become so much a commonplace among advanced sociologists and even enlightened factory owners that they do not seem in any way revolutionary to the contemporary reader. We have to see them in relation to the working and living conditions generally considered sufficient for industrial workers in the 1880's to realise that they were then quite daring proposals.

In Kropotkin's view the most spiritually destroying feature of capitalist society was that "division of labour" which, following Adam Smith, economists had elevated to a necessary principle. In *The Conquest of Bread* he merely sketches his objections to this system, and we will leave his more developed arguments until we discuss *Fields, Factories and Workshops*; here it is sufficent to note his eloquent remark that:

"The division of labour means labelling and stamping men for life—some to splice ropes in factories, some to be foremen in a business, others to shove huge coal-baskets in a particular part of a mine; but none of them to have any idea of machinery as a whole, nor of business, nor of mines. And thereby they destroy the love of work and the capacity for invention that, at the beginning of modern industry, created the machinery on which we pride ourselves."

Similarly, there appear in *The Conquest of Bread* references to decentralisation of industry, and to intensive agriculture, which are also more amply treated in *Fields, Factories and Workshops*, and which we note here merely to show that these preoccupations were already troubling Kropotkin during the 1880's, at least ten years before he elaborated them in his larger book.

There remains one important chapter of *The Conquest of Bread*, provocatively entitled "Objections", in which Kropotkin dismisses some of the more important difficulties associated in the general mind with the application of anarchist communism, and which can be summarised in the question: "What is to be done with the man who will not work?" Anarchist communism, as we have already explained, repudiates the wages system because it is a form of compulsion in the spirit of the Biblical threat, "He that will not work, neither shall he eat", and also because it seems impossible to arrive at a just decision as to how much a man is entitled to receive as his share of the common production. Therefore the anarchist communist suggests the abolition of remuneration, whether in money or, as the Owenites had suggested, in labour cheques, and the recognition of the fundamental principle, "From each according to his ability, to each according to his needs": by which is meant that all men will do what essential work they wish, regulating relationships with their neighbours by voluntary contract, and will receive from the common pool as a natural right whatever they need in order to satisfy their reasonable desires. In other words, an anarchist communist society would be one "that recognises the absolute liberty of the individual, that does not admit of any authority, and makes use of no compulsion to drive men to work".

Against this is commonly raised the objection: "If the existence of each is guaranteed, and if the necessity of earning wages does not compel men to work, nobody will work. Every man will lay the burden of his work on another if he is not forced to do it himself." To this Kropotkin has a number of pertinent answers.

Firstly, he points out that in the past, when men have been freed from compulsion, as in the emancipation of the French and Russian peasants, they have worked for themselves with much more vigour than they had ever toiled for the masters whose chattels they formerly were. In fact, far from compulsion having been an incentive, it has always made men work less willingly and well than they might have done in better conditions. On the other hand he contends :

"Well-being—that is to say, the satisfaction of physical, artistic and moral needs, has always been the most powerful stimulant to work. And where a hireling hardly succeeds to produce the bare necessities with difficulty, a free worker, who sees ease and luxury increasing for him and for others in proportion to his efforts, spends infinitely far more energy and intelligence, and obtains products in a far greater abundance. The one feels riveted to misery, the other hopes for ease and luxury in the future. In this lies the whole secret. Therefore a society aiming at the well-being of all, and at the possibility of all enjoying life in all its manifestations, will give voluntary work, which will be infinitely superior and yield far more than work has produced up till now under the goad of slavery, serfdom or wagedom."

Nowadays, says Kropotkin, everybody tries to avoid his share of basic manual work, because of the stigma of inferiority attached to it and the bad conditions under which it has to be done. But when the merit of work is seen in its social necessity, and when it is carried on in free and pleasant conditions, the general attitude will change. Here, although Kropotkin does not use it, we might instance the not uncommon case of the city worker who despises the agricultural labourer because of his inferior social status and his poverty, but who himself gladly spends his spare time energetically cultivating his garden. Similarly, the majority of sports can reasonably be regarded as a form of perverted manual labour, performed voluntarily by those who are inhibited by social prejudice from ploughing or carrying bricks.

But even when it has been granted that men will generally work as well or even better under a voluntary system, there still remains the objection that the real danger lies in the loafers who will wish to take advantage of the conscientious members of the community. Kropotkin's first answer is that a free society could protect itself from this danger without using authoritarian penalties or sanctions. In all societies there are moral standards independent of authority which deter men from certain actions because of the disapproval of their fellows. A free society would be no different, and a group threatened by idlers would undoubtedly make use of this method of influencing recalcitrant members. Kropotkin in fact composes a little exhortation which an imaginary commune might make to those who sought to join it, and in which, after asking the recruit to work twelve hundred hours a year in some socially useful occupation of his own choice, it would continue:

"But if not one of the thousands of groups of our federation will receive you, whatever be their motive; if you are absolutely incapable of producing anything useful, or if you refuse to do it, then live like an isolated man or like an invalid. If we are rich enough to give you the necessaries of life we shall be delighted to give them to you. You are a man, and you have the right to live. But as you wish to live under special conditions, and leave the ranks, it is more than probable that you will suffer for it in your daily relations with other citizens. You will be looked upon as a ghost of bourgeois society, unless some friends of yours, discovering you to be a talent, kindly free you from all moral obligations towards society by doing all the necessary work for you.

"And finally, if it does not please you, go and look for other conditions elsewhere in the wide world, or else seek adherents and organise with them on novel principles. We prefer our own."

Clearly Kropotkin thought that even if an anarchist society would not need the economic or physical coercion employed in other societies, it might on occasion be justified in applying moral pressure to save itself from anti-social individuals; which might be held to constitute moral coercion. However, most anarchist theoreticians, from Godwin onwards, have regarded the use of public opinion as a necessary means of restraining anti-social individuals. And it must be admitted that Kropotkin gave very good reasons to suggest that in a society which had returned to a condition of equilibrium, such cases become rare, since, as he points out, most idleness is due to sickness, psychological maladjustment, or the lack of proper training. Indeed, in a healthy human being it is such a rare phenomenon that it is very unlikely to be a real danger in a society where every effort is made to reduce maladjustment and where work has a real incentive. Even the rich are not really idle; usually their days are filled with activity which, although often a futile waste of energy, shows that man naturally needs occupation and that if circumstances prevent him from finding it in a natural way, he will do so in a perverted manner. Therefore the danger of the lazy man is slight, and this key objection of those who oppose a free society falls to the ground.

In writing *The Conquest of Bread* Kropotkin became even more aware of the importance in any social revolutionary programme of certain subjects which had not previously received sufficient attention from theoreticians, and particularly the question of the increase of production. He therefore set about investigating the agricultural and industrial systems of his time, and the means by which they might be improved to give the greatly increased production necessary for realising general well-being. In his *Memoirs* he links this investigation with his criticism of contemporary economists and his attacks on the current myth of over-production. All these questions are, indeed, discussed in the final chapters of *The Conquest of Bread*, but Kropotkin was not content with a mere sketch of this subject. He recognised that such unorthodox arguments would need to be supported by a mass of carefully documented information, and that they should be presented in a form, devoid of sectarian language, which would appeal to men not as propaganda but as scientific argument. For some years he worked conscientiously at this research, using what he called the inductive-deductive method, by which he meant that having formed certain generalised conclusions from an observation of social tendencies, he now began to sift all the relevant facts with the intention of supporting or modifying his conclusions. It may perhaps be contended that a true scientist should gather his facts first and then elaborate his theory. But in practice very few research workers have begun without certain preconceptions, and at whatever stage it is reached, a scientific theory requires a certain act of intuition before the maze of facts begins to assume shape.

The result of Kropotkin's research was *Fields, Factories and Workshops*, a treatise on economic regionalism and the integration of industrial activities. He begins by considering that even in his own day the specialisation of certain countries in industrial production was being broken down by the spread of factories in what had formerly been consumer areas. He regards this tendency as an excellent correction of the top-heavy structure of nineteenth-century industrialism, and as a beginning of that disintegration of economic imperialism which is necessary before the anomaly of exporting goods widely, while their producers are in need, can be brought to an end.

He sees regional specialisation in industry as another aspect of that division of labour which he condemns in the field of individual work, and advocates decentralisation and the local and individual integration of work as a necessary basis for healthy social and personal lives.

> "Political economy has hitherto insisted chiefly upon *division.* We proclaim *integration*; and we maintain that the ideal of society—that is, the state towards which society is already marching—is a society of combined, integrated labour. A society where each individual is a producer of both manual and intellectual work; where each able-bodied human being is a worker, and where each worker works both in the field and in the industrial workshop; where each aggregation of individuals, large enough to dispose of a certain variety of natural resources—it may be a nation, or rather a region —produces and itself consumes most of its own agricultural and manufactured produce."

He acknowledges that such a change in the processes of production is not likely to take place when conditions allow "the owners of land and capital to appropriate for themselves, under the protection of the State and historical rights, the yearly surplus of human production". But capitalist industry, with its crises and tendencies towards recurrent imperialist wars, carries within itself the seeds of its own destruction, and he is more concerned with the errors of those socialists who think to dispense with the evils associated with the present relationship of capital and labour without taking such factors into consideration.

> "A reorganised society will have to abandon the fallacy of nations specialised for the production of either agricultural or manufactured produce. It will have to rely on itself for the production of food and many, if not most, of the raw materials; it must find the best means of combining agriculture with manufacture—the work in the field with the decentralised industry; and it will have to provide for 'integrated education', which education alone, by teaching both science and handicraft from earliest childhood, can give to society the men and women it really needs."

From his first general survey of the tendency towards the expansion of industry more evenly over the world, Kropotkin proceeds to a closer examination of the possibilities of a highly increased agricultural production, particularly in the industrial countries.

This question of integrated agriculture had occurred to him originally in his days as an agitator, and it then took the form of a problem in revolutionary tactics. His study of the revolutions of the past had taught him that the question which took precedence over all others in the long run was that of bread, of the provision of sufficient food for the people. Scarcity, he realised, had always played into the hands of enemies of the revolution, both by giving them a means to starve out the people while they were firm in their support of a revolutionary change, and also by enabling them to exploit any weakening of that support. In a city like Paris a complete seizure of all the food and other necessities might enable starvation to be halted for a period. But if, at the end of that time, arrangements had not been made for growing a vastly increased supply in the areas controlled by the revolutionary people, all their achievements would be at the mercy of blockade without or speculators within, as it had been during the French Revolution. The first task of a revolution must therefore be to institute an efficient agricultural policy, by which intensive methods and a sufficient supply of labour, machinery and fertilisers would ensure a rapid increase in the productivity of the soil. It was mostly from this point of view that Kropotkin discussed the matter in *The*

Conquest of Bread. But he soon saw that the question of intensive farming had a much wider application, and that it took its place in the greater sociological concept of an integrated society in which a regional and individual balance of functions might be obtained.

He views the situation existing in his own day, and still persisting in ours, in which most manufacturing countries grow insufficient food and import large quantities from abroad. From a conscientious consideration of agricultural potentialities, he comes to the conclusion that it is in fact possible for countries like Great Britain to feed their present populations in abundance. His calculations are based on the actual results of intensive methods used regularly by market gardeners, and even by ordinary peasants in some countries. While he makes reference to exceptional results obtained under special conditions, he does not use these instances as the bases of his main calculations. At present we cannot go into all the figures he produces, and in any case they are now rather out of date, since present cultivation techniques are even more advanced. Some years ago one of the authors of the present book carried out an investigation of the potential agricultural production of Great Britain, and his conclusions fully confirmed Kropotkin's, since he found that if the arable acreages of 1870 were recovered, if the pastures that have declined into rough grazing and waste land were reclaimed, if the ordinary standards of cultivation of Denmark, Holland and Belgium were equalled, and if grass were cultivated as in Switzerland, all the basic foods at present used in this country could be grown with ease, and without even resorting to the more intensive methods of the laboratory.*

Kropotkin is a fervent advocate of regional self-sufficiency in food production, but not merely for tactical reasons. He recognises that the food, being fresh, would be more healthy, he sees the spread of land work as a contributory factor in social regeneration, and he considers that the extra labour required would be met by eliminating "the amount of labour that must be spent for obtaining them under an irrational culture, for collecting them abroad, for transporting them, and for keeping armies of middlemen".

From agriculture he turns to industry, and shows with equal

* See *New Life to the Land* by George Woodcock, London, 1942.

detail that despite the spread of large factories much industry has been left to small localised workshops, which are more efficient for many forms of production and which the diffusion of electric power has helped to maintain. Here again his examples have been superseded, but it would certainly be very easy to produce similar figures to show that in our own day, however far large-scale industry may have spread, small factories and workshops still hold their own; though it would be difficult to argue that the domination of the larger units had in any way been reduced since the turn of the century.

Looking into the future, Kropotkin foresees that under the stimulus of modern technics it will be possible for a decentralised and regionalised industry to replace the large factory aggregations, and here again he visualises the possibility of a great enrichment of life in the mingling of agriculture and industry, not only by making factories rural, but also by allowing people to alternate field with factory work.

> "The scattering of industries over the country—so as to bring the factory amidst the fields, to make agriculture derive all those profits which it always finds in being combined with industry and to produce a combination of industrial with agricultural work—is surely the next step to be taken, so soon as a reorganisation of present conditions is possible. . . . This step is imposed by the very necessity of *producing for the producers themselves*; it is imposed by the necessity for each healthy man and woman to spend a part of their lives in manual work in the free air; and it will be rendered the more necessary when the great social movements, which have now become unavoidable, come to disturb the present international trade, and compel each nation to revert to her own resources for her own maintenance."

In advancing these views of the integration of rural and urban life, Kropotkin was the precursor of a whole movement which has become much more self-conscious today than it was fifty years ago, and which embraces not only the theories of men like Patrick Geddes and Lewis Mumford, but also the garden-city experiments of Ebenezer Howard and the schemes for satellite towns which have formed a feature of post-war plans of reconstruction. In the practical field his ideas have been confirmed by a general tendency (by no means wholly fulfilled) towards the industrialisation of agriculture, and a parallel tendency, whose extent it is difficult to estimate, for factories to move into the rural areas. But these are no more than tendencies, and the complete social transformation of which Kropotkin would regard them as symptoms lies yet in the free society of an unpredictable future.

This process of social integration, Kropotkin contends, can only become complete if it is accompanied by a change in the outlook and education of individuals in the direction of an "integration of capacities", involving the abolition of division of labour and the acquisition of a variety of occupations, embracing both hand and brain work and giving an understanding of the whole productive process in which at a given moment the worker may be involved in one specific operation. To this end he anticipates more recent educationalists by advocating an "integral education", which will replace the old academic intellectual training by methods cultivating mental and physical aptitudes at the same time.

Finally, from all these changes both in social environment and in training individuals, Kropotkin foresees a society in which a steady improvement will result from the full application of scientific resources—unrestrained by vested interest—to increasing production and reducing toil. All this, he warns, will be conditional on men realising that "in order to be rich they need not take the bread from the mouths of others", but can gain by their own united skill and intelligence "all imaginable riches". In these circumstances, he prophesies:

> "Technics and science . . . will reduce the time which is necessary for producing wealth to any desired amount, so as to leave to everyone as much leisure as he or she may ask for. They surely cannot guarantee happiness, because happiness depends as much, or even more, upon the individual himself as upon his surroundings. But they guarantee, at least, the happiness that can be found in the full and varied exercise of the different capacities of the human being, in work that need not be overwork, and in the consciousness that one is not endeavouring to base his own happiness upon the misery of others."

III

In putting forward these propositions, Kropotkin was always faced by a powerful set of arguments which had the support of many scientists and which, until dealt with on their own ground, threatened to destroy the edifice of reasoning he had built up. These arguments were connected with the fashionable Darwinian theory of evolution, and claimed that in nature there is never enough for all and that, indeed, it is undesirable that there should be, since the most potent force in the evolution of the animal world, and therefore of mankind, is the struggle for existence within the species which by procuring the survival of the fittest acts as a means of natural selection to ensure the progress of the race. These ideas were readily adopted by capitalist apologists of unrestricted competition, and also by the Marxists, who saw in the proletariat the "fittest" class.

The main exponent of the struggle-for-existence theory in the nineteenth century was Thomas Henry Huxley, but the fundamental basis of the discussion, and its use as a justification for the existing social order, was much older than the nineteenth century or the evolutionary controversy in its modern form. During the seventeenth century the authoritarian philosopher Thomas Hobbes, author of *Leviathan*, had based his justification of the State and of monarchical authority on the theory that primitive man is naturally given to fratricidal struggle and that the social virtues can be implanted in him only by the force of a superior authority. At the end of the eighteenth century the argument was carried into the realm of economics, and by what can hardly be regarded as a coincidence was connected intimately with the first appearance of anarchism as a mature and complete social doctrine. In 1793 William Godwin published his *Enquiry concerning Political Justice*, which in its time enjoyed a vast intellectual influence, and in which he advocated universal benevolence as the basis of human relationships (a view not far removed from Kropotkin's idea of mutual aid), and suggested, like Kropotkin, that if all men did their share of manual work, if all kinds of socially wasteful activities were eliminated, and if the potentialities of science were exploited fully for the benefit of all, it would be possible to enjoy well-being at the cost of a much smaller expenditure of energy than had been customary in previous societies.

For some years Godwin's arguments went virtually unanswered. But then appeared a clergyman, T. H. Malthus, who contended that there was a natural tendency for population to increase in a higher ratio than any possible increase in the supply of food. This process would clearly result in disaster if there were not certain "positive checks" to the increase in population—that is to say, such natural phenomena as disease and famine, and such social phenomena as war and the general struggle among individuals by which the weaker goes to the wall. In order to preserve what well-being existed, Malthus argued, it was necessary that this process should be left unchanged, and he therefore denounced Godwin's doctrine of universal benevolence as a conception which would upset the natural limitation of population and defeat itself by producing a society in which the growth of population, outstripping the increase of food supply, would naturally bring disaster and famine to all, instead of to the minorities who are cut off before their prime in the normal process of unrestricted competition. The final result of any attempt at change would therefore be a return, through terrible trials, to the old situation. Things, in fact, were as they were bound to be, and this Pangloss in real life concluded that all talk of improvement in human society was quite chimerical.

It was a consoling doctrine for the factory owners, the generals, and the poor-law administrators in those ruthless days of the early industrial revolution, and no doubt many a capitalist whose child employees were stunted in the mephitic atmosphere of his cotton mills, many a landowner who took away the common lands and helped to turn a well-fed peasantry into a starving rural proletariat, was comforted by the consolation of the Rev. Malthus's assurances. The theories of this amiable Christian were given classic status in the Victorian system of economics, and although it is difficult to realise this in our own day, were accepted by many scientists of standing. But even at the time their basis of reasoning and mathematics was effectively destroyed, not only by Godwin's belated answer in 1820, but also by Hazlitt's prompt *Reply to Malthus*. Today, when the possibility of vastly increased production of essential goods has been placed beyond reasonable doubt, and when it has been shown by experience that greater well-being and education result in a falling birth-rate, Malthus's basic theory has become untenable, and those who seek a reason to support their argument that the condition of humanity cannot be changed must seek it elsewhere.

The advent of Darwin transferred the argument from the economic to the biological field. In formulating his theory Darwin distinguished himself from previous evolutionists, like Lamarck, Buffon and his own grandfather, by giving emphasis to the struggle for existence as the mechanism by which "natural selection" sorted out favourable variations and destroyed unfavourable ones; he admitted that in reaching this conclusion he was strongly influenced by Malthus's theory of the positive checks to an increase in population, which he felt could also be regarded as potent factors in weeding out inferior individuals in the struggle for life. While Darwin at times gave warning against using the term "struggle for existence" in a too literal sense, it seems clear that he envisaged not only a struggle against environmental factors but also a struggle between individuals, as being dominant in the evolutionary process. While in later years he acknowledged that co-operation was also important, he never developed this idea to any marked degree, and the main basis of his conception of evolution remained the idea of conflict.

Thomas Henry Huxley, his chief apostle and populariser, pushed this tendency to its extreme by his talk of the animal world as "a gladiators' show", and of the life of primitive man as "a continuous free fight". Competition, struggle, animosity, envy, hatred, were the qualities that automatically emerged from Huxley's view as necessary factors in progress. Strife between groups and individuals alike was, according to him, a law of life. Not only was it desirable as a condition of progress, but it was also inevitable.

It will be seen how this theory pleased the apologists of nineteenth-century capitalism in that age of scepticism when the values of orthodox religion were losing their power; scientific materialism of the Huxleyan type, violently opposed on its first appearance, rapidly became as respectable as the untenable doctrines of the Church. Those who felt uneasy about basing their actions on a dubious divine law were very glad to find that natural law had been interpreted by Professor Huxley as an equally strong justification of unlimited competition. Clearly, if such doctrines were true, the basic anarchist theory that men are naturally co-operative was jeopardised. Any conception of a society based on voluntary agreement must be supported by an effective answer to the neo-Malthusian evolutionists, and this Kropotkin gave in *Mutual Aid*.

His preoccupation with this aspect of evolution dated from the years before he became concerned with revolutionary theories, for already in the 1860's he and his brother had discussed Darwin's theory of variation at great length and had formed doubts on the question of inheritance, while during his Siberian explorations he had been puzzled to find that there was in fact less evidence of struggle than of co-operation between individuals of the same species. Later, when he became an anarchist and was seeking to found his beliefs on a scientific basis, he was once again troubled by this question. We have already noted his defence, in 1882, of mutualist solidarity as an evolutionary factor, and his introduction, at Clairvaux, to the ideas of Kessler. But it was Huxley's extreme statements about the ferocity of the struggle for existence in 1888 that finally decided Kropotkin to take up the challenge. It must be emphasised that, in spite of Huxley's uncouth behaviour in connection with the petition for his release from Clairvaux, Kropotkin never bore any personal animosity and was always ready, even when pointing out the danger of Huxley's perversions of Darwinism, to praise the courage, learning and intelligence with which he had originally defended the general evolutionary theory against ecclesiastical orthodoxy.

Kropotkin begins *Mutual Aid* with an examination of the life of animal species. His study is packed with instances from the writings of field naturalists and from his own observations which show that sociability or mutual aid between individuals of the same species is so widespread in all levels of the animal world, from the insects up to the highest mammals, that it can be regarded as a law of nature:

> "Those species which live solitarily or in small families only are relatively few, and their numbers are limited. Nay, it appears very probable that, apart from a few exceptions, those birds and mammals which are not gregarious were living in species before man multiplied on the earth and waged a permanent war against them, or destroyed the sources from which they formerly derived food."

Not merely is mutual aid a law of nature except among animals living under somewhat artificial conditions, or among dwindling species, but it is also, in Kropotkin's view, the most important factor in the evolution of social species:

"Life in societies enables the feeblest animals, the feeblest birds, and the feeblest mammals to resist, or to protect themselves from, the most terrible birds and beasts of prey; it permits longevity; it enables the species to rear its progeny with the least waste of energy and to maintain its numbers albeit a very slow birth-rate; it enables the gregarious animals to migrate in search of new abodes. Therefore, while fully admitting that force, swiftness, protective colours, cunningness, and endurance to hunger and cold, which are mentioned by Darwin and Wallace, are so many qualities making the individual, or the species, the fittest under certain circumstances, we maintain that under *any* circumstances sociability is the greatest advantage in the struggle for life. Those species which willingly or unwillingly abandon it are doomed to decay; while those animals which know best how to combine have the greatest chance of survival and of further evolution, although they may be inferior to others in *each* of the faculties enumerated by Darwin and Wallace, except the intellectual faculty."

Intelligence, nurtured by language, imitation and accumulated experience, Kropotkin regards as "an eminently social faculty". Moreover, the very fact of living in society tends to develop, in however rudimentary a form, that "collective sense of justice growing to become a habit" without which social life becomes impossible.

The evidence presented in support of these arguments turns Huxley's view of "nature red in tooth and claw" into a lecture-room scientist's nightmare. But Kropotkin does not wholly dismiss the struggle for existence. It plays its part, he admits, metaphorically in the form of the struggle against adverse circumstances. But in the form of competition within the species it is present only in exceptional circumstances, and even then is injurious rather than advantageous since it dissipates the advantages gained by sociability. Natural selection, far from thriving on competition, seeks out the means by which it can be avoided.

If these ideas apply almost universally to the animal kingdom, they apply also to primitive man, who owes ascendancy in the animal world to his sociability and the aptitudes he cultivates in society. Huxley's vision of primitive man engaged in a perpetual vendetta between individuals and families, like Freud's hypothesis of the primal horde centred round the father, has been proved completely false by three generations of anthropologists. From the time of Lewis Morgan down to the present day, students of primitive man have found everywhere a tendency to live, not in family groups, but in tribal aggregations among whom law as such is unknown, being replaced by a complex system of customs ensuring co-operation and mutual aid. Nor is there any evidence that primitive man was other than a social species; indeed, the relics of early cultures give abundant indication of his primeval sociability and co-operativeness.

Kropotkin, drawing on the accounts of pioneer anthropologists in his own day, proved that within the primitive tribe mutual aid was the rule rather than the exception, and showed how among the barbarians the area of mutual co-operation grew into the village and, through the emergence of the early form of guild, even assumed national and international proportions. Finally, the role of mutual aid in human institutions reached its highest development in the mediæval free city. Kropotkin, even in his youth, had done much research into the nature of social relationships in these cities, and he was able to bring forward a mass of evidence, gleaned from contemporary records, which showed that the current nineteenth-century ideas of mediæval life were almost completely wrong, and that within the walls of the free cities and before their decay in the Renaissance, a rich communal life had existed in which mutual aid and co-operative communism played a great part.

These chapters of Kropotkin's book are written with enthusiasm, and it may be that he has tended to gloss over the dark side of life in such societies. Yet he is very conscientious in revealing the internal weaknesses which led to the collapse of the communal spirit at the end of the Middle Ages. And, taking his information as a whole, it makes a most impressive case for the important part mutual aid has played in the development of social activity, and its vital role as the organic bond between human beings. Even today, although the State has assumed such menacing importance in human life, mutual aid survives as the most important factor in the intercourse of men and women, considered as individuals.

PETER KROPOTKIN ON HIS DEATHBED

"... Neither the crushing powers of the centralised State, nor the teachings of mutual hatred and pitiless struggle which came, adorned with the attributes of science, from obliging philosophers and sociologists, could weed out the feeling of solidarity, deeply lodged in men's understanding and heart, because it had been nurtured by all our preceding evolution.... What was the outcome of evolution since its earliest stages cannot be overpowered by one of the aspects of that same evolution. And the need of mutual aid and support which had lately taken refuge in the narrow circle of the family, or the slum neighbours, in the village, or the secret union of workers, reasserts itself again, even in our modern society, and claims its rights to be, as it always has been, the chief leader towards further progress."

Mutual aid and sociability, in fact, are the foundations of every creed of social ethics, every practice of co-operation, and if they did not naturally condition almost all our daily acts towards our fellows, the most austere tyranny could not prevent the disintegration of society.

It was this ethical aspect of mutual aid which Kropotkin developed in his later years, when he wrote his monumental but unfinished work on *Ethics*, which we shall discuss in our final chapter. Here it is necessary to notice briefly its precursor, a pamphlet entitled *Anarchist Morality*, first published in 1890. In this work Kropotkin distinguishes between the so-called moral codes which attempt to govern men's lives from above, and the innate moral sense which naturally plays its part in determining their attitude towards their fellow beings. The former he sees as the heritage of primitive superstitions, taken over by priests and rulers in order to buttress their own authority. It is the instinctive moral sense, based on the sympathy and solidarity inherent in group behaviour, that constitutes true morality. This is expressed in mutual aid, itself the necessary condition of any successful social life, and the basic rule of mutual aid is none other than the ancient maxim, "Do to others as you would have others do to you". But there is more in morality than this, for "if societies knew only this principle of equality; if each man practised merely the equity of the trader, taking care all day long not to give others anything more than he was receiving from them, society would die of it". A greater moral quality is needed, and it emerges in that superabundance of devotion, that desire to give more than is asked, which has always inspired the men whose actions contribute most to the progress of mankind.

If *Anarchist Morality* represents an extension of the mutual-aid theory into the realm of ethics, *The State* represents its application in the field of social history. Here Kropotkin shows how human communities based on mutual aid were successful and prosperous, and how, when they deserted that principle and accepted instead the domination of authority, they failed and eventually died away, while the descendants of their members lived progressively more miserably under the over-riding authority of the State. Much of this pamphlet repeats in condensed form the information and arguments of *Mutual Aid.* But it differs from the longer work in that here Kropotkin examines the evolution of human institutions and reaches the partisan conclusion that anarchy, society without rulership, is the only social form in complete accord with the beneficial principles of social co-operation. Thus, *The State* can in a way be regarded as the final chapter of the book.

It begins with a description of the free societies, primitive and mediæval, which existed before the development of centralised power in the modern era (or which, in the case of certain primitive societies in Kropotkin's own day, even contrived to exist in a world for the most part dominated by increasingly centralised States). There follows a description of the way in which these free societies disintegrated under the impact of the rising power of authority in the late Middle Ages and the Renaissance. And finally, analysing the way in which the State has developed since its origin, Kropotkin reaches the conclusion that, if it is allowed to expand unrestrictedly, it will mean social destruction and a new and more terrible Dark Age:

"Either the State will be destroyed and a new life will begin in thousands of centres, on the principle of an energetic initiative of the individual, of groups, and of free agreement, or else the State must crush the individual and local life, it must become the master of all the domains of human activity, must bring with it its wars and international struggles for the possession of power, its surface revolutions which only change one tyrant for another, and inevitably, at the end of this evolution—death."

In this pamphlet Kropotkin adopted a more scientific attitude than was shown in the early optimism of his prophecies of the ending of centralised social forms, and his warning has been amply fulfilled in a world of all-pervasive government and ever more destructive wars. For this reason we shall return later to these significant contentions.

The last work we have to consider is *The Great French Revolution*, a lengthy and exhaustive study of events from 1789 to 1793. It is one of the less celebrated of Kropotkin's works, but it is nevertheless an exceptionally good piece of historical writing, and can stand comparison, both for its quality and for the authenticity of its information, with any of the more celebrated histories of this period.

From childhood, from the days of his tutor M. Poulain, the French Revolution had exercised a fascination over Kropotkin's mind, and as we have seen, it was not long after his escape from Russia that he first began the long research into its history which continued, with interruptions, for nearly thirty years. It was after his arrival in England in 1886 that he actually planned *The Great French Revolution*, which he conceived on a completely different basis from the works of his predecessors, since, regarding the causes of revolutions as economic, he thought it necessary to stress the struggle of the common people for the necessities of life rather than to concentrate on political intrigues and the romantic dramatisation of leading figures which had been practised by so many other historians. Without this study of economic causes, he remarks justly, "the history of the period remains incomplete and in many points incomprehensible". He himself describes thus the evolution of his book:

"It was with the intention of throwing some light upon these economic problems that I began in 1886 to make separate studies of the earliest revolutionary stirrings among the peasants; the peasant risings of 1789; the struggles for and against the feudal laws; the real causes of the movement of May 31, and so on. . . .

"Believing that it would not be easy for the reader to appreciate the bearing of separate studies of this kind without a general view of the whole development of the Revolution understood in the light of these studies, I soon found it necessary to write a more or less consecutive account of the chief events of the Revolution. In this account I have not dwelt upon the dramatic side of the episodes of these disturbed years, which have been so often described, but I have made it my chief object to utilise modern research so as to reveal the intimate connection and interdependence of the various events which combined to produce the climax of the eighteenth-century's epic."

But with the spirit of the true historian, Kropotkin was not concerned merely with the period he discussed. He saw it as a climax in a long past and future development, and sought to conjure up a picture not only of the events which were his immediate subject, but also of "the mighty currents of thought and action that came into conflict during the French Revolution—currents so intimately blended with the very essence of human nature that they must inevitably reappear in the historic events of the future".

The result is a very skilful and absorbing book, with great momentum, an active and readable style, and a capable use of a mass of details regarding the more obscure but no less important aspects of the French Revolution. Beginning with the causes of economic discontent which actually precipitated the revolution and realised the hopes of the pre-revolutionary thinkers, it preserves a continuous and well-sustained narrative through the complex series of incidents which constituted the stormy history of the revolution, down to the final triumph of reaction on the 9th Thermidor, placing emphasis always on the basic struggle of the people to gain satisfaction for their economic needs and social demands, yet not neglecting the superimposed pattern of political manœuvring which frustrated their expectations, and here and there giving the most vivid representations in miniature of revolutionary incidents and personalities. All the theories on the nature, course and needs of revolutions which Kropotkin put forward in his active days of agitation here take their place in the historical pattern, and are supported by convincing evidence and analysis. He illustrates the interaction of economic distress and intellectual discontent; the generation of the revolution in the heart of the people and its sweeping progress beyond the will of the leaders it threw up; the continual tendency of the revolutionary government to retard progress, to cling to power in the face of popular pressure, and finally, by revealing a fundamental cleavage in the revolutionary ranks, to open the way for the counter-revolution. And, lastly, there runs as an undercurrent through his narrative the insistent cry of the masses for bread, and he shows how great a part was played in the eventual disaster by the failure of the revolutionaries to fulfil this basic demand.

Yet, although the revolution failed to achieve its great object of "Liberty, Equality, Fraternity", it did, according to Kropotkin, accomplish two great tasks which put France in the forefront of the European social movement—the abolition of absolutism and that of serfdom. On these achievements, and on the "communist" ideas which he regarded as having been originated by the French Revolution, he based that inordinate admiration for Republican France which later amounted to a kind of patriotism. Despite this one fault of excessive partiality, *The Great French Revolution* remains an excellent historical study and a fine vindication, in the field of practical example, of the theoretical ideas concerning the nature and needs of revolutions which Kropotkin had put forward in his two earliest books, *Paroles d'un Revolté* and *The Conquest of Bread.*

CHAPTER VIII

THE EXILE

I

KROPOTKIN left Russia in 1876 with the fixed intention of returning to resume his work there. That he did not go back within a few months was due partly to a realisation that his escape had assumed a wider importance in the eyes of the Russian authorities than he had thought likely, and partly to the way in which, after the beginning of 1877, he became involved in the active and varied work of the international anarchist movement. Personal differences cut him off from those Russian anarchists like Ralli, who still hoped to transmit propaganda from Western Europe to Russia, and theoretical differences parted him from other revolutionaries, like Stepniak, who had constitutional aims. Indeed, the only Russian with whom he was to collaborate at all closely for some years was Cherkesov.

It also seems that, at least during his first years in Western Europe, Kropotkin had little direct contact with revolutionary elements within Russia.The Chaikovsky circle was completely broken up, and many of its leading members, like Klemens, Stepniak and Chaikovsky himself, had left Russia for America or Western Europe. It was not until the middle of 1877 that he was able to write to Robin: "At last I have been given work from Russia. A booklet about propaganda by deed. So I have got this started and must now finish it." Whether this pamphlet was completed we do not know, but, if it was, it does not seem to have had any effect in encouraging an anarchist tendency among the revolutionaries within Russia, for not very long after, in 1879, he wrote:

"I no longer think of Russia. The tendency there is so moderate—which is strange in view of the executions—that I feel, and all agree with me, I would stand there absolutely alone. The tendency is towards a constitution. The secret organ (*Land and Liberty*) calls itself socialistic, but writes only against autocratic government. I doubt if I could ever get accustomed to this tendency."

Nevertheless, at this time he was roused to a passing enthusiasm by the attempt of the revolutionary Soloviev against the Tsar, and after his execution in 1879 printed a pamphlet in connection with *Le Revolté*, in which he hailed Soloviev as the expression of the discontent of all classes in Russia against the autocracy, spoke of the resentment caused in the towns by the execution of the revolutionary, and said that among the peasants, "insurrection, the precursor of the revolutions, is already growling. The 1793 of the Russian peasant can be felt in the air."

Undoubtedly this lack of any pronounced anarchist trend within the movement in Russia partly explains Kropotkin's long period of comparative inactivity in the affairs of his own country, which lasted until 1895. There was the one interval, during 1881–2, when his strength of feeling over the execution of Sophie Perovskaya and her friends led him for a while to carry on spoken and written propaganda for the People's Will, and even to offer to go to Russia on their behalf. In the short but eloquent pamphlet which he wrote at this time on the executions, he devoted a special chapter to the memory of Sophie Perovskaya, and ended with the moving words:

"By the attitude of the crowd she understood that she had dealt a mortal blow to the autocracy. And she read in the sad looks which were directed sympathetically towards her, that by her death she was dealing an even more terrible blow, from which the autocracy will never recover."

But the continued concentration of the People's Will on propaganda for a constitution, and the conspiratorial nature of their activity—of which Kropotkin did not approve, since he regarded it as isolating them from the people—soon led him to withdraw from this connection, and for many years he did not try on any large scale to influence Russian affairs. Even after his arrival in London he found himself at first isolated in the

Russian colony there, and as late as 1888 Reclus wrote of him to a Swiss author:

"... In London, where he lives and where all the Russians are his friends, there is *none* who completely shares his ideas. All are more or less constitutionalist, all have still the illusion of the State, all follow from afar the movement which leads Russian youth into the paths of a revolution with a parliamentary ideal."

It was for this reason that a few years afterwards when the majority of the Russian emigrés in London united with some radicals and Fabians, led by Spence Watson, to found the Friends of Russian Freedom, which aimed at a constitutional form of government in Russia, Kropotkin, while maintaining a friendly attitude, took no responsible part in the work of the organisation.

His reasons for not attempting to start his own anarchist propaganda in Russia are evident. He had a long-standing opinion that it was impossible for emigrés to conduct propaganda work within their own country; he had thought this way during his own period in Russia, and afterwards remained consistent. If there had been any anarchist organisations at home he would have co-operated with them. But the groups founded by Ross and his associates had been broken up and for nearly twenty years no others replaced them. His own return to resume underground work was out of the question, and it was only during the period of emotional stress in 1881 that he ever considered it. His health was too delicate to stand undue privations, while it was unlikely that he would have escaped arrest. His growing celebrity as a revolutionary in Western Europe had given the Tsarist government a fear of him out of all proportion to his real danger, and the inaccurate reports of the spies abroad kept the secret police in a perpetual agitation over his return. In January 1879, for instance, the Third Section received information that he "intended to penetrate into Russia in secret", and telegrams were immediately sent to the frontier posts, while circulars ordering his arrest went out to the police all over the country. In October 1880 there was a further scare about his supposed "arrival in Russia between the 1st and 15th November". It is very unlikely that he would have long evaded the police net even if he had succeeded in crossing the frontier, and an arrest would almost certainly have meant a return to the Peter-and-Paul fortress, with probably fatal consequences. But he did not attempt it, and the police reports were based on false information, provided by spies in Western Europe who felt they must somehow justify their living.

Outside Russia Kropotkin became the most personally respected of the exiles, particularly in England, but this did not mean that he was influential in the Russian movement of revolt. Indeed, although the most celebrated anarchists have been Russians, anarchism has always been a relatively small minority movement in Russia itself.

On the other hand, it must not be forgotten that there was at least some indirect influence of the anarchist theories on almost all revolutionaries except the Marxist groups up to 1917. Even though the Populists made their first demand a constitution, nevertheless, following their writers, they distrusted the State and shared the Bakuninist respect for the people. For this reason it is often difficult, even in 1917, to find much tangible difference between the moderate anarchists and the extreme Social Revolutionaries. When an abridged Russian version of *The Memoirs of a Revolutionist* was published in 1902, it was, according to Breshkovskaya, widely disseminated by the Social Revolutionaries, who seem to have been, unlike the Marxists, by no means averse from distributing anarchist literature. The failure of anarchism to arise as a significant current within Russia until well into the twentieth century is due very largely to the fact that the creeds with which it had to compete, while constitutionalist, were not strictly authoritarian, and emphasised communal organisation. It is significant that it should have begun to spread after the rise of Marxism and the appearance of an influential movement of avowed State socialists.

Nevertheless we must not minimise the fact that, although personally respected by all Russian liberals and revolutionaries except the social-democrats, Kropotkin was not nearly so ideologically influential in Russia as in the Latin countries, or so well known for his scholarship as in Great Britain or the United States. But as his interest in Russian affairs resumed a growing importance from the 1890's onward, and as it finally dominated the last period of his life, it is biographically necessary to give special attention to this subject.

His increasing activity as a participant in preparing and transmitting propaganda to Russia can be traced from the middle of the 1890's, when anarchist groups began to reappear both in exile and home. The last Russian anarchist propaganda in Western Europe had been carried on by Ralli and Zhukovsky through the Geneva *Rabotnik* during the 1870's, and from that date there is a long gap until the early 'nineties. A group called "The Anarchist Library" was then founded in Geneva by Dr Alexander Atabekian, whom we have already encountered as an Armenian student visiting Kropotkin in England during that decade.

This period marked a temporary relaxation of the autocratic terror within Russia. We know, from several of his friends, that about this time Kropotkin received, in Mavor's words, "a message to the effect that full amnesty would be granted him, and that he might return to Russia provided he undertook to refrain from political agitation". It was even suggested that his estates might be returned. Kropotkin, however, had no intention of committing himself to refrain from political activity, nor did he trust the good faith of the Tsarist authorities, while he preferred to live by his own efforts rather than from inherited income. However, he did send a request that at least part of the income from the estates might be devoted to the maintenance of his brother's family. This was refused, and all he received was a box of books and papers which had been seized on his imprisonment and were now relinquished by the police department.

It was at this time of relative calm that Atabekian began his work in Geneva. As yet there were no resources to publish a periodical, and "The Anarchist Library" concentrated on the production of pamphlets, of which the first was Bakunin's *The Paris Commune and the Nature of the State*, with an introduction by Kropotkin. Atabekian and his group established connections with individuals within Russia, and it is also probable that some of Kropotkin's young converts returned there, for towards the end of the decade the first groups since the 1870's were formed clandestinely. Meanwhile, revived interest in Russia had led Kropotkin to a wider consideration of the whole field of its culture and thought, and a result of this was the series of lectures on Russian writers given at Boston in 1901, and eventually embodied in *Ideals and Realities in Russian Literature*, published in 1905.

This interest was closely connected with Kropotkin's revolutionary ideas, for he maintained that literature had a unique influence in Russian social life as the only way of reflecting its real currents of development.

"In no other country does literature occupy so influential a position as it does in Russia. Nowhere else does it exercise so profound and so direct an influence upon the intellectual development of the younger generation. There are novels of Turgenev, and even of the less-known writers, which have been real stepping-stones in the development of Russian youth within the last fifty years.

"The reason why literature exercises such an influence in Russia is self-evident. There is no open political life, and with the exception of a few years at the time of the abolition of serfdom, the Russian people have never been called upon to take an active part in the framing of their country's institutions.

"The consequence has been that the best minds of the country have chosen the poem, the novel, the satire, or literary criticism as the medium for expressing their aspirations, their conceptions of national life, of their ideals. It is not to blue-books, or to newspaper leaders, but to its works of art that one must go in Russia in order to understand the political, economical, and social ideals of the country—the aspirations of the history-making portions of Russian society."

Kropotkin's exposition is executed from a social standpoint, and this necessarily affects its character. His criteria of appreciation are not narrow, and he seeks to give credit not merely to anarchists, or even to revolutionaries, but to any work that may represent some stage of resistance to the prevalent autocracy. This attitude gives his book catholicity, but it has corresponding disadvantages, since it makes him concentrate on content rather than on form, on intention rather than achievement, and also to ignore aspects of the author's work which are not strictly social. He tries to speak well of everybody, which is in his nature and which also suits his purpose, but which makes analysis at times superficial. And he shows an almost complete failure to understand the religious mind, so that his treatment of Tolstoy's Christianity is too elementary, while he does not appreciate the spiritual duality of Dostoevsky and the social views he expressed towards the end of his life. It may be that Kropotkin himself was too secure and serene in his single-mindedness to understand the intellectual torment that impelled these two great masters of the Russian novel.

With men like Turgenev and Chekhov, whose attitude had a clarity and coherence resembling his own, he is much more at home, and there is admirable conciseness and accuracy in such judgments as this:

"Chekhov's heroes are not people who have never heard better words, or never conceived better ideas, than those which circulate in the lowest circles of the Philistines. No, they have heard such words, and their hearts have beaten once upon a time at the sound of such words. But the commonplace everyday life has stifled all such aspirations, apathy had taken their place, and now there remains only a haphazard existence amidst a hopeless meanness. The meanness which Chekhov represents is one which begins with the loss of faith in one's forces and the gradual loss of all those brighter hopes and illusions which make the charm of all activity, and then, step by step, this meanness destroys the very springs of life: broken hopes, broken hearts, broken energies. Man reaches a stage when he can only mechanically repeat certain actions from day to day, and goes to bed, happy if he has 'killed' his time in any way, gradually falling into a complete intellectual apathy and a moral indifference. The worst is that the very multiplicity of samples which Chekhov gives, without repeating himself, from so many different layers of society, seems to tell the reader that it is the rottenness of a whole civilisation, of an epoch, which the author divulges to us."

Of Turgenev, Kropotkin claims that "for the artistic construction, the finish and the beauty of his novels", he was "very probably the greatest novel-writer of his century". There will be many to debate this assertion in the interest of either Dostoevsky or Tolstoy, yet it can reasonably be admitted that, though Turgenev may not have had the great breadth or the intense passion of either of his contemporaries, his novels are formally nearer perfection, while his psychology, devoid of the moralism of Tolstoy or the morbidity of Dostoevsky, is more acutely perceptive of real human character.

Kropotkin had known Turgenev towards the end of the novelist's life. Turgenev, having heard that he was in Paris during 1878, sent an invitation through Lavrov to dine in friendly celebration of the escape from Russia. Of that evening, and of the meetings which followed whenever Kropotkin was in Paris, the latter has left an interesting account in his *Memoirs of a Revolutionist* and the important points are worth quoting at length, since they give some guidance to the author's better understanding of Turgenev than of many other Russian writers.

"His appearance is well known. Tall, strongly built, the head covered with soft and thick grey hair, he was certainly beautiful; his eyes gleamed with intelligence, not devoid of a touch of humour, and his whole manner testified to that simplicity and absence of affectation which was characteristic of the best Russian writers. . . .

"His talk was especially remarkable. He spoke, as he wrote, in images. When he wanted to develop an idea he did not resort to arguments, although he was a master in philosophical discussions; he illustrated his idea by a scene presented in a form as beautiful as if it had been taken from a novel. . . .

"He knew from Lavrov that I was an enthusiastic admirer of his writings; and one day, as we were returning in a carriage from a visit to Antokolski's studio, he asked me what I thought of Bazarov. I frankly replied, 'Bazarov is an admirable painting of the nihilist, but one feels that you did not love him as much as you did your other heroes'. 'On the contrary, I loved him, intensely loved him', Turgenev replied, with unexpected vigour. 'When we get home I will show you my diary, in which I have noted how I wept when I had ended the novel with Bazarov's death.'

"Turgenev certainly loved the intellectual aspect of Bazarov. He so identified himself with the nihilist philosophy of his hero that he even kept a diary in his name, appreciating the current events from Bazarov's point of view. But I think he admired him more than he loved him. In a brilliant lecture on Hamlet and Don Quixote, he divided the history-makers of mankind into two classes, represented by one or the other of these characters. . . . He himself and several of his friends belonged more or less to the Hamlets. He loved Hamlet and admired Don Quixote. So he admired also Bazarov. He represented his superiority admirably well; he understood the tragic character of his isolated position; but he could not surround him with that tender, poetical love which he bestowed, as on a sick friend, when his heroes approached the Hamlet type. It would have been out of place. . . .

"I saw him for the last time in the autumn of 1881. He was very ill, and worried by the thought that it was his duty to write to

Alexander III—who had just come to the throne and hesitated as to the policy he should follow—asking him to give Russia a constitution, and proving to him by solid arguments the necessity of that step. With evident grief he said to me: 'I feel that I must do it, but I feel I shall not be able to do it.' In fact, he was already suffering awful pains occasioned by a cancer in the spinal cord, and had the greatest difficulty even in sitting up and talking for a few moments. He did not write then, and a few weeks later it would have been useless. Alexander III had announced in a manifesto his intention to remain the absolute ruler of Russia."

These reminiscences suggest that personal knowledge had given Kropotkin a special insight into Turgenev's character, and may explain the aptness with which he puts forward on Turgenev's behalf a claim which the unbiased reader cannot fail to find sympathetic.

Taken as a whole, *Ideals and Realities in Russian Literature* provides a good and comprehensive introduction to Russian writing up to the end of the nineteenth century. As his particular interest is in the nineteenth-century rebels, Kropotkin deals briefly with the older literature, from the early folk poems to Pushkin. But when he reaches the later writers of the nineteenth century, from Gogol onwards, his study becomes both comprehensive and sufficiently detailed for general purposes. Every writer of significance is discussed, and every class of serious literature is included, criticism as well as novels, and political writing as well as poetry. It is clear that, despite his other varied activities and his years of exile, Kropotkin always found time to continue that thorough reading of Russian literature which he began in childhood. He did not, like so many revolutionaries, allow social preoccupations to blunt his literary and artistic appreciation, and *Ideals and Realities in Russian Literature* is another proof that he always retained a wide and humane culture.

While we are discussing Russian literature, it is not inappropriate to consider Kropotkin's relationship with Tolstoy which, although indirect, since the two men never met, was marked by a strong mutual respect. Their ideas had much in common; both hated the State and any kind of institution that interfered with the freedom of individual conscience and actions, both denounced property, both believed that man's innate moral sense should be sufficient to prevent all those ills for the cure of which governments try to persuade us to accept the greater evils of police and armies, laws and punishments. But they differed on two important issues. Firstly, Tolstoy condemned violence unreservedly and in all circumstances, while Kropotkin, despite his intense personal feelings, was ready to admit its necessity under certain extreme conditions. And secondly, Tolstoy held that the change in society must come as an individual moral change, a realisation that "the Kingdom of God is within", which will in turn affect men's actions towards their fellows and so alter the whole pattern and morality of social relationships. This element certainly had its place in the teachings of Kropotkin and many other anarchists, but it tended to become obscured by a doctrine of social strife, which Tolstoy regarded as a mere perpetuation of the old evil. Instead of counter-violence, he preached the withdrawal of co-operation from the State and its subsidiary institutions and the complete refusal to obey.

Tolstoy respected Kropotkin as a man of integrity who had sacrificed a great deal for his opposition to Tsarism. Kropotkin regarded Tolstoy as a great writer who had thrown his life and prestige into the cause of the oppressed, and who had risked much by his fearless denunciations of Tsarist policy even within Russia.

Their first contact seems to have come with the arrival in England of Tolstoy's leading disciple, Vladimir Chertkov. This exiled Tolstoyan had, by an odd coincidence, been an officer on duty at the St Petersburg Military Hospital at the time of Kropotkin's escape. They became close friends, and Chertkov was a regular visitor at Kropotkin's Bromley home. Soon after their meeting, Kropotkin asked Chertkov to transmit a message of friendly esteem to Tolstoy. He seems to have made some reference to their difference of opinions on the question of violence, for Tolstoy wrote to Chertkov shortly afterwards:

"Kropotkin's letter has pleased me very much. His arguments in favour of violence do not seem to me to be the expression of his opinions, but only of his fidelity to the banner under which he has served so honestly all his life. He cannot fail to see that the protest against violence, in order to be strong, must have a solid foundation. But a protest for violence has no foundation and for this very reason is destined to failure."

Chertkov read these words to Kropotkin, who was very disturbed by what he regarded as a misunderstanding of his attitude, for he replied: "In order to understand how much I sympathise with the ideas of Tolstoy, it is sufficient to say that I have written a whole volume to demonstrate that life is created, not by the struggle for existence, but by mutual aid."

The cordial feelings of the two great opponents of government continued. Visitors to Tolstoy in Russia, like Mavor and Nevinson, would be given special messages of friendly greeting for Kropotkin, and in January 1903 the old novelist wrote to Chertkov: "One has time to reflect when one is ill. During this illness I was particularly occupied with recollections, and my beautiful memories of Kropotkin were given special preference." A month later he wrote again: "Send my greetings to Kropotkin. . . . I have recently read his *Memoirs* and I am delighted with them." In 1905 Nevinson found Tolstoy full of interest in *Fields, Factories and Workshops*, which he thought of using as a basis for starting a recovery of Russian agriculture.*

It may be that, just as Kropotkin saw in Tolstoy the great writer inspired by an unbounded love of humanity, so Tolstoy saw in Kropotkin what Romain Rolland has indicated, the man who actually practised the renunciation which he himself had been able to achieve only in thought and writing.

At last, in November 1910, when it was tragically too late, Tolstoy made the break with his old life which he had so long felt necessary. He disappeared from home, and a rumour circulated that he had entered a monastery and would probably recant his former objections to the Orthodox Church. Kropotkin immediately went to his defence, writing to *The Times*:

"As to the possibility of 'recantation' by Tolstoy of his religious opinions, I can say it is absolutely improbable. It so happens that for the last two years I have been studying almost passionately and writing about the inner drama of Tolstoy's life as it appears from his novels, and other writings, and from the biographical material

* It is an interesting fact that Tolstoy's greatest disciple, Gandhi, was an enthusiastic reader of Kropotkin, whose influence can be seen in the Indian leader's idea of a society of village communes.

which he has himself permitted his friend, P. A. Biryukov, to publish; and I am sure that, having devoted the last thirty years of his life to the working out of a universal rationalist religion, divested of all the mystical elements of modern Christianity, a religion which, he says, would be equally acceptable to the Christian, the Buddhist, the Hebrew, the Musulman, the follower of Lao-Tse and to every ethical philosopher, and after having so passionately proclaimed in his latest writings the supreme decisive right of reason in religious matters, Tolstoy will certainly not return to the teachings of the Greek Orthodox Church.

"I am not astonished to learn that Tolstoy had decided to retire to a peasant house where he might continue his teachings without having to rely upon anyone else's labour for supplying himself or his family with the luxuries of life. It is the necessary outcome of the terrible inner drama he had been living through the last thirty years—the drama, by the way, of thousands upon thousands of intellectuals in our present society. It is the accomplishment of what he was longing for a long time."

Kropotkin ended by expressing the hope that "our great, venerated, beloved writer's" life would not be poisoned by the Russian church authorities. At least this wish was granted, for a few days later came the news that Tolstoy had been seized with pneumonia on his last journey of escape, and had died, with a few friends about him, in a remote stationmaster's house of Central Russia. Kropotkin was much afflicted by the news, and wrote several articles of appreciation, in which he referred to Tolstoy as "the most loved man, the most touchingly loved man, in the world".

II

Our discussion of Kropotkin's interest in Russian writers has led us rather far from the path of his connection with the revolutionary struggle in that country, and it is therefore necessary to turn back again in time, to the beginning of the century.

The struggle against the autocracy was rapidly gaining strength and depth in popular support, and Kropotkin followed its development with the warmest interest. In July 1902 he remarked to Guillaume that the news made it seem as though "the history of 1789" were "repeating itself in Russia: the constitutional movement against the background of Jacquerie and uprisings in the towns". There was at least some justification for this opinion, for throughout 1902 and the early months of 1903 took place a whole succession of peasant revolts, student demonstrations, and strikes among industrial workers, who were rapidly becoming a militant force in Russian affairs. There even began a widespread disaffection among the professional classes and in the army, and on at least one occasion the Cossacks refused to be used for police duties. The final result of all these disturbances was a manifesto of the Tsar, promising all kinds of reforms, which Kropotkin denounced in two articles for the *Daily News*, where he contended, correctly, that it was merely a device of the government, calculated to deceive all classes, and that the promises would never be translated into reality.

During this period, from 1897, when the student protests had been crushed with brutality and tortures, up to his illness in 1915, Kropotkin constituted himself a spokesman of the Russian opposition, and sent continual letters to *The Times*, the *Daily News* and other newspapers, exposing the persecutions instituted by Nicholas II and his ministers. The most important feature of these letters was their wide sympathy with all enemies and victims of the Russian tyranny. When it came to protesting against injustice, Kropotkin was no party man. He defended the victims, whatever their opinions, and in writings of this kind never attempted to make capital for his own point of view.

These events had strengthened the small anarchist groups in Russia, and also increased the number of young emigrés in Switzerland, France, and London, many of whom fell under the influence of Kropotkin's writing and also of Cherkesov's active personal proselytising. Eventually, in the summer of 1903, a group in Geneva decided to start an anarchist periodical. Kropotkin was not present at the original meetings in which this project was discussed, but he and Cherkesov promised full support, and in August 1903 appeared the first number of *Hleb i Volya* (*Bread and Freedom*). The editor, and the most active member of the Geneva group, was a Georgian, G. Goghelia, who worked under the double aliases of K. Orgheiana and K. Illiashvili. This has been described as "the first Russian anarchist paper", a distinction which might be disputed in the name of some of the Bakuninist papers. But *Hleb i Volya* was certainly the first Russian anarchist paper to have any influence within Russia. According to G. P. Maximov, a leading anarchist in the 1917 period, almost all the two or three thousand copies printed were transported illegally to Russia, and the contents were prepared with that end in view. *Hleb i Volya* provided a basis for anarchist underground propaganda, and from 1904 the number of groups in the larger Russian towns began to increase. It is significant of the influence of the paper that for a long time their rivals in the revolutionary struggle called the anarchist communists "Hlebovoltsi".

Kropotkin's share in this work was considerable. He wrote a series of eight articles, mostly unsigned, on questions of particular Russian interest, such as "The Russian Labour Union" or "The Russian Revolution", or of general theoretical interest, such as "The Peaceful Aim of Revolution" and "Organisation or Free Agreement". Ideologically, the *Hleb i Volya* group was much influenced by him, and indeed, the whole Russian anarchist movement was always dominated by his theoretical ideas, although there were, as we shall see, several important differences of opinion on the question of tactics between him and many groups in Russia and even Western Europe.

He was at first very pleased with the new paper, and on the 16th August wrote to Cherkesov: "No doubt you saw *Hleb i Volya*. Very good. Everything all right—the ideas as well as the style." But it was not long before there appeared an advocacy of terrorism which moved him to express strong disapproval. He told Cherkesov that the article impressed him "most disagreeably", and pointed out that it was not for the anarchist to call for terrorist acts from afar, since "this sort of propaganda can only be done by example". He complained that "such a tone" had not been seen in the anarchist press since the days when the police spy Serreaux tried to discredit the movement with *La Revolution Sociale*. On the main issue, he remarked that "generally speaking, to raise terror to a system is, in my opinion foolish". And in this particular case, he suggested, the article might have the most unfortunate effects, since only recently

Burtsev, the well-known Social Revolutionary, had been arrested by the Swiss authorities for making an outspoken attack on the Tsarist regime, and the government might well decide to clamp down similarly on *Hleb i Volya*. The alternative was little better, since:

"In case the government does not do it, what impression will it make among the Russians? Everybody will ask himself 'why such a privilege?' And in consequence the rumour will inevitably start that our comrades have fallen into the hands of some rascal of the same kind as Michael Serreaux. You say that this article should be circulated here. Read the first part. It would be better not to circulate it at all."

There is no evidence that the article in question had either of the results Kropotkin feared. But terrorism remained a constant source of disagreement between him and many Russian comrades. We have already given attention to the question in Western Europe and North America. But Russia offered a different problem, both in its general situation and also in the character of its revolutionary movement. The autocracy was more brutal than any other European regime; the pervasiveness of its repression had rendered the tasks of ordinary propaganda always difficult and at times almost impossible, while the police themselves had from the beginning introduced into the struggle between them and the revolutionaries an element of extreme violence. Faced by the failure of other methods, the revolutionaries had resorted to terrorist acts to express indignation and weaken the regime. It was a policy followed by all groups and parties until the advent of the social-democrats, and it is a moot point how far it was effective, since, although terroristic acts in themselves never resulted in any direct change, they provided a heroic revolutionary tradition, and helped to preserve the flow of young men and women who sacrificed themselves freely for the cause of the people. However, this result might have been obtained by other means, and even in Russia the case for terrorism is still unproved. The only point on which it really differed from the same phenomenon elsewhere lies in the fact that in the atmosphere of widespread hatred for the government, which permeated almost every stratum of the population, it did not arouse the same almost universal disapproval as in Western Europe.

Kropotkin's attitude towards terrorism in Russia did not differ fundamentally from that he adopted towards it in other circumstances. Despite his own dislike for violence he did not condemn specific acts, but he would not support terrorism conceived and followed as a definite policy, since he thought that this drove any movement that practised it into conspiratorial action and so divorced it from the people, a consequence which, both as an anarchist and a former *narodnik*, he could in no way approve. How this affected his attitude towards the Russian anarchist movement, which often manifested diametrically opposite tactical views, will be seen later. But for the present it is necessary to turn to the wider scene of Russian social developments at this period.

In the early weeks of 1904, having followed for some years a provocative policy of expansion in the Far East, the Russian Empire found itself at war over the Manchurian question with the rising Asiatic power of Japan. To Nicholas II and his evil genius, the minister Plehwe, the war was at first not unwelcome, since it seemed to provide a means of placating rising social discontent by an appeal to patriotism. But they had reckoned without several important factors. The corruption and brutal discipline of generations had made the Russian army, while efficient in suppressing peasants, wholly useless in warfare, particularly as its equipment was outdated and inadequate. The Japanese, on the other hand, had adapted rapidly and with great efficiency the Western techniques of industry and warfare, while their military system was not nearly so corrupt as the Russian. Their efficiency did not end on the military plane; they even attempted political warfare, and tried to get the leading Russian revolutionaries abroad to accept payment in order to increase their subversive work in Russia. Kropotkin was approached by their agents, but refused; he did not intend under any circumstances to enter the pay of a government; he was too good a patriot to side with the enemies of Russia, even to destroy her government, and he realised that if he were known to be associated with the Japanese it would do irreparable harm to the anarchist cause throughout the world. Pilsudski, then a Polish socialist, was among the few who were ready to accept the Japanese offer, but his case was different, since he was not an anarchist and he *was* a Pole who regarded the Russians as foreign invaders in his own country.

However, the Japanese need not have gone to all this trouble, since the Russian people were so discontented with the Romanovs that the war, far from becoming an incentive to the renewal of patriotism, was merely an added reason for hating the autocracy. Defeatism spread rapidly, and the military disasters only increased it and revealed to the disaffected people the weakness of the government. Finally, in July 1904, Plehwe was assassinated by the Social Revolutionaries, despite the elaborate precautions which he had taken to surround himself with a close system of police protection. Nobody could be found to continue his system of government by terror, and when Prince Mirsky finally agreed to take office, it was on the understanding that representatives of the Zemstvos should be called together to discuss a scheme of national representation. They met, and presented to the Tsar a strongly worded memorandum demanding constitutional guarantees; their action was supported by similar demands from barristers and magistrates, municipal councillors, and even a few provincial Assemblies of the Nobility. The educated and liberal section of the nation had come into the open, but it was propelled and supported by a great and open unrest among the whole population.

A new factor appeared in the first month of 1905, when the working men of St Petersburg joined the movement. The January events make very strange telling. A certain Father Gapon, who was later found to be a double agent, working for the authorities and the revolutionaries at the same time, managed during 1904 to gain a great influence among the workers of St Petersburg, and when he suggested that they should go *en masse* to the Tsar and present a petition for constitutional guarantees, 70,000 men pledged themselves to take part in the demonstration, and on the chosen day, the 22nd January, nearly 200,000 working people came out into the streets to march on the Winter Palace and lay their grievances before the Autocrat, in whose paternal feelings they still had a childish faith. The exact intentions of Gapon have never been satisfactorily explained. It is certain, however, that the authorities knew of the projected demonstration long before it took place, and made no attempt to prevent it, or to warn the people of the likely consequences of their action. Instead, elaborate military arrangements were made secretly, and when the people appeared before the Winter Palace they were received with massed volleys, which killed nearly two thousand of them.

If the government hoped by such brutal means to halt the wave of revolution they were disappointed. For in one stroke they had destroyed one of the chief bulwarks of their power, the faith of the people in the Tsar's goodwill, and from this moment the working people of Russia began to pursue a more revolutionary path. A few days afterwards a wave of strikes broke out in Poland, followed by more bloody massacres. It was clear to those with any insight that a revolutionary situation already existed, and on the 23rd January Kropotkin wrote enthusiastically to Guillaume about the initiative shown by the workers, comparing it with the stale phrasemongering of the Russian social-democrats. A few days later, in the early days of February, he showed optimism on an even greater scale by remarking to the Russian anarchist, Yanovsky, "The best way to help the revolution in Russia is to begin the social revolution in all the civilised countries".

The Russian revolution, needless to say, was not helped in this way, but although the anarchist movement as a whole was too tiny to have any real influence, many individual members worked well in the ensuing months, and took active parts in the great movements later in the year, particularly the strikes of October and November which wrung great, though temporary, concessions from the Tsar. But it was an uprising that fulfilled the theories of the anarchists much more completely than if it had been fought under their banner. For one cannot examine the amazing history of these days, when events marched far ahead of parties, without being impressed by the truth of Kropotkin's remark: "It is not Social-Democrats, or Revolutionary Socialists, or Anarchists, who take the lead in the present revolution. It is labour—the working man." All the anarchist conceptions of revolution were being confirmed, and the results of October also showed the efficiency of the weapon of the general strike which the anarchists had long advocated. The fact that later on all the gains of 1905 were lost to the superior manœuvres of the reactionaries does not disprove these contentions; it merely shows that the revolutionaries were too unaccustomed to success to take steps that would prevent a counter-revolution.

During this period the Russian anarchists were much concerned with the problem of tactics, and two conferences in which Kropotkin took an active part were held in London, in December 1904 and in October 1906, to discuss these vital questions, as well as an informal meeting during his visit to Paris in September 1905. Since the problems raised at these gatherings were closely related, we shall discuss them together.

Kropotkin's views on tactical questions were very rigid and strongly held, and Marie Goldsmith, a Russian Jewish anarchist who attended these meetings and worked in the London group of *Hleb i Volya*, has given, under the *nom de plume* of M. Corn, a description of his attitude in these discussions with the young comrades from Russia.

"All who at this time were present at Peter Alexeivich's conversations with the young remember how he listened with an affectionate smile and gentle gaze. . . . But, indulgent as he was with every sincere enthusiast, he was always severe in the choice of the means of struggle. There were methods of propaganda which Peter Alexeivich could not endure. His voice then became hard and stern and his censure was uncompromising. Above all, he referred with absolute aversion to the principle that 'the end justifies the means' and to everything that in the slightest recalled this principle, whether in questions of organisation, methods of collecting money, attitude to the hostile camp, or relations with other parties. On his lips the word 'Nechaevism' was always a strong rebuke."

The meeting in December 1904 was a very small one, and was not a conference in the true sense of the word, since none of those present came as delegates, but only as individuals appearing on their own responsibility to discuss their problems and Russian affairs in general, and to obtain Kropotkin's advice. The attitude of the meeting towards the revolution which everybody regarded as imminent was embodied in a resolution setting forth a characteristically anarchist view of the unity of the revolutionary process.

"In view of the approaching Russian revolution we cannot remain indifferent to the outcome of the movement organised against autocracy in Russia. Regarding autocracy as one of the most harmful forms of government, we consider at the same time that our task is not so much to assist its overthrow as to widen the struggle, directing it simultaneously against capital and the State in all its forms. We do not recognise it as possible to divide our struggle into two successive periods—one for the achievement of political upheaval and the other for economic reforms of new State institutions."

The resolution ended by proclaiming the right of both the masses and individuals to rebel and carry out revolutionary deeds, and added that "individual acts" cannot be decided by organisations but must be left to men on the spot to carry out if they judge them necessary and possible.

From this followed a discussion of the attitude to be adopted towards the constitutional agitation then proceeding in Russia. The *Black Banner* group took the logically extreme position of hostility towards every political agitation that went no farther than advocating the overthrow of the autocracy. Kropotkin regarded this attitude as impractical, and contended:

> "Let the liberals do their work; we cannot be against it. Our business is not to fight with them, but to bring into the existing revolutionary ferment our own ideas, to widen the demands which are raised."

But the question which aroused most discussion was that of "expropriation". In its specialised Russian sense this word had only the most tenuous connection with the general expropriation of the means of production which Kropotkin envisaged as likely to play a significant part in the social revolution. In the Russian sense it meant obtaining money by theft or fraud for financing revolutionary groups. It was used by all the revolutionary parties; and in his early days as a social-democrat even Generalissimo Stalin attained distinction as a bank robber. Like the other parties, many anarchist groups used these methods, and most of the comrades who came from Russia were in favour of their continuance. Kropotkin, however, came out categorically against "expropriation". He contended that it led inevitably to demoralisation within the movement, and resulted in the unnecessary waste of young lives. He also claimed that this practice violated the principle of labour, and that only work should be the source of income, whether for private living or for underground activities. "Our propaganda should be supported by sympathisers, workers, readers; bourgeois money is not necessary to us—either as donations or as thefts." He showed by example how such practices had retarded the movement in other countries.

His plea was eloquent, and we are told that at least one of his opponents burst into tears. But most of the men from Russia persisted in their attitude, and, since anarchists do not accept majority decisions, no agreement was reached on this important point. The groups at home continued to indulge in "petty" expropriation, but with such bad results that, according to Marie Goldsmith, most of its advocates eventually accepted Kropotkin's strictures.

The actual revolution raised new problems for the Russian anarchists, and the Paris discussions of September 1905 centred mostly round the problems of syndicalism and participation in the Soviets of Workers' and Peasants' Deputies, which in that year made their momentous appearance in Russian history. All were agreed that direct action should be the basis of struggle, in opposition to the parliamentary methods advocated by the social-democrats, but there were important divisions on the question of how this action should be carried on. One extreme section believed that the revolutionary spirit was to be found only among the vagabond elements of the masses, and regarded participation in trade unions or similar bodies as a concession to the idea of organisation and therefore a deviation from the anarchist ideal. They adopted a rather individualist attitude, and feared that, if they ceased to act independently, the anarchists would be submerged in the great masses of the population, which were not genuinely revolutionary. The anarcho-syndicalists, on the other hand, were concerned with the problem of organising a free society, and saw the trade unions as important instruments of the day-to-day struggle and also as basic organisations on which to build the network of voluntary co-operation which was their aim. Kropotkin did not put much faith in the "vagabond elements", and gave qualified support to the anarcho-syndicalists.

The same split was evident on the question of the Soviets. The individualists were opposed to participation, the anarcho-syndicalists in favour of it. Kropotkin conceded that "One may enter the Soviets, but certainly only as far as the Soviets are organs of struggle against the bourgeoisie and the State, and not organs of authority". But he added: "I, however, would personally prefer to remain among the working masses."

The third meeting, in October 1906, was again held in London, in an atmosphere of mingled hope and disillusionment. The achievements of 1905 were already being submerged by the new advance of reaction; on the other hand, the revolutionary feeling of the Russian people was stronger than ever before, and the anarchists, although still a small minority movement, in comparison with the Social Revolutionaries or the Social-Democrats, had certainly increased their influence. The time had come for a reassessment of the situation, and the meeting seems to have been rather longer than on previous occasions, for Kropotkin delivered two more or less formal lectures, other anarchists also spoke, while a series of resolutions was afterwards adopted, and the whole of the documents were finally published in 1907 as a pamphlet entitled *The Russian Revolution and Anarchism.*

In view of later developments in Russia, Kropotkin's lectures are of sufficient interest to be paraphrased at some length. His first subject was "The Political and Economic Revolutions". He claimed that developments in Russia corresponded roughly with what had happened in Western Europe during 1789 and 1848, and contended that it was impossible to concentrate wholly on the economic struggle and ignore the struggle against autocracy, which had been in progress for half a century. But he disputed the contention of the social-democrats that Russia must necessarily go through a parliamentary stage, like Germany, for that country had not experienced a revolution, but had received her constitution from above, as a means of preserving the monarchy. The strength of the government in Russia, the amount of political freedom, the durability of bourgeois rule, all depended on the energy manifested by the extreme anti-government party.

As regards practical achievements, all the land should go to the people who tilled it, but the mistakes of the French Revolution must be avoided, and, instead of being divided for private ownership, it should be vested in the communes, who would deal with its use and distribution. Similarly, factories, workshops, mines and means of transport should be run, not by new ministries, as the social-democrats proposed, but by the men who worked in them, organised in free unions or syndicates.

The anarchists must leave their isolation and become a real revolutionary force, capable of helping the people to find new roads in the organisation of Russian life. Without the masses nothing could be achieved, and therefore the anarchists should seek always, like the old *narodniks*, to be "with the people, among the people".

Here, in the insistence that the land must go to the peasants and the factories to the workers, we have the emergence of that demand for which the anarchists fought in 1917, and which was actually taken over by the Bolsheviks before the latter could persuade the Russian people to confirm them in an authority which they used for taking the land and the factories out of the hands of the people and putting them into those of the State. It was the anarchists who first realised these aspirations of the Russian people, and the Bolsheviks only used the idea because it provided a road to power.

The second lecture dealt with the attitude of anarchists towards the unions of workers and peasants which were being formed all over Russia. Kropotkin demonstrated that what had been achieved in Russia was not the work of any party, but sprang from the self-sacrifice of the working masses. The anarchists, who should be in the forefront of such action, were few in numbers and divided by theoretical differences, but they should join the trade unions and seek to demonstrate that direct action is more effective than parliamentary methods. He criticised as untrue the defeatist idea that all urban workers were influenced by the social-democrats and all peasants by the Social Revolutionaries, and recalled what had been done by anarchists in Western Europe, and particularly in Spain. Their task was to see that the unions did not become subsidiary organisations of political parties.

These lectures seem to have had a considerable influence on the comrades assembled at the conference, for, after bringing in the traditional resolutions regarding the destruction of capitalism and State and the expropriation of the means of production, they went on to state that anarchists should take an active part in workers' organisations, build new anarchist unions wherever possible, and elsewhere enter all unions not attached to political parties. Clearly at this point the success of mass strikes sufficiently impressed many Russian anarchists to convert them, at least temporarily, to Kropotkin's attitude.

The events of 1905 were not without their effect on Kropotkin's personal life. His nephew, Nicholas Alexeivich Kropotkin, who had come to Europe for a prolonged visit in 1903, stayed some time at Bromley towards the end of 1904 and during the early days of 1905, when the news of the revolution began to arrive. Nicholas and his uncle had already discussed the current events in Russia, and Kropotkin had shown particular interest in the tendencies among the peasants and students—the two revolutionary classes in Russia with whom he had enjoyed most direct contact. Nicholas Alexeivich remarked that: "In spite of what seemed to me a certain idealisation of the Russian people, he looked far more soberly at events in Russia than the Paris emigrés."

Kropotkin was ill in bed when the news about Father Gapon and the demonstration of the St Petersburg workers arrived; he became very excited, and translated the reports from the English papers for his nephew's benefit. "One of these days," the latter recounts, "Peter Alexeivich's house was besieged by innumerable reporters who wanted to interview him about events in Russia. He did not receive them, and the only thing they obtained from him was a short note, written with my pencil, on which only 'Down with the Romanovs!' could be found."

Kropotkin immediately began to think of returning to his own country, and discussed with his nephew a scheme for publishing a large newspaper designed especially for the peasants. Nicholas Alexeivich thought his uncle might have been very successful at this task, since he knew the needs of the peasants, could express himself very plainly and, despite his long exile, had retained a rich Russian vocabulary. As Marie Goldsmith also mentions this proposal, it seems to have been discussed fairly widely among Kropotkin's friends.

Meanwhile, the desire to return became steadily more acute; in August, Kropotkin discussed it with Brupbacher in Brittany, and in November Nettlau encountered him at the British

Museum and heard his plans. He confessed that he had spent several free hours practising with a rifle in a shooting gallery, since "he was curious to know, after a long lapse of time, whether he could still hit his mark—and he was satisfied he could". He emphasised that if he went to Russia under the recent amnesty, "situations might arise where all might be driven to street fighting, and, old as he was, he was satisfied that he could still be of some use". Perhaps Kropotkin, who had a romantic view of revolutions, still hoped that life would give him those days on the barricades which had been granted so abundantly to Bakunin, but denied so completely to himself.

But there were great difficulties in the way of returning, since it was by no means certain, even after the events of 1905, that the Russian government would leave him unmolested. To Guillaume, on the 12th November, he wrote that he was going soon, but did not know when. He feared that the authorities might rake up an old accusation which was raised against him in 1873, "of trying to persuade two workers to kill the Tsar (an absurdity!)", and that they might also discover his relations with Russian anarchists. "I was told from Russia that they would arrest and keep me in prison for a month or two, pending the Court's decision." But he insisted, "Nevertheless we are going soon". A month later he wrote to Guillaume, "We are almost certain that I shall go in January".

In December the defeat of the Moscow rising swamped any hopes of further revolutionary success in the near future, and made a strengthening of Witte's government inevitable. Guillaume and other friends urgently warned Kropotkin not to return in a hurry. However, he did not wholly abandon his plans, and early in the New Year wrote again to Guillaume, saying that the government had postponed its order to arrest the leaders of revolutionary groups, but that its policy towards exiles had still not been clarified and that he had therefore decided to wait a little while. Besides, there were other reasons why it might be better to delay, for "Madame Lavrov advised me, when she wrote a month ago, that it is better to come before the onset of winter (to get used to it), than to arrive in the very middle of the frost".

He continued to be optimistic, and remarked :

"This wave of reaction will not be protracted, though the revolutionaries have been forced to postpone for some time any attempt at armed insurrection. I must, however, tell you that we do not propose to go before the first days of February. So much has to be arranged, especially as regards work which I began for the *Encyclopædia Britannica.*"

His desire to return was increased by the news that a number of his books and pamphlets, such as the *Memoirs of a Revolutionist, Paroles d'un Revolté, An Appeal to the Young,* were being published in St Petersburg and Moscow, legally and illegally, during 1905 and 1906, and were attaining some popularity, while several small biographical pamphlets on his life and ideas had appeared. They only enjoyed a brief run of open publication, for very shortly the editions were confiscated by the police. Delays and doubts continued, and June 1906 still found Kropotkin talking of packing his trunks, to be sent "some day" to Russia. By the end of July he had become more resigned to the real situation, and wrote to Guillaume:

"I would so like to go to Russia now, but this would only lead to my arrest during the first week. Ah, if I were only somewhat younger! I could then live underground."

Meanwhile, after the counter-revolution of 1906, the anarchist movement within Russia began to spread rapidly in the cities, where the workers were becoming disillusioned by the reverses they had suffered under the leadership of the social-democrats. Anarchist groups appeared in all the major towns, and became particularly strong in Ekaterinoslav, Odessa, the Ukraine generally, and parts of Poland and the Urals. It is difficult now to disentangle the complicated relationships of the various groups, but at least three general currents can be detected, anarchist communism, anarcho-syndicalism, and individualism. All groups, whatever their theoretical approach, were more touched by individualism in action than were the movements in Western Europe. Almost all militants, as well as carrying on propaganda by literature and inciting strikes, practised terrorism and expropriation, and however much they may have respected Kropotkin's general theories, few seem to have regarded his warnings in the matter of tactics. There were even extremists who believed in "terror without motive", and in general the anarchists were more feared by the authorities, as the last chief of the Tsarist police, Vassilyev, has admitted, than any other movement.

In Western Europe the number of Russian anarchist refugees increased, and the days of Kropotkin's isolation among the mass of Russian constitutionalists were past. The groups in London, Paris, the Swiss towns and American cities, reflected the differing ideas within Russia, though it seems that Kropotkin's influence over them was more complete. Nor should we forget in this connection the considerable movement of Russian Jewish workers in the East End of London, who gathered round the *Workers' Friend* and were inspired by the German, Rudolf Rocker, who worked very energetically among them. This large Jewish group represented the only really compact mass of anarchist workers in England, and certainly the most considerable emigré Russian group in Europe. Its attitude tended towards syndicalism and its members were extremely devoted to Kropotkin, who himself was always glad to be among them.

The revolution of 1905 temporarily disorganised the work of propaganda from Western Europe. Most of the active young comrades returned to Russia, including even the editors of *Hleb i Volya*, and the paper ceased publication after November 1905. The need for a new emigré periodical became evident, and in October 1906, as a result of the conference in that month, a group in London started *Listki Hleb i Volya*. Kropotkin took from the beginning a very active part. He was always a member of the editorial board, and when, shortly after its formation, most of his collaborators moved to Paris, he continued it himself, assisted editorially by Marie Goldsmith and technically by Alexander Shapiro. He told Guillaume in December 1906, "... Since I began to publish our Russian paper, *Listki Hleb i Volya*, all my time is taken by this work, and I have not even had an opportunity to write anything for that paper. It has eight pages, twice a month. ... But most of the time is taken up by endless correspondence, and my thoughts are always with this work." He added optimistically: "The real anarchist party, in the true sense of the word, is in the process of final formation in Russia."

Marie Goldsmith says that Kropotkin filled their paper with his own articles when sufficient material was not available, found interesting extracts from Russian letters, provided bibliographical data, so that the paper was "rich in valuable literary material". It was largely supported from America, cheques for fifty or a hundred dollars frequently arriving from sympathetic groups or individuals. Unfortunately, according to Marie Goldsmith, "the paper did not possess an adequate technical equipment for conveying it to Russia, and circulating it there", and Kropotkin told Guillaume in March 1907 that a very large proportion of the three or four thousand copies printed actually went, not to Russia, but to the emigrants in the United States. The same letter showed him still maintaining confidence in the Russian situation, and again toying with the idea of going back.

"All of us are now much occupied with the idea of returning to Russia. To be paralysed there or to remain paralysed here—is it not the same? In any case, I feel that there I would have some influence, even if I do not have a newspaper at my disposal.

"At the present time a number of anarchist groups have already been formed in Russia. Trade unionism, which at one time was in the background and in neglect, begins to make headway. The Social Revolutionaries, and the Social-Democrats are trying to get it into their hands, and now in Russia there is a fine field for work if I can help the comrades with words of encouragement or advice to save the independence of the unions. . . . But work goes very badly and any minute one can expect a reactionary *coup d'état*, and then nothing can be done. Notwithstanding this, all three of us thirst to go to Russia, at least for a stay."

But he did not go. For soon there came the dissolution of the second Duma, and the triumph of counter-revolution was complete. Writing in *Temps Nouveaux*, he recognised that the revolutionary period was over, and that it was time to jettison any hope of further achievements along the path of constitutional liberalism. Now, he claimed, must begin preparation for the second period of the revolution, which would only be achieved through the masses.

"The work of demolition can only be accomplished by the direct participation of the whole of the people. And they will only act in the name of their immediate and popular needs. The land to the peasant; the factory, the workshop, the railway and the rest to the worker."

His words were prophetic, for the events of 1917 took place under the very slogans he here advanced. But they were used, not by a Kropotkin, but by a Lenin, and not to liberate but to enslave the people.

Anarchism within Russia did not retain the momentum gained in 1906. During 1907 it seems to have reached the end of expansion; there was a limit to the self-sacrifice which had sent its young men in dozens to the gallows. While still growing in numbers, the anarchist groups did not increase greatly in proportion to the Social Revolutionaries or the two sections, Bolsheviks and Mensheviks, into which the social-democrats were divided; of the four currents of Russian revolutionary activity during the period from 1907 to 1917, anarchism remained much the weakest. Outside Russia its fame was deceptively great, owing largely to its mistaken identity in the ordinary European mind with nihilism and terrorism.

In London, Kropotkin could find nobody to take the regular burden of editing *Listki Hleb i Volya*, and eventually, after carrying on for nearly a year and devoting a very great proportion of his time to it, he abandoned it in July 1907, owing to his frequent absences from England for the good of his health. This did not mean a diminution of interest in Russian affairs. After the termination of *Listki Hleb i Volya* the group in London began to publish, under his guidance, pamphlets and even books. Several of his own works were translated into his native language for the first time, the most ambitious effort being the production of *The Great French Revolution*, completed during 1914. Kropotkin himself did a good deal of work on a volume of selections from Bakunin's writings, finally completed by Cherkesov and published in 1915.

During 1910 *Hleb i Volya* was revived for a few numbers in Paris, and Kropotkin contributed articles, but it was again impossible to assemble a sufficiently active and permanent staff, and the paper was finally abandoned. But other emigré papers appeared, and Kropotkin wrote for them whenever he found time. The most important was *Rabochi Mir*, which began in 1911, and later, in 1913, became the organ of the Federation of Russian Anarchist Communists, formed at a congress of all the existing Western European groups. It was suspended in 1914, at the beginning of the Great War. From 1913 Kropotkin contributed regularly, but he would not join the editorial board, partly because he was already involved in the preliminary work on his *Ethics* (he had said shortly beforehand that he was now able to work only five or six hours a day), but also because, according to Marie Goldsmith, " . . . he did not like official 'organs' of parties and federations, which always had to express the views of all the members or some 'middle' opinion of the organisation. He preferred the organs of small groups."

Before we end our discussion of Kropotkin's Russian activities prior to 1917, it is necessary to discuss two other incidents which lay outside his purely anarchist interests. The first was the Azev affair, to which we have already referred in passing. Azev, like Gapon, was one of those strange double agents who played such a persistent role in the Russian revolutionary movement. As head of the battle organisation of the Social Revolutionaries, he was responsible for killing a number of Russian dignitaries, including an archduke, yet at the same time he acted as an informer to the Tsarist secret police. In his role as a revolutionary terrorist he showed such enterprise that it was long before his comrades harboured any doubt of his integrity, and when another Social Revolutionary, Burtsev, brought an accusation of treachery against him, it was decided to arraign Burtsev before a Jury of Honour for spreading scandalous rumours.

Kropotkin was invited to become a member of the jury, and this fact is an interesting reflection of the cordiality of his relationship with the Social Revolutionaries, who, as heirs of the *narodnik* tradition, were nearer to the anarchists than any other political party in Russia or elsewhere. He was on terms of close personal friendship with many of them, and next year took a prominent part at the meeting organised to welcome Vera Figner to London. His attitude towards them was in sharp contrast to the hostility which usually existed between him and the social-democrats of both factions.

The other members of the Jury of Honour were two leading revolutionaries of unimpeachable repute, Lopatin and Vera Figner. At first everybody thought it was merely a question of pacifying Burtsev; he was attacked by Chernov and Natansohn, one of Kropotkin's old comrades in the Chaikovsky circle, and at the beginning all the jury except Kropotkin seem to have thought there was no foundation in his accusations. Kropotkin, however, with a great experience of spies and *provocateurs*, held that where suspicions had been aroused against a person in different circles over a long period they had usually some substance. He was right, for after a month of tiresome discussion, Burtsev produced evidence which proved Azev's guilt. Burtsev was exonerated, and here Kropotkin's responsibility ended. Azev, who had kept away from Paris during the inquiry, was unmasked by the Social Revolutionaries. The incident had one rather annoying aftermath so far as Kropotkin was concerned, for the Russian police now tried to associate him with their discredited spy, and in February 1909 he was forced to make an announcement, printed in *The Times*, to the effect that he had met Azev only once, and that accidentally.

It was in 1908 that the second instance of more general participation in Russian affairs also commenced. At this time the reaction in Russia had become wholly triumphant; Nicholas II and his minister Stolypin were embarking on a campaign of repression which included execution, imprisonment, exile, torture, and beatings on a scale unprecedented in recent Russian history. Much indignation was aroused in England at the revelations of these brutalities, and a Parliamentary Committee on Russian affairs was formed by a few M.P.s sympathetic to Russian liberation. Its avowed object was to collect and disseminate genuine information concerning events in Russia, and to keep the subject before the attention of Parliament. The ultimate aim was a wide propaganda campaign to stress the need for supporting the revolutionary movement in Russia. The leading Russian exiles all took part in this work. A monthly *Bulletin* was edited by David Soskice and Felix Volkhovsky, Sophie Kropotkin gave lectures at various places in the country, and Kropotkin undertook the preparation of a "Statement on the White Terror in Russia", which it was originally intended should be printed in the Committee's *Bulletin*, with the object of furnishing authenticated data for the use of speakers at meetings on the Russian question.

But there was so much information continually coming in that the statement grew steadily until it reached the proportions of a small book. Some of the English members of the Committee, and particularly H. W. Nevinson and H. N. Brailsford, assisted in collating material, but both of them found Kropotkin's methods so chaotic that co-operation was difficult. Eventually, however, when all the material was collected, he wrote the pamphlet rapidly, and it was published in 1909, a compact work of nearly eighty pages, which had a very wide circulation. It was written as a mere statement of facts; Kropotkin kept out all the stormy emotions which his collaborators say swayed him strongly when he was doing this work; he recorded neither comment nor judgment. Only the facts were left to tell their unhappy tale against the Tsarist regime, and the work represented a fine example of condemnation by the mere presentation of evidence. It had a considerable influence on British opinion in its time; today its interest is merely historical, but it does present a good illustration of the extent of its writer's interest in, and knowledge of, what was happening within Russia at this period.

III

It is impossible to consider Kropotkin's attitude towards the Great War of 1914 apart from his position in the Russian revolutionary tradition. In the past chapters we have given some indication of the constancy of his anti-German feeling, its rapid growth in the late 1890's, and its connection with both his admiration for France and his general position as a Russian radical. Here, before proceeding to discuss his attitude during the war period, we must pause to dwell briefly on the background against which it arose.

Ever since the early days of progressive and revolutionary movements in Russia, there had been a tendency for rebels to develop a particular hatred towards Germany. Originally this was due to the fact that German influence had played a strong part in developing the autocracy of the Romanovs. Peter the Great had sought to introduce German methods into his new Russia, and had used German experts and officials in furthering his policy of centralisation. Catherine the Great was actually a German princess by birth, and since her time the ruling family had been German in feeling and largely also in blood. Nicholas I had modelled his military methods on the Prussian army, and had sought unsuccessfully to build a Junker class similar to that which formed the military backbone of Germany, while, among the aristocracy, the German gentry of the Baltic provinces proved most reliant in their support of the autocracy. Finally, it always seemed to Russian liberals that the proximity of a strongly centralised military State like Prussia provided a bad example and also a bulwark to Russian absolutism. If the Prussian and later the German State had not been there, they argued, it would have been so much easier to overthrow the Tsars.

There was much reason behind this attitude, but, instead of specifically opposing the German State, many Russians tended to identify with it both the country and the people, and thus to arrive at a general detestation of Germans and all things German. This was so in the case of Herzen who, despite his Prussian mother, always detested Germany and even German ideas. His attitude was later adopted by Bakunin. In his early days the latter had been a devotee of German philosophy, an admirer of Hegel and even of Marx, and at Dresden in 1849 a fighter for the freedom of Saxony. But the rise of the imperial State under Bismarck, the long intrigues of Marx and the cultivation of State socialism by the social-democrats made him see Germany as a country hostile to the libertarian socialism at which he aimed; when the Franco-Prussian War began in 1870 he hoped for the destruction of the German armies, but he was consistent in his revolutionary beliefs, since he did not wish for this through a rival French State or army, but by the rising of the communes and a revolutionary war on an international scale. Marx, on the other hand, supported Germany, because he thought the defeat of imperial France would encourage the spread of authoritarian socialism on a world basis, at the expense of Proudhon's federalist ideas, which then dominated the French labour movement.

Kropotkin followed Bakunin's lead, and in his case the distaste of the Russian radical for German ideas, and of the anarchist for victorious Prussia and growing Marxism, were supplemented by the love of France, which his almost obsessive interest in the revolution of 1789–93 had converted into a kind of adoptive patriotism. He might expose fiercely the corruption of the French government and of French society, but he nevertheless regarded the Third Republic itself as something better than any other society in the world; the protestations he had always made that no kind of government is better than another were in practice relaxed in its favour, and the misdeeds of individual ministers and cabinets were dismissed as the errors of individuals who sullied the revolutionary tradition rather than as symptoms of flaws in the Republican State itself.

Thus, while in the 1880's he was talking in Bakuninist terms of an uprising of the communes and a revolutionary war against the invader, without armies or military organisation, by the early years of the twentieth century, although still believing theoretically that the international rivalry of States was the prime cause of conflict, he was actually ready to go into a war on the side of one of these same States. In 1906, in a reply to Gustave Hervé, then a fervent anti-militarist, he had said that if France were attacked, socialists should not stand aside and see the republic defeated by a reactionary monarchist power. And, while it is true that he mentioned the need for a social revolution to overthrow the present regime, he cancelled this out by speaking against the anti-militarist propaganda of the syndicalists, and by asking that the anarchists should agree to conscription, which was both unanarchist and an indirect support of the State that conducted the conscription.

The fact that he assumed a position which few anarchists would support must have been evident to Kropotkin after the Amsterdam Congress of 1907, if not before, but he persisted with the obstinacy which became steadily more evident in his nature in later years. Neither logic nor the knowledge that his actions would eventually entail a breach with many loved and respected comrades could move him from his position.

In 1912, for instance, he received a number of anarchist friends, including Rudolf Rocker, and discussed with them the question of the coming war. He placed the blame for it unequivocally on the shoulders of the German rulers, and here it may not be amiss to quote his semi-prophetic statement:

"I am firmly convinced today that unless an absolutely unexpected turn takes place war is bound to come. I even believe that we are already walking in its shadow. They have already gone too far in Germany to make a retreat now. After you have rattled the sabre for so long, so that the whole world feels itself threatened, you cannot suddenly exchange the trumpet for the shepherd's flute, particularly if you fear to lose face. Through its foreign policy Germany has divided itself more and more from Western Europe. Since Bismarck's departure the situation has become more and more acute from year to year, for the present power-holders in the Reich are lacking in deeper insight. Their entire policy has rested until now on the use of terror. The growing isolation of Germany shows them that this means is no longer effective, and they are becoming frightened. . . . But fear is always a bad counsellor. In order not to lose your last allies you believe it necessary to overtake events, and this will finally lead to catastrophe. They only wait for a favourable excuse, and as soon as that is found there will be no stopping them.

"Secret diplomacy everywhere has been to school with the devil. Yet the present rulers in Germany are more responsible than all others, as they have been the cause of the militarisation of Europe and have determinedly refused any suggestions of disarmament. In that way they have created a condition which must inevitably lead to catastrophe, because there is a limit for even the richest countries. If that is reached, and they have not come to their senses, which rarely happens in such cases, then war remains the only way out for these rulers. England and France have nothing to gain but much to lose from a war. Even a victorious end would inflict frightful wounds on both countries which could not be healed easily. A war, which today could only be a war on the greatest scale, and which would spread over many countries, would have as its result the thorough disruption of European economic life and lead to endless crises, the effects of which could not even be measured today. For Germany the situation is much more favourable. Should she win the war, she will be in a prevalent position in Europe for a long time."

Kropotkin's arguments were not without a basis of reason. It was not, as many of his critics have tried to infer, a question of senility. A looseness of thought had led him to identify peoples with States and think in national terms, as distinct from the international terms of anarchist thought, and once he had accepted this false basis, his reasoning beyond it was clear. It was true that German imperialism and militarism were largely responsible for the international chaos, but the diplomacy and intrigues of other countries, and the ferocious imperialism of all major European countries in the nineteenth century, had also played a part in provoking the war situation. It was a condition of the capitalist world as a whole, of which German swashbuckling was merely an extreme symptom, and Kropotkin, on the basis of his own analysis of the causes of war, should have seen that for a general disease there could not be a particular remedy, such as supporting a bad side against a worse, but only the general remedy of a complete change in the social structure.

When the war actually came, in 1914, Kropotkin was unwittingly connected with the incident which touched off the guns—the now half-forgotten murder at Serajevo. The Balkan provinces of Bosnia and Herzegovina, with their mixed population of Serbs, Croats and Moslems, had been virtually annexed by Austria-Hungary in 1878, and since 1908 had been *de jure* part of the Hapsburg empire. About the latter year there began among the Serbian youth a movement aimed at liberation from Austrian domination and fusion with the population of Serbia. Right from the beginning it had a strongly anarchistic flavour, which was due partly to Bakunin and his followers having always taken a strong interest in Balkan affairs and having advocated the liberation of all the Slavs from Hapsburg authority, and partly to the absence of any constitutional outlet for rebellious impulses, so that the anarchist weapons of terrorism and strikes in schools were readily accepted by the Serbian youth of the subjugated provinces.

After a series of strikes and disturbances, the Austrian government decided in 1910 to grant a charter and a Diet, in the hope of dividing the opposition. This aroused indignation among the more revolutionary elements, and a student named Zherajich, who had steeped himself in the writings of Kropotkin, decided to commit an act of protest. Without telling his comrades, he lay in wait for the Austrian governor-general when the latter returned to his palace after the opening of the first Bosnian Diet. He fired at the Austrian, missed, and immediately shot himself. As he lay bleeding to death in the street, the governor-general walked up, kicked his body several times, and then walked away.

Zherajich's attempt left a deep impression on the young Serbs, who made him an almost legendary hero, and decided to avenge his memory. However, several attempts failed, and, although Kropotkin's works were read and retained much influence in student circles, the youth movement began to lose its anarchistic character through the upsurge of Serbian nationalism as a result of the Balkan wars of 1912–13. At last, in 1914, the young Serbs heard that the Archduke Franz Ferdinand, heir to the Hapsburg throne, was to visit Bosnia, and they decided that this was the opportunity to avenge Zherajich and to draw world attention to the plight of the subjugated Slavs.

The plotters consisted of a group of young Serbian nationalists, and they were joined by one genuine anarchist, the printer Chabrinovich. It was actually to an Italian anarchist group in Trieste that they first applied for bombs, and only after failure in that direction did they accept the assistance of a secret nationalist group of Serbian officers in Belgrade, the Black Hand.

The anarchist Chabrinovich threw the bomb at the Archduke. Failing to kill him, he tried to commit suicide by swallowing poison and jumping into the river, but was arrested and revived by the police. Half an hour later Princip fired his revolver successfully. At the trial Chabrinovich admitted that he had worked in an anarchist printing establishment in Belgrade, while Princip, although describing himself as a radical nationalist, mentioned Kropotkin and Bakunin as the revolutionary writers who had influenced him.

In showing Kropotkin's intellectual influence on the Serajevo assassins, it must be emphasised that he was clearly in no way responsible for the act itself. On the other hand, the absorption of his theories brought the young men into the revolutionary milieux in which such acts were regarded with favour, and there is little doubt that he would not have condemned the attempt, even if he did not specifically approve of it.

The Serajevo incident precipitated the outbreak of war which Kropotkin had long dreaded. Before it began he knew what his attitude would be, and held it without wavering and with a manifest sincerity, even though he knew it would mean the end of his relationships with many old friends. H. W. Nevinson, who did not share his attitude, said that "when it (the war) came, he certainly welcomed it. He hoped and believed it would end despotism and the military State for ever. Perhaps he was the only man of distinction who sincerely believed in 'the war to end war'. His faith in humanity was inexhaustible."

To an American visitor just after the outbreak of war he expressed his support in strong terms, and, if he did not win the approval of many of his friends, he certainly gained that of some he would once have regarded as enemies, for on the 27th August the *New York Times* appeared with a flattering editorial calling him "the veteran Russian agitator and democrat". But even this paper found it difficult to swallow his optimistic opinion that whatever the outcome of the war, the alliance with England and France would result in "a strengthening of the liberalising forces in Russia". He was quite convinced that there would be important changes in Russia after the war, and this was one of his main reasons for supporting it. He was not wrong in his prophecy, but the changes came (as we shall see) not from the inspiration of the war, but in reaction against it.

By September he was already riding the high belligerent horse, as shown by a fiery letter to Grave in which he asked, "What world of illusions do you inhabit to talk of peace?" and demanded a war to the bitter end, since "the conditions of peace would be imposed by the victor". Gone was Kropotkin's past advocacy of a popular rising to expel the invader. Now all Kropotkin did, like any militarist, was to talk of bigger and better cannons, to exhort his friends to "defend themselves *like wild beasts*", and to repeat the current exaggerated atrocity stories of the Germans "fighting like devils and trampling on all the rules of humanity".

If official opinion in England and France was pleased with his attitude, within the revolutionary movement it caused consternation to his friends and delight to his enemies. A few leading anarchists shared his opinion, but the mass of the movement remained opposed to it. It was probably among the Russians that he caused most initial confusion. The anarchists within Russia, and the majority of the emigrés, decided to resist the war, following the same revolutionary defeatist line as the Bolsheviks. Only a few close personal followers supported Kropotkin, and some of these, like Yanovsky, changed their minds later.

But the Bolshevik leaders were pleased to make capital

against the anarchists as a whole by attacking this "lost leader". Already, in December, Lenin in his article on "The National Pride of the Great Russians", was writing of Kropotkin and Plekhanov as "chauvinists by opportunism or spinelessness". In 1915 he talked of the "lamentable fate" of the "bourgeois" Kropotkin; later in the same year he demoted him to a "petty-bourgeois" and afterwards to "anarcho-chauvin". Meanwhile, Stalin wrote in a personal letter to the Bolshevik leader, "I have recently read Kropotkin's articles—the old fool must have completely lost his mind". And Trotsky, in his later *History of the Russian Revolution*, expressed a view he held already in 1914:

> "The superannuated anarchist Kropotkin, who had had a weakness ever since youth for the *Narodniks*, made use of the war to disavow everything he had been teaching for almost half a century. This denouncer of the State supported the Entente, and if he denounced the double power in Russia, it was not in the name of anarchy, but in the name of a single power of the bourgeoisie."

In comments of this kind the Bolshevik leaders were completely within their rights, since Kropotkin did seem, to all but himself and a few close friends, to have gone back on his past record and theories. Where Lenin and his followers were unjustified was in their use of Kropotkin's error to discredit the whole anarchist movement; during 1917, in *The State and Revolution*, Lenin claimed that "few anarchists" had "still preserved a sense of honour and conscience", and suggested that the majority had been following Kropotkin and Grave in becoming "social-chauvinists". In fact, nothing of the kind happened; only about a hundred anarchists signed the various pronouncements in support of the war; the majority in all countries maintained the anti-militarist position as consistently as the Bolsheviks.

It was his break with the main anarchist movement that formed the most tragic event of Kropotkin's life. The dispute began with the Freedom Group. Already, before the war, it had become evident that a large section, consisting of almost all the active members, did not agree with his attitude. Nevertheless, no attempt was made to inhibit the free expression of his views, and he fully availed himself of this tolerance by publishing in the October 1914 issue of *Freedom* a letter to his Norwegian friend, Professor Steffen, justifying his attitude to the war, and also, in later issues, two articles attacking traditional anti-militarism.

His arguments were the familiar ones. Germany was responsible for the militarism in Europe which led up to the Great War. Germany had prevented the free development of the libertarian tendency in France by the presence of her armies. Germany had been the "chief support and protection of reaction" in Eastern Europe and particularly in Russia. He conjured up a justified nightmare of Europe dominated by Prussia, but then hastened to whitewash Tsarist Russia by suggesting that unity in war would make a return to autocracy impossible. All the old pacifist and anti-militarist dreams were pointless. A general strike could not end the war, and the German working class were as bad as their rulers. The main work of the day was to clear the invaders from Belgium and France. Then could begin the attack on the main evils of capital and the State.

All this was a vast shift from the contention that the radical evils, capital and the State, must be abolished, and then war and militarism could be brought to an end in the general social reconstruction which would follow the successful uprising of the people against invader and native ruler alike. Perhaps in some ways the traditional libertarian attitude was too simple. But so was Kropotkin's new nationalist view of social changes, and many historical facts, such as the refusal of the German sailors to continue fighting in 1918 and the palpable failure of the Great War to ensure either freedom or peace, have proved that in a war the march of events will upset the calculations and hopes of the best-intentioned man.

Immediately after the appearance of his articles a number of protests were sent to *Freedom*, and printed with editorial impartiality. Among them, perhaps the most significant was that from Malatesta, which states concisely the attitude of the majority of the anarchists who stood against Kropotkin on the issue of the war. After defining anti-militarism as "... the doctrine which affirms that military service is an abominable and murderous trade, and that a man ought never to consent to take arms at the command of the masters, and never to fight except for the Social Revolution ...", Malatesta goes on to argue:

"Kropotkin seems to have forgotten the antagonism of the classes, the necessity of economic emancipation, and all the anarchist teachings; and says that an anti-militarist ought always to be ready, in case a war breaks out, to take arms in support of 'the country that will be invaded'; which, considering the impossibility, for the ordinary workmen, of verifying in time who is the real aggressor, practically means that Kropotkin's 'anti-militarist' ought always to obey the orders of his government. What remains after that of anti-militarism, and, indeed, of anarchism too?

"As a matter of fact, Kropotkin renounces anti-militarism because he thinks that the national questions must be solved before the social question. For us, national rivalries and hatreds are among the best means the masters have for perpetuating the slavery of the workers, and we must oppose them with all our strength. And as to the right of the small nationalities to preserve, if they like, their language and their customs, that is simply a question of liberty, and will have a real and final solution only when, the States being destroyed, every human being, nay, every individual, will have the right to associate with, and separate from, every other group.

"It is very painful for me to oppose an old and beloved friend like Kropotkin, who has done so much for the cause of anarchism. But for the very reason that Kropotkin is so much esteemed and loved by us all, it is necessary to make known that we do not follow him in his utterances on the war. . . ."

He went on to admit that he and the other anarchists had been mistaken in not recognising the importance of Kropotkin's "Franco-Russian patriotism and in not foreseeing where his anti-German prejudices would lead him", but said that he would " . . . never have dreamt that Kropotkin could invite the workers to make common cause with the governments and masters".*

But Kropotkin was not moved by this appeal of an old friend, and the other letters exposing his inconsistency merely drove him to fury. In order to try to settle the dispute, Keell, then editor of *Freedom*, went down to Brighton to talk with him. He was received angrily in a room where flags of the allies stood on the mantelpiece, and was subjected to a fierce barrage

* It should be noted that, although Kropotkin and Malatesta were close personal friends up to 1915, they did not always agree on tactics or general ideas. Malatesta was a practical revolutionist, with a tendency towards conspiratorial action. The most realist of the great anarchists, he did not always share Kropotkin's optimism, and, while he accepted anarchist communism, regarded it in the light of a hypothesis to be revised and reconsidered according to changing circumstances.

from Kropotkin, who complained of "offensive personal letters" in *Freedom* and accused Keell of not having the courage to reject such contributions, and therefore being no good as an editor. Since there was nobody to take his place, Kropotkin suggested that *Freedom* should cease publication. He emphasised that every honest man must support the Allies, and would not agree that the German workers had been deceived, but maintained that they acted consciously as Pinkertons for their rulers. He refused to discuss the question of Russia, contenting himself with accusing all his opponents of knowing nothing. His whole attitude throughout the visit seems to have been that of an initiated omniscient, and he was supported in all he said by Sophie, who claimed that anyone who did not share their opinion was a coward. We have taken this information from a private notebook which Keell kept at the time, so that there is little likelihood of exaggeration on his part, particularly as other evidence bears out his opinion of Kropotkin's attitude at this time.

The dispute over *Freedom* continued, and Cherkesov called a meeting, to which he invited only the members who shared his and Kropotkin's views on the war. Keell attended as editor, but no other active London anarchist was called. Kropotkin was ill and did not attend, but Sophie represented him. All the supporters of the war childishly refused to speak to Keell when he arrived, and a very violent discussion ensued. All except Keell wanted *Freedom* to be suspended; he said he would continue it as an anti-war paper until he was censured by a general meeting of active anarchists. Cherkesov then forgot himself so far as to shout: "Who are you? You are our servant!"

The meeting broke up in disagreement, and the final result was that the active London anarchists continued *Freedom* as an organ of the considerable anti-war majority. Kropotkin's connection with the paper which he had done so much to found and develop was ended, and it marked the termination of his connection with the militant anarchist movement in Western Europe.

But he was not alone in this attitude. Not only Cherkesov, but also Jean Grave, Charles Malato and Paul Reclus (the son of Elisée), all leading French anarchists, and Christian Cornelissen, the important Dutch anarchist, supported his attitude, and it was natural that these men should come closer together when confronted by the hostility of the anarchist movement as a whole.

During much of 1915 and 1916 Kropotkin was prostrated by illness. In January 1915 he wrote to Mrs Dryhurst: "I am ordered *not* to travel to London all the winter!", and in March he underwent two operations on his chest. The rest of this year he was almost completely confined to his bed, and even in 1916 was still an invalid wheeled about Brighton in a bath-chair. But he kept up an extensive correspondence with those friends who shared his point of view, and in 1916 Jean Grave and his wife crossed the Channel to spend a few weeks with him in Brighton.

Naturally enough, they discussed the war. Kropotkin declared that if he had been young enough he would have taken part in the struggle as a combatant, and when Grave suggested that they should issue a declaration supporting the war, he at first refused to participate because he was unable to take an active part in fighting. At last, however, he was persuaded, and the two friends collaborated in their manifesto. The exact authorship is difficult to determine, since Grave claimed that he wrote the document and Kropotkin revised it, while the anarchist historian Maximov asserted that Kropotkin wrote it and Grave merely suggested one or two alterations. However, the resultant declaration was clearly much inspired by Kropotkin, and, since it more or less repeated all his old arguments about Germany, there is little need to examine it at length, except to point out that it clearly under-estimated the strength of the war weariness that would arise in all countries engaged in the war.

This manifesto was signed by fifteen well-known anarchists, including Kropotkin, Guérin, Cherkesov, Grave, Malato, Cornelissen and Paul Reclus. It attained celebrity as the Manifesto of the Sixteen, because Husseinday, the home of an Algerian signatory, was taken as an extra name. For some unknown reason, Guillaume, who also supported the war, did not add his signature. It was printed in a pro-war sheet called *La Bataille Syndicaliste*, which the Marxists, rightly or wrongly, accused of being subsidised by the French government.

The Manifesto of the Sixteen merely confirmed the split

which existed in the anarchist movement. Already, in February, a strong group of English, Swiss, Italian, American, Russian, French and Dutch anarchists had issued a statement opposing the war. They included two out of the three secretaries of the corresponding bureau elected at the meeting of the Anarchist International in 1907, Malatesta and Shapiro, as well as Domela Niewenhuis, Emma Goldman, Berkman, Bertoni, Yanovsky, Harry Kelly, Tom Keell, Lilian Wolfe and George Barrett, and represented the most active and militant elements in Europe and America. The remaining member of the international bureau, Rocker, was interned, but also opposed the war. This manifesto claimed that war is the natural consequence of an exploiting system, and therefore the blame cannot be placed on any particular government, nor can any real distinction be drawn between offensive and defensive war. In the modern age, wars are the results of the existence of States. "The State has arisen out of military force, and it is still on military force that it must logically rest in order to maintain its omnipotence." The anarchists must recognise only one war of liberation, that waged by "the oppressed against the oppressors, by the exploited against the exploiters". They must seek to spread "the spirit of revolt", to organise revolution against all States and show men "the generosity, greatness, and beauty of the anarchist ideal: social justice realised through the free organisation of producers; war and militarism done away with for ever, and complete freedom won by the abolition of the State and its organs of destruction".

It was not to be expected that the signatories of such a document should agree with Kropotkin and his friends. Malatesta made a protest on their behalf against the Manifesto of the Sixteen, and others joined their voices, including Luigi Fabbri, the Italian writer, Sebastian Faure, editor of the *Anarchist Encyclopædia*, the editorial boards of *Freedom* in England, *Mother Earth* in America, *Le Libertaire* in France, and the majority of other anarchist papers, as well as the Continental individualists led by E. Armand, editor of *L'Unique*. Indeed, it was clear that a solid majority of the really important anarchists were opposed to Kropotkin, and that he and the bare hundred friends who could be persuaded eventually to support the Manifesto of the Sixteen were really a minority slight in numbers if not in names. For a while this group thought of starting a new organisation; Cornelissen issued a manifesto advocating a new international, and plans were set on foot for founding an anarchist-communist paper to support Kropotkin's view. But these ventures met so little support that they were abandoned.

Kropotkin, indeed, put a bold face on the matter in a letter to Grave at the beginning of April, which refers not only to the war, but also to his health and the varied interests he and Sophie contrived to maintain even at this time of isolation and anxiety.

"Guérin writes me a post-card, and tells me that our declaration has 'made the comrades jump' and that the Marxists slander us grossly. We must wait. It does not play their game—the game of the Marxists. But it is sad that our comrades also are angry. . . .

"But if our comrades—some among them would be enough—only gave themselves the trouble to re-read the events of 1875, when Bismarck was ready to march on France to take away Champagne (that morsel coveted by all the conquerors of Gaul), not for its wine, but for its agricultural wealth in general and 15 milliards of indemnities, and to install himself in the heart of France, still nearer to Paris. 'To have all the French colonies, it would be enough to take Paris', Bismarck said openly. 'It is in Paris that Algeria will be conquered.' Always Paris! . . .

"But enough! I have just been called to go out for a walk. My health is not too bad. The wound had opened just a little. But, in general, it seems likely to heal for good. A year since the first operation has now passed; it was the 25th March.

"Sophie is well. Her talk on 'The Effects of Prohibition on the Sale of Alcohol in Russia' will take place on the 10th.

"You know, my instinct did not deceive me on Dostoevsky. In *The Brothers Karamazov* the type of the prostitute who falls terribly low comes, they say, from the *Miseries of Foundlings* by Eugene Sue (have you that book?). As for his famous speech of the Grand Inquisitor, it is wholly inspired by the volumes of *Memories of the People*, where Sue speaks of Christ, and later of the *auto-da-fe*, and still later of Loyola. . . ."

Kropotkin's actions had isolated him from the main anarchist movement, and he never regained contact with it. In the eyes of many of his former disciples and many of his socialist friends he lost standing. Clearly, he was always very sure of the rightness of his own attitude, and many of his close personal friends were with him on the question of war. But he must have felt strongly the loss of contact with old friends like Malatesta and Dumartheray, and with the mass of the young and lively comrades who had admired him in the past but who were now grieved or angered by his defection from the libertarian tradition.

With very few of the anti-war anarchists did he retain any friendly relationship. Rocker and Shapiro were exceptions, but both were interned. For the last two years his life became lonely in comparison with the crowded years up to 1914. Few of his friends living in England maintained any further contact with him, and the calls of people motivated by petty curiosity can hardly have been a compensation for the comradely visits of past years. Some trade unionists like Tillett and Bowman, a few scientific and literary friends like Keltie and Cobden-Sanderson, occasionally travelled down to Brighton, a little group of working men from the Brighton Trades and Labour Club visited him once a week to talk over their problems, and the neighbours were kind and friendly. It looked like a dull end to an active life, and in March 1917, when the news came through from Russia that the people had revolted and the autocracy was at an end, we can safely guess that a part of Kropotkin's joy was due to the personal hope that his last days might after all be saved from isolation and futility.

CHAPTER IX

THE NEGLECTED SAGE

I

WHEN Kropotkin heard the news of the February Rising, it seemed as though the moment had come for which he and his friends in the Russian cause had struggled all their lives, and he looked forward with joy to the idea of returning and taking part, old as he was, in the work of reconstruction. Almost immediately he wrote to May Morris:

> "Is it not grand? All the old region authorities *in the villages* and provincial towns swept away, free democratic self-government instead, the soldier becoming a citizen—almost nobody to take the defence of the rotten regime, capital punishment abolished, the prisons opened, *the Finnish constitution restored*, the Red Flag floating on the Peter-and-Paul fortress . . . all, all that realised with comparatively very little bloodshed."

He mentioned the great number of letters and telegrams he had received, recalled the "beautiful days of 1886–90", and ended :

> "Need I tell you how we are happy for Russia, and also for our friends who must be now on their way from the hard labour jails of Siberia to Russia. And freed, not by a Tsar's 'clemency', but by the will of the people."

In the same letter he talked optimistically of the "events that *will come* in Germany and Austria", meaning that he hoped these countries would soon follow the lead of Russia. But even at this moment he did not cease to be preoccupied with the war against Germany, and in a telegram to the Russian newspaper *Rech* a few days later he urgently demanded active continuance of the war. Military events made it impossible for him to go there yet, but he exhorted:

"Men, women and children of Russia, save our country from the Black Hundreds of the Central Empires.

"Do not waste a single hour. Oppose to them a strong, united front. Now, when you have dealt so valiantly with the internal enemy, every effort which you make for the expulsion of invaders serves for the strengthening and further growth of our liberty and a lasting peace."

When a great meeting of Russian organisations was held in the Kingsway Hall on the 2nd April he was ill and unable to attend, but he sent a message on which he went even farther in his militaristic ideas by attributing the success of the revolution to the inspiration of the war.

"Many English friends are astounded by the unanimity with which the revolution was accomplished. The reason for this was that for the past two and half years the army felt that it had its best, true friends in the nation at large, which supported the army in thousands of ways in the rear, while the government proved at every step its incapacity and, still worse, its treacherous pro-Germanism. In such conditions the people and the army stood together."

By referring to the Empress as "the German woman", and to the Romanovs in general as "secular supporters of German imperialism", he further sought to give the impression that the great force behind the unity of the revolution was the desire to prosecute the war more effectively. He ended:

"The main point for Russia—just as it is for England, France, and Belgium—is to drive the German invaders from the territories they have occupied. . . . We mean to retain our conquests, and surely the people of Russia will consolidate them by further developing the constructive creative work it has been doing in the past years—thus preparing the way for the socialisation of the country's natural riches, its production and its exchange."

It is clear that Kropotkin was very ill-informed about the actual situation in Russia and particularly about developments beneath the surface. The unity of the February revolution was deceptive, as soon became evident. And to say that the mass of Russians revolted because the war was not being carried on efficiently was wholly fallacious. In fact, the soldiers "voted with their feet", as Lenin put it, against all the privations and sufferings they had undergone in the last years; they did not want to fight any longer. The workers and peasants realised that this was a moment for putting forward their economic demands and overthrowing the autocracy. But only a tiny minority of business men, officers, and liberal politicians were anxious for a more efficient prosecution of the war. The people as a whole were tired of fighting, they wanted "peace and bread", as was shown by their actions in the months to come.

Among those who supported the revolution in 1917 there were two opinions regarding the war. The Liberal Cadets, many Mensheviks and right-wing Social Revolutionaries, and a tiny group of anarchists who followed Kropotkin faithfully, were in favour of continuing. The Bolsheviks, as well as some of the Social Revolutionaries and Mensheviks, and most of the anarchists, wished to see the immediate ending of hostilities, so that the work of the revolution might be carried on without this distraction. Whatever their motives, which varied a great deal according to party, the advocates of peace were more realistic and closer to popular desires.

It was, indeed, owing to this initial miscalculation of the situation within Russia and to an obstinate clinging to his error until the Brestlitovsk peace had removed the cause of controversy, that Kropotkin failed to realise, until it was too late to intervene, how the real revolutionary currents were being diverted by the Bolsheviks to their own ends. The reason for his continued and even intensified advocacy of the war, even after returning to Russia, can be found partly in his anti-German feeling, which had grown during the conflict, and partly, no doubt, in an idea that events had turned the war against Germany into a revolutionary fight and thus justified his apparent apostacy.

In accordance with his views, Kropotkin gave support while he remained in England to the pro-war Russian elements, writing in April an appeal for their "Liberty Loan", and in May accepting the chairmanship of the Correct Information Committee, which aimed at providing the Press with facts supporting the new regime in Petrograd.

Yet he did not wholly lose sight of his anarchist aims, and in May 1917, when his plans for departure were well advanced, he wrote to two old working comrades of the hopes they had in common. To Dumartheray, on the 21st May, he said:

"I cannot tell you how happy I was to see your lines and read your message! Yes, dear old friend, something great has happened in Russia and something which will be the beginning of still greater events almost everywhere.

"This revolution was unquestionably impending for eighteen months. But what struck me very much is the profound good sense of the masses of workers and peasants in comprehending the import of the movement and its promise. It is because they have been prepared since 1861 when—under the influence of the Russian refugees in London and the remains of the Fourier circle in Russia (that of Chernyshevsky)—propaganda was begun from the midst of the people. From that time on, circles of propaganda in the fields and factories have succeeded each other from year to year. . . .

"You understand that we are leaving for Russia. *You, George, and the Jurassians will know that I am not going there to occupy any governmental position whatever.* But a life well spent, experience and also some study sometimes allow one to understand events better, and Sophie, Cherkesov, and myself think that I may be useful."

There follows a paragraph in which Kropotkin once again puts forward his theory of the patriotic origin of the revolution, and claims that the voluntary war-time organisations represented a step towards free communism and thus facilitated the uprising. He ends with this somewhat bizarre version of events in March 1917:

"What they reproached us with as a fantastic Utopia has been accomplished without a single casualty. The free organisations which sprang up during the war to care for the wounded, for supplies, for the distribution of provisions, the unloading of trains, and so many other ends, have replaced on 2nd March the whole ancient litter of functionaries, police, etc. They have opened the prison-gates, declared the ancient government non-existent, and what is best, have one after another disarmed and expelled all the police, high and low."

It is surely unnecessary to refute at length this version of revolution by the Russian equivalent of the Boy Scouts and Red Cross; an earlier Kropotkin would have recognised the spontaneous rising of the masses in 1917 as something fundamentally similar to that of 1905, bred of impatience with war and a natural tendency to co-operation in moments of rebellion. It was also the kind of revolution of which he had dreamed in

Paroles d'un Revolté and in *The Conquest of Bread*, with the old order giving way to the new in an almost bloodless manner.

But in the final paragraphs, bidding farewell to his early comrades, the old Kropotkin emerges again, full of hope and enthusiasm at the prospect of returning to work in his own land:

"It is necessary to put our shoulders to the wheel. We are going there with the fervour of youth. We are both fit. Sophie, despite her sixty years, bears incredibly well the fatigue of the last three weeks of sorting all kinds of papers accumulated during thirty years of life in England, since Clairvaux. You can well imagine what a task it was! At last we are near the end.

"You will know that after the operation (the two, in fact) I have dragged out a whole year without being able to go outside except in a little wheelchair. But now it is better, except that my lungs are badly affected and threaten pneumonia. That is why two doctors have absolutely forbidden me to undertake the semi-arctic voyage that is necessary in order to enter Russia before the cold sets in. Now the departure will depend on the boats. It will probably be towards the end of the second week in June."

And to Yanovsky, who had left England, he wrote a few days later that he would like to visit Paris, to bid farewell to all his friends and comrades, but that this was impossible.

"After all the struggles which we have experienced together, I would be so happy to talk about the future, the new horizons which are opening before us, about the progress which our anti-State, egalitarian and communist ideas have made since the beginning of the war.

"But the events in Russia, the revolution which has already accomplished so much, and which is continuing to develop there, needs everybody's strength, and we are going to place ourselves at the service of the popular revolution."

After leaving their home at Brighton, Kropotkin and Sophie went to London for the remainder of their sojourn in England. Peter began to say good-bye to his old friends, visiting Rocker at the internment camp, writing May Morris a letter "full of high hopes and happiness at the thought of Russia's new life", and breaking his long connection with *Nature* in a note recalling how he read its first numbers in his Russian prison more than forty years before. He received an illuminated address from his friends of the Brighton Trades and Labour Club, and presented them with a chair and a writing-table that had belonged to Richard Cobden. His last evening in London was spent with the Cobden-Sandersons at Hammersmith; he was in a state of "feverish excitement".

He wished Grave to see him in London during the few days before departure, but he had to join his ship at Aberdeen earlier than he had first anticipated, and it was finally by letter that he bade farewell to this old friend who had shared his opinions for so long.

"I cannot tell you how it annoys and saddens me to go away without saying goodbye to you, you and dear Mabel. Sophie is very sorrowful. After so many years of work together—almost forty years —not to say goodbye, not to talk of a thousand things! It is more than sad!

"... The order has come to go, and I write this from Scotland, and this letter will only be sent to you, my friends, when we are in Norway, if the submarines do not change our plans and send us to the bottom of the sea. Such is war!

"Poor Sophie is completely tired out. As for myself, although I am exhausted, I am very well. . . ."

He finally embarked at Aberdeen on a ship bound for Bergen, travelling under the name of his Russian friend, Professor Turin, in order to avoid any demonstration. Before the ship sailed he handed Turin a farewell letter to the British nation, published a few days later in *The Times*. He thanked all his friends for their kindness to him personally, and the radical section of the British public for its continual interest in Russian affairs and its insistence on preserving the right of asylum for exiles. He mentioned the many letters of congratulation he had received and regretted he had been unable to reply to more than a few. The rest of the letter was devoted to a repetition of his views concerning the war, praise of the Western Powers "striving to achieve progress through a steady growth of inner forces, economic and intellectual", and a hope that the Russians would continue to fight.

Another letter, to the working men of the West, had been handed to John Turner, the trade-union leader. It opened with a message recalling the old days of struggle.

"After having worked in your midst for forty years, I cannot leave Western Europe without sending you a few words of farewell.

From the depth of my heart I thank you for the reception—more than fraternal—that I found in your midst. The International Workingmen's Association was not for me a mere abstract word. Amidst the working men of Switzerland, France, Britain, Spain, Italy, the United States, I was in a society of brothers and friends. And in your struggles, each time I had the opportunity to take part in them, I lived the best moments of my life. I deeply felt that wave of human solidarity and oneness of man, disregarding all frontiers, which represents one of the greatest promises for man in the future."

Again he talked of the war, and threw the whole blame on Germany, against whom he called for a great military effort. But he also stressed the need for constructive action:

"The production of all that is necessary for the nation, as well as the distribution of the produced wealth, must be organised in the direct interest of all. It is no more a matter of struggling for adding to the wages a few shillings, which usually are soon swallowed by all sorts of exploiting intermediaries. The workers, the producers, must become the managers of the producing concerns. They must settle the aims and the means of production, and society must recognise their right of disposing of the capital that is needed for that."

This message seems to have evoked little attention among his former comrades, and most of them probably shared the attitude of his old paper, *Freedom*, which commented:

"In bidding farewell to Kropotkin on his return to Russia, we can but hope that by contact with the Russian workers he may realise the errors of his attitude on the war, and with them work in the building of that anarchist society of which he was such an enthusiastic exponent prior to the war. His numerous anarchist books and pamphlets will be read and remembered long after his patriotic backsliding in this war has been forgotten."

The voyage was uneventful, though on the ship entering Norwegian waters it was followed by a German submarine, which hastened away on the approach of warships. Kropotkin perceived with annoyance among his fellow passengers a number of "Germanophiles" from London, Russian exiles who supported an early peace. There were also delegates from two Russian divisions fighting on the French front. "One division", he says, "had sent good delegates, valiant, bold, loyal, the other what are called *Bolsheviks*."

Although he had left England *incognito*, his identity seems to have become known as soon as he landed in Norway, and at Bergen he was greeted by "an imposing demonstration of workers", while at Christiania dozens of students approached his carriage with "marvellous flowers". From Bergen he sent a post-card to Cobden-Sanderson, saying, "Au revoir, dear good friends! Our next meeting will take place, let us hope, in Russia!" It was the last time they ever heard from him.

In Sweden his triumphal progress continued. He arrived at Stockholm in the early morning, and was met by Branting, the social-democrat leader, who talked with him for an hour. The subject of their conversation was the impending congress of social-democrats at Stockholm to discuss the early end of the war. Kropotkin suspected it as a German trick, and was all for fighting out to the bitter end, but he recognised Branting's sincerity. He went on to the reception organised by a local committee of friends of the Russian revolution. There were many Russians, and he renewed old friendships, made new acquaintances, and submitted to the attentions of newspaper interviewers. He was pleased to find in Sweden that *Mutual Aid* and the *Memoirs of a Revolutionist* had been very widely read.

Finally, at Torneo he crossed, for the first time after forty-one years, the old frontiers of Imperial Russia into the province of Finland. The Russian officers and soldiers were extremely friendly towards him, and he had to speak to them from the top of a car, a practice he was forced to repeat at every stopping-place along the route. He did not wish to make a speech, but chatted with the men. He was followed by an ex-prisoner of war, and then a Leninist who was answered, he noted with satisfaction, by an officer who spoke unprovocatively, but with vigour and plenty of spirit.

At Uleaborg there came deputations of Finnish workers carrying tulips, and a hundred soldiers playing the "Marseillaise" and shouting, "Long live free Russia! Long live free Finland!" He was deeply moved. Everybody here told him that the Leninists had enjoyed great success, but that their time had passed. Nevertheless, some at least of the officers do not seem to have felt so confident, for Kropotkin was continually asked to address the soldiers in order to offset "strong Bolshevik propaganda". At Rikhimiaki, where the old anarchist was welcomed with presented arms and the regimental flag, he induced the soldiers to take a mutual oath to die rather than allow the Germans into Petrograd. At Vyborg alone his appeals were unsuccessful; there the soldiers remained silent during his speech, and turned their attention towards a Bolshevik speaker.

But this indifference was compensated by the reception at Petrograd, when they arrived at two o'clock in the morning. As the train pulled slowly into the station, to the strains of the "Marseillaise" played by military bands, and the cheers of the Semenovski regiment of Guards, sixty thousand people waited to welcome Kropotkin, and he was deeply moved by the sight of "that crowd of intelligent, bold, proud faces, celebrating the triumph of light over the shadows, of truth over falsehood, of freedom over slavery". The cheering people surged forward to the train, and Kropotkin and Sophie, in their modest effort to avoid being carried in triumph, were almost crushed. They were saved by a group of Guardsmen who formed a chain and led them to the hall in which were waiting the ministers Kerensky and Skobelev, as well as Sasha, who with her husband had gone to Russia during the war, and many old friends, including Chaikovsky. They were also greeted by representatives from the socialist parties, from various popular organisations, and from the anarchists who shared Kropotkin's views. Those of his comrades who opposed the war did not come, and thus the breach which had begun in Western Europe was perpetuated.

There followed an exhausting period of activity. Many visitors came, and on some days followed each other without interruption. Most of them were "useful people", and it was often very late at night before the last departed, so that Kropotkin hardly had the strength to write, or the time to prepare for the meetings he addressed. These, indeed, taxed his strength greatly, for he was always carried away by enthusiasm and emotion. On the first occasion, in the Grand Theatre, he began "like a young man", with a very sonorous voice, advocating an offensive against the German armies. But he had caught a cold on arrival; his voice soon became hoarse, and he felt that something had gone wrong in his lungs. He was put to bed and cupped in time to halt any serious effects, and in a day or two was on his feet again, still as hoarse as if he had "drunk too much", but attending meetings, sometimes twice a day.

His position as an anarchist who supported the war led him at times into equivocal company and situations. Even before his arrival he was not among the most popular of the revolutionaries, for at the election of the Executive Committee of the Congress of Peasants' delegates early in June he did not gain sufficient votes to be returned, although Brechkovskaya and Vera Figner were elected. No doubt he was not anxious for election, but the incident was an indication of his relative obscurity in the public eye.

Indeed, in some respects he stood in great isolation. Most of the Russian anarchists held aloof from him, and he was out of favour with all the social-democrats, with the left Social Revolutionaries, and with the growing movement among the masses, who longed for peace and bread and were already beginning to take the situation into their own hands. And his relationship with those who supported the war, most of whom were also in favour of constitutional government, was equally uneasy.

During the war, under the stress of what he regarded as the prime necessity of defeating German militarism, he had established relationships with the Cadets, a constitutional liberal party who had no revolutionary aims and represented the more enlightened middle class. In May 1916 Paul Miliukov, the Cadet leader who became Foreign Minister for a short time after the February revolution, visited him at Brighton, and while still in England he began to write articles expressing his belligerent views in the Cadet newspaper, *Russkiye Vyedomosti*, which were continued after his return, and eventually collected in a booklet published, ironically, after the October Revolution.

On his arrival he established cordial relationships with Kerensky, then Prime Minister and Prince Lvov, his predecessor, to both of whom he took "a great liking". Kerensky was very anxious to use his name, and offered him any place in the government he might choose. Kropotkin refused, and remarked to Emma Goldman afterwards: "I told him that I fought all my life against government, as a corrupting factor, and never did I intend to take part in it." His exact words are said to have been: "I consider the trade of shoeblack more honourable and useful." But, although he refused so indignantly a ministerial post, a pension of 10,000 roubles, and a lodging in the Winter Palace, he did not hesitate to give his advice to Kerensky and the other members of the government, and said more soberly in a letter to Turin:

"You certainly know already through the newspapers of the proposition which has been made to me; I naturally refused it immediately, but to the full extent of my strength, I will help the people to agree on a programme and to direct their strength towards the reconstruction of the internal life of the country, which is moving towards a great downfall."

Finding the strain of Petrograd life more than he could endure, he moved out for the summer to the village of Kamenny Ostrov, in the middle of a pleasant forest near Petrograd. He was accompanied by Sophie, Sasha, and Boris Lebedev, and they stayed in a villa which his niece, the widow of the archæologist Poloviev, had taken from the Dutch consul.

It was a time of much bewilderment and sorrow. There is no doubt that Kropotkin felt strongly his detachment from the popular masses and his own comrades, while he did not always find it easy to understand the course of events set going by this revolution for which he had worked so long. To one friend he wrote of "the mass of impressions which are piled on top of each other, sometimes marvellously beautiful, sometimes profoundly sad, to such an extent that I have never encountered or lived through anything like it, either in life or in books". The July attempt of the Bolsheviks to seize power, with its revelations of a deep cleavage of the revolutionary forces, was very disturbing, and he said that during the weeks following this event he "could only pass from pity to horror, and from horror to pity". During this period, Lvov, before departing to Moscow, came to see Kropotkin in his country retreat, where they "wept together"; he regretted Lvov's departure from the government, since the Prince and his fellows of the Zemstvos had worked honestly and well to organise decentralised autonomy on democratic principles.

The military situation was bad; he declared that if his health had been better he would have gone to the front long ago. But he also thought of leaving Petrograd in another direction, for "some people advise me to go to Moscow, saying that from there will come the spiritual *élan*, not by heroic means like that of women's death battalions and shock brigades, but by the contagion of the general force; yet I hesitate, I feel that it is here that I can be useful in the critical moment, and this is the most dangerous post, for Riga is not far away".

In August he finally decided to depart for Moscow, where he at first seems to have been more happy than in Petrograd. He met many friends, and discovered a good apartment with some kind people, while Sophie found catering more easy. They decided to spend the winter in the old capital. He continued to speak in favour of the war, appearing with his old friends, Breshkovskaya and Vera Zasulich, at a meeting for this purpose in the Michael Theatre. Later in August he took advantage of the departure of a visitor who was returning to England to send a message to his friends which, for its undertone of nostalgia, is worth recording:

"You return now to England and my thoughts fly with you to the many, many friends I would have been so happy to meet again, to express to them all my brotherly love and to tell them of the bonds which unite me with them across the distance which separates us. And now I regret that my health has been so poor for the last ten years that I have not seen enough of my friends, and especially of those personally unknown people among the working classes and social reformers from whom I might have learned so much that would have been so useful now. Give all of them my brotherly love."

It was in the spirit of evoking an even older past that he paid a visit to his childhood home in Moscow. He described the house as "charming". A servant showed him over it in the absence of the owners in the country, and he went into the room where his mother had died.

Then, at the end of August, came the so-called State Conference of all parties in Moscow, when Kerensky made an attempt to gain general support. The split between those who supported the war for various motives and those who opposed it was clear. Kropotkin was not at first among the speakers, but it was later proposed that he, Brechkovskaya, and Plekhanov be invited as veteran revolutionaries, and Kerensky gladly agreed. On the issue of the war, Kropotkin declared himself opposed to the Bolsheviks:

"I join with those who have called upon the Russian people to cast loose from Zimmerwaldism once for all, and as one man, to stand up in defence of their country and the Revolution. In my opinion Russia and the Revolution are inseparable. If the Germans defeat us, the consequences of their victory will be so terrible, that even to mention it fills the mind with horror."

But he went beyond mere patriotism, and, while "fully acknowledging" the right of the coming Constituent Assembly to "the sovereign decision" on the future status of Russia, spoke in favour of a federal republic. Since such an argument represented a further clear departure from his own denunciation of any form of revolutionary government, it is only fair to allow him to make his own justification, in a letter to Turin shortly after the conference:

"I had proposed it [the Republic] in an extremely moderate form (up to then nobody had pronounced the word 'Republic') and notably in such a way as to avoid infringing in advance on the rights of the supreme Constituent Assembly, but simply in order to facilitate its task: I asked the Conference to express its suffrage in favour of the Republic. The whole hall rose and improvised a tumultuous ovation. It lasted a long time—one or one and a half minutes. I looked round in embarrassment; the whole floor was on its feet, all the Left in the boxes, and, to my stupefaction, all the Right as well; what struck me particularly was the balcony of industrialists and financiers who had not ceased to maintain a significant silence during the democratic ovations of the Left.

"Kerensky was right to say in his declaration that the Republic was accepted unanimously by the Conference. Unfortunately, by virtue of the principle laid down in advance, it had not the right to take any decision. That was why I expressed myself in such a moderate fashion."

But this moderation was fatal, for the sight of the old anarchist advocating war and a republican government similar to that of the United States, deferring to the Constituent Assembly and quoting Lloyd George's activities as a sign of the spread of socialism, can only have been encouraging to the advocates of authority whom he had fought so long, and discouraging to those friends who had drawn from him their inspiration for years of struggle against war and the State. It was a classic example of the danger of compromise, and was used by the Bolsheviks to rob Kropotkin of much of the devotion that still existed towards him, and also to discredit further the whole anarchist movement, which did not support him on such issues.

The excitement of the Moscow Conference brought a new setback in his health, and his illness prevented him from accompanying Lvov to Petrograd where, at "the tragic moment" of Kornilov's attempt to seize the capital and set up a new Tsarist government, the Prince had gone to assist Kerensky.

A few days later he wrote pessimistically of the condition of Russia, whose great misfortune he found in the "complete disorganisation of the army", due to many causes, including "tiredness, inaction, demoralisation, the traditional admiration for Germany and ignorance of the Latin world". There was also a danger of famine, but he thought Russia would emerge after a peaceful transition from the present collapse. His own proposals for practical action were vague, and it is significant that he ignored the Soviets, to whose policy on the war he was opposed, as a factor in reconstruction, and said nothing of the great movement for the seizure of the land which even before October was going on apace in various regions, and which he himself had advocated in 1905. Instead, he proposed, as soon as he had recovered, to assist in "organisation and the Conquest of Bread" the new Social Revolutionary Municipality of Moscow.

But he saw that here the difficulties were "not slight". He also talked of the Zemstvos, or county councils, but recognised pessimistically that the majority of them were of little use, showing neither knowledge, nor experience, nor the habit of work. He spoke sadly of the influence of the Bolsheviks, particularly among the Vyborg garrison, where he now said that "the Germans have particularly directed their forces". By this he seems to have meant *propaganda* forces, for there were no military operations in this area. Like many other people at the time he honestly believed that some of the Bolsheviks were in German pay, and this belief was not without reason.

From early September until the end of 1917 there is little word of Kropotkin; we have no record of his activities during the October Revolution, and the only contemporary opinion of that event which has survived is his remark to Atabekian during the struggle: "This buries the Revolution." He certainly deplored the triumph of the Bolsheviks and their anti-war associates, and failed to perceive the real popular forces behind the October movement.

For the actual rising merely consecrated a tendency which had been developing for some months among the people. The peasants had been taking land into their own hands, the workers had been assuming control of factories and transport, the soldiers had been implementing their hatred for the war by a widespread desertion which increased to vast proportions during the harvest months. Parallel with Kerensky's attempt at constitutional government had risen the network of Soviets of Workers', Soldiers' and Peasants' Deputies, which represented a much nearer expression of the revolutionary forces. Kerensky's policy had in fact become unworkable. The soldiers would no longer fight, and the people would no longer listen to the nominal government. A genuine revolutionary situation had arisen, and the universal recognition of the Provisional Government's bankruptcy was shown by the relatively bloodless character of the actual insurrection.

Thus far, the events of October had taken place on the traditional anarchist pattern; the people had overthrown their rulers by mass action, the peasants had seized the land and the workers the factories. The decrees by which the Bolsheviks made these facts legal during the brief halcyon days of the revolution merely recognised an accomplished situation. The majority of anarchists, while opposing the government, had seen the necessary and revolutionary nature of these demands and given them their support. And the sequel to October, the seizure of power by the Bolsheviks while at the same time opposing the government, was also a vindication of the anarchist theory of revolutions—this time the part which teaches that even in a revolution governments are the enemies of freedom.

Yet, although Kropotkin may have been disturbed by the October Revolution and have disagreed with the armistice which Lenin asked from the Germans, the current of events, by removing from actuality that war issue which had caused so much disagreement with his fellow anarchists, drew Kropotkin's attention back to the more concrete realities of social organisation and individual freedom; and by the end of 1917 we reach a termination of his sad period in the wilderness and a return to a renewed faith in fundamental principles, a faith which Kropotkin resumed too late for his change to be effective. The period from 1918 to his death is no less tragic than that of the war years, but the tragedy is of a man who adheres to his ideals and is no longer swayed by adventitious forces of circumstance.

II

The October Revolution seems to have made little immediate change in his personal circumstances; he and Sophie had two well-warmed rooms, and the people with whom they lived had relieved Sophie of the need for standing in queues to obtain their food. His books were at last beginning to appear, printed legally, and in the first letter after October (3rd January, 1918), he talked of "tiring his eyes" over the proofs of the *Memoirs of a Revolutionist*. He was helped in his work by Marie Goldsmith, whom he described as "a charming collaboratrice". His general tone was sad and dispirited. Expressing thanks for some books, he continued:

> "But alas! what good is all that? I ask myself. Everything is in such a mess that it is impossible to get any work done. It is hardly permitted to write in *Russkiye Vyedomosti*, and I feel like giving it up completely. When we were installed here I had the intention of occupying myself with a great work, with some of our friends, on demobilisation and social reconstruction, which are inevitably linked. But what is the good? Life goes on at much too smart a pace. . . ."

The work to which he referred was that of a group of Moscow intellectuals who had set themselves the task of investigating the means of carrying out further revolutionary changes without bloodshed, but in the swift passage of events after the October Revolution their work never really got under way. In the same letter Kropotkin mentioned the Society of Relationships with England, of which he was president, and which was publishing a bulletin to counter the Germanophile influence in Petrograd. But this again was a well-meant venture which was lost in the changing pattern of Russian affairs.

A fortnight later, on the 16th January, Kropotkin began to write of the tightening of the Bolshevik regime. He had put some faith in certain elements among the Zemstvos as a possible help in pulling Russia out of her difficult position. His friend Prince Lvov had left Moscow for the south, but the "conversations which I had enjoyed with certain of their members . . . had made me believe that there was among them that living strength which would effectively help the people to emerge from a truly frightful situation. But I learn today that even this last centre is destroyed, dispersed, annihilated."

However, his constitutional optimism still shone through these repeated disappointments, and he declared:

"That Russia will emerge from the collapse I do not doubt for a second. But it will have to live through two or three hard years. Afterwards I foresee years of vigorous, healthy, intelligent development. The elements are there, and of an extreme richness."

But he did not minimise the difficulty of the present time. Although it had been a mild winter Moscow was threatened with famine, and food supplies were already short, so that anything the English or Americans could do to feed the people would be accepted gratefully; he showed his renewed sense of the importance of concrete organisation by pleading also for assistance in the rebuilding of communications. "A gift of a thousand locomotives would be welcome; a thousand locomotives and a few workshops ready to start work with all the necessary material on repairing 'sick' locomotives."

During the early months of 1918 there was still one work which Kropotkin and those associated with him carried on vigorously; this was the fight against governmental centralisation, through the Federalist League. The League was a comparatively small group of persons interested in sociology who hoped, by publishing important economic and social data, to encourage the various localities to attempt their own industrial and agricultural recovery without relying on the dubious efficiency of the central authorities.

At one of the earlier meetings of this group, on the 7th January, 1918, Kropotkin delivered a lecture in which he pleaded for an abandonment of the idea of one centralised hegemony over the many peoples of the Russian Empire:

"The impossibility of directing from one single centre 180 million people spread over an exceedingly checkered territory, considerably larger than Europe, becomes every day clearer, as it becomes daily clearer that the true creative power of these millions of men could only exert itself when they will feel they possess the fullest liberty to work out their own peculiarities and build their own life in accordance with their aspirations, the physical aptitudes of their territories and their historical past. Thus the thought of a federative union of regions and peoples which were part of the Russian Empire grows steadily among thinking people. More than that: a conscious feeling is born that only through a federative agreement is it possible to found a union, without which the valleys of Russia risk becoming the apple of discord between its fighting—present and future—neighbours. That the true path to the unity of heterogeneous elements of which the Russian Empire is made up lies in this direction is proved by contemporary history. It is full of instances of how federation led to unity and how the opposite path of centralisation has led to discord and to disintegration."

He quoted the example of the British Empire, in which attempts at centralisation in the case of Ireland had shown complete failure, while those of decentralisation in the case of the Dominions had resulted in greater unity and a richer social and economic development.

Of the League's work, he told Professor Turin:

"At this moment we are trying to develop the federative element. I see in it the only counterbalance to the monarchist appetites which are developed assiduously by the propaganda of the two camps, the Prussian and that of the Holstein-Gottorps."

But he also lamented that they were meeting "a crowd of obstacles, both internal and external", and that "faith in centralism is still strong".

The activity of the Federalist League continued until the summer of 1918, but Kropotkin's account of its work shows a pathetic mixture of good intentions, hard work, and complete frustration in actual achievement:

"We have undertaken . . . a great work; we shall publish four volumes of twenty sheets each on federalism and all its aspects—geographical, ethnographical, economic, political, historic, etc. Each volume consists of a dozen articles, all by specialists.

"The contributors of each volume examine minutely the contents of every article. It promises to be a good and indispensable work. We meet at my home, and I am the editor-in-chief. The collaborators are mostly professors, teachers, etc."

Only the first volume of this work was fully completed, but it never saw the light of day, for not long afterwards the Bolsheviks, who in the spring of 1918 began their general attack on minority groups threatening their own aim of centralised authority, decided to suppress the League, despite its primarily scientific character, and to confiscate its documents.

Kropotkin was personally untouched in this persecution, but he did not find life pleasant in Moscow. In the spring of 1918 he had to leave his apartments, and, although the *Memoirs of a Revolutionist* and *The Great French Revolution* had appeared, he said in May that it was six months since he had written in the newspapers. This may have been due partly to immersion in federalist propaganda, but it also seems likely to have been as much attributable to the fact that there was no longer any platform for the opinions he wished to express. Physically he was weak, and could hardly walk, while mentally he became steadily more depressed. At the end of the month he wrote to Turin:

"We live as though in the past. Life is difficult, my friend. The future is black. Our friends still succeed in obtaining a little bread. But our morale is low. That is why I write to nobody. . . ."

It was during this period that Edgar Sisson, the representative of President Wilson in Russia, visited Kropotkin in Moscow, at the request of Sasha, whose husband was working for the Americans. Sisson found him living in "a cold though otherwise liveable suite of rooms in one of the beehive blocks of flat buildings"; he seemed "far yet from being drained of vigour". He told his visitor that he was not in want, but that he felt "lonely and distressed, grieving for the downfall of his country". There followed an attack on the Bolsheviks, whom he called "aliens, enemies of Russia, robbers and gangsters, set upon looting and destruction". He went on to say, according to his interlocutor:

"They have deluded simple souls. The peace they offer will be paid for with Russia's heart. The land they have been given will go untilled. This is a country of children, ignorant, impulsive, without discipline. It has become the prey of the teachers who could have led it along the slow, safe way. I am too old to lead any longer and I am without that sort of ambition, but I returned to Russia to observe, to share in the new bounty of liberty offered by the downfall of Tsarism, to be warmed by home fires. There was hope during the summer. The war was bad—I am the enemy of war, but this surrender is no way to end it. The Constituent Assembly was to meet. It could have built the framework of enduring government."

Even allowing for the almost inevitable failings of the narrator's memory and the errors in interpreting Kropotkin's words, even granting that he probably did not use the phrase "enduring government" (which is unlikely since he himself had so emphatically refused any governmental post), it is clear that his ideas on revolution had changed a great deal since the 1880's, that the tendency towards gradualism already noticeable in his English days had vastly increased, and that his faith in the Russian people had suffered a great setback when he saw them following the Bolsheviks. But there was no lessening of his old indignation against dictators in his attack on Lenin, which was apt and acute:

> "Lenin is not comparable to any revolutionary figure in history. Revolutionaries have had ideals. Lenin has none. He is a madman, an immolator, wishful of burning, and slaughter, and sacrificing. Things called good and things called evil are equally meaningless to him. He is willing to betray Russia as an experiment."

He ended by saying sadly that he did not expect to live to see a better future. Sophie, "who seemed frailer than he", joined occasionally in the conversation, but was much more anxious for news of her daughter.

The Bolshevik terror which began in 1918 tended to draw Kropotkin closer to his old anarchist friends. He had supported the war, they had supported the October Revolution. But the war was over, and the anarchists found themselves among the first victims of the Bolshevik repression, for already in April 1918 there began that series of arrests and suppressions of anarchist organisations and periodicals which soon ended in the complete extinction of an organised movement in Russia.

After he reached Moscow, Kropotkin began to take a closer interest in the work of the militant groups than in the days at Petrograd. He read their papers with interest and re-established individual contacts. On several occasions he called at anarchist editorial offices, and gave advice on propaganda methods. Some of his old disciples began to visit him, and Shapiro in particular became a regular caller; he and Kropotkin had long and friendly discussions on the situation in Russia, in which both of them studiously avoided any reference to the war. G. P. Maximov and Volin, two of the most active anarchist writers of this period, also came, and general relationships resumed much of their former cordiality.

In the ensuing years Kropotkin's position under the Bolsheviks was to become similar to that of Tolstoy under the Tsarist regime. Day after day he saw his comrades and disciples, the men who had adopted the ideas he preached and who strove to turn them into reality, persecuted and harried by the government while he was left in peace. Partly, no doubt, this was because of his age and comparative harmlessness, but it was undoubtedly also due in a great degree to the fact that, like the Tsarist government in the case of Tolstoy, the Bolsheviks realised that to make a martyr of such a world-respected revolutionary could only harm themselves. So, while they persecuted the lesser-known anarchists, they left Kropotkin alone and even made unsuccessful attempts to gain his active co-operation. The sight of the anarchists again becoming a persecuted minority added to his unhappiness, and he was increasingly conscious that he achieved nothing by staying in Moscow, while city life was bad for his health, and a second removal owing to the requisitioning of apartments made it seem as though there was a deliberate attempt by the Bolsheviks to make his life there uncomfortable.

Accordingly, his friends began to seek some dwelling-place in the country, and eventually, after a long search in which Tolstoy's former secretary, Bulgakov, took a friendly part, a house was discovered at the village of Dmitrov, in the Moscow province, some forty miles north of the new capital. He decided to move there in June 1918.

The day before he departed there arrived as a chance visitor a man who was shortly to become a guerrilla leader of almost legendary fame in the Ukraine. This was Nestor Machno, a peasant who had already carried on anarchist propaganda in the Ukrainian villages. In 1917 Machno and his comrades in his native village had heard with delight of Kropotkin's arrival in Petrograd and had written asking his advice on the organisation of the movement and the action anarchists should take during the revolution. They received no answer; this may have been due to the chaos of Russian communications at this period, but it may also have been caused by Kropotkin's own ideas, so confused at the time of his war-offensive propaganda, of what anarchists really could do in Russia. When the news came through of his speech at the August Conference in Moscow, these peasant anarchists were much grieved, but they did not cease to respect and love Kropotkin for his teachings.

In the spring of 1918 Machno came to Moscow and worked there two or three months. One day, when he was delivering copies of a Russian translation of *The Conquest of Bread*, his companion suggested he should pay a visit to Kropotkin before he returned to the Ukraine. Machno agreed, since he wanted the advice of the *starik* (old man) on the attitude to adopt towards the Austro-German army of occupation in the Ukraine and towards the various political groups there. He tells of his visit with the peasant-like simplicity which characterised this modern Stenka Razin.

> "I went to see our dear *starik*, Peter Alexeivich. I caught him the day before he moved to Dmitrov. He received me tenderly. . . . He talked a great deal to me about the Ukrainian peasants.
>
> "To all the questions I raised he gave me satisfactory answers. But when I asked him for advice about my intention of making my way to the Ukraine to carry on revolutionary activities among the peasants, he flatly refused, saying: 'This question, comrade, is associated with great risk to your life, and only you can properly decide it.'
>
> "Only when we were saying goodbye did he tell me: 'It is necessary to remember, dear comrade, that the struggle has no room for sentimentalities. Self-denial, firmness of spirit and will, can defeat everything in the way of achieving one's objectives.' "

This was the only meeting of the two men, very different in their characters and abilities, yet strikingly similar in the essential sincerity of their outlook. Machno went to the Ukraine, and there began his amazing career as the leader of the guerrilla bands of Ukrainian peasants who long fought successfully against the Austro-German armies and Petlura's nationalist bands, and who eventually played a decisive part in the defeat of Denikin's White Army, only to be finally beaten in the last struggle against the centralist action of the Red Army. But in all his sweeping activities Machno did not forget Kropotkin's final words, and says that he always tried to act according to them.

Dmitrov, Kropotkin's last place of residence, was a small town which in the Tsarist days had been a fashionable airing-place for the wealthy Muscovites, who came in winter for carousals and in summer for country excursions, bringing their mistresses and making life very gay. But the revolution had changed all that, the town was quiet and all the fashionable houses were empty or inhabited by peasants.

The house in which the Kropotkins were installed had formerly been a summer dwelling of Count Olsufev. Contrary to some reports, it was not very tiny, and was probably as large as any of the homes Kropotkin had inhabited in England. It contained six rooms, as well as a kitchen and a hall. A large garden, filled with old birch and lime trees, surrounded it, and a high wall gave privacy from the street. Kropotkin had a little room looking northward, which he used for both sleeping and working. It contained a couch, a plain table which he used as a desk, and a few bookshelves. He set himself a very strict regimen, so as to economise his limited strength, and arranged as regularly as health and weather would permit his times of work, meals, rest and walks.

The shortage of food and such essential things as fuel and lighting made life difficult at Dmitrov. For food, indeed, the Kropotkins were better off than most Russians, particularly the town-dwellers. Both of them received the special academic ration, which was larger than the ordinary; Peter had at first refused it because he did not wish to be placed in a privileged category, but according to Emma Goldman, Sophie later accepted without telling him, and received it herself as a botanist. In addition, they had been given a cow by the local co-operators, and were allowed to keep the milk, and when Margaret Bondfield visited them in 1920 they had also a few chickens. And there was the vegetable garden, where Peter worked whenever he felt fit enough for a little light toil, but which was mostly cultivated by Sophie; both of them took great pride in her achievements. One season they grew a large surplus of potatoes; some they exchanged for fodder, and the rest Sophie gave away to the neighbours who had insufficient vegetables. In addition, they received occasional parcels from foreign visitors and from comrades in the Ukraine.

Kropotkin was always very particular about gifts, and would not accept anything which might come from an official source. "At the same time", according to a local co-operator, "he received gifts very easily and simply from those who seemed friendly and who gave with a good heart". Such presents, however, were only occasional, and much of the time, as his son-in-law has said, "Kropotkin fed like all Russian citizens, on *casha* (a porridge of buckwheat or millet) and potatoes; he never complained to anybody, but naturally he needed meat or a chicken . . . ". Indeed, far from complaining, he was furious if rumours of his "starvation" were put about; when some Swedish friends began making a collection to send him food, he wrote and asked them to desist and use the money they had received for some social purpose.

Perhaps he felt more keenly the lack of warmth and light, and of the proper facilities for carrying on his work. Although the Dmitrov area is surrounded by forests, it became very difficult, owing to the lack of labour and the cost of transport, to obtain enough wood to keep the house warm, so that during winter the family had to live in one room and Kropotkin's tiny study. Oil was also scarce, and most of the long evenings they had to be content with a small paraffin lamp. Once Victor Serge sent a large bundle of candles, but a gift of this kind was a rare event.

Writing paper was hard to get, and Kropotkin could no longer obtain the copious supply of learned periodicals which had been available in Western Europe. For the most part, the only periodicals he saw were the government papers, *Pravda* and *Izvestia*, and even these he had to fetch from the village shop. An occasional English or French magazine was a great treat; some visitors, like George Lansbury, undertook to send periodicals from Western Europe, but, though the promises were doubtless kept, the papers rarely arrived. He felt this intellectual starvation much more acutely than the shortage of food. His circumstances also hindered him in the actual work of writing. He obtained an old typewriter, but was too poor to employ a typist. For a time the stenographer of the Dmitrov co-operative gave some assistance in his work, but later he had to do everything himself, typing slowly and painfully because of his feeble strength.

His main relaxation consisted of music, occasional gardening, and talking to visitors. He still played the piano, and the last two months of his life were made unhappy because, owing to the lack of fuel, it was too cold for him to play. Once a week two women friends came to spend a musical evening, and Peter enjoyed greatly the singing on these occasions.

Visitors were not frequent, particularly in the early days at Dmitrov, although during 1920 a number of foreign travellers began to regard his home as a necessary place of pilgrimage. But there were occasional anarchist callers, like Yelensky, Emma Goldman, Berkman, Shapiro, Atabekian, Maximov and Nicholas Lebedev, and sometimes bewildered intellectuals would come for advice. Sasha and her husband stayed whenever they could, but their work in Moscow and Petrograd necessarily made their visits intermittent.

The lack of visitors was compensated to an extent by friendships formed in Dmitrov. His attitude towards the government made Kropotkin's relations with the local Soviet very guarded, but with the Dmitrov Co-operative Union he was on good terms. He regarded the co-operatives as voluntary institutions which were not yet subservient to the centralised government, and as early as January 1918 he lectured to the consumers' co-operative in Moscow. In Dmitrov he took quite an active part in the social life of the union, interesting himself particularly in the library, museum and book-store. One of the members of the organisation remarked that:

"Peter Alexeivich was interested in the purely co-operative work of the union. He regarded co-operation as a slow but sure way of bringing about socialism. He attached particularly great importance to craft co-operation, and often referred to the English home craftsmen who achieved great successes in their production, thanks to the application of technical improvements."

In December 1918 the managers first invited him to a meeting of the union. The whole room stood up to welcome him, and henceforward he established good relationships with the co-operators, and attended their meetings regularly, right up to November 1920, after which the central authorities began to persecute them and make their work impossible. He was popular with his fellow members, talked to everybody without affectation or show of knowledge, and loved to tell about his youth and his travels. He was particularly pleased when the gathering indulged in music and sang Russian songs. When a photograph was taken at one of the meetings, he and Sophie were invited to sit in the place of honour, and on another occasion the craft artel showed its esteem by presenting him with a bookcase made by the local joiners.

But the particular activity which interested him was the museum, with its educational projects. When he arrived it had only just been founded in the burst of voluntary activity which followed the revolution, and was still in a chaotic state. One of its workers has described it as a "sombre room with a stove in the middle and encumbered with all sorts of material". There was the usual unsorted muddle of small museums the world over—tables with specimens of rocks and ores, pressed plants, branches of trees, lichens, insects and aquaria. Kropotkin, drawing on his memories of English and French museums, gave advice on its reorganisation, and when it was ready, presided at the public opening. He attended the deliberations of the museum committee, and took a particular part in the work of the geological section, becoming a member of the commission investigating the local marsh lands, for whom he prepared a paper on the effects of the ice age and gave assistance in making maps. Indeed, in the small sphere at his disposal he returned to the geographical interests of his youth with great zest, preparing a report on the geology of the Dmitrov area, and, in the last autumn of his life, giving a lecture to local teachers on the tasks of museums and his own practical experience in this field fifty years ago in Siberia.

Almost immediately after his arrival in Dmitrov he began work on the final draft of his last book, and as early as January 1919, he wrote to Nicholas Lebedev, "I am diligently working on *Ethics*, but I have little strength, and I am compelled at times to interrupt my work". But his attention was not wholly devoted to this last great work. He still watched with lively interest the train of events in Russia, and for all his dislike of the Bolshevik regime, was completely opposed to the policy of intervention and blockade practised by the Western Allies, which he felt could only do harm in Russia and hinder the work of the genuinely revolutionary elements. He expressed these feelings in a letter written at the end of April 1919 to his Danish friend, Georg Brandes.

He began by denying the rumour of his arrest which had been spread in Western Europe, and said that he was in reasonably good health. He recounted his activities and remarked: "At my age it is practically impossible to participate in public affairs during a revolution and it is not in my nature to occupy myself with them like an amateur." He went on to discuss the situation in Russia, comparing it with the French Revolution, the Bolsheviks assuming the same role as the Jacobins.

"The Bolsheviks are striving to introduce, through the dictatorship of a fraction of the social-democratic party, the socialisation of the land, industry, and commerce. This change which they are now trying to accomplish is the fundamental principle of socialism. Unfortunately the method by which they seek to impose a communism recalling that of Babeuf in a State strongly centralised—and in paralysing the constructive work of the people—makes success absolutely impossible. Which is preparing for us a furious and evil reaction. The latter already seeks to organise itself in order to bring back the ancient regime while profiting by the general exhaustion produced first by the war and then by the famine we are undergoing in Central Russia and by the complete disorganisation of exchange and production, inevitable during a revolution so vast and accomplished in so many stages.

"They speak, in the West, of re-establishing 'order' in Russia by the armed intervention of the Allies. Well, dear friend, you know how criminal towards all social progress in Europe, in my opinion, was the attitude of those who sought to disorganise the power of resistance of Russia—which prolonged the war for a year, brought us the German invasion, under cover of a treaty, and cost oceans of blood to prevent conquering Germany from crushing Europe under the imperial heel. . . .

"Nevertheless, I protest with all my strength against any kind of intervention of the Allies in Russian affairs. Such intervention would result in an access of Russian chauvinism. It would once more bring about the chauvinistic monarchy—signs of it are already apparent—and, mark this well, it would produce among the entire people of Russia a hostile attitude towards Occidental Europe—an attitude which would have the saddest results. The Americans have already comprehended this well.

"They perhaps imagine that by supporting Admiral Kolchak and

General Denikin they are supporting a liberal republican party. But that is already an error. Whatever may be the personal intentions of the two military chiefs, the great number of their partisans have other designs. Of necessity, what they would bring us would be a return of the monarchy, reaction and seas of blood."

He then gave a realistic description of the famine and the drastic shortage of essential goods for production, under which "a whole generation is fading away", and showed that Russia's greatest need was assistance in its emergence from economic disorganisation.

"It is to work out a new future by the constructive elaboration of a new life that is already unfolding, despite all odds, that the Allies ought to help us. Come without delay to the aid of our children! Come to help us in necessary constructive work!"

And he asked that the Russians be sent, "not diplomats and generals", but food, agricultural implements and economic organisers.

This plea, which was later circulated widely in the Western European Press, had no perceptible effect on the actions of the Western Allies, but the knowledge that it had been made, and that Kropotkin had declared himself unequivocally opposed to intervention, may have been in part responsible for the effort the Bolsheviks shortly made to establish friendly relations.

Towards the end of April, Lenin himself expressed a desire for a meeting. The arrangements were made through a leading Bolshevik, Bonch-Bruevich, and it was in his house in Moscow that the meeting took place in the early part of May. Only Kropotkin, Lenin and Bonch-Bruevich were there. The discussion ranged over many subjects, including the co-operatives, which the Bolsheviks were already beginning to attack, the coercive methods used by the government, the steady growth of the bureaucracy, and the course of development which the revolution should henceforward take. Kropotkin expounded his idea that it should grow through the genuine organisations of the workers and peasants, the unions and co-operatives. Lenin replied by setting out his own plan of revolution through the State. Kropotkin then remarked:

"We start from different points of view. Our methods of organisation and action are different, but our goal is the same and I am not going to refuse to help you and your comrades. But this help is going to be negative. I shall draw your attention to all wrong and irregular doings."

Lenin asked Kropotkin to do this. With how much sincerity he spoke we cannot tell, but it is certain that on the three occasions when Kropotkin wrote to the Bolshevik leader, his words had little effect. Early in 1920 he spoke on the general condition of the country and the difficult economic position of the postal workers in Dmitrov. Later, on the suppression of non-Bolshevik periodicals, he gave a warning against State control of literature, pointing out that it was a danger to all progress and free thought, and that it would make really creative work almost impossible. Maxim Gorki made a similar gesture at the time, but in vain. Finally, he wrote his celebrated protest against the taking of hostages by the Bolsheviks, a courageous denunciation to which we shall return when we discuss the final months of his life.

It seems likely that Lenin's main object was to secure Kropotkin's name as a support during the difficult days through which the Bolsheviks were passing, particularly as such a declaration of partiality might assist in undermining Machno in the Ukraine. Certainly he spared no effort at reconciliation, for not long afterwards Lunacharsky, the People's Commissar for Education, offered to pay 250,000 roubles to publish Kropotkin's collected works. Kropotkin replied that he had never received anything from the State, and did not intend to start doing so now. Privately he said that since the Bolsheviks had expropriated others, they might as well help themselves to his books, but would never do so with his consent.

Indeed, the actions of the Bolsheviks led him into ever stronger criticism. In the early days of 1920 he was visited by two Spanish trade-union delegates, Angel Pestaña and Vilkens; the latter had been imprisoned by the Cheka for speaking too frankly in criticism of the regime. The Spaniards brought a generous supply of butter, sugar, jam, sweets, and white bread, all of which the Kropotkins now saw only as luxuries. Sophie jested, "Here are the new bourgeoisie; they have everything", and provided a soup and boiled potatoes which were all she could muster. Kropotkin was delighted to see friends from Spain; it reminded him of his visit in the days of the old International, and he showed with pride a "turnip" watch which had been sent him by a group of working men from Corunna.

When the conversation turned to Russian affairs, he was open in attacking the Bolsheviks.

> "The Communists, with their methods, instead of putting the people on the path to Communism, will finish by making them hate its very name. Perhaps they are sincere, but their system hinders them from introducing in practice the least principle of Communism. And, seeing that the revolutionary work does not advance, they augur from this 'that the people are not ready to swallow their decrees, that there must be time, and diversions'. It is logical: the history of political revolutions repeats itself. The saddest thing is that they recognise nothing, do not wish to acknowledge their errors, and every day take away from the masses a fragment of the conquests of the revolution, to the profit of the centralising State."

But, despite his personal difficulties and physical hardships, despite the evident failure of the revolution, he repudiated any desire to leave Russia. "No," he said, "after forty years of exile, I have no other desire but to die in the country I love so much and where I believe it to be my duty to assist in all phases of the revolution."

III

This attitude he adopted throughout his last years. There were rumours that he had applied for a passport, and that the request had been refused, but these reports were untrue. It was at one time suggested that he, Korolenko, and Vera Figner should be invited to go abroad in order to beg assistance for the Russian children, but Kropotkin himself did not agree to this, partly because he was physically too feeble, and partly because of his conscientious scruples about leaving Russia in its hour of crisis.

For a time, from the beginning of 1920, he began to show more confidence in the future. But he still realised the vast difficulties that lay ahead before any genuine free society could be reached, and never returned to the old optimism of the 1880's, when ten years seemed a long time to look forward to the revolution. In particular, he admitted freely the complicity of the workers of Western Europe in the tragedy of 1914–18; and it is significant of a change of attitude since 1917, that in the epilogue to the Russian edition of *Paroles d'un Revolté*, written in December at Dmitrov, he included them in his condemnation while continuing to blame the Germans for their part in the aggression of 1914. He also condemned the British and French workers for aiding the imperialist expansion in Asia and Africa, which had contributed to the atmosphere of national competition and hastened the war. And he spoke in a vein of acute prophecy when he foretold the danger of even greater tragedies unless a general change of attitude took place.

"Under such conditions it is clear that for the civilised peoples the future holds a whole series of yet more bloody and savage wars, unless they themselves accomplish a social revolution and reorganise their lives on new and more social principles. The whole of Europe and the United States, with the exception of a minority of exploiters, is feeling this need."

But the experience of Bolshevism had already led him back to his early conviction that a lasting and radical change could come, not from the use of authority, but only from the kind of awakening consciousness and responsibility among the people which the anarchists have always envisaged:

". . . We must hope that this lesson will be understood, that everywhere in Europe and America earnest efforts will be applied to the creation, among the entire toiling class—the peasants, the workers and the so-called intelligentsia—of the cells of the forthcoming revolution, not acting on orders from above, but capable of working out by themselves free forms of the new economic order."

The emphasis on the need for decentralisation appears with a remarkable consistency in all Kropotkin's pronouncements to his various visitors at this period. To the *Daily News* correspondent, Meakin, he expressed his hostility towards the coercive economy the Bolsheviks were trying to impose. To the Austrian, Augustin Souchy, he advocated an attempt to rebuild the communes, saying:

"We should have communal councils. These should work independently. They should for instance see to it that, in the event of a poor harvest, the population did not lack the bare necessities of life. Centralised government is, in this case, an extremely cumbersome machine, whereas, on the other hand, a federation of the councils would create a vital centre."

He did not, however, minimise the useful work that could be done through syndicalist propaganda. At that time anarchist ideas had made some headway in certain sections of the Russian trade-union movement, particularly among the bakers, and when a young comrade wrote to ask for guidance, Kropotkin advised him and his group to concentrate on this work.

During this period he re-established contact with Atabekian, who was now practising as a doctor, and in May 1920 he wrote him a long and significant letter. It is a moving document, of mingled resignation so far as his own life was concerned, and hope for the general future.

"I have undertaken to write on Ethics because I regard that work as *absolutely necessary*. I know well that intellectual movements are not created by books, and thus just the reverse is true. But I also know that for clarifying an idea the help of a book is needed, a book that expresses the bases of thought in their complete form. And in order to lay the foundations of a morality freed from religion and higher than the religious morality which expects rewards from the other world, the help of clarifying books is indispensable. The need for such books is particularly urgent now, when people struggle between Nietzsche and Kant. . . .

"I have only a little time left to live. My heart has beaten about as long as it is capable of doing. Today I almost fainted, without any particular cause. . . . Thus, dear friend, I am consecrating all my strength to ethics, so much the more because, even when we worked together so long ago, I felt with little personal conviction that anything serious could be done in Russia. . . . What is going on now had been preparing for thirty years, and against it there were only our exceedingly modest forces, which even so were not wise enough to unite. . . .

"I believe profoundly in the future. I believe that the trade-union movement, to whose congress the representatives of twenty million workers recently came, will become a great power for laying the foundations of an anti-State communist society. If I were in France, where at this moment lies the centre of the industrial movement, and if I were in better health, I would be the first to rush headlong into this movement in favour of the First International—not the Second or the Third, which only represent the usurpation of the idea of the *workers'* International for the benefit of a party which is not half composed of workers.

"I also believe that for the organisation of a socialist society, or better still a communist society, among the peasants, the co-operative movement will present in the next half-century a nucleus of communist life. . . . And the impulse in that direction will come from Russia and perhaps in part from the United States.

"I am convinced of this. But I feel that in order to breathe living strength into these two movements, in order to mould them, to elaborate them, to help them transform themselves from the instruments of self-defence into a powerful instrument of the communal transformation of society, forces younger than mine are necessary, and particularly collaboration among workers and peasants. Such forces will be found. They already exist here and there, although they do not reckon with the future that awaits them. They have not grown up to it; they are not imbued with the socialist ideal. . . ."

Unfortunately the personal task which Kropotkin set himself was never completed, and the hopes he had for the world in general have not come to fruition. The forces he saw in the trade unions and co-operatives were represented only by minorities within these movements, which in recent years have become steadily more centralised and subject to outside control. But this very tendency arouses new forms of discontent, new desires to escape from authority, and it is always possible that a widespread movement towards individual and local independence might divert the forces of genuine solidarity into more constructive currents.

Ethics was not finished. Failing strength, lack of technical assistance, the very magnitude of such a task for an aged man, combined to prevent this, and when Kropotkin died, nine months later, he left only the first volume—an analysis of the development of ethical thought—complete, together with a mass of notes for the second, in which he intended to put forward his own conclusions. But the sketch of his developed theory is already implicit in the one published volume, of which, even in its incomplete form, Herbert Read has justly said: "No better history of ethics has ever been written."

In considering this book it should be first emphasised that Kropotkin did not intend to write a propaganda treatise, a specifically "anarchist" ethics. As Nicholas Lebedev has said:

"Whenever this subject was broached to Kropotkin himself, he invariably answered that his intention was to write a purely *human* ethics (sometimes he used the expression 'realistic').

"He did not recognise any *separate* ethics; he held that ethics should be one and the same for all men. When it was pointed out to him that there can be no single ethics in modern society, which is subdivided into mutually antagonistic classes and castes, he would say that any 'bourgeois' or 'proletarian' ethics rests, after all, on the common basis, on the common ethnological foundation, which at times exerts a very strong influence on the principles of the class or group morality. He pointed out that no matter to what class or party we may belong, we are, first of all, *human beings*, and constitute a part of the general animal species, *Man*. . . . And in his plans for the future of society Kropotkin always thought simply in terms of human beings—without that sediment of the social 'table of ranks' which has thickly settled upon us in the course of the long historical life of mankind."

What he sought was to establish a system of ethics divorced from the supernatural or the metaphysical; in other words, a morality concerned for once with its real function, the relationship of man to man.

He was quite convinced that ethics could be brought down from the transcendental realms of philosophy and take its place among the sciences, as a development into all human relations of his characteristic doctrine of mutual aid, enhanced by a disinterestedness that goes beyond mere equality. "Without equity," he declared, "there is no justice, and without justice there is no morality." But equity alone is not enough; there must be that element of voluntary giving which creates and upholds the brotherhood aimed at by all true ethical systems.

It was in order to seek the source and development of this conception that Kropotkin made his lengthy examination of the ethical systems of the past. He discussed the emergence of morality in the animal world as mutual aid, and its extension into the world of primitive man, the development of the idea of justice among the thinkers of antiquity, and the final growth, in Christian and post-Christian thought, of the greater conception of self-sacrifice, of giving more than is required by justice.

His study of the various ethical philosophers is just and balanced. However opposed he may be, for instance, to organised religion, he does not seek to depreciate the genuine ethical teachings of such men as Buddha or Christ, and he effectively defends a philosopher like Epicurus from the distortions which have been attributed to him. There is a masterly analysis of the moral philosophers of the Enlightenment, and, though the nineteenth-century section is incomplete and deals often with philosophers, like Spencer and Guyau, whose works are neglected today, he nevertheless presents very well the intellectual climate of the age.

Ethics was eventually published after Kropotkin's death; he had wished that his notes should be used by some friend to complete the whole work, but technical and perhaps to an extent even political reasons made this impossible, and all that eventually appeared was the uncompleted first volume.

We have already mentioned in passing some of the visitors who called at Dmitrov during 1920. But there were others who left accounts which have a more personal character, and give a better idea of Kropotkin's domestic life. In March, Emma Goldman and Alexander Berkman were in Moscow and anxious to visit him. They heard that George Lansbury, then editor of the *Daily Herald*, had been given facilities, in the form of a special train, to visit Dmitrov; at Sasha Kropotkin's request, Lansbury agreed to take Berkman, Emma Goldman and Shapiro.

They were all shocked by Kropotkin's appearance. Emma remarked that "he looked old and worn", Berkman observed his "emaciation and feebleness". But all found in him the old gentleness and charm. The talk, as usual, was of the Bolsheviks, of whom Kropotkin said, "They have shown how the revolution is *not* to be made", by subordinating its interests to their own dictatorship, and by destroying the co-operatives which might have bridged the interests of the workers and peasants. He and his friends, indeed, were so critical that Lansbury, who then tended to be dazzled by the communists, remarked: "It was not at all a nice night's talk: all these men held fast to their anarchist creed and refused to see or hear anything but evil spoken about the Bolshevik regime." When asked why he had not raised his voice against the government, Kropotkin said that as long as Russia was blockaded by the Western Powers, he would not join the chorus of ex-revolutionists who only helped by their denunciations the enemies of the Russian people. He preferred to keep silent. And he added sadly, "We have always pointed out the effects of Marxism in action. Why be surprised now?"

Later, in the middle of the summer, Emma Goldman paid a further visit to Dmitrov. She found Kropotkin very much changed for the better, largely because of the sun and ampler food.

"He appeared healthier, stronger, more alive than when I had last seen him. . . . He looked young; he was almost gay, his conversation sparkling. His power of observation, his keen sense of humour and generous humanity were so refreshing, he made one forget the misery of Russia, one's own conflicts and doubts, and the cruel reality of life."

Once again the talk turned on the Revolution. Kropotkin thought there was no reason to lose hope. What had happened was still more momentous than the French Revolution, even though the Bolsheviks, "the Jesuits of Socialism", were distorting it by their use of a strangling bureaucracy. He criticised the anarchists because they had talked much of revolutions, but, in general, had made little preparation for the actual work to be done. "The real facts in a revolutionary process do not consist so much in the actual fighting—that is merely the destructive phase necessary to clear the way for constructive effort. The basic factor in a revolution is the organisation of the economic life of the country. The Russian Revolution had proved conclusively that we must prepare thoroughly for that. Everything else is of minor importance."

Kropotkin's generally improved state of mind was also witnessed by his last letter to Turin, written towards the end of June, in which he told his friend:

"We are alive, which is already a great deal to say. In good health, mentally alert, despite all our tribulations. Naturally, we have aged; that is to say, I have, not Sophie. She is alert and very much occupied with the garden and haymaking."

In June he was visited by Margaret Bondfield, who had gone to Russia as a member of the British Labour Delegation. She was received with delight by the family, who were obviously glad to see a visitor from England and quickly prepared a meal out of their scanty rations.

"Madame Kropotkin seemed tired, but, otherwise, better than I had expected to find her. Peter Kropotkin at this moment seemed extremely well, with rosy cheeks and an appearance that gave abundant evidence of the great care taken of him by his devoted wife."

After they had talked for a while on the problems of Russia, the local Soviet rang up to invite Margaret Bondfield to address the villagers. They also intimated that they would regard Kropotkin's presence as an honour. What he thought of this is not recorded, but he went to the school where the meeting was to be held, no doubt from a feeling of obligation towards his guest. He was greeted by cheering, and at the end of the meeting the chairman made a speech in which he paid "a tribute to the great services which the proletariat of the whole world owed to the distinguished man who lived among them". An American journalist who was present told Roger Baldwin that Kropotkin was highly embarrassed at this attempted friendliness on the part of an institution he had repudiated. He was "uneasy" when the meeting cheered him, and after the chairman's speech, "he arose, half pleased and half angry, grew very red, and sat down without speaking a word".

When Margaret Bondfield left, Kropotkin gave her a document which he asked should be published abroad, and which was reproduced as an appendix to the report of the British Labour mission. It was a *Letter to the Workers of the Western World*, and was written with a clarity and a sense of reality which showed no diminution of its author's intellectual powers.

Kropotkin began by calling on the workers and all progressive elements to demand an end to the blockade and war of intervention, since such hostile actions, far from saving the good elements in the revolution, would "necessarily result in a reinforcement of the dictatorial power", hinder the work of Russians anxious for genuine social reconstruction, and promote antagonism towards the West. He then put forward his own idea of Russia as a federation of autonomous peoples, breaking down into a looser federation of rural communes and free cities, and pointed out that a speedy *rapprochement* between Russia and the Western nations could help to minimise the centralist tendencies.

The second part of his letter was an exhortation to the people of other lands to learn from the errors made in Russia. In attempting to achieve economic equality, the Russian revolution had taken a step beyond its English or French counterparts. But the Bolsheviks' attempt to achieve this by means of a centralised party dictatorship had merely shown "how communism should not be imposed".

Kropotkin described the original conception of the Soviets controlling the life of the country as a "grand idea", since it would have led to the direct participation of the real producers. But under a party dictatorship these Soviets, or Labour Councils, were reduced to a passive and insignificant role.

"A Labour Council ceases to be a free and valuable adviser when there is no free Press in the country, and when we have been in that position for nearly two years, the excuse for such conditions being the state of war. More than that, the Peasant and Labour Councils lose all their significance when no free electoral agitation precedes the elections, and the elections are made under the pressure of party dictatorship."

The ways of overthrowing a weak government are already well known from historical examples. But the constructive tasks offer a much more difficult problem, requiring the maximum devolution of initiative.

"The immense constructive work that is required from a Social Revolution cannot be accomplished by a central government, even if it had to guide it in its work something more substantial than a few socialist and anarchist booklets. It requires the knowledge, the brains, and the willing collaboration of a mass of local and specialised forces, which alone can cope with the diversity of economic problems in their local aspects. To sweep away that collaboration and to trust to the genius of party dictators is to destroy all the independent nuclei, such as trade unions (called in Russia 'Professional Unions') and the local distributive co-operative organisations—turning them into bureaucratic organs of the party, as is being done now. But this is the way *not* to accomplish the Revolution; the way to render its realisation impossible."

He foresaw socialism making progress in all parts of the world, and called upon the workers to make sure that their forces were not dissipated, and to erect a new International unaffiliated to any party but based on the free co-operation of producers, organised in trade unions, "in order to free the production of the world from its present enslavement to capital".

These were bold words, when one considers that they were to be published in the Western Press and that the Bolsheviks, who had already imprisoned thousands of people for less thorough disagreement, would certainly read them. But Kropotkin, whatever might have been his errors, was never devoid of moral courage, and now, like Tolstoy years before, he raised his voice wherever he could against the abuses of power, and if he was heard only by a few in Russia itself, it was because he had not the means of publicity of which even the Tsarist autocracy could not wholly deprive Tolstoy.

In the ensuing months, as the ruthless nature of Lenin's régime became more evident in practice, Kropotkin's indignation increased, and at last, in the autumn of 1920, when the Bolsheviks began the repulsive mediæval practice of taking hostages in order to protect themselves against the possible violence of their opponents, he was moved to write his famous letter to Lenin on this subject, a document which, for its forthright courage and honesty, deserves to stand with Tolstoy's *I Cannot Keep Silent*, written under very similar circumstances twelve years before. There was no hesitation, no moral doubt, in these ringing tones:

"I have read in today's *Pravda* an official communiqué from the Council of People's Commissars, according to which it has been decided to keep as hostages several officers of Wrangel's army. I cannot believe there is no single man about you to tell you that such decisions recall the darkest Middle Ages, the period of the Crusades. Vladimir Ilyich, your concrete actions are completely unworthy of the ideas you pretend to hold.

"Is it possible that you do not know what a hostage really is—a man imprisoned not because of a crime he has committed, but only because it suits his enemies to exert blackmail on his companions? These men must feel very much like men who have been condemned to death, and whose inhuman executioners announce every day at noon that the execution has been postponed until the next day. If you admit such methods, one can foresee that one day you will use torture, as was done in the Middle Ages.

"I hope you will not answer me that Power is for political men a professional duty, and that any attack against that power must be considered as a threat against which one must guard oneself at any price. This opinion is no longer held even by kings; the rulers of countries where monarchy still exists have abandoned long ago the means of defence now introduced into Russia with the seizure of hostages.

"How can you, Vladimir Ilyich, you who want to be the apostle of new truths and the builder of a new State, give your consent to the use of such repulsive conduct, of such unacceptable methods? Such a measure is tantamount to confessing publicly that you adhere to the ideas of yesterday.

"But perhaps, with the seizure of hostages, you do not try to save your work, but merely your own life? Are you so blinded, so much a prisoner of your authoritarian ideas, that you do not realise that, being at the head of European Communism, you have no right to soil the ideas which you defend by shameful methods, methods which are not only the proof of a monstrous error, but also of an unjustifiable fear for your own life?

"What future lies in store for Communism when one of its most important defenders tramples in this way on every honest feeling?"

It seems that Kropotkin was not merely content to voice in writing his protest over this offence against common humanity, but actually paid a visit to Lenin in Moscow to reason with him on the question. It is unlikely that the trip was made solely for this purpose; during the early autumn a new anxiety descended on the family, for Sasha was taken ill with typhoid fever, her mother went to the capital in order to nurse her, and Peter no doubt travelled to Moscow at the same time rather than stay at Dmitrov alone.

He may, indeed, have paid two visits to the Bolshevik leader during this autumn, for in September he wrote to Armando Borghi, the Italian syndicalist, saying that he had been to see Lenin in order to ask him not to continue the attacks on the co-operatives; his interest in this matter certainly remained very strong, for as late as December 1920 Berkenheim, the co-operative leader, visited him for a long conversation on the situation of the movement. The incident of the hostages took place in October or later, after the letter to Borghi, so he appears to have made at least two visits to Lenin during 1920.

Atabekian saw him after this last interview. Kropotkin was very agitated, and took his friend aside into a room where they would not be disturbed. He then asked whether he would not censure him, since he had been to intercede with Lenin for a former emigré friend on the list of hostages. Atabekian replied that he would approve of pleading even to the Tsar to save those who were condemned to death. Kropotkin then said that he had also asked Lenin to abolish altogether the system of hostages, and executions generally, and reminded him of the ill effects of such a policy during the French Revolution, and its final end in reaction. Rather naïvely, he concluded, "I frightened them a little".

It is true that about this time certain changes were made, for the right of local sections of the Cheka to carry out executions was abolished, but it is not certain that this had anything to do with Kropotkin's plea. Moreover, the improvement was only temporary, and throughout the civil war executions were carried out on the battlefield, with little regard for Lenin's overt decrees.

Yet, though he was fully aware of the terrible trials through which Russia and the revolution were passing, Kropotkin still had some hope for the future, and in November he wrote to a friend, "You know how I always believe in the future. . . . Without disorder, the revolution is impossible; knowing that, I did not lose hope, and I do not lose it now." But to Volin, the anarchist writer who had taken part in Machno's work in the Ukraine and who visited Dmitrov in November, he was more pessimistic and genuinely clear-sighted, saying sadly that the centralisation of development under the dictatorship of a single party State had produced "a typical unsuccessful revolution", which he believed might lead to "a profound reaction".

It seems, indeed, that his mood varied greatly, and also that he spoke his inmost thoughts only to close friends and trusted comrades, for another acquaintance of this period recorded him as saying:

> "I of course take a negative attitude about a great deal that is happening, and I have said so directly and frankly to many of those who stand at the head of the present government. They behave well towards me, and many of the things I asked were carried out. They even proposed that I should take part in their work, but I refused. As an anarchist, I cannot reconcile myself to any government."

And later he returned to his optimistic vein, saying that he believed in the future of Russia, and remarking of the present difficulties: "All this is history; it must be like that, but it will be better than it was before." His chief regret was the comparative inactivity of the anarchists, particularly in Moscow.

Sophie on this occasion took a more melancholy view of the situation, complaining about the shortage of food and the general discomforts caused by the condition of the country, and looking pessimistically into the future.

At last, in the end of November, Kropotkin made an effort, at the request of his friends, and particularly of Sophie and Sasha, who had apparently been exhorting him for some time, to make a statement of what he thought the anarchists might do in Russia. Evidently the effort to admit all his deepest feelings at this time caused him a great emotional disturbance, for when he called his wife and daughter in the room to read what he had written, his manner was agitated, his voice trembled, and his handwriting, usually clear and even, was almost illegible.

This statement, entitled "What to do?" is perhaps the most despairing and tragic document that ever came from Kropotkin's pen, for, looking candidly at the world around him, he saw nothing that could be done to halt the steady decline and eventual death of the revolution. A revolution, he pointed out, was a vast social phenomenon, in which individuals had little real influence, small groups hardly more, while even large parties could only ride on the surface of events and use them to their own advantage. The revolution had taken a different course from that for which the anarchists had prepared, but there was now no means of halting the rush of events.

"The revolution will advance in its own way, in the direction of the least resistance, without paying the slightest attention to our efforts.

"At the present moment the Russian revolution is in the following position. It is perpetrating horrors. It is ruining the whole country. In its mad fury it is annihilating human lives. That is why it is a revolution and not a peaceful progress, because it is destroying without regarding what it destroys and whither it goes.

"And we are powerless for the present to direct it into another channel, until such time as it will have played itself out. It must wear itself out.

"And then? *Then—inevitably will come a reaction.* Such is the law of history, and it is easy to understand why this cannot be otherwise. People imagine that we can change the form of development of a revolution. That is a childish illusion. A revolution is such a force that its growth cannot be changed. *And a reaction is absolutely inevitable*, just as a hollow in the water is inevitable after every wave, as weakness is inevitable in a human being after a period of feverish activity.

"Therefore the only thing we can do is to use our energy to lessen the fury and force of the oncoming reaction. But of what can our efforts consist?

"To modify the passions—on one side as on the other? Who is likely to listen to us? Even if there exist those who can do anything in this role, the time for their *début* has not yet come; neither the one nor the other side is as yet disposed to listen to them. I see one thing; we must gather together people *who will be capable of undertaking constructive work in each and every party after the revolution has worn itself out.*"

This document Kropotkin did not intend to publish; it was meant only for a few close friends. He did not wish the whole world to see the despair that faced him when he looked into the depth of his mind. It may have been the last considered statement he made on the Russian Revolution, although he also left an unfinished essay which was probably started at about the same time, entitled "The Ideal of the Revolution". Here he said that the task of the Russian Revolution had been made difficult not only because it took place during a great war, but also because it was not animated by the same "high moral ideal" which had inspired both the English and French Revolutions. This lack he blamed on to the infiltration from Germany of economic materialism during the past decade, and he saw the only hope in the possibility that "the common sense of the Russian people will come to the surface" and enable them to get rid of the plague of autocracy "which threatens to weaken the Russian Revolution and make it barren".

IV

Volin in November had found Kropotkin well and alert, but with the approach of winter his health again declined, and he no longer found it possible to leave Dmitrov. The Moscow Tolstoyans invited him to join them in a celebration of the great novelist's anniversary, but he had to decline, writing on the 21st November:

"I would have so ardently wished to spend two or three days with you all, evoking the memory of him who has taught men love and fraternity, who has awakened the conscience within them, and whose powerful voice has called upon them to construct a new society on fraternal foundations and without masters—of him whose words would be so necessary precisely at this time. Unfortunately, my bad health forces me to decline your kind invitation. But my thoughts join you with all my soul—and all those to whom the name of Leo Nicolaevich is dear."

However, a week or so later his condition seems to have improved, and on the 14th December Sasha wrote from Moscow to Margaret Bondfield:

"Father is very well. We are all annoyed that people think he is at present dying of hunger. Compared with many people, he is well off. Mother has aged a great deal with the hard work of this summer and of my illness."

December was his final month of reasonable health, and two days before Christmas, on the 23rd December, he wrote the last letter that can be traced from his pen. A Dutch anarchist, P. de Reyger, had invited him to spend the rest of his days in Haarlem. Kropotkin was already too feeble for travel, and in any case he still maintained his decision not to desert his country in time of crisis. So he wrote to decline the invitation, and since this is his last letter, we quote it in full:

"Dear Comrade de Reyger,

"Please accept my cordial thanks for your friendly letter of last November which has at last reached me. All three of us, my wife, my daughter, and myself, are deeply moved by your letter and your invitation. But, as you will probably know already, through the letter which I sent to the comrades of *der Syndikalist*, our situation is not so bad at the present time as it was last year. We have the necessities for living, and as this is not the case in all the countries of Europe, it is already a great deal. A thousand thanks for your invitation. If I again go to Western Europe, I will do my best to pay you a visit in Haarlem.

"The social revolution has unfortunately assumed in Russia a centralist and authoritarian character. It nevertheless shows the possibility of a transition from a capitalist to a socialist society. And this thought will doubtless encourage the socialists of Western Europe in their efforts at reconstituting society on the basis of an anti-militarist equality. At the same time, the centralist errors committed by the Russian communist revolution will certainly contribute to make us avoid similar mistakes by the workers of other lands.

"Fraternal greetings,

"Peter Kropotkin.

"P.S. We are living in a little town 60 kilometres north of Moscow, where we have a little vegetable garden which is cultivated by my wife. Unfortunately, I myself am in no condition to undertake physical labour, so it is my wife who provides us with nearly all the vegetables we need. I am working on a great book on Ethics *on a naturalistic basis*. You can write to me in Dutch. I understand it well, but I cannot write it."

He never went to Haarlem, for barely a month later, in the middle of January, he was prostrated by an attack of pneumonia which proved his last illness. His condition was immediately recognised as serious, and Sasha in Moscow engaged a Russian nurse, E. Lind, who had been trained in England and who has left one of the most complete accounts of her patient's last days. Emma Goldman, who was a trained nurse, offered to go as well, but Sasha declined because of the scanty accommodation at Dmitrov, and Emma, hearing that Kropotkin's situation was not immediately critical, went to Petrograd.

Atabekian went to Dmitrov to give medical attention, and Lenin decided to send by special train a group of five eminent Moscow physicians, led by Professors Pletnev and Shurovsky. There can, indeed, be no doubt that in these last weeks Kropotkin had every medical care that Russia could then provide, while Sophie, Sasha and the nurse looked after him very devotedly.

But his body was now too feeble to withstand this final sickness. It began alarmingly, with severe heart attacks, which weakened him greatly and made him think that his death was near, although this feeling did not prevent him from being comparatively cheerful. The first examinations of the doctors made them decide, however, that his constitution and the healthy life he had lived in recent years might yet enable him to recover, and on hearing this opinion he remarked that he did not want to die, for there was still work he wished to complete, and that he would therefore do his best to recover.

At the beginning he was restless, and almost resentful that he could not dispense with help. His brain was very active, and the continual new ideas, which he insisted on discussing with whomever might be present, tired him and sometimes prevented sleep. As if intent on cramming the last scrap of activity into a well-spent life, he still wrote when he had the strength to do so, and one night spent his wakeful hours making an elaborate word picture of an anarchist commune.

He talked of the past, returning persistently to early childhood memories, speaking often of his mother, and sometimes of the Empress Marie Alexandrovna, the wife of Alexander II, whom he always respected and pitied.

After a time it seemed as though his illness was growing no worse, and the nurse returned to Moscow. But a few days later he had a seizure which resulted in a temporary paralysis of the brain and deprived him of speech for a few hours. He recovered, but was left considerably weaker. Sasha and Boris Lebedev came, and friends in Moscow and throughout Russia waited anxiously, for they felt he could not recover.

In these last days he was patient, never complaining of his condition, never regretting the death he now knew to be inevitable, and always considerate, saying "How painful to give trouble to so many good people".

Towards the end he became indifferent to all around him, and would lie for hours without asking for anything, but sometimes inquiring about people of whom he thought. Once he murmured, after a long silence, "What a hard business—dying". Almost to the last he recognised his friends, and two hours before his death he was still jesting with them.

He died just after three o'clock on the morning of the 8th February, 1921, in silence and at last unconscious. His wife and daughter, as well as Atabekian and Boris Lebedev, were with him. Emma Goldman, delayed by the bad train service, arrived too late, and Berkman, with a group of leading Russian anarchists, came from Moscow on the same day.*

* William Henry Chamberlain was told by Emma Goldman that Kropotkin's last words were, "Why has the revolution no noble side?", but as Emma was not at his death-bed and as none of the actual witnesses has mentioned this fact, we merely record it. A "supernatural" element was introduced by his son-in-law into his account of the last days, for he recorded that shortly before Kropotkin's death he and Sasha went out on to the verandah of the house, ". . . and I was suddenly struck by an extraordinary spectacle; on the dark vault of the sky I saw an immense meteor with a long tail and dazzling green light which lit up the sky and the earth. It fell slowly and disappeared on the horizon. I had never seen anything like it in my life. We stood as if fixed to the spot. It seemed to us that there was a mysterious relationship between the falling star and the dying revolutionary."

The Bolshevik government immediately offered a State funeral for Kropotkin; his family and friends declined, for they all knew that the old anarchist would have regarded this as an insult. A Funeral Commission was therefore formed by representatives of the Russian anarchist groups in order to carry out the arrangements for the ceremony.

Immediately difficulties were encountered. Owing to the nationalisation of all public conveyances and the closing of independent printing houses, they had to apply to the Moscow Soviet for assistance. The question of conveyance was settled easily, but the printing arrangements were more complicated. After some negotiation, the authorities agreed to sanction the printing of two small leaflets and a single-day newspaper in memory of Kropotkin, but when the anarchists asked that these publications should be uncensored, their request was categorically refused. Eventually they took matters into their own hands, opened an anarchist press which had been sealed by the Cheka, and printed two uncensored leaflets bearing appreciations of Kropotkin.

Meanwhile, at Dmitrov, the great man lay on the couch in his study, where he had worked and lived for the last three years, while workers, peasants, intellectuals, even soldiers and Bolshevik officials, filed unceasingly through the little house. Then the coffin was taken to the station and put on the special train that would carry it to Moscow. The schools were closed for the day, and the children strewed pine boughs on the snowy ground before the procession. The whole population of the village accompanied it to the station, including the local Red Army garrison who, in deference to the dead man's opinions, came unarmed.

At Moscow, a great crowd awaited the arrival of the funeral train at a station in the suburbs, and accompanied Kropotkin's body, with revolutionary music, to the Palace of Labour where he was to lie in state. This building had formerly been the Palace of the Nobility, and in the Hall of Columns where Kropotkin now lay had taken place, long ago, the ball at which, dressed as a little Persian prince, he had been presented to the Tsar Nicholas I. For the next three days thousands of people passed through to pay their tribute.

Meanwhile, a further dispute had arisen between the Funeral

Commission and the authorities, this time over the anarchists who were incarcerated in Moscow prisons for speaking their views too openly. Some were held in the Special Department of the Cheka, others at the terrible Tsarist Butirky prison which Tolstoy immortalised in *Resurrection*. The Funeral Commission immediately sent a wire to Lenin, asking that the imprisoned men be released for the funeral day. The Central Executive Committee of the Soviets recommended the Cheka to release the prisoners, "wherever possible", in order to take part in the funeral. The Cheka refused unless a guarantee were given for their return, but when this was done they replied that there were no anarchists in prison for them to release. This was known to be untrue, since Berkman had gained access to both the Butirky and the Special Department prisons and had talked to the anarchists held there.

On the morning of the funeral the anarchists decided to take direct action, and on behalf of the Commission, Sasha Kropotkin telephoned Kamenev at the Moscow Soviet, saying that if the prisoners were not released a public announcement of the Bolshevik breach of faith would be made to the crowds assembled within and outside the Palace of Labour, and the Bolshevik wreaths would be removed from the bier. American and British newspaper correspondents, including the English author Arthur Ransome, were present, and the mood of the people in the hall was becoming truculent. Victor Serge, who was there, tells us that:

"The shadow of the Cheka was everywhere; but the crowd was large and responsive. . . . With his austere head, smooth high forehead, chiselled nose and snowy beard, Kropotkin looked like a sleeping prophet, while around him angry voices whispered that the Cheka was breaking Kamenev's promise. . . . The black flags, the speech, the frightened whispering, whipped the crowd into a kind of frenzy. . . ."

Kamenev pleaded for time, and promised that the imprisoned men would arrive in twenty minutes. For an hour the crowds waited in the bitter cold, and then only seven, the men from the special prison, appeared. The Cheka assured the Commission that the men from the Butirky prison were on their way, and the funeral began, but these prisoners never came.

The orchestra of the Moscow Opera played the First and the Pathetic symphonies of Chaikovsky, which Kropotkin had always loved, and as the bier was being taken from the hall a choir of two hundred singers from the Opera performed the requiem, *Eternal Memory*, which had also been sung for Tolstoy.

In the streets a great procession of a hundred thousand people followed the coffin in its five-mile progress to the cemetery of the Novo-Devichi monastery, on the riverside, opposite those Sparrow Hills where Herzen and Ogarev in boyhood had sworn to devote their lives to the Russian people. The banners of the political parties, the trade unions, scientific and literary societies, and student organisations, interspersed by the black flags of the anarchist groups, waved above the crowd as it marched to the tune of revolutionary music. (Only the "Internationale" was not played, in deference to Kropotkin's dislike of this song, which he likened to "the howling of hungry dogs".) Unarmed soldiers and sailors and groups of children mingled with the ranks, and there were many old friends, such as Vera Figner and Armand Ross, who had introduced Kropotkin to anarchism forty-nine years before. The students and workers formed a chain of linked hands around the procession, and it moved with a self-imposed order. It was, nevertheless, the last great demonstration against the Bolshevik tyranny, and many of the people were there as much to call for freedom as to pay their tribute to the great anarchist. The banners bearing in flaming letters the words "Where there is authority there is no freedom" and "Anarchists demand liberation from the prison of Socialism" expressed the mood of that day.

On the Tolstoy Museum the black anarchist flag was flying in tribute and a draped bust of Tolstoy stood on the steps, while a band of Tolstoyans played Chopin's *Funeral March* as the procession halted. Outside the Butirky prison there was a second halt as the prisoners shouted their farewell from the barred windows.

Finally, the cemetery was reached, and the coffin was lowered into a grave under a silver birch tree. The speakers stood up one after another to make their tributes—a student, a Tolstoyan, representatives of the Social Revolutionaries and Mensheviks, Mostovenko for the Bolsheviks and Rosmer for the

Third International, Emma Goldman for the foreign anarchists, and six Russian anarchists, the last of them Aaron Baron, one of the paroled prisoners, who created a sensation by his bold attack on the government. "Emaciated, bearded, wearing gold spectacles," as Victor Serge describes him, "he stood erect and cried out in defiant protest against the new despotism, against the butchers at work in the dungeons, against the dishonour that had been brought upon socialism, against the violence by which the government was trampling the revolution under foot."

The sun was already setting on the short winter's day when the last orator had spoken to the silent crowd in the cemetery, and as the earth was filled in over the dead revolutionary the procession began to make its way back to the city, marching again to the tune of revolutionary songs. The anarchists returned to the prisons from which some of them would never emerge; their comrades who remained outside became the subject of continued and intensified persecution from the Bolshevik authorities. The government that had wished to pay State honours to Kropotkin systematically set about eliminating those who preached or attempted to practise his doctrines.

A town on the steppes and one or two schools were named after the anarchist sage, the street in which the Tolstoy Museum stood was renamed Kropotkin Street, and the old house in which he had been born was presented by the Moscow Soviet to the Funeral Commission for use as a museum (oddly enough, the street in which it stood was named after Tolstoy). Nicholas Lebedev was in charge of it, and Sophie lived there and often showed visitors round the collections. Twice, in 1923 and 1929, she came to Western Europe. She remained always hostile to the Bolshevik regime, but died unmolested in 1938 (Lebedev had already died in 1936). After her death the museum was suppressed by the government, the collections dispersed among other museums, and the building handed over to the Academy of Sciences.

CHAPTER X

THE PROPHET

To those who knew Kropotkin, the man seemed often more important than his works, and throughout our account we have had to record the strong impressions of amiability and goodness left by him. He had many ideological enemies, but few men of celebrity in their own time have had so few personal foes; even those who were bitterly opposed to his teachings usually found his modesty and sincerity difficult to resist.

In general, he can be said to have embodied the best attributes of the Russian people, and he in turn believed in the Russian people because he recognised in the peasants those very qualities of warmth and generosity which he himself displayed. Thus it is not inappropriate that he should have gained a wider repute than any other Russian exile of his time, and have become regarded in the Western world as the representative of those Russians who resisted the Tsarist autocracy in the name of liberty and the well-being of the people.

His ideal of human solidarity was no vague conception, nor was his amiability a superficial virtue. They were continually manifested in his daily life, and, although he may at times have fallen into error, there is nothing in Kropotkin's acts or writings of intellectual dishonesty. He always spoke what he thought to be right, and was ready to take the consequences, whether it meant imprisonment or—what was much worse to a man of his character—the loss of old and respected friends. He was always kind, anxious to avoid giving pain or inconvenience, and conscious of the needs of others. His hospitality was wide, his sympathy abundant, his generosity as unlimited as his resources allowed. In the difficult roles of husband and father he seems to have been exceptional, for there are no records of those stormy family disorders which mark the biographies of so many other Russian writers and rebels.

Indeed, his mature life was so well-balanced that there is little material which the psychologically minded critic can use to explain away his actions, and if we seek for frustration as a motive it can be found very simply in his early rebellion against an unsympathetic father. Even this motive should not, however, be exaggerated, for there was enough in nineteenth-century Russia to turn any sincere and sensitive man into a rebel, without relying too heavily on the consoling explanation of the Œdipus complex.

Nor should we be content with the impression of Kropotkin as a saint. Obstinacy and intolerance had their place in his character, though he never erred into conscious injustice. He held his views steadfastly, and, once he had reached an opinion, he was not easily turned aside. On the other hand, he was generally receptive to ideas, had a great facility for absorbing new knowledge, and always did his best to examine thoroughly all information connected with any subject in which he was interested. In this he was assisted by a brilliant faculty of generalisation, which was balanced by a weakness for over-simplification in almost all the issues he discussed.

The latter characteristic is connected intimately with his constitutional optimism. That this quality, with its tendency to expect rapid and painless solutions to vast problems, amounted at times to a fault, was evident not only to hostile critics, but also to some who shared his fundamental ideals, for even his old friend and comrade, Malatesta, the most realistic of all anarchists, said after his death that he had leaned too much towards excessive optimism and theoretical fatalism.

This optimism, which was so evident in Kropotkin's actions and works, can be traced to more than one cause. Important among them was the romanticism which had influenced him in childhood. The romantic movement had a kind of delayed flowering in Russia, long after its decline in England, France, and Germany, and it survived even into the third quarter of the nineteenth century. The romantic tendency was particularly strong among the young aristocrats, with their partly Western background, and Kropotkin was almost as much influenced by the lingering effects of this trend of thought as his predecessors, Herzen and Bakunin, had been. The memory of his Byronic mother, the literary discoveries of his early years, all played their part, and his concrete image of the revolution seems for many years to have been that of Delacroix's barricades, while his chivalry, his idealisation of women and his puritanism sprang from the same root. But the optimism of romance, when faced with disappointment, turns quickly into the blackest despair, and more is needed to explain the persistence of Kropotkin's attitude.

One of its roots lies in the prevalent scientific and political atmosphere of the time. The nineteenth century was *par excellence* the age of progress. The scientists believed that unrestricted research would lead to a pattern of gradual but continuous amelioration of human existence. Politically, it was thought that the domain of freedom was expanding steadily, that the lower classes were beginning to take their part in administration, that the submerged races were entering the community of nations. The spread of education, the rise of a popular Press, the growth of trade unions and co-operative movements, the opening of the vast unexploited areas of America and Australia, the steady increase in material wealth, all contributed to create an almost irresistible atmosphere of confidence in the future. In such a century only a few singularly cross-grained pessimists among the educated classes persisted in a negative attitude towards progress, and doubted that it was inevitable.

The labour movement was no less infected by this spirit than the worlds of literature, science, or industry. Since the beginning of the century, the stream of working-class activity had increased steadily; there had been setbacks, some of them tragic, but on the whole, by the 1890's, the workers of Europe showed a far greater militancy than in the year of Waterloo, and had made advances both in their organisation and in the material conditions under which they lived.

It must be admitted that in the last years of the nineteenth century there was much to be said for optimism. Nobody doubted that there would be obstacles in the future, but very few realised that they would be so formidable or that progress itself would also have such destructive aspects. Kropotkin had his full share of this happy faith, and it cannot be said that in this respect his optimism was any more gross than that of most of his contemporaries; indeed, it was in some ways even less so, for he at least recognised the threat of a European war clearly enough and had an uneasy vision of the kind of harm it was likely to entail.

As a further important reason for his optimism and his broad faith in humanity, we might place the fact that he had been generally fortunate in his own career and in his personal relationships. From the beginning he had found people who loved and cared for him—his mother, the loyal servants at his home, his brother Alexander, his comrades in the Chaikovsky circle, and finally Sophie. In Siberia, among the Doukhobors and the other colonists, he saw the Russian peasant at his best, and his only intimate contact with the workers of Western Europe, in the Jura Federation, had shown him a group of devoted men who were certainly not representative of the proletariat as a whole, while the cultured middle-class people who treated him so kindly in England were equally untypical of their class, of the hard business men, the cunning financiers, and the insensitive squires of Victorian England. Thus he gained, from a schooling among the Russian *narodniks* and an imperfect experience elsewhere, a rather naïve romanticisation of the workers and a tendency to depreciate the will to resist social change among the propertied classes.

He had also found easy success in those activities which he considered important in life. In his childhood he won distinction as a scholar, and when he was a very young man recognition as a geographer. Even his imprisonment in Russia ended in the fantastic good fortune of his escape, while on settling in Western Europe he quickly became and remained the leading anarchist teacher of his time. A few years later in England he made yet another reputation as a writer and scholar of varied accomplishments. Only rarely was he in real want, and the modest competence he earned provided him with the means to carry on his work, which was all the luxury he asked. It was only in his very last years, as a result of the difficulties and disappointments of the Russian Revolution, that despair fell heavily upon him.

This combination of personal success with the generally confident atmosphere of the nineteenth century certainly fostered Kropotkin's natural optimism and also the theoretical fatalism which Malatesta noticed, and which at times made him fall into a belief, similar to that of the Marxists, that history shared his social aims and would proceed in its own good time to the free society of his dreams.

But, while excessive confidence was in some respects a fault in Kropotkin, making him expect improvements in society or mutations in human consciousness too quickly or too easily, it also had its advantages, since it fostered that ease with which he approached the most difficult problems and that tireless energy with which he worked all his life for the attainment of his aims. A man who had been less certain of the ultimate and not very distant realisation of his ideals could not have achieved or even attempted all that Kropotkin did in a long life packed with unceasingly creative activity.

The breadth of his achievements in his own time we have already shown in our narrative. Our aim now must be to consider how these achievements stand in the perspective of history. What significance do his theories have today, in a society still searching for a solution to ills that seem inherent in its constitution?

The first phase of his contribution to knowledge can be passed over briefly, since it belongs to the relatively uncontroversial science of geography. He made a few explorations in unknown corners of Asia; his journeys were in themselves unspectacular in comparison with the hazardous and sensational travels of Livingstone or Stanley, but they gave him the basic facts for elaborating the three theories, of the structural lines of Asia running diagonally instead of along the parallels of latitude, of the ice cap covering the whole of Northern Europe, of the desiccation of Eurasia, which represent his now undisputed contributions to geographical knowledge.

The second phase of his activity is that of the anarchist militant, the builder of a social idea. Here it must be emphasised that Kropotkin did not create a new movement. He came into an intellectual tradition as the fourth of its great thinkers, in succession to Godwin, Proudhon and Bakunin; he entered a movement of propaganda and agitation that had already been in progress for some years and had gained many of its distinctive characteristics before he appeared. It was, moreover, a movement in continual flux of growth and change. In 1872, when he first became an anarchist, the International was about to split into its mutually hostile sections. In 1877, when he finally settled as a militant in Switzerland, Bakunin was already dead and the part of the International which had followed his lead was declining. If anarchism survived this crisis, it was at least in part due to Kropotkin's work.

His activity in Switzerland and France, from 1877 to 1882, showed rare qualities of initiative and energy. He proved himself an able editor, a simple and convincing journalist and pamphleteer, a sincere and moving orator. He was industrious and resourceful, in manual as well as intellectual work, and very shortly after his first initiation into theoretical writing, he produced the best advocacies of the libertarian idea that had been written since Godwin.

In Switzerland he was unable to halt the decay of the Jura Federation, but there is no doubt that by founding and editing *Le Revolté* he did much to keep the anarchist idea alive, and to bridge the difficult period between the decline of the old International and the rise of the new French movement and a fresh international impetus in the years after 1881. His influence in France was certainly great, both through *Le Revolté* and his early books, which were published first in France and inspired intellectuals as well as workers. Even his imprisonment there helped to spread anarchist ideas, and it might reasonably be claimed that, with the possible exception of Louise Michel, he was the greatest single influence on that considerable libertarian movement which still exists in France. Nor should it be forgotten that the anarchists were the pioneers of the renaissance of the labour movement after the destruction of the Paris Commune.

In Spain and Italy, where anarchism has long traditions and still maintains a relatively wide influence, Kropotkin has been more a respected thinker than a formative influence, for already, when he became active, the movements in these countries had assumed their own ideological tendencies and organisational forms. In Germany, despite his efforts to spread anarchist propaganda from Switzerland, his theories were for long disputed by Johann Most, and when the German and Austrian libertarians finally accepted his ideas their influence had already dwindled in the face of advancing Marxism. And the large Dutch anarchist movement, while accepting his theoretical ideas, remained tactically under the influence of its pacifist leaders Domela Niewenhuis and Bart de Ligt.

In England the small anarchist movement was largely his creation; the newspaper *Freedom*, which he founded, still appears, with a circulation greater than in his day. But anarchism in contemporary England is more an intellectual and literary current than a revolutionary grouping, and Kropotkin's disciples here are to be found among writers rather than among agitators, in an indefinite libertarian cult of decentralisation rather than in a tendency towards militant action. In America today a similar influence among a group of intellectuals persists, showing a tendency to revive and spread among the young.

Finally, in his own country, Kropotkin's personal prestige was always greater than his influence as a militant or a thinker. The anarchists were in a small minority, and even they, while respecting him as a theoretician, agreed little with his tactical ideas. During the revolution their only real successes lay in the Ukraine, and these were achieved through the dynamic personality of Machno. Today, under the communist dictatorship, Kropotkin's name has probably less meaning in his own land than anywhere else.

As a writer, in his long series of books on many aspects of social thought, Kropotkin brought order into the chaos of anarchist thought. As a systematic thinker he was inferior only to Godwin, and he had the added advantage of a scientific background and a faculty for simple writing. After the tortuosities of Proudhon and Bakunin's rambling rhetoric, with its passages of brilliant insight, Kropotkin's writings are remarkably clear. He deliberately endeavoured to make them understood by men of little education, and the result was highly successful, so that among all the more celebrated works of the socialist tradition they are remarkable for the ease with which they set forward arguments that are often profound and complicated. There is a sincere fervour about almost all his work which brings warmth into scientific discussions and infuses even statistics with a feeling that human needs have not been forgotten in favour of numbers. Today, nearly half a century after most of them were written, these books still retain their freshness of thought, and are remarkably free from the scaffolding of nineteenth-century pseudo-philosophy which marred most contemporary political writing, and particularly that of the "scientific" socialists. It is not without reason that the anarchists still use them as text-books and that some contemporary sociologists regard them as important basic works in their science. All his books, even where he thought to give them a general scientific form, were influenced strongly by his libertarian ideals. Whether he was considering mutual aid in the animal world or the possibilities of increased agricultural production, the economic origins of the French Revolution or the social evils of the wages system, he had always before him his vision of a peaceful anarchy, and was busily engaged in constructing some part of the intellectual basis on which it would be built. That his inquiries should have gone so far afield is indicative of the imaginative nature of his scientific outlook and the great breadth of culture which enabled him to find room in his thoughts for so many aspects of the problems he faced.

In a sense, he was one of the last descendants of those Renaissance geniuses who aspired to universal knowledge; he would have understood the complex outlook of men like Leonardo da Vinci and Pico della Mirandola much more easily than most nineteenth-century revolutionaries. It was this breadth of interest in the human aspects of science that enabled him to take the important place he holds among the pioneers of sociology considered as a science rather than as a series of temporary political expedients. That he had always in mind the ways and means of converting men to a recognition of the necessity and feasibility of a free society did not detract from the genuinely scientific spirit with which he carried out his inquiries.

Of his many books the most celebrated and influential is undoubtedly *Mutual Aid.* It was a timely work, since when it appeared the majority of biologists still accepted with a surprising lack of criticism the views on the struggle for existence which were being advanced by Huxley As an antidote to these teachings, *Mutual Aid* was extremely valuable. It was a genuinely scientific work, based on a painstaking collection of the relevant facts, and it undoubtedly played a great part in changing the intellectual climate of its time and in bringing about a modification of evolutionary theory, and a general recognition among biologists and anthropologists of the important role played by co-operation in animal and human life and progress.

But it is on the question of the State that we come to the core of Kropotkin's arguments, for the controversy of the State versus the free society has always represented the fundamental difference between State socialists and anarchists. The socialists, with their emphasis on the economic man and their goal of material security, have always regarded capitalism as the chief enemy of the oppressed classes. The anarchists, from Godwin onwards, have declared that the chief enemy is the State, by which they mean the whole system of authority and coercion which maintains and consecrates property relationships.

Kropotkin's main criticism of the State, and his prophecies of what would happen if it were allowed to continue its development and its increasing domination over human affairs, have been proved correct by events. The State finds its highest development in State socialism, and it has become evident that in this system freedom is steadily more restricted, while even the temporary material advantage which is in some measure secured to the people is cancelled out by the danger of recurrent and steadily more terrible wars.

Today capitalism, at least in its private form, is dying, not from the action of the exploited classes but from the action of the State—this happened in Nazi Germany as well as in Communist Russia, and it is happening in Britain today. The expropriators are indeed being expropriated, but not quite in the way Marx and his followers foresaw, while the State, gaining strength from its absorption of economic power, interferes more with individual freedom, becomes more oppressive and more belligerent than ever before.

Kropotkin, as we have shown, prophesied that if the State were allowed to continue, it "must crush the individual and local life, it must become the master of all the domains of human activity, must bring with it its wars and internal struggles for the possession of power, its surface revolutions which only change one tyrant for another, and, inevitably, at the end of this evolution—death!" He also warned the workers against accepting the bread and circuses of the modern State, since such material gifts would be more than cancelled by loss of freedom and life.

Today these warnings seem even more real than they can have done to the people of the 1890's who first read them in the days when State socialism was still something of a beautiful mirage in the distant future. Today we are much advanced in the evolution he foresaw, and the justice of his contentions can be seen by comparing any modern State with one of the national aggregations of Kropotkin's day. The classic case is his own country, Russia, which is presented to us as the apogee of State socialism, the fine fruit of a century of Marxist development.

Tsarist Russia was one of the most tyrannical States of its time; it lived by terror and murder, by secret police and knouting Cossacks, yet even within that terrible autocracy there were places in which freedom could live and even thrive. Among the peasants there still existed the commune, which united the lives of the villagers on a basis of voluntary co-operation. The emigrating peasants were allowed to occupy Siberia as they thought fit and to establish the communistic institutions they desired. Today all this has been at an end for many years, and the forced collectivisations, the requisitioning of crops, the persecution of independent farmers, and the deportation of millions of the peasant population into the Arctic death camps, are crimes beside which those of the Tsarist nobility and police officials seem puny indeed.

Intellectual freedom has been wholly crushed in this model State. The Tsarist government suppressed radical writing but left literature relatively free, and an author of international celebrity, like Tolstoy, could attack the State and go untouched. Consequently, intellectual vigour flowered in a great mass of creative writing. The Bolshevik State, however, immediately recognised the danger of creative art in fostering personal thought and criticism. It instituted a crude system of standards to which all art must conform—not only in its political teachings but also in its form. It must be propagandist, and must administer its propaganda according to a uniform technique. The consequence is that the great achievements of the nineteenth-century Russian writers have been replaced by a level of journalistic mediocrity difficult to parallel in any other country.

What can be said of the influence of the State in Russia on the lives of peasants and writers applies to its influence in every other respect. The bureaucratic regime exceeds the Tsarist government, perhaps not in the degree of its brutality, but certainly in the fact that while the Tsarist authority was sporadic and inefficient in its attacks on the individual, the Bolshevik government is thorough and efficient, and has steadily reduced the means by which the individual can retain any kind of life outside the State. The State has extended its scope from political to economic government, and in this way the two forms of power which in the previous phase still stood apart have coalesced in a totality governed by a united class of officials, which regulates every aspect of the community and steadily advances its net of regulation about the lives of the individuals within it, so that even its own members are not immune from the ever-recurrent purges.

Nor has State socialism in Russia even reduced the problems it set out to solve. Political freedom, as we have demonstrated, is even less substantial than it was under the last Tsar. Economic freedom does not exist, since not only the factories but also the trade unions are organs of the State, and the working man has no say in his conditions of employment, nor the chance of finding more congenial circumstances in which to work. Inequality, whether political or economic, has in no way been liquidated, for a privileged minority of picked party members holds all the bureaucratic and managerial posts, while the differences of wages between high industrial executives and ordinary labouring workers is much wider than in Western Europe. Economic instability still exists, and this is intensified by a failure of the centralised State economy to evolve an agricultural system that will obviate the risk of famine, or to provide a sufficient production of consumer goods to raise the standard of material comfort among Russian workers to that obtaining in Western Europe or the United States. Industrial and technical efficiency, despite a vast succession of trials for "sabotage", remain at a very low level in Russian factories, partly because of the poor standard of living among the workers and partly through the lack of any real incentive except the negative one of coercion, economic or physical.

Nor has the socialist State of Russia found it possible to do without the nationalism, militarism, and imperialist expansion which were characteristic of preceding types of State. "Soviet patriotism" has become a well-known slogan, any attempt at genuine internationalism is derided and suppressed as "bourgeois cosmopolitanism", and Marx's famous dictum that "the worker has no fatherland" has long been negated by the rulers of Russia. The forcible incorporation of the Baltic States, the establishment of a hegemony over Eastern Europe, are manifestations of the imperialist side of modern "socialist" nationalism in its belligerent aspects. Nor will the argument that Russia is forced to act in this way by the hostility of capitalist States any longer explain the aggressiveness of its nationalist policy, since it finds itself at loggerheads not only with social-democratic governments like that of England, but also with Communist States of the same pattern, like Jugoslavia.

We have taken Russia as our example because it proves amply that the socialist State, in taking freedom away from the individual, provides none of the material compensations or solutions which were supposed to be the reward for his subjugation. But the same kind of development has been going on at a slower pace in other countries, even including those which retain some title to democracy; it was analysed brilliantly some years ago by the American writer, James Burnham, in *The Managerial Revolution*. Burnham put forward the theory that capitalism is in a state of decline, that the capitalist class as such is losing all real power, and that virtual control is passing into the hands of a new ruling class, the 'managers', by whom he means the administrators of industry and government. The recent nationalisation projects of the British Labour Government provide an excellent illustration of this passage of industries into the hands of a managerial autocracy, which includes the more able of the former capitalists, without any perceptible change in the status of the workers.

The subservient condition of the workers, while politically due to the presence of the State, is, as Kropotkin has pointed out, economically due to the existence of the wages system. We have already shown the reasons which Kropotkin put forward for regarding as absurd any attempt to assess the relative value of each man's labour. But here it is necessary to indicate that in practice his indictment of the wages system has proved as pointed and prophetic as his attack on the State. The wages system was the means by which the capitalist kept his control over the worker, by holding in his hands the gift of the means of existence. It is always the outward manifestation of a society in which some individuals control the means of production and divide the product, while others work and receive payment; in other words, a society where there is a class of masters and a class of servants. In the socialist societies of the present day this has not changed, and the workers remain in the power of those who dispense the means of living, the managerial bureaucracy. Nor have the rulers of Soviet Russia or any other similar States failed to use the tactic of creating an *élite* of well-paid workers by the use of differentiated wages. The relationship of employer and worker is not peculiar to capitalism. It exists wherever there is a division between the operation and the control of the means of production, where, in other words, the worker continues to be a wage labourer instead of a partner sharing in the work product to the full extent of his needs. Its perpetuation in the socialist State reveals that even here the worker is as far from partnership as he ever was in the days of capitalism.

The Marxist idea of the liberation of mankind through the dictatorship of the proletariat and the use of the State and organised violence has clearly failed, for it shows no signs of a concrete result in really increased happiness or safety for the people. All it offers is the prospect of further violence and yet more repression, with the perspective ending in the most destructive and inhuman war of history.

What is our alternative? Clearly it is impossible, even if it were desirable, to retreat through history to the society of individual capitalism. And the only other choice left to us is a society based, not on organised violence, but on peaceful understanding, not on the State, but on a decentralised network of voluntary co-operation. It is here that we see how impossible it was for the collaboration between anarchists and social-democrats to have continued beyond the end of the nineteenth century, since their fundamental values are totally different. Marxism aimed at reaching the millennium by organised violence; anarchism aimed at establishing a society of peaceful agreement by the co-operation of uncoerced individuals and groups. Marxism, in spite of its talk of eventual freedom, finds its apotheosis in a moralistic State governed by "our beloved teacher of genius"; anarchism is based on the multiplicity of individual and local responsibilities. Marxism is a doctrine of class hatred, giving a Messianic role to a fragment of one class and desiring to subjugate society to its dictatorship; anarchism is a doctrine of human brotherhood which desires, not the triumph of any class, but the elimination of all class distinctions.

Kropotkin, at least for a long part of his career, thought that the destruction of the State and the passage to a free and peaceful society would be a comparatively simple and rapid progress. His optimism made him often ignore the long struggles of the past for social betterment, and he also saw the future in a foreshortened perspective. Moreover, like almost all the revolutionaries of his time, he did not foresee in its full strength the power which the State would achieve in the modern age.

It did not occur to him that capitalism would die in such a way that the oppressed classes would have no chance to state their claims to the inheritance, since the transition would be a hidden one from capitalist control to that of the State, duly embodied in its managerial class. Nor did he fully realise the magnitude of this class, or the security of its control over the vastly more powerful technical means of organisation which have enabled it to achieve, in turn, a far wider centralisation of control over production and administration. And a further error into which he fell was to assume, like most of his fellow anarchists, that the contradictions within the State would necessarily prevent it from providing security for the workers. In fact, during the last fifty years, and despite the effects of war, there has been a steady increase in certain forms of material security, e.g. security from starvation, for the workers in many countries. What they have lost are personal freedom and comparative immunity from the effects of war. Finally, Kropotkin did not take into full account the hold nationalism and racialism would still have over the popular imagination, which would enable them to be used, even in the middle of the twentieth century, as a means of solidifying the power of totalitarian States.

On the positive side, Kropotkin erred in his estimate of the forces opposed to the State, and particularly in his confidence in the popular revolutionary drive. This sprang from his *narodnik* past, and also from the fact that his contact with workers had always been with men of particularly strong character, such as the militants of the old Jura Federation, and of the revolutionary clubs in London. He did not know the ordinary workers, and did not realise how far, even in his own day, they had been conditioned by State education and discipline into obedience and fear of responsibility. Since that time, Marxist propaganda has also played its part in leading them astray by dreams of well-being through State socialism, and, although many people no doubt realise the falsity of such promises, their reaction at present is too often to sink into apathy.

Thus the dissolution of the State seems in our day immeasurably more difficult than it did to Kropotkin. Nevertheless, hard of achievement though it may be, some form of decentralised free society, with co-operative ownership and the spreading of social responsibility among individuals and local and functional groups, does seem the only means of gaining a stable liberty and a cessation of the destructive wars which are inseparable from giant States. There is little doubt that every sensible man or woman sees the desirability of a solution similar to that posed by Kropotkin; as all the great anarchist thinkers have indicated, even the capitalist would be happier and would enjoy more real emotional security in a society where he was assured peace and freedom from anxiety.

Yet the task of carrying out a fundamental change in society (whether by peaceful or violent means) has been vastly complicated by the increased technical power of the State and the present tendency of the majority of the people to regard material security as more important than freedom or life. Libertarians of all kinds, and even people who merely value their freedom more than their security, are still in a minority everywhere, and all they can do at present is to carry on the work of education in the ideas of freedom and responsibility which is the necessary prelude to change. But even this is important since, as Kropotkin realised, a high moral development and a great sense of responsibility are essential for the enjoyment of real freedom.

Pessimism regarding the future of mankind is as irrational as optimism. Laws of historical development are rightly suspect, but one thing that history does teach is that no social order is stable over a long period of time. It must either develop or decline, and it is at the periods of decline, when its rulers have become unable to cope with its economic and social contradictions, that the patience of the people breaks its bounds and revolutionary situations arise spontaneously. At such moments social orders which had only shortly before seemed stable are seen to be obsolete and vanish for mere lack of support, leaving behind them a flux of change. In the history of all great revolutions—the English, the American, the French, the Russian, this kind of situation has arisen, and there seems no reason why it should not be repeated, particularly since in our own day the tempo of social change has been vastly increased.

Real revolutions are not made by revolutionaries. They come from the people, and any attempt to anticipate them is bound to fail. Nobody can prophesy when a stage of social dissolution will be reached which will indicate the advent of a fundamental change in society.

But, while no group can itself radically alter society, it is still possible to prepare the intellectual climate in which such an alteration may occur, as the writers of the Enlightenment elaborated for nearly a century the ideas on which the French Revolution was fought. The situation which may lead to a new social order cannot itself be produced artificially, but the mental attitude in which it begins can be influenced, and therein lies the importance of the kind of sociological investigation and education on which Kropotkin spent a lifetime.

Since it is the people who must make the revolution, the question which Kropotkin posed can be re-phrased in terms which take into account the alterations in the society since his day. Do they want the comforts, the illusory security which the State can offer, when these must be bought not only by the loss of personal freedom but also at the risk of violent death? It is a question which confronts people in all lands today, and which events will sooner or later force upon their attention in an acute and tragic form.

In relation to this question Kropotkin's arguments, shorn of their romantic superstructure, take on a new realism. The continued existence of the giant State can only lead to death, and the sole alternative to a renewed State, with its faults resurrected, is a world federation in its turn comprised of federations of regions and towns, in which peace, freedom and well-being are guaranteed by a balanced economy and a co-operative organisation of life.

This kind of society would involve a radical change in the direction of social organisation; it would not be the first time in history that such a change has taken place. It would also involve sacrifices, but it is for the people to decide whether they are willing to make them voluntarily, or to retain their present form of society with all its national rivalries and the vastly greater sacrifices which its wars will entail.

As the free society is recognised by more people to be the only genuine alternative to the total State, the chance of its eventual attainment will increase; and in any approach that is made towards decentralisation and voluntary co-operation, Kropotkin's work has still a part to play, for even though some of his tactical theories and his more detailed sketches of anarchy may inevitably be outdated, his general conceptions of organisation and outlook will still remain applicable. When mankind emerges from the present epoch of violence and hatred, oppression and misery, Kropotkin, at present half forgotten, will, unlike many of his contemporaries, be honoured as one of the leading pioneers of a better and happier world. And then, and only then, will humanity be able to realise its full debt to Peter Kropotkin, the anarchist.

BIBLIOGRAPHY

I

Almost all of Kropotkin's works were published in several languages, and at least some of his writings appeared in volume form in most European languages, including Yiddish and Esperanto, as well as in Chinese, Japanese, and Hindustani; they also appeared in the United States and most South American countries. The following select list, including all the works published in volume form as well as the principal pamphlets, follows the procedure, which seems most convenient for our readers, of indicating the first English edition, where such exists, and otherwise the first edition in the original language.

Appeal to the Young (translated by H. M. Hyndman). London, 1885.

Paroles d'un Revolté (edited with an introduction by Elisée Reclus). Paris, 1885.

Law and Authority. London, 1886.

In Russian and French Prisons. London, 1887.

Anarchist Morality. London, 1890.

Fields, Factories and Workshops. London, 1898.

Memoirs of a Revolutionist. London, 1899.

Mutual Aid. London, 1902.

The State. London, 1903.

Ideals and Realities in Russian Literature. London, 1905.

The Conquest of Bread. London, 1906 (a translation of the French original, published in Paris, 1892).

The Great French Revolution. London, 1909.

The Terror in Russia. London, 1909.

Modern Science and Anarchism. London, 1912 (the translation of a Russian original, published in London in 1901).

Ethics (edited with an introduction by Nicholas Lebedev). London, 1925.

A valuable collection of Kropotkin's pamphlets was published in New York in 1927 under the title of *Kropotkin's Revolutionary Pamphlets. . . .* Edited with introduction, biographical sketch and notes by Roger Baldwin". A volume of selections from Kropotkin's principal works, compiled by Herbert Read and prefaced by an illuminating introduction, was published in London in 1942 under the title of *Kropotkin—Selections from His Writings*.

Articles and letters by Kropotkin will be found in many periodicals of the time, including *The Times, Daily Chronicle, Nature, The Nineteenth Century,*

Fortnightly Review, *Atlantic Monthly*, *Le Revue Scientifique*, *The Geographical Journal*, *Freedom*, *Le Revolté*, *Temps Nouveaux*, *L'Avant Garde*, *Commonweal*, *Hleb i Volya*, *Listki Hleb i Volya*, *L'Intransigeant*, *Voice of Labour*, *Newcastle Daily News*, *Daily News*, *Arbeiterfreund* (London), *Tierra y Libertad* (Madrid), *Bataille Syndicaliste* (Paris), *The Speaker*, *Le Soir* (Brussels), *Ecole Renovie* (Brussels), *La Protesta* (Buenos Aires), *Probuzhdenie* (Detroit), *Golos Truda*, *Delo Truda*, *Independent* (New York), *Politiken* (Copenhagen), *The Alarm*, *El Productor* (Barcelona), *Avant Courier* (Oregon). Reports of his addresses to the British Association, the Royal Geographical Society in London, and the Russian Geographical Society appear in the proceedings of these bodies. He also contributed to various learned compilations, such as the *Encyclopædia Britannica*, *Chambers's Encyclopædia*, *Le Geographie Universelle*, etc.

A collected edition of Kropotkin's works is now being prepared by Freedom Press, the publishing group founded by Kropotkin in 1886, which still publishes *Freedom*, the periodical originally edited by him.

II

Up to the present day the only full-length book attempting to give a complete life of Kropotkin is a 200-page biography entitled, *Kropotkine, descendant des Grands Princes de Smolensk, Page de l'Empereur, Savant illustre, Revolutionnaire international, Vulgarisateur de la Pensée anarchiste*, by Fernand Planche and Jean Delphy, published in Paris during 1948. This, however, contains little material not already fairly generally available, and treats its subject very superficially. During the present century a number of pamphlets giving biographical sketches of Kropotkin have appeared in Russia and in the Latin countries, but none of these has contributed anything of importance to our studies. We would, however, make special mention of two very interesting brochures on limited aspects of Kropotkin's thought which have been published in England during recent years and which we found of considerable assistance; they are Camillo Berneri's *Kropotkin—His Federalist Ideas*, and John Hewetson's *Mutual Aid and Social Evolution*.

The really important source-book for Kropotkin's early life is, of course, his *Memoirs of a Revolutionist*, and for his youth we have been able to supplement this by two volumes of letters between him and his brother which were edited and published by Nicholas Lebedev in Moscow during 1932–3. We have obtained letters written by Kropotkin during his later years from many published sources. The principal was a very large selection from the years 1876 to 1914, which were published in the February 1931 and other issues of the Detroit Russian anarchist periodical, *Probuzhdenie*. They were edited by the well-known anarchist historian, Max Nettlau, who contributed a number of articles on Kropotkin to the same periodical. We were indebted for further letters, unpublished articles, and copious biographical details to several books by this writer, including his *Bibliographie de l'Anarchie* (Brussels, 1897), *Der Anarchismus von Proudhon zu Kropotkin: Seine historische Entwicklung in den Jahren 1859–1880* (Berlin, 1927), *Anarchisten und Sozial-revolutionäre 1880–1886* (Berlin, 1931), and his biographies of Kropotkin's friends, Reclus and Malatesta. A selection of important letters from Kropotkin after his return to Russia in 1917 was published in *Monde Slave* (Paris) in 1925, and further important documents appeared in the Russian periodicals *Katorga i Ssylka*, and *Volna*. To the Italian anarchist monthly review *Volonta*, we are indebted for the text of Kropotkin's famous protest to Lenin against the taking of hostages. Finally we had access, through the kind assistance of various institutions and individuals, to many unpublished letters of Kropotkin. In particular, we would mention the letters to William and May Morris and Mrs Dryhurst in the British Museum, letters to English anarchists like Tom Keell, Alfred Marsh, and George Barrett, which were made available by their friends and relatives, and various communications of which we were kindly furnished with copies by the librarians of Harvard University, McGill University, Montreal, The Royal Geographical Society, London, and the National Library of Scotland. Other important manuscript sources included the diaries of William Morris and John Burns preserved in the British Museum.

Much important and otherwise unavailable information was gleaned from various memorial volumes and special editions of periodicals devoted to Kropotkin. Prominent among these are the Memorial Volume published by Joseph Ishill, New Jersey, in 1923, the Memorial Volume edited by N. Lebedev and Alexander Borovoi and published in Moscow in 1921, *P. A. Kropotkin i ego Uchenie*, edited by G. P. Maximov (Chicago, 1931), two pamphlets of appreciations entitled *Kropotkine* and prepared by Jean Grave for the Groupe de Propagande par l'Ecrit (Paris, 1921), *Centennial Expressions on Peter Kropotkin, 1842–1942* (Los Angeles, 1942), the special issues of *Mother Earth* (U.S.A.) and *Il Pensiero* (Rome), which were published on Kropotkin's seventieth birthday in 1912, and special numbers of *Temps Nouveaux* (Paris, 1921), the Russian magazine *Byloe* (1921), and the New York Jewish paper *Freie Arbeiter Stimme* (1942).

Information regarding Kropotkin's career as a geographer was provided by the diary which he kept from 1862 to 1867 and which was published in Moscow in 1923, by various issues of *The Geographical Journal*, by Professor Dudley Stamp's *Asia*, and by the account of Kropotkin's Siberian travels in *Puteshcstviya P. A. Kropotkina*, by S. Anisimov, published in Moscow in 1943. Pages 123–9 of this book contain a useful bibliography of Kropotkin's geographical and geological works and accounts of journeys which were published in Tsarist Russia.

Many books have given us specific information regarding precise aspects and periods of Kropotkin's life, and the following are particularly worthy of mention: *L'Internationale*, by James Guillaume (Paris, 1905–10), the *Correspondence* of Elisée Reclus, the autobiography of Professor James Mavor and the journals of T. J. Cobden-Sanderson, Jean Grave's *Le Mouvement libertaire sous la Troisiéme Republique* (Paris, 1930), Emma Goldman's *Living my Life* (London, 1931), and *My Disillusionment in Russia* (London, 1925), *Mihailu Bakuninu 1876–1926, Ocherki istorii anarchicheskogo dvizheniya v Rossii*, edited by Alexander Borovoi (Moscow, 1926), and finally the *Chronique du Mouvement Socialiste en Russie*, of which a confidential limited edition of 100 copies was published in French by the Russian Ministry of the Interior in 1890. We have also taken copiously from the memoirs, diaries, and autobiographies of the period, which contain many friendly references, but we have not sufficient space to list these in detail or to refer specifically to the various papers and magazines in which there is mention of Kropotkin.

Our thanks are due to Rudolf Rocker for allowing us to use passages from his memoirs, yet unpublished in English, to the Editor of *Politics* for extracts from part of Victor Serge's autobiography published in his excellent review, and for various information, assistance, advice and encouragement to Ingeborg Woodcock, who typed the final version of this book, to the late Marie Louise Berneri, Lilian Wolfe, V. Richards, the late Harry Jones, G. P. Maximov, B. Yelensky, Dr H. Frank, H. N. Brailsford, Li Pei Kan, Joseph Ishill, Colin Ward, Miss E. M. Heath, Mrs Katherine Bruce Glasier, Mr and Mrs Edward Pease, George Bernard Shaw, and many other friendly correspondents whose help has contributed so much to our work.

We would also acknowledge our debt to the various institutions and libraries of whose facilities we made copious use, including the British Museum, the Public Record Office, the London Library, the London School of Economics, the Fabian Society, the Bibliothéque Nationale and the Institute of International Documentation in Paris, to the directors of the National Archives in Paris, the Royal Archives in Brussels and the Cantonal Archives in Geneva for the valuable information which they have given us, and to the editors of the English, American, French, and Italian periodicals who published our letters asking for information. Among the institutions whose help we asked was the International Institute of Social History in Amsterdam, which has certain documents relating to Kropotkin but, as they had not been sorted, could not make them available to us. Most of this material was, however, used by Nettlau in his various volumes, and we feel certain that he could have left little of significance unnoticed.

Apart from the Tolstoy Museum in Moscow, none of the Russian institutions we approached vouchsafed a reply to our requests for information, nor did the VOKS representative in London. We would also mention the refusal of the French Ministry of Foreign Affairs to give us any information regarding their records concerning Kropotkin, and a similar refusal on the part of the Aliens Department of the British Home Office.

INDEX